Ethics Done Right

Practical Reasoning as a Foundation for Moral Theory

Ethics Done Right examines how practical reasoning can be put into the service of ethical and moral theory. Elijah Millgram shows that the key to thinking about ethics is to understand more generally how to make decisions. The papers in this volume support a methodological approach and trace the connections between two kinds of theory in utilitarianism, in Kantian ethics, in virtue ethics, in Hume's moral philosophy, and in moral particularism. Unlike other studies of ethics, *Ethics Done Right* does not advocate a particular moral theory. Rather, it offers a tool that enables one to decide for oneself.

Elijah Millgram is E. E. Ericksen Professor of Philosophy at the University of Utah. He is the author of *Practical Induction* and the editor of *Varieties of Practical Reasoning*. He has written on moral philosophy, coherence theory, and late British Empiricism. He has been a Fellow of the Center for Advanced Study in the Behavioral Sciences and of the National Endowment for the Humanities.

Ethics Done Right

Practical Reasoning as a Foundation for Moral Theory

ELIJAH MILLGRAM

University of Utah

CAMBRIDGE
UNIVERSITY PRESS

CAMBRIDGE UNIVERSITY PRESS
Cambridge, New York, Melbourne, Madrid, Cape Town, Singapore, São Paulo

Cambridge University Press
40 West 20th Street, New York, NY 10011-4211, USA

www.cambridge.org
Information on this title: www.cambridge.org/9780521839433

First published 2005

Printed in the United States of America

A catalog record for this publication is available from the British Library.

Library of Congress Cataloging in Publication Data
Millgram, Elijah.
Ethics done right : practical reasoning as a foundation for
moral theory / Elijah Millgram.
p.   cm.
Includes bibliographical references and index.
ISBN 0-521-83943-2 (hb) – ISBN 0-521-54826-8 (pbk.)
1. Ethics.   2. Conduct of life.   3. Reasoning.   4. Thought and thinking.   I. Title.
BJ1012.M545   2005
170–dc22   2004060554

ISBN-13   978-0-521-83943-3 hardback
ISBN-10   0-521-83943-2 hardback

ISBN-13   978-0-521-54826-7 paperback
ISBN-10   0-521-54826-8 paperback

Cambridge University Press has no responsibility for
the persistence or accuracy of URLs for external or
third-party Internet Web sites referred to in this book
and does not guarantee that any content on such
Web sites is, or will remain, accurate or appropriate.

56809586

For (and against) John Rawls

Contents

Acknowledgments

"What's the Use of Utility?" appeared in *Philosophy and Public Affairs* 29 (2), Spring 2000: 113–35. © 2000 by Princeton University Press.

"Mill's Proof of the Principle of Utility" appeared in *Ethics* 110 (2), January 2000: 282–310. © 2000 by The University of Chicago. All rights reserved.

"Does the Categorical Imperative Give Rise to a Contradiction in the Will?" appeared in *Philosophical Review* 112 (4), October 2003: 525–60.

"Murdoch, Practical Reasoning, and Particularism" appeared in *Notizie di Politeia* 18 (66), 2002: 64–87.

"Was Hume a Humean?" appeared in *Hume Studies* 21 (1), April 1995: 75–93.

"Hume on 'Is' and 'Ought'" appeared (under the title "Hume on Practical Reasoning") in *Iyyun* 46, July 1997: 235–65. Reprinted with the kind permission of the editor of *Iyyun*.

"Incommensurability and Practical Reasoning" reprinted by permission of the publisher from *Incommensurability, Incomparability, and Practical Reason*, edited by Ruth Chang, pp. 151–69, Cambridge, Mass.: Harvard University Press. Copyright © 1997 by the President and Fellows of Harvard College.

"Commensurability in Perspective" appeared in *Topoi* 21 (1–2), 2002: 217–26. © 2002 Kluwer Academic Publishers, with kind permission of Kluwer Academic Publishers.

"Varieties of Practical Reasoning and Varieties of Moral Theory" (originally titled "Varieties of Practical Reasoning") appeared in Georg Meggle (ed.), *Analyomen 2: Proceedings of the 2nd Conference "Perspectives in Analytical Philosophy"* (de Gruyter, 1997), vol. III, pp. 280–94.

I am grateful for fellowship support from the National Endowment for the Humanities and the Center for Advanced Study in the Behavioral Sciences; financial support was provided through the Center by the Andrew W. Mellon Foundation.

Ethics Done Right

Practical Reasoning as a Foundation for Moral Theory

Introduction

The Method of Practical Reasoning

In philosophy, choice of method matters. You're about to read an adver-
tisement for a method: namely, that the right way to do moral philosophy
is to start by working out your theory of practical reasoning. By way of
introducing the book-length argument, I want first to explain what I
mean by that. Then I'll give some reasons for using the method, and
hand out some promissory notes for the reasons I can't give up front; I'll
also flag some of the issues I won't be taking up here. By way of clearing the ground, I'll discuss so-called reflective equilibrium, which has
been, for some time now, the method of choice, or anyway the default
method, for moral philosophers of the analytic stripe. I'll briefly indicate
the advantages my proposed method has over the reflective equilibrium
competition.

Next I'll provide a site map for the volume, which will describe how the
subsequent chapters advance the main argument. Almost all of these were
originally written as freestanding papers, and have agendas of their own;
since they are (with occasional exceptions) unrevised, their respective
conclusions are not always the contributions I want them to be making to
the argument of the book. Accordingly, I'll provide more or less chapter
by chapter orientation and reading instructions. Finally, I'll wrap up by
looking beyond the work I do in this volume, to some of the further
possibilities of the Method of Practical Reasoning.

1

First, terminology. Substantive moral or ethical theories[1] answer questions like: What is it morally permitted for me to do? (Is it all right to

cheat on my taxes?) What actions are morally required? (Do I have to help out my neighbors, even if I dislike them for very good reasons?) What kind of person should I be? (Ambitious? Modest?) What sorts of outcomes count as generally positive, or as generally negative? (Is *happiness* a positive outcome? Everyone's happiness, or just my own?) How should I treat my fellow human beings? (With respect? Even if they've done nothing to earn it?)

Substantive theories of practical reasoning, on the other hand, answer questions further upstream: What considerations should I look to in making decisions? (Am I just looking for ways to achieve my goals?) What makes one kind of consideration as opposed to another count as a reason to do something? (If it's a reason this time, does it *always* have to be a reason?) More generally, what's the right way to figure out what to do? (For example, should I be aiming for the very best, or is "good enough" good enough?)

If you were to try to give a step-by-step rendering of the Method of Practical Reasoning, it would look something like this. First, get an overview of as many different theories of practical reasoning as possible. Second, puzzle out what moral theories those accounts of practical reasoning give rise to (or anyway, leaving aside for a moment issues of what's responsible for what, which of the former are yoked to which of the latter). Third, without appealing to any substantive moral theory, determine which theory of practical reasoning is correct. Fourth and last, adopt the moral theory with which you have paired it.

The stepwise rendering is too clunky to be realistic philosophical procedure, and when you get there, you'll notice that the claims defended in subsequent chapters are more complicated than it suggests. But it will do as a first approximation, one which will help explain what's new about the present approach. A moral philosopher attending to practical reasoning is nothing new: Immanuel Kant called his second critique *The Critique of Practical Reason*; Thomas Hobbes and David Gauthier built political and moral theories around their respective instrumentalist accounts of practical reasoning; and it is one of the higher priority items on the agenda of this volume to locate the theories of practical reasoning at the centers of the better-known philosophical moralities. What I am demanding over and above what we already find in the field is a systematic overview of the options, both of the theories of practical reasoning and the moral theories, with priority being given to the selection of a theory of practical reasoning.

Let me support the claim that it's important for an overview to precede the choice of a moral theory. For most of the past, philosophers have not been especially self-aware when it came to their opinions about practical reasoning. Typically they didn't notice more than one or two possibilities, and typically one of those seemed to them obviously right, and not to need much in the way of sustained argument or defense. But it is a good rule of thumb in philosophy that one's positions will not be well constructed or well chosen if one does not keep a range of live alternatives in mind. For one thing, one's arguments are not normally worth much if one is not attending to the variety of objections they will have to endure. And since those objections are normally launched from the standpoint of an alternative or opposing position, if one doesn't have those alternative positions available, one's arguments for one's own position probably won't be very good. An overview of the alternative theories will allow us an intelligent, and intelligently argued, choice of moral theory.

Why should we be giving priority to practical reasoning over traditional moral issues? For starters, if you don't have good reasons to act on what your moral theory tells you – if doing what it says doesn't count as a good decision – then, practically speaking, morality isn't all that important for you. (Why do what it says? No reason.) So, conversely, if morality *is* important, then a successful moral theory will be shaped so that you have reasons to do what it says. This means in turn that the shape of your moral theory should be constrained by what reasons for action can be like. A theory of practical reasoning tells you what your reasons for action can be like. All of which suggests that, if morality is important, to figure out which of the many available (or possible) moral theories is the right one, you should look to your theory of practical reasoning. If the Method of Practical Reasoning works, it gives you a moral theory with a built-in advantage: you know why you have a reason to do what it says.

Some points (like that one) we can make up front; others we can be confident about only later on, after we've seen how they play out: a lot of the time, the proof of the pudding really is in the eating. Whether the Method of Practical Reasoning will work is something we can't know up front, and no manifesto, however inspiring, will carry the day if we can't get the Method to do its job. Since the best way of showing that a method is usable is to actually use it, I intend the papers in this collection to be taken as a feasibility demonstration. Singly or in groups, the papers trace connections between various substantive theories of practical reasoning and the moral or ethical theories with which they are coordinated, and in the course of the survey I hope to convince you of the following claims.

First, the strong moral theories of the past – the moral systems that have passed the test of canonization – have distinctive takes on practical reasoning.

Second, central structural features of those moral theories are consequences of the understandings of practical reasoning that underlie them.
When you show *how* moral theories pair off with theories of practical reasoning, you gain theoretical insight into the deep structural features of
your moral theories.

Third, problems in the moral theories can often be traced back to
problems in the underlying theory of practical reasoning. This turns
out to be important when the time comes to fix them; if you haven't
identified the level at which a difficulty originates, your response will be
(what computer scientists call) a kludge, a perhaps clever but unprincipled and fragile trick, rather than graceful and effective philosophical
engineering.

Fourth, the train of thought sketched a moment ago shows that your
theory of practical reasoning ought to provide constraints on your moral
theory, but, so far as the argument has progressed, possibly quite weak
constraints, constraints perhaps almost any moral theory would satisfy.
I want to defend a stronger claim than that: the treatments assembled
below are meant to persuade you that theories of practical reasoning
are the *engines* of strong moral theories, and that, once you focus on
the otherwise viable candidates, the Method of Practical Reasoning is a
powerful selection technique.

Fifth, if the Method of Practical Reasoning is successful at the second stage of the step-by-step rendition, that is, at pairing off theories of
morality and of practical reasoning, it will prove to have a second built-in
advantage: the moral theory it selects will come with an argument that it
is the correct one. Such arguments will be of the form: Each viable moral
theory presupposes a different theory of practical reasoning. *This* is the
correct theory of practical reasoning. Therefore, the moral theory that
presupposes it is the correct one; the competing moral theories, which
presuppose incorrect theories of practical reasoning, are mistaken. The
theory by theory survey is meant to convince you that the pairings are
tight enough to support such arguments.

2

This volume focuses on the pairing-off stage of the Method of Practical
Reasoning, and because the pairing is just one phase of the larger argument, I'm going to ask you to put aside a handful of worries and objections
for the present.

First of all, if the differences among the canonical moral theories are to
be accounted for by different underlying theories of practical reasoning,

then there have to be sufficiently many distinct theories of practical reasoning in play. This is not the occasion to argue that there are sufficiently many live options to make exploring the range of alternatives they generate intellectually interesting. But to make the point that there *are* many different theories of practical reasoning, I've edited another volume, suitably titled *Varieties of Practical Reasoning*, which surveys a number of them.[2]

Second, why think that you can settle on the right theory of practical reasoning without appealing to your moral theory? If your theory of practical reasoning isn't independent of your moral theory, won't the Method of Practical Reasoning prove to be viciously circular? I expect that we will be able to proceed without circularity, but this is another point we can't be sure about up front. In the meantime, here are three stopgap (but not decisive) considerations. One, most practical reasoning is directed toward decisions whose subject matter is, by almost anyone's lights, nonmoral. (What shall we choose as our evening's entertainment? Should I redecorate my apartment, or take a trip to the Canary Islands? What gauge of track is the subway we're designing going to use?[3]) If the logic of action and choice does not vary with the subject matter, then we ought to be able to determine the forms it takes, using subject matter to which moral considerations are irrelevant as a testbed. Two, you can find plenty of examples of arguments for and against theories of practical reasoning that do not invoke moral views: some in the anthology I have just mentioned, some in an earlier monograph of my own.[4] Whether or not you accept that those particular arguments establish their conclusions, the examples may persuade you that arguments of the *sort* that the Method of Practical Reasoning requires are there for the assembling. Three, contrast the presumption about the burden of proof that the objection expresses with the similarly situated but opposite presumption regarding theoretical rationality (that is, reasoning about matters of fact). When it comes to the forms taken by theoretical inference, just about no one thinks that you can only choose your logic on the basis of your substantive theory of the world (your physics, your chemistry, and so on).[5] Why, when it comes to practical logic, should it be the other way around?

Third, I'm going to leave the selection of the correct moral theory for another occasion. (I even want to leave it open whether what we get will be systematic and orderly enough to count as a *theory*.) What I mean to be demonstrating now is a *method*, a point about the order of argument, and not a substantive moral conclusion. I want you to agree that a theory of practical reasoning ought to be an input to your choice of moral theory, and that it ought to go a long way toward determining the output. I don't want my own preferences over the inputs and outputs to occupy center stage, and I'm not insisting that you accept them – although I haven't suppressed them, and as you read along it will be fairly obvious what they are.

Fourth, I am trying to persuade you that focusing on practical reasoning gives you leverage on, and interesting results in, moral philosophy, because theories of practical reasoning pair off, pretty much one to one, with the canonical moral theories. But you might be wondering whether (and why) I am treating the canonical moral theories as though they were the only viable ones. Perhaps the right theory of practical reasoning is compatible with more than one moral theory, because not all moral theories are in the canon. There have been many attempts to graft a moral superstructure of one sort onto a theoretical base that canonically has supported a superstructure of a different sort. And what about hybrid theories, which try to get the best of two or more worlds by taking a bit of one moral theory and sewing it together with a bit of another?

At the end of this Introduction, I'll return to the possibility of moving beyond the canonical moral theories. In the meantime, it's an observation, and one which needs to be explained, that both hybrid and grafted theories fade from philosophical consciousness fairly quickly. My take on the matter (but this has to be made out by examining the cases, and, as before, isn't something we can be sure about up front) is that hybrid and grafted theories vanish because they're not viable, and they're not viable because they don't have a cohesive and unified theory of practical reasoning at their core. There are two likely explanations. One, inconsistencies between the theories of practical reasoning embedded in the grafted or hybridized components make theoretical failure a foregone conclusion. And two, the motivational impetus that the canonical moral theories derive from the understandings of practical reasoning to which they are yoked go missing in hybrid and grafted theories. But these proposals won't be supported here.[6]

Fifth, and last for now, you might be wondering whether the Method of Practical Reasoning is in competition with one or another position in metaethics. That question, at least the way it's usually put, seems to me to express what used to be called a category mistake. The contrast between moral theories and theories of practical reasoning cuts across (and is not the same as) the contrast between substantive ethics and metaethics. I introduced substantive moral or ethical theories as taking up questions like: What ought I to be doing? (Is lying always wrong?) By contrast, metaethical theories take up questions like: What does that "ought" *mean*? (What are you doing, when you describe something as "wrong"?) The same (or an analogous) contrast can be made out within the study of practical reasoning. A substantive theory of practical reasoning will tell you whether the reasons for action are (say) your desires, or universalizable maxims, or maximally coherent clusters of intentions, or whatever, and it will tell you what conclusions follow from what reasons; that is, a substantive theory of practical reasoning is a theory of the forms taken by (legitimate or correct) practical inference. (It will tell you what makes one kind of consideration count as a reason, as opposed to another kind.) A metaethical account of practical reasoning would take up questions like: What does it mean to say that something is a "reason" for action? What is meant by calling the conclusion of a practical inference "incorrect"? (It will tell you what it is for a consideration to count as a reason *tout court.*)

There are important connections between the substantive theory of practical reasoning and its metaethics, and we won't be able to leave these entirely to one side. For instance, Chapters 6 and 7 tease out Hume's metaethical arguments for his own theory of practical reasoning; the postscript to Chapter 3 tries to account for Kant's substantive theory of practical reasoning by attributing to him a (not fully articulated) view lying on the border between the substantive and the metaethical; Chapters 9 and 10 trace connections between value theory – more or less, the metaphysics of values – and practical reasoning. Nevertheless, the topic of this volume is the way in which substantive theories of practical reasoning drive substantive moral or ethical theories. Distinguishing the questions isn't meant to discourage metaethics-based moral theory, but does suggest the form it should take. If you would like to use metaethical considerations to select a theory of practical reasoning, and thereby a moral theory, by all means give it a go.

3

It is a familiar and characteristic part of the practice of philosophy to stop in one's tracks and look around for a new and different way of thinking about things. But of course it is not *always* appropriate. So why, you may be wondering, does moral philosophy need a new method, when we already have a method that does perfectly well, that is, the method of reflective equilibrium? By way of forestalling this objection, I now want to explain why I think the Method of Practical Reasoning is a better choice. I'll give a brief (and, I hope, uncontroversial) description of reflective equilibrium, and then go on (more controversially) to describe the more important advantages of the new method over the old.

Reflective equilibrium was introduced into the contemporary philo-sophical repertoire by Nelson Goodman, with the following characteri-zation of how we determine rules of inference for reasoning: "A rule is amended if it yields an inference we are unwilling to accept; an inference is rejected if it violates a rule we are unwilling to amend."[7] Its current popularity is due to John Rawls, who adapted it to the political problem of determining how basic social institutions should be configured. Early on in his enormously influential *Theory of Justice*, Rawls explained how to select an idealized bargaining situation, one in which social principles get chosen:

> if . . . [our] principles match our considered convictions of justice, then so far well and good. But presumably there will be discrepancies. In this case we have a choice. We can either modify the account of the initial [bargaining] situation or we can revise our existing judgments, for even the judgments we take provi-sionally as fixed points are liable to revision. By going back and forth, sometimes altering the conditions of the contractual circumstances, at others withdrawing our judgments and conforming them to principle, I assume that eventually we shall find a description of the . . . [bargaining] situation that both expresses rea-sonable conditions and yields principles which match our considered judgments duly pruned and adjusted. This state of affairs I refer to as reflective equilibrium.[8]

It has become routine to distinguish between "narrow" and "wide" reflective equilibrium.[9] The "narrow" recipe for using reflective equilib-rium in moral theory has come to look roughly as follows. First, collect a number of moral reactions to actual or imagined circumstances. (These are usually called "moral intuitions," but philosophers no longer think of them as the deliverances of some special faculty; sometimes, following Rawls, they just call them "considered moral judgments.") Then formu-late a general principle whose instances or consequences largely agree with the intuitions. Lastly, negotiate the remaining disagreements: for each point at which principle and intuition conflict, either allow the principle to override the intuition, or, where you can't bring yourself to do that, adjust the principle to accommodate the recalcitrant intuition. Iterate until done, and adopt the revised principle.

"Wide" reflective equilibrium differs in taking into account not only judgments about particular instances, but further principles to which you have an antecedent commitment, background theories, values, argu-ments of all sorts, and in fact just about anything that might be considered relevant. Since the requirement is that everything be made to hang to-gether, it is an ethics-specific variant of what in epistemology gets called coherence theory. So much for what I mean to be an uncontroversial and fair characterization of the opposition.

It's an indication of how respectable the notion has become that on occasion I see "reflective equilibrium" typed into the method blank of a philosopher's grant or fellowship application. Probably an even more important indication of its respectability is the family of overlapping responses you encounter when you press practicing philosophers on the reasons for using reflective equilibrium: One, what *else* could you do? Two, you do it *anyway*. Three, you don't *need* to give an argument for it, or any special reason for doing it *this* way. And four, you *can't* argue for something as basic as this. Call these the Coffeeshop Responses, because you get them over coffee, after class, and during Q & A sessions. Answers like the Coffeeshop Responses are normal practice only when what's being defended is itself normal practice.

A tendency to identify reflective equilibrium with wide reflective equilibrium makes the Coffeeshop Responses seem reasonable, but also makes the notion uninteresting: *any* philosophical argument (with a qualification I'll get to in a moment), including putative alternatives such as my own, ends up counting as an application of the method of (wide) reflective equilibrium. And so *of course* reflective equilibrium is what you do anyway (Coffeeshop Response One), something to which there is really no alternative (Coffeeshop Response Two), and a method which requires no special justification (Coffeeshop Response Three). And what would *count* as an argument for doing – well, *anything*? (Coffeeshop Response Four). But if *anything* you do counts as an instance of Method X, then Method X is not a *method*.

Narrow reflective equilibrium may be a method that gives real guidance, but it isn't supported by an argument to the effect that it's a method appropriate for moral theory; rather than try to supply one, ethicists have almost uniformly abandoned it in favor of wide reflective equilibrium, presumably because it is visibly unsuited to the domain. Wide reflective equilibrium comes with *something* like an argument (the Coffeeshop Responses), but isn't a method. The Method of Practical Reasoning comes with the arguments we've already reviewed, and it promises the guidance one expects from something that advertises itself as a method.

Wide reflective equilibrium is almost content-free, but not entirely. The residual content is the methodological commitment to giving up principles (or values, or theoretical views, or whatever) when they generate (a large enough number of) consequences at which one balks. Now you might think that this is what one does whenever one engages in theory construction, and so it can't possibly be a problematic aspect of the method. But notice that one balks at a consequence of a *moral* theory (in the fancier vocabulary, one has a moral intuition or considered moral judgment that the consequence is to be rejected) when one does not *like* the consequence. (Which does not preclude accepting some very inconvenient consequences, say, the theory's insistence that you keep your promises: one's dislike may be quite impersonal.) Consequently, adopting wide reflective equilibrium as a method amounts to deciding to give up your moral theories when you don't like their results (or, anyway, when you *really* don't like their results). That is to say, wide reflective equilibrium is a method formally indistinguishable from intellectual dishonesty.

The Method of Practical Reasoning does not have this kind of built-in invitation to complacency. As we will see, it has the potential to produce results that are not only genuinely surprising, but very hard to take. Both approaches give you results in which you have a stake, but the kind of stake is very different in the two cases. Reflective equilibrium gives you a theory that agrees with most of what you already think. The Method of Practical Reasoning gives you a theory on whose dicta you have reason to act. Your stake in your prior opinions is inertial, a matter of habituation or emotional comfort (thus the invitation to complacency); whereas what you have reason to do may not match your prior opinions on any point (thus the potential for hard-to-take results).

If you think that moral theory ought to be powerful enough, in principle, to tell us that we have been thoroughly mistaken in our ethics, then the Method of Practical Reasoning should look much better than reflective equilibrium, wide or narrow. The motivation I am trying to invoke now is not metaethical: my worry about reflective equilibrium arises *within* ethics. If you're about to adopt a method which guarantees that what you happen to already think can't be *very* wrong, you need to show – and this is a *moral* demand – that it's not just an expression of self-righteousness, or smugness, or laziness, or an aid to self-deception. After all, if you were very wrong about moral matters, and you made reflective equilibrium your sole method of ethics, you'd never find out. So it would be a tempting method to adopt if, deep down, you suspected, or worse than suspected, that you *were* very wrong ... so tempting, in fact, that you'd better have a convincing argument that this isn't what's going on. I've never seen such an argument, and so, I think we're better off with the Method of Practical Reasoning.[10]

Let's now turn to a chapter by chapter overview of the links between theories of practical reasoning and the canonical (and a couple of less than canonical) moral theories.

4

Instrumentalism is the view that all practical reasoning is means-end reasoning: that the thinking that goes into deciding what to do consists solely in figuring out how to get what you already want. Utilitarianism – not so much a theory as a family of moral theories – directs you to bring about the greatest utility, where that means, roughly, happiness understood subjectively (in terms of the satisfaction of desires or preferences, or, a bit archaically, in terms of pleasant and painful feelings). Instrumentalism is still the default theory of practical reasoning, and utilitarianism, while less fashionable than it used to be, remains one of the canonical moral theories. "What's the Use of Utility?" (Chapter 1) and "Mill's Proof of the Principle of Utility" (Chapter 2) put on display some of the ways in which instrumentalist understandings of practical reasoning and utilitarian ethics travel together.

An instrumentalist understanding of practical rationality naturally – with a caveat I'll get to – gives rise to one or another of the central forms of utilitarianism. Suppose that to adduce a reason for action is always to point out an end to which the action is a means. That end may be a means to a further end, and that further end a means to yet a further end. But eventually, at the terminus of the chain, reasons will bottom out in ends that one *just* has (that is, has without further reasons). It is natural (and traditional) to take them to be determined by brute psychological facts: your final ends are what you just *want* or *prefer*. Alternatively, and in an older way of thinking, they are what give you pleasure (and do not give you pain).

Since what matters and what is important ought to give you reason to act, and since what gives you reason to act is, on this way of filling out the instrumentalist account, your desires, preferences, pleasures, or what have you, it is also natural for instrumentalists turning to moral theory to construe what matters or what is important as an amalgamation of feelings of pleasure, or as a complex of satisfied desires or preferences – in either case, as built up out of the psychological states which determine your final ends. And so instrumentalists will find themselves, other things being equal, with what we have conventionally come to call *utility* at the center of their moral theory. Since reasoning about what to do is, on the

instrumentalist approach, the pursuit of goals, and since utility is introduced as a complex of goals, it is likely to occupy the role of an overall or
all-embracing end in an instrumentalist's moral theory. This is sometimes
remarked upon as the "consequentialist" character of utilitarian theory.
Since utilitarian moral theory directs you to rank outcomes (in terms of
the utility they produce or involve), and then to attempt to achieve the
highest-ranked outcome, it is always looking to the consequences of your
actions.

The instrumentalist's final ends – once again, the ends at the termini
of chains of means-end reasons – are set by brute psychological facts, and
are not themselves the products of practical reasoning. So as far as reason
is concerned, there is no need for them to change, and while they may
change on their own, as it were, they will not be expected to change con-
tinuously and systematically, as the result of ongoing practical reasoning
whose function is precisely to modify final ends. This presumptive stability
is (partly) why it makes sense to treat utility as itself a large or overarching
end, one which moral agents are bound to pursue.

Suppose you have available an alternative theory of practical reasoning
on which there *is* a pervasively operating mode of reasoning that adjusts
and modifies final ends. Such a theory ought to serve as a springboard for
a criticism of utilitarianism, and "What's the Use of Utility?" develops one
criticism of this kind, using what I've elsewhere called *practical induction*
or *practical empiricism* as the alternative theory of practical reasoning. This
is the idea that part of deliberating about what to do is learning, from
experience, what is important and what matters. The chapter sketches
one way such learning occurs, and suggests that the cognitive role of
pleasure is not that of a goal; rather, pleasure is a regulator whose function
is to control the adoption and abandonment of goals.

Suppose that this criticism of utilitarianism is effective, provided that
the practical-inductive theory of practical reasoning is correct. That
would confirm my claim that instrumentalism is part of the machinery of
utilitarian moral theory. If it is right, then it is good policy to redirect arguments about utilitarianism to the question of which theory of practical
reasoning is correct. And if the criticism of utilitarianism is (again, con-
ditionally) effective, then we have shown that attention to its underlying
theory of practical reasoning gives us interesting and useful insights into
the workings of utilitarian moral theory. To reiterate, while practical induction happens to be my own preferred theory of practical reasoning,
I'm not asking you to accept it now; I *am* asking you to agree that the
tension between utilitarianism (a moral theory) and practical induction

(a theory of practical reasoning) is real, and thus, that a theory of practical reasoning can be a constraint on what moral theories you adopt.

"Mill's Proof of the Principle of Utility" was originally published as a primarily exegetical piece. I no longer want to stand by my interpretation of Mill's argument, but I have another use to which I am going to put the discussion here. Because I haven't rewritten the papers collected here, this one requires special reading instructions. First, I'll describe what the paper purports to do; then I'll recount the bug in the argument; I'll explain how it nonetheless puts on display the connections between instrumentalism and utilitarianism that are my present concern; finally, I'll sum up where I think the exegetical question stands.

Instrumentalism is generally introduced as an account of each individual's own practical reasoning, and the instrumentalist takes the pleasures or desires or preferences that guide an individual's practical reasoning to be the individual's own.[11] Utilitarians want their moral theory to be a *socially* suitable set of guidelines, not just an affirmation of widespread individual selfishness. If utility is assembled out of the psychological states that terminate chains of means-end reasons, the moral psychology which seems to drop out of instrumentalism dictates an exclusive concern, on the part of each individual, with that individual's *own* utility (pleasures, desires, and preferences). But a socially satisfactory moral theory will have to take into account the collective or overall utility (defaultly, *everyone's* pleasures, desires, and preferences). This problem – call it the Bridging Problem, because what you are looking for is the right kind of theoretical bridge between individual and collective utility – crops up in Mill in the form of a famous fallacy, allegedly found in his proof of the Principle of Utility. Chapter 2 reconstructs Mill's proof in a way that avoids the fallacy; that is, it attempts to map out Mill's solution to the Bridging Problem.

The short version of the story runs as follows. Like most instrumentalists, Mill introduces a device for correcting the psychological states that are to determine your final ends. A typical way of correcting desires nowadays is to stipulate that the right desires are the ones you *would* have if you had all the relevant information; Mill's older proposal is that your preferences are to be corrected by the preferences of the more experienced. (This sounds like reasonable enough advice in low-key circumstances: if you're wondering whether to see the movie, ask someone who has already seen it how they liked it.) There is a Millian argument to be made that anyone's preferences, corrected in this way, *are* preferences for the general happiness: that the general happiness counts as the most important good to anyone, whether he happens to be aware of it or not. So anyone ought to make choices that promote the general happiness.

As I mentioned, I no longer wish to endorse that interpretation of Mill's argument. The reason is a passage in one of Mill's letters, brought to my attention by Geoffrey Sayre-McCord. In 1868, one Henry Jones wrote to Mill with a criticism of the latter's proof of the Principle of Utility (as a warmup to asking Mill's help in finding a job). In the course of developing his objection, he proposed a reading of one of the phrases in Mill's argument that is more or less my own:

> I . . . understand ["the general happiness is a good to the aggregate of all persons"] to mean that the general happiness is a good to the great majority of persons (or perhaps all.) . . . I mean . . . A's, B's, C's etc. ad inf. happiness (the meaning I take it of "the general happiness") is a good to A, to B, to C, etc.

Mill's response to the construction Jones proposed to put on that step of the argument was as follows:

> As to the sentence you quote from my "Utilitarianism"; when I said that the general happiness is a good to the aggregate of all persons I did not mean that every human being's happiness is a good to every other human being; though I think in a good state of society and education it would be so. I merely meant in this particular sentence to argue that since A's happiness is a good, B's a good, C's a good, &c., the sum of all these goods must be a good.[12]

Mill is disavowing the idea that each person's utility (partially or largely) consists in the summed utilities of all persons. That is, read in conjunction with the letter to which it is a response, Mill's letter flat out denies my reading of one of the conclusions of his argument.

I'm not a great fan of the correspondence theory of truth – I mean, of the view that the correct reading of a philosophical text is to be found in its author's correspondence – but in this case I'm willing to take Mill's word for it.[13] I think we can afford to be relaxed about the historical point because even if we let it go – even once we drop the parts of the interpretation tied to the reading of the phrase Mill has glossed for Jones – "Mill's Proof of the Principle of Utility" usefully displays what the Bridging Problem looks like in Mill's development of utilitarianism, how it arises out of the instrumentalist foundations of the moral theory, and why it will be an urgent issue for any such theory, including our own contemporary variants. In showing how one could assemble a response to it using the intellectual resources provided by Mill's philosophical system (whether or not that response was Mill's own), the chapter works as a full-dress rehearsal for further attempts on the Bridging Problem, and it exhibits the kind of difficulties that have to be overcome. My main concern in exhibiting these difficulties on this occasion is to show how easy it is to end up papering over the deeper problem in the theory of practical reasoning. In particular, the solution Chapter 2 assembles out of Mill's writings has a family resemblance to moves in moral theory that are popular today, and so the points made about it are of current interest. Altogether, whether it has the history right or not, the argument as it stands confirms the intimate connection between instrumentalist and utilitarian moral theory.

Let's take stock of the interpretive state of play, still on the assumption that Mill's letter is decisive. Mill's proof of the Principle of Utility is philosophy's Leaning Tower of Pisa, a glaring architectural flaw turned into a perpetual tourist attraction. If the solution proposed by Chapter 2 was not Mill's way of fixing it, then the interpretive question, of how Mill thought the problem was to be addressed, remains open, and the tour buses can keep coming. We should not be misled by the passage quoted from Mill's letter into thinking that it was his solution to the Bridging Problem (or rather, that we understand what he meant by it). Because philosophers with what we would now regard as professional training were few and far between, Mill's writings were meant for both lay and sophisticated audiences, and so he would often put his points as straightforwardly as possible, deferring to other occasions the argumentation and glosses that the handful of sophisticates would need. Moreover, Henry Jones was not just a layman, but an importuning fan, and his letter, in which he described how Mill's philosophizing had complicated his life, must have been awkward and even embarrassing to read. While Mill no doubt meant what he said, he did not bother, in his curt reply, to explain to Jones *why* (or how) he meant it. But Mill was quite aware that the additivity of the goods of different people required an explanation.[14]

There is one more point to make about Mill's letter to Jones. At the time, utilitarianism was in the first place a political movement, and it had a party line, set out in the main by Bentham. Mill was sharper and philosophically more sophisticated than his movement's founders, but also entirely loyal to them. He dealt with the ensuing tensions not by disagreeing verbally with his fellow Radicals, but by finding interpretations of the party line with which he could live. Much of Mill's proof of the Principle of Utility echoes the first chapter of Bentham's *Introduction to the Principles of Morals and Legislation*, and so does the response to Jones: Bentham says that "the community is a fictitious *body*, composed of the persons who are considered as constituting as it were its *members*. The interest of the community then is, what? – the sum of the interests of the several members who compose it."[15] When Mill tells Jones that "the sum of all these goods must be a good" he is repeating the party line; that does not tell us how Mill had (re)interpreted the party line so as to satisfy his own intellectual scruples, or what arguments he had found to support the crucial additivity claim.

Utilitarianism is motivated by the instrumentalist understanding of practical reason. Chapter 1 shows that it can be criticized from the standpoint of alternative theories of practical reason; Chapter 2 shows that any variant of the view will have to resolve a delicate structural problem whose source is to be found in instrumentalism. If all that is correct, the claims I have been making for the Method of Practical Reasoning are borne out as far as the utilitarian family of moral theories is concerned.

5

Kantian moral theory has gotten a lot of attention recently, and these days, it looks like the theory to beat. Kant's own exposition came with apparently metaphysical baggage that contemporary philosophers do not want to claim, and the present popularity of Kantian ethics is due to the success of a number of commentators, especially Onora O'Neill, Barbara Herman, and Christine Korsgaard, at recasting the position in a more palatable register. "Does the Categorical Imperative Give Rise to a Contradiction in the Will?" (Chapter 3) takes up their version of Kant's Universal Law Formulation of the Categorical Imperative, and, as the title suggests, argues that it is actually self-refuting. I have been suggesting that robust moral theories are normally tightly tied to theories of practical reasoning; in Kant's case the connection is so tight that he scarcely distinguishes them: the subject matter treated by the *Critique of Practical Reason* is continuous with that of the *Groundwork for the Metaphysics of Morals*, which is in turn continuous with that of the *Metaphysics of Morals*. That continuity notwithstanding, the problem the argument of Chapter 3 exhibits has to be understood as a difficulty in Kant's theory of practical reasoning, rather than, say, as a mistake in his moral judgment.

At one level of description, it is fairly clear what the difficulty is. The requirement of universalizability imposed by the Categorical Imperative, first formulation, is, very roughly, that you be able coherently to will that everyone act as you propose to; the counterargument developed in Chapter 3 points out that you cannot coherently will that everyone act in accord with that requirement. In the *Republic*, Plato suggests looking at the city, where we will be able to see justice writ large,[16] and the universalizability requirement, as expressed in the so-called CI-procedure, systematizes that approach. The CI-procedure requires us to project problems onto the backdrop of the 'perturbed social world' (the world in which everyone does as you intend to do), and the counterargument turns on projecting that very requirement onto that very backdrop. What the argument of Chapter 3 exhibits there, writ large, is the unwillingness to regard your practical inferences as (to introduce the relevant bit of quasi-technical vocabulary) *defeasible*: the unwillingness of others to grant exceptions (which I argue you cannot will) is just the way the CI-procedure represents your own insistence on operating with rules that could, in principle, have no exceptions.[17]

This is a concern that generations of Kant's readers have felt, in one way or another. But the concern usually takes the form of a complaint about the too harsh or too demanding nature of Kantian morality (that is, of a complaint about Kant's moral judgment). This has put Kant's opponents in the compromising position of arguing that a moral theory shouldn't be harsh and demanding, and his defenders in the equally compromising position of arguing that Kantian ethics is less harsh and demanding than it sounds. The concern as it is developed here, however, is formal; as Aristotle recognized long ago, in practical deliberation the warranted exceptions are (just about) always endless: practical inference is *characteristically* defeasible.

As we will see, Korsgaard tries to make room for defeasibility by introducing a notion of "provisional universality," the suggestion being that we are settling for less than full, exceptionless universality only for the meantime, and that even if full universality is unattainable (even if it is a limit concept), it is something we approach as we revise our maxims. That is very implausible, and something on the order of a logical mistake. The function of *ceteris paribus* clauses ("all else equal" clauses, in Korsgaard's discussion) is not to mark something else that might be equal, and that when filled in would make inference deductive rather than defeasible; it is, rather, to mark nonmonotonicity in inference.[18] Provisional universality requires Alfred Jarry's pataphysics – "the science of the particular . . . [which] will examine the laws governing exceptions" – and pataphysics was a Dadaist joke.[19]

If the objection to the Kantian universalizability requirement (to the Categorical Imperative, first formulation) is formal and logical, then what looks like a moral problem with the theory (its being unreasonably harsh and overdemanding) bottoms out in the theory of practical reasoning (a mistake about what practical inference patterns can look like). This confirms the usefulness of according priority to the theory of practical reasoning when thinking about moral theories.

What motivated (and still motivates) views of this kind? This question is a reminder of what comes next in the Method of Practical Reasoning: once you have figured out which theory of practical reasoning a given moral theory depends on, you will want to turn to the further question of what is moving that theory of practical reasoning. The postscript to Chapter 4 suggests that what was moving Kant's position on practical reasoning was something less than clearly formulated claims or arguments. (In this, I think, he was not atypical, and so he can be, for most of us, a valuable object lesson.) The Principle of Sufficient Reason, in this context, is the idea, which you still find kicking around in a lot of different forms today, that a *proper* (a *full* or *complete*) reason for action is one which accounts, all on its own, for the practical conclusions drawn from it. Kant never got around to connecting the dots, but he wrote *as though* the Principle of Sufficient Reason was the premise that anchored the Categorical Imperative. Because he didn't connect the dots, he never gave the Principle anything like the kind of argument or full on examination that it needs.

Here Kant's position resembles our own. I am arguing that our moral theories are grounded in our theories of practical reasoning, but we are (still) at a stage of our philosophical development where logic – not the subspeciality of mathematics, but the part of philosophy that asks what makes inferences correct or incorrect – is one of the hardest topics to think about. And so we find that, at two removes, the considerations supporting our ethical and moral views are scarcely thought out at all.

6

Kant's moral theory, together with its underlying view of practical reasoning, occupies the right-wing extreme on a spectrum of views about the universalizability of reasons: if it's a reason, it's *always* a reason. Further to the left, we have Aristotelian theories of practical reasoning, which are focused on defeasibility management. On these sorts of views, if it's a reason, it's normally or presumptively a reason on other occasions; but there are (also normally) indefinitely many exceptions to the general rule, because your presumptive reason can be overridden by other considerations. Aristotle's theory of the practical syllogism captures this understanding of practical reasoning, and "Reasonably Virtuous" (Chapter 4) sketches how his virtue ethics is organized around it. (The chapter then goes on to generalize Aristotle's approach to virtue so as to allow us to exploit the plurality of theories of practical reasoning, and it sketches a number of alternative pictures of virtue that would accompany them; I'll touch on this side of the chapter at the end of this Introduction.) Aristotelian ethical theory is another of the canonical approaches in moral philosophy, and it too stands or falls with the theory of practical reasoning that it is possible to locate at its core.

Still further to the left, we have particularism, according to which, even if something is a reason *here*, so to speak, it may not be a reason *elsewhere* (in a different context) . . . and not because it is being overridden by some other reason. "Murdoch, Practical Reasoning, and Particularism" (Chapter 5) takes up particularism; it tries to show that Iris Murdoch's insights about practical reasoning explain much of her own substantive moral view, and can serve as a theoretical substructure for current particularist moral theory.

At the extreme left or anarchist end of the spectrum would be the view that reasons are like kleenex: you use them once and you throw them away. (On the extreme view, that it's a reason now creates no presumption whatsoever that it will be a reason on any other occasion.) Kleenex reasons may well be unintelligible, and in my view particularism is interesting because it approaches this limit as closely as we are likely to get. Because the extreme anarchist position can look like a philosophical abyss, and because particularism seems dangerously close to it, there has been a tendency among some particularists to try to assimilate particularism to the Aristotelian position one step to the right.[20] This looks to me to be a strategic mistake, and Section 2 in Chapter 5 argues that Aristotelian ethical theory is a bad fit for the central insight of the particularist movement. If I am right about the structure of the spectrum I have been describing, it is mistaken intellectual strategy for a further reason as well. It is easy to be dismissive of reasons that are only good for the occasion; they are, well, hard to wrap one's mind around. But it is good practice to do one's best to make sense of extreme hypotheses, which in this case means articulating a position that is as close as possible to the far end of the spectrum. That in turn means treating objections to particularism as challenges to which one ought to rise, rather than unanswerable rhetorical questions. Whether you find particularism an attractive position or not, you should hope for deeper and more powerful renderings of it.

The Method of Practical Reasoning tells us to expect that variation in the underlying theory of practical reasoning will produce variation in the ensuing moral or ethical theory. On the spectrum we have just been examining, what varies in the account of practical reasoning is the reach and rigidity of reasons for action. Can we make out features of these moral theories that vary along with it?

The traditional claim that the virtues are unified comes up in both Aristotelian ethics and in Murdoch's particularism, and it's instructive to contrast them. For an Aristotelian like McDowell, the doctrine of the unity of the virtues is a way of talking about how the resolution of competing considerations into a decision goes ahead in the agent. The difficult part of reasoning with the Aristotelian practical syllogism is defeasibility management: for example, the considerations expressive of one's courage, when they are invoked in a practical syllogism, can be defeated by considerations expressive of one's honesty; only if the courageous considerations are overridden just when they should be does one count as properly courageous, and so one is properly courageous only when one is also honest – and likewise for the other virtues. (So if you have one virtue, you have them all.) One's awareness of when some consideration should override some other expresses one's grasp of how apparently conflicting objects of choice are unified in "eudaemonia," Aristotle's word for the well-lived life. Aristotelian defeasibility-oriented practical reasoning, done right, is both a producer and product of a unified agent. Considered from the point of view of a theory of practical reasoning, rather than as a moral claim, unity of the virtues, in Aristotelian ethics, is unity of agency; so unity of agency is at the very center of Aristotelian moral theory. (Section 5 of Chapter 4 discusses and criticizes the overidealization involved in this model of practical reasoning and agency.)

In Murdoch's writing, unity of the virtues turns up as a paradigmatic instance of how disparate objects of choice can be seen in a way that resolves conflict: if doing the honest thing, properly described, is also doing the brave thing, apparent conflict between the demands of courage and of honesty is, in the end, only apparent. Murdoch's central insight is that the hard part of figuring out what to do is getting the description of your circumstances right, and that the terms in which your description is to be given are not themselves given to you. (Everyone – from utilitarians on down – ought to agree that you have to describe your circumstances correctly if you're going to make the right decision, but the utilitarian, for example, is certain in advance that the utility of an outcome is going to be part of the right description.) She expects her readers to have been convinced, before they encounter her writing, that the virtues are unified, and so the virtues make a good illustration of a deliberative move which she discusses; but it is obvious that it cannot be merely a consequence of her theory of practical reasoning (as it is in Aristotelian ethics) that the virtues always travel together. Unity of the virtues is neither central to Murdoch's theory nor a theoretical guise assumed by unity of agency.

Murdoch's take on practical reasoning counts as particularist because there is no recipe for arriving at the right description: what are at first glance very similar situations may be, it turns out, correctly described very differently, and you will accordingly have very different reasons for action in each. As a businessperson, you may lobby to prevent the regulation of the carcinogenic pollutants your factory produces; as a major stockholder, you may feel it incumbent upon yourself to donate substantial sums to cancer research; as a homeowner, you may sue to prevent factories like yours from opening up nearby. In other words, the activities of a Murdochian agent are likely to exhibit a sort of patchwork agency. The particularist's virtues may (or may not) turn out to be unified, but that doesn't mean that the particularist agent will be.

Particularism is not as well worked out a moral theory as one would like. I have not tried to develop it further myself, but I will indicate some issues that are worth thinking about, and which would give us a clearer picture of how substantive moral theory depends on its underlying theory of practical reasoning in this instance.

Particularism, as a position about moral matters, looks to some observers like old-fashioned antinomianism, and Chapter 5 rehearses a complaint fielded against it, that it does not accommodate the aspects of morality having to do with social control. We all know people who deploy what looks like particularist reasoning in order to evade their obligations, and while Murdoch acknowledges "the *moral* dangers of . . . specialised and esoteric vision and language," she ends up saying merely that "we know roughly how to deal with these dangers and part of the moral life is dealing with them."[21] An important open question for particularist moral theory is whether there is a more convincing response to the problem than that.

One possibility is that of contesting the objection's assumption that particularist deliberation is inimical to social regulation. Notice that social roles typically function as contexts that change what count as one's reasons. For instance, if you have come across evidence that would pin a crime on its perpetrator, that is reason to come forward with it; but if you are the perpetrator's defense attorney, you instead have reason to conceal it, and to get the evidence ruled out on procedural grounds. Our practices of social regulation are *already* particularist.

Even if particularist moral theory does less well than its competitors on some aspects of social regulation and control, we need to remind ourselves of its compensating strengths. Take a point made by Stanley Kubrick's extended cinematic critique of utilitarianism, that the political tradition descended from it has a great deal of difficulty in making out what is morally wrong with certain ways of *seeing* things.[22] Murdoch's account is able to explain what has gone wrong where utilitarian theory flails.[23] Briefly, particularism may well have the resources needed to address problems on which more traditional theories get stuck.

Finally, and returning to the contrast we were highlighting between Aristotelian ethics and particularism, as we approach the extreme left of the universalizability spectrum, agency becomes more chaotic. Most moral theories require or presuppose highly unified agency, and treat cases in which agents cannot live up to that demand as deviant or "nonideal" cases.[24] But on particularist theories of practical reasoning, disunified or patchwork agency is the result of arriving at one's decisions *correctly*, and so we ought to expect of particularist moral theory that it accommodate disunified agency more generously. It is a very interesting question what such a moral theory might come out looking like.

7

"Was Hume a Humean?" (Chapter 6), "Hume on 'Is' and 'Ought'" (Chapter 7), and "Hume, Political Noncognitivism, and the *History of England*" (Chapter 8) take up Hume at some length. As he is usually read, he is likely to be regarded as evidence that there is less to the Method of Practical Reasoning than I have been promising. Hume is standardly interpreted not just as an instrumentalist, but as the *locus classicus* of instrumentalism. (In fact, it's common to use "Humean" where I use "instrumentalist.") But although Hume has sometimes been described as an "English Utilitarian,"[25] his view is structurally very different from utilitarianism as I have described it here. Sayre-McCord has noticed that "utility," in Hume, is the trigger of a response perhaps most familiar, in the contemporary United States, from encounters with The Sharper Image and its competitors, retailers whose gadgets are intended to strike you as clever and elegant solutions to practical problems.[26] (Remember how often customers purchase the gadgets even when they do not actually have the problems the gadgets are supposed to solve.) The term is not a label for the aggregate built out of end-determining psychological states that we encountered in our earlier discussion of utilitarianism.

If Hume were an instrumentalist, but not a utilitarian, then the Method of Practical Reasoning would not provide as useful a selection principle as

I have been suggesting: choosing the instrumentalist theory of practical reasoning would still leave two structurally very different moral theories in play, rather than telling you which one of them is correct. Utilitarianism, as I have already remarked, is a *family* of moral theories, so I'm not insisting that the Method of Practical Reasoning always produces unique results. Nonetheless, I want to show that it is more effective than that complaint would have it. "Was Hume a Humean?" and "Hume on 'Is' and 'Ought'" argue, in opposition to the standard reading, that Hume is not an instrumentalist after all, and that he actually has the most minimal possible theory of practical reasoning: he does not believe that there is any such thing.

A moral theory that cannot help itself to reasons for action will have to make do with other materials, and various commentators have pointed out several interesting aspects of Hume's attempt to get by with only human emotional responses as his building blocks. I have already mentioned Hume's deployment of an emotional response which is not usually appealed to by moral theorists. Korsgaard has noticed how Hume manages a surrogate for normativity (though she does not think of it as a second-rate substitute herself) by turning one's emotional responses on those very responses: if you approve of your approval, it's good to go. Merritt has realized that virtues – the ethical subject matter of most interest to Hume – will end up being understood from the outside in: both as picked out by patterns of (primarily others') approval and disapproval, and as shaped and enforced by those patterns.[27] These observations jointly give us a partial sketch of what a moral theory constructed around the null theory of practical reasoning can end up looking like.

"Hume, Political Noncognitivism, and the *History of England*" (Chapter 8) adds to these observations an overview of how Hume tried to make sense of our practice of moral argument – an accomplishment you might have thought had been preempted by his account of practical reason. The moral theory of the *Treatise* provides a way of classifying character traits into virtues and vices on the basis of people's emotional reactions to them. But our practice of moral argument consists in a great deal more than pointing out that most people approve of *this* and disapprove of *that*. As an intellectually responsible theorist, Hume was concerned to demonstrate that his philosophical views would not make an insoluble puzzle out of the texture of our ethical lives. Philosophers usually address worries of this kind by producing one or two small-scale, toy treatments; Hume instead wrote a six-volume *History of England*, an extended episode of moral and political argument (or rather, "argument," but I won't keep adding in the scare quotes), which displays, first, how such argument can be conducted consistently with a nihilist position on practical reasoning, and second, how one's strategies of ethical argumentation (and not just one's moral theory) are shaped by one's theory of practical reasoning.

There is a further problem that Hume was attempting to address, and because it is a focus of the chapter, I will just mention it now. We often act, especially in political debate, as though nihilism about practical reason were true, or, to put it differently, as though a much cruder treatment than Hume's captured the force of our self-declared reasons. Hume was trying to come to terms with the novel system of party politics that had recently emerged in England (and from which America's is descended), and he thought of it as a practical problem: how can we bring people to conduct political argument, not as a shouting match teetering on the brink of civil war, but as a method that can bring citizens to agreement on policy? His *History* displays his thinking about that topic also, which makes it an ancestor to the current discussions of deliberative democracy. It is instructive to consider Hume's attempt on a problem with which we subsequently have had so little success.

8

The next two chapters are meant to preempt another apparent alternative to the Method of Practical Reasoning. Sometimes philosophers (and other people) talk and write as though there were these *things* – values – that are just like medium-sized physical objects, except that where furniture and gardening tools have spatial dimensions (length, width or height), values have *evaluative* dimensions. Alternatively, you can find philosophers treating deliberation as though it consisted of episodes in a kind of mental bubble chamber, where the mental particles interact and emit a decision; just as the outcomes of the collisions of physical objects are determined by physical properties (like mass, velocity, or rigidity), so, on this way of looking at things, the deliberative outcomes are determined by properties of the mental particles: especially, by the strength, weight, or intensity of the desires.

If you think those dimensions or properties are just *there*, it makes sense to try to read your ethics off of them. Moorean intuitionism is the *ur*-instance of such a philosophical response: Moore thought he could just see what was good. More typically, however, it is formal features of the values that will seem to dictate the structure of a philosopher's moral theory. For instance, if happiness is a fungible substance, if it comes in *amounts*, and it is something we want greater quantities of, then utilitarianism becomes the obvious moral theory. But if persons are supremely valuable, in a way that doesn't admit of tradeoffs, then something on the order of Kantian respect for them is called for.

Where do our views about this odd class of fact come from? Mackie thought that values were projections of our emotions onto the world.[28] Be that as it may, their formal features (such as their fungibility), which are mostly what matter for the moral theories, *are* projections of either our theories or our practice of practical reasoning. And this point is perhaps most vividly made by taking up the debate about incommensurability, that is, the question of whether, when you compare the values (or their internal mental surrogates, such as desires), you are guaranteed to find that one of them is either more weighty, less weighty, or just as weighty as the other.

"Incommensurability and Practical Reasoning" (Chapter 9) takes the position that commensurability is a product of practical reasoning, and not its precondition (as instrumentalism, the most popular theory of practical reasoning, presupposes). A question like, "Are values commensurable?" shouldn't be expected to have a metaphysically guaranteed yes-or-no answer; rather, values will turn out to be commensurable to one degree or another; commensurable in some ways, but not in others. "Commensurability in Perspective" (Chapter 10) argues that because two of the more important forms of practical reasoning work to undermine commensurability, full commensurability is not even an ideal that successful practical deliberation will approach. On the contrary, if you find someone whose values or ends are fully commensurable, you can be quite sure that he has a history of irrationality. The methodological point I want to underline here is that value theory is not the starting point in the process of selecting a moral theory, but rather a detour on the way there. The formal features of values that are relevant to the choice of moral theory are projections of (explicit or implicit) theories of practical reasoning. They do not explain anything on their own account, and so should not themselves drive the choice of a moral theory. Better instead to take care of your theory of practical reasoning first, and only then see what its consequences are for the metaphysics of values.

9

Let's wrap up the chapter by chapter survey, and step back to consider where the Method of Practical Reasoning can take us. After reviewing the motivations for the Method of Practical Reasoning we have already seen, "Varieties of Practical Reasoning and Varieties of Moral Theory" (Chapter 11) suggests that the Method can do more than just help us to choose from among the moral or ethical theories that we already have.

Each of the three main streams of substantive moral theory – utilitarian or consequentialist, Kantian or deontological, and Aristotelian or virtue-centered – looks back to a distinguished ancestor and a hoary tradition. But that is not necessarily a good thing; in philosophy, a hoary ancestry and a distinguished, even mythologized, founder are not advantages. Appealing to them, whether explicitly or tacitly, is tantamount to an appeal to authority, and if there's any one thing that's off limits in philosophy, it's arguments from authority. On the contrary: if these views are old, they have had a long time to persuade the world of their correctness, and have failed. Moreover, by the time we have reached the final chapter of the volume, we will have added our own objections to the history of deadlock. Prior chapters will have argued that utilitarianism is built on a theory of practical reasoning containing a hard-to-fix bug, and that it misconstrues the cognitive function of desires and of pleasure; that Kantian moral theory is self-refuting, and that it is motivated by the very implausible Principle of Sufficient Reason; and that Aristotelian ethics, because it is built around the practical syllogism, requires an impossibly overidealized agent.

When presidential candidates run and lose, we expect them to step aside, so that other people, with different (and perhaps better) ideas can take a shot at it instead. That's a procedure which, it seems to me, would benefit moral philosophy. Now I have been suggesting that theories of practical reasoning can be paired off with characteristic moral theories: that, in fact, theories of practical reasoning shape and motivate the strong moral theories. That suggests generating novel moral theories by thinking about those theories of practical reasoning that have not yet been embedded in moral theories of their own. Practical reasoning is a field which has only just come of age, and new accounts of practical reasoning are appearing at a relatively rapid clip. So there is new material to be exploited, and we should expect new moral theories to be in the offing.

Sheer intellectual curiosity would be motivation enough for this line of investigation. For instance, what *would* it look like if one were to build an ethical theory around a coherentist account of deliberation – around "inference to the most coherent plan"?[29] Or how *would* a thoroughly inductivist or empiricist moral theory tell us to live? Or again, the bounded rationality tradition has it that what counts as proper inferential procedure will be determined in part by our cognitive limitations. (This is one of the standard arguments for satisficing, that is, the idea that instead of aiming for the very best, you ought to choose the first option to come along that's good enough.[30]) How about moral theories which take bounded rationality seriously?

Turning to new theories of practical reasoning might also allow us to sidestep a source of resistance to allowing views of practical reasoning to dictate moral theories. The more traditional theories of practical reasoning are relatively minimalist: for instance, instrumentalism, which is nowadays the default theory, says that there is only one form that practical reasoning takes, namely, the means-end form. It's hard to get everything moral philosophers tend to want from their moral theory out of such stripped-down accounts of practical reasoning, and so every now and again, you see a moral philosopher's frustrated rebellion against paying attention to practical reason at all.[31] But if there are many available alternatives to the more minimalist theories of practical reasoning, we may find that there is no shortage of construction materials for a full-featured moral theory. Philosophers should not be driven away from the Method of Practical Reasoning by the feeling that it gives them nothing to work with.

That's not meant as reassurance that we will, after deploying the Method of Practical Reasoning, get back a moral theory conforming to our preconceptions of what such theories look like. On the contrary, the likelihood that we will come up with moral theories that do not fit our preconceptions is, in my opinion, the most important payoff promised by the Method of Practical Reasoning. "Reasonably Virtuous" (Chapter 4) gives a foretaste of how that possibility might play out. It develops profiles of virtuous characters suitable to a number of different theories of practical reasoning, some of which notably do not conform to our antecedent conceptions of virtue.

The Method of Practical Reasoning may force us to reconsider and revise our understanding of what a moral theory looks like, and what it does. Kant protested that he was not in the business of moral innovation, because it would be unreasonable to claim to have discovered new moral principles. But *is* innovation in morality so unreasonable? Look around. The moralities we have been living by perform erratically at best, dismayingly at worst. If the Method of Practical Reasoning promises to expand the menu of moral theories, and to allow us to rethink what it is we want a moral theory to do, isn't that, on its own, a weighty reason to adopt it?

Notes

I'm grateful to Lanier Anderson, Chrisoula Andreou and Sarah Buss for comments on earlier drafts, and to the Helen Riaboff Whiteley Center for a congenial place to write one of them.

1. I'll explain what I mean in qualifying the theories as "substantive." To keep things short, in this Introduction I'll use "moral" and "ethical" interchangeably; one contrast conventionally marked by those terms will be introduced in Chapter 4.
2. Millgram, ed., 2001; see ch. 1 for an overview.
3. The examples are from Williams, 2001, p. 80, Kolnai, 2001, pp. 267–8, and Latour, 1996, pp. 89–91, respectively.
4. Millgram, 1997.
5. There are exceptions, e.g., Putnam, 1979. For my purposes, it suffices that Putnam understood himself to be advancing a highly unconventional proposal.
6. See Scheffler, 1994, for an example of a hybrid, and Chapter 11, note 2, for examples of grafted theories. Joseph Perkins has pointed out to me that hybrid theories ought to be the normal output of the competing method of reflective equilibrium. So, and this is something to bear in mind while reading the next section, one explanation for the paucity of hybrids is that reflective equilibrium is actually used a good deal less than the frequency of appeals to it might suggest.
7. Goodman, 1983, p. 64, emphasis deleted.
8. Rawls, 1971, p. 20; the passage comes with a citation to Goodman.
9. The distinction was given wide currency by Daniels, 1979, who takes it from Rawls, 1999. See also Daniels, 1980.
10. But if Goodman is correct, aren't theories of inference, and so, theories of practical reasoning, arrived at via reflective equilibrium? And in that case, isn't the Method of Practical Reasoning really reflective equilibrium in the end? However, the anthology I've mentioned provides a survey of the arguments deployed for and against theories of practical reasoning (Millgram, ed., 2001, see esp. p. 19 for the beginnings of a list). The survey shows that appeals to narrow reflective equilibrium make up only one of the many forms of argument used. And wide reflective equilibrium excludes so little that we do not have to worry about the objection that theories of practical reasoning are arrived at using it.

    Advocates of reflective equilibrium sometimes claim that their method can produce surprises and extensive corrections. Given the way the method works, results of that sort would be, by that very token, very surprising: I'll believe it when I see it.
11. Of course, instrumentalist theories of practical reasoning will normally be meant to apply as well to the deliberation performed by, for example,

bureaucracies, and such institutions don't obviously have desires and so forth in the same sense that individuals do. I'll leave these complications to one side right now.

12. Mill, 1967–1989, XVI:1414, Sayre-McCord, 2001; the correspondence is archived in the Special Collections of the Johns Hopkins Library.

13. The letter dates to a period during which Mill's correspondence was largely written by Helen Taylor, and the younger Taylor was quite willing to express her views in Mill's persona. (A striking example: in a letter to Florence Nightingale, Taylor begins a sentence with, "Myself (but then I am a man) I cannot help thinking that. . . . ") Why think that what we have in the letter to Jones is Mill's authoritative expression of his own intent, rather than an inexpert opinion offered on his behalf by his stepdaughter?

The letter is traditionally given a split attribution, on the basis of a notation on the envelope of Jones's letter. In (as far as I can tell) Mill's handwriting, it reads, "first two paras by H. T." This seems to imply that the final paragraph, that is, the passage I just quoted, is by Mill himself. (I'm grateful to Jo Ellen Jacobs for tracking down the source of the attribution.) The letter was re-copied in Mill's hand; this would have given Mill the chance to correct any mistakes Taylor might have made about his views. And the recordkeeping suggests that Mill anticipated the publication of his letters, which in turn suggests that they were written for public consumption.

And there is a second and more compelling reason to avoid attributing the passage to Taylor rather than Mill. Mill's best-known works were the results of a similar collaboration with Harriet Taylor. Methodological parity would mean separating out Harriet Taylor's contributions from Mill's as well; that would mean fragmenting the Mill corpus beyond usability. (Himmelfarb, 1990, has a very interesting account of Mill's collaboration with Harriet Taylor, which also illustrates the dangers of the approach. She ends up attributing *Utilitarianism* and *On Liberty* to different authors: the former to Mill, and the latter to the joint author consisting of Mill and Harriet Taylor.) In making sense of Mill, one has no real alternative to proceeding on the assumption that the collaborations in which he participated produced a philosophically unified point of view; the alternative would make the body of writing scarcely worth philosophical attention.

14. Let me say briefly why I don't think that the alternative reading proposed by Sayre-McCord, 2001, is satisfactory. First, additivity: On Sayre-McCord's view, "Mill assumes that whatever turns out to be of value [i.e., happiness] is such that we ought to maximize it, and assumes too that the value to be maximized is additive." But Mill did not always assume that goods added up in the way that, say, money does. For instance, the "lower" pleasures are distinguished from the "higher" in that the lower don't add up to parity with the higher. (See Chapter 2, note 38.)

The willingness to ascribe the additivity claim to Mill as an undefended assumption is part of a broader problem. Sayre-McCord takes Mill to be pointing out that people want happiness because they find happiness valuable, in something like the way you might want cake because it's good. The *stuff* – the rich, moist, chocolate cake – is a good *for you*, because it's good, regardless of *who* gets it. The various consumers of the cake, all of whom find it to be a good, are valuing different parts of the same homogenously valuable thing.

However, in Mill's treatment, happiness or utility just is the sum of the things that you want (or perhaps the sum of the things that you *really* want); we can read this point off the argument, in Chapter 4 of *Utilitarianism*, that people desire only happiness. (The argument turns on counting anything someone wants as *thereby* part of his happiness.) When people seem to want different things, and find different things valuable, Sayre-McCord is committed to thinking of them as rather like the blind men in the story, who felt the elephant, gave different accounts of it, but were really sensing different parts of a coherent underlying object. Millian happiness is not like that, because, unless desires are drastically corrected (this is the exegetical option that Chapter 2 explores, and which I am giving up), people's desires are unconstrained by consistency, by similarity, in fact, by anything at all.

A suitable replacement for the parable of the blind men and the elephant might be Philip K. Dick's "Faith of Our Fathers" (1992). In this story, a Mao-like leader appears the same to all of his television viewers, but there is a hallucinogen in the tap water. When the antidote is taken, the shared image vanishes, and the leader appears differently to different people: to one person, he looks like a robot; to another, like a whirlwind; to a third, a sea-monster, and so on. Millian happiness or utility is like *that*: not a shared and homogenous stuff, but a category label masking disparate elements that (unless there is some regimenting device) have nothing in common over and above being desired by someone or other. Getting *this* sort of utility to be well-behaved by the lights of a Cornell moral realist – to be a sort of moral plasticine which can be stuck together, pulled apart, and which remains good by everyone's lights – is a surprising accomplishment. The good behavior cannot be something Mill *assumed*, and it requires an inevitably ambitious explanation.

Note that I am not trying to cast Mill as an esoteric writer; it is not that his writings are supposed to take a secret and Straussian interpretation. But I think there is more to *Utilitarianism* than, for example, Jacobson, 2003, allows, when he takes it to express merely a lowest common denominator of the various utilitarians' doctrines.

15. Bentham, 1789/1970, ch. 1, sec. 4; compare also sec. 11 with Mill's discussion, at the outset of *Utilitarianism*, ch. 4, of the nature of the proof of the Principle of Utility. (Bentham: "Is it susceptible of any direct proof? it should seem not: for that which is used to prove every thing else, cannot itself be proved: a chain of proofs must have their commencement somewhere. To give such proof is as impossible as it is needless.")

16. *Rep.* 368b–369a.

17. For further explanation of defeasibility, see Chapter 4, Section 1, and p. 173. Recall, under this heading, Kant's complaint, in the second *Critique*, about taking happiness as a guiding light: it is "far from sufficing for a law because the exceptions that one is warranted in making upon occasion are endless and cannot be determinately embraced in a universal rule" (Kant, 1902–, vol. 5, at Ak. 28). David Dick has pointed out to me that Kant's arguments

against treating happiness as a practical guide are, *mutatis mutandis*, also arguments against Kant's own use of the mandatory ends put in place by his arguments for imperfect duties. I am not at all clear that there is a way to render Kant consistent on this score.

18. The point is made by Brandom, 2001, sec. 4, and by an unpublished manuscript of John Searle's.

19. Jarry, 1996, p. 21; I'm grateful to Jerry Dworkin for directing me to this very amusing book.

20. Little, 2001a, is an example.

21. Murdoch, 1998, pp. 334, 91–2.

22. Kubrick, 1971. For instance, viewers register *A Clockwork Orange* as misogynist, and initially pin that evaluation on violence to which the female characters are subjected – a mistaken explanation, because the male characters are subjected to just as much violence. More careful attention reveals that viewers are responding to the camera work, the musical cues, and the other aspects of the point of view which the film invites its consumers to inhabit vicariously.

23. What is perhaps her most famous example treats a case of just this type. Murdoch, 1970, pp. 17–23.

24. Jaworska, 1999, is an exemplary discussion of this kind.

25. E.g., Albee, 1957, ch. 5.

26. Sayre-McCord, 1996.

27. Korsgaard, 1996b, pp. 51–63; Merritt, 2000.

28. Mackie, 1977, pp. 38–42.

29. See Thagard and Millgram, 1995, for the slogan, and for one model of coherence. Possibly the view that Nehamas, 1985, attributes to Nietzsche belongs to this family, and can give us some sense of what such theories would be like.

30. Simon, 1957, chs. 14 and 15.

31. Warren Quinn's title, "Putting Rationality in its Place" (1993a), could serve as the excelsior of these recurrent rebellions; however, and confusingly, the best place to find the view in Quinn is not in that paper but in Quinn, 1993b.

We can use a couple of cases already on the table to analyze the frustration. I'm claiming that Hume endorses the null theory of practical reasoning, and so you might expect that, if the connection between theory of practical reasoning and moral theory is as strong as I say, he would have no moral theory at all. Nevertheless, he does produce a moral theory out of the materials available to him. Utilitarianism evidently presupposes instrumentalism, but instrumentalism does not straightforwardly produce utilitarianism, as opposed to, say, egoistic hedonism: this, recall, was the Bridging Problem. I have never seen a plausible solution to the Bridging Problem that was not overly clever; that cleverness is needed and supplied shows that utilitarian moral theorists are working hard to get something that does not come easily.

What both cases show us is that theorists have inherited a conception of what territory a moral theory ought to cover, and more or less how it ought to cover it. That's confirmed by a point I registered earlier, that most people do not think of a moral theory as just a summary or systematization of all of the applications of practical reasoning, correctly performed. The scope of practical reasoning is thought to be broader than the scope of moral theory; but if many choices are not taken to be morally fraught, then there must be a conception of morality that excludes them. It is evidently the mismatch between the inherited conception, on the one hand, and the scanty materials supplied by minimalist theories of practical reasoning, on the other, that gives rise to the frustration.

1

What's the Use of Utility?

The title of this chapter may sound like a question that doesn't need an answer. Utility is one of those things that is obviously good, just plain intrinsically valuable; good in itself, and not *for* anything else. On some views, it's the only such thing, and utilitarianism is the natural upshot. I'm going to present arguments against two varieties of utilitarianism, arguments which will put us in a position to advance an answer, or rather, two related answers, to the question: what *is* the use of utility?

There have been different ways of understanding the notion of utility, and so there have been correspondingly different varieties of utilitarianism in play. I can't (and won't try to) consider all of the many bearers of the name. The two I do want to discuss here are interesting (despite a notable shortfall of adherents) because they are perhaps the clearest expressions of the thought that, it seems to me, moved the better-known utilitarians: that things matter because we have a stake in them, and not the other way around; we do not have a stake in things because they already matter. In trying to make sense of having a stake in something, in a way that could be explanatorily prior to that something's importance, utilitarians came to understand having a stake as *psychological*, and they went on to look for the classes of mental states in which having a stake consisted.[1] What they found was determined by the available ways of thinking about the mental. Against the background of British Empiricism, nineteenth-century utilitarians took the mattering-making mental states to be pleasure and pain, understood on the model of sensations. Later on, with the advent of propositional-attitude psychology, the mattering-makers became propositional attitudes, viz., desires and preferences. I will be focusing here on two resulting subjectivist forms of utility (and the corresponding forms of utilitarianism), beginning with utility construed as a matter of intrinsically valuable phenomenal states, paradigmatically, pleasure, and proceeding in due course to utility as a matter of the satisfaction of desires or preferences.

1

Utilitarianism recommends taking actions or adopting policies that maximize utility.[2] It is thus committed to what we can call the Presumption of Effectiveness: that, normally, there are available policies and actions, choice among which will make a significant difference to utility. And it is committed to a more fully spelled-out version of the Presumption of Effectiveness, call it the Contoured Presumption of Effectiveness, roughly that since differences in utility are, according to utilitarianism, what matter, when moral choices that matter are at hand, differences in utility that can make sense of, and guide us, in those moral choices must also be at hand. That is, the contours of the moral landscape match the contours of the utility landscape, and, in particular, if significant moral choices are to be made on the basis of the differences they make to utility, the differences should be significant rather than trivial differences in utility. We can think of the Contoured Presumption of Effectiveness as an expression of our interest in moral theory. (I do not intend it to be supported by "intuitions" as to what counts as a moral choice.) What we want to know, when we look for a moral theory, is: how should we go about making *these* decisions? (Should I break my promise when keeping it will mean betraying my friend? How should I think about my responsibilities toward my charges?) If a would-be moral theory fails to answer enough of these questions, and to answer them compellingly, then, whatever other merits it may have, it is not what we were looking for.[3]

The Presumption of Effectiveness seems quite innocent. It goes without saying that, typically, our morally important choices make a significant difference to the utilities of those involved, whether these are construed in terms of hedonic tone or in terms of preference satisfaction, just because our actions in general have consequences that affect our utilities. The frequent votes on whether gambling should be legal in this or that location are bound to have large consequences for the utilities of those who might start playing the lottery; driving decisions can have enormous effects on the utilities of those on the road. After all, if you win the lottery, you will be very happy for a very long time; whereas if you are permanently crippled in an automobile accident, you will be miserable.

The Presumption of Effectiveness goes without saying; but, I am about to argue, it is nonetheless false. If it is false, then utilitarianism is deeply misguided. This implication seems to have been acknowledged by John Stuart Mill, perhaps the most subtle and influential advocate of the theory; he writes that "if no happiness is to be had at all by human beings, the attainment of it cannot be the end of morality or of any rational conduct."[4] Utilitarianism proposes as the criterion of moral choice that the option be selected that will most increase (or least decrease) overall utility. But if it were true that in normal circumstances nothing one does is going to make much of a difference to anyone's utility, or is not going to make the right kind of a difference, then utilitarianism would not have in fact provided a satisfactory criterion of moral choice. As it turns out, something like this is actually the case. For while Mill was right in thinking that claiming happiness to be entirely impossible would be "at least an exaggeration," there are more ways to fail to make the right kind of a difference to utility than not producing any at all.

I remarked a moment ago that if you were to win the lottery, you would very probably be much happier than you are now, and if you were to be permanently crippled in an automobile accident, you would very probably be devastated. There is not much of a mystery here; or there would not be, if it were true. But it is not. In a study that had lottery winners and accident victims assess their happiness, "lottery winners and controls were not significantly different in their ratings of how happy they were now, how happy they were before . . . , and how happy they expected to be in a couple of years." While recent "accident victims . . . experienc[ed] their present as less happy than controls . . . the paraplegic rating of present happiness [was] still above the midpoint of the scale, and . . . the accident victims did not appear nearly as unhappy as might have been expected."[5] The subjects were interviewed between a month and a year after their respective strokes of good or bad fortune, and so this should not be all that surprising. If good fortune strikes, you will be briefly elated. But as you become accustomed to your new situation, the elation will wear off, you will find new things to be dissatisfied about, and very soon you will be about as happy (or as unhappy) as before. If, on the other hand, disaster strikes, after a painful period of readjustment you will once again find things in which to take pleasure; upon getting used to your new circumstances, you will find that they do not make that great a difference to how you feel.[6]

Once the phenomenon has been pointed out, it is easy enough to see how widespread it is. Changes in one's circumstances bring about temporary changes in one's hedonic tone. But over the long haul how happy one feels is mostly a matter of temperament rather than circumstance. If one's utility or happiness is thought of as being a matter of how one feels, then, modulo short-lived fluctuations, it does not look like there is much in the normal run of things that one can do to make people more or less happy. And if that is true, then the Presumption of Effectiveness is false, and utilitarianism fails.

2

My denial of the Presumption of Effectiveness is meant to be the minimum needed for the job. The Contoured Presumption has it that significant differences in utility can be identified when moral decisions are at hand. So denying the Presumption means holding that there are clumps of our moral world for which the Presumption fails, and that these clumps are too large to sweep under the rug. It does not require holding that we cannot find decisions that make a significant difference to utility. I want to allow that sometimes people get depressed, and stay that way. I am willing to allow that there may be severe trials that permanently affect one's ability to be happy – even if being maimed in an automobile accident is not quite enough. And, of course, minor variations in utility are ubiquitous: people become upbeat or down in the mouth, buoyant or glum; utility fluctuates.

Minor choices typically produce minor effects on the utilities of those involved, but when the choice is minor, a minor effect is just the right basis on which to make the choice. When I miss the movie and become annoyed and irritable, the utilitarian can point to these effects as a perfectly good reason for not having missed the movie. If we are allowing that extreme circumstances can produce permanent effects on one's happiness, then we should also allow that utilitarianism can give us guidance when such circumstances come up: it might tell us not to torture people or send them to death camps. And if, as I have suggested, one's long-term happiness is mostly a matter of one's temperament, it may be that utility can be affected indirectly, by bringing about circumstances that cause a change in one's temperament, and that a utilitarian moral theory could keep us gainfully employed in improving our fellow man's character.[7]

Minor effects on utility are proportionate to minor decisions, but not all decisions are minor. Even if choice makes a significant difference to utility in extreme situations, extreme situations are, thankfully, rare. It is not enough, for the Presumption to be borne out, that such effects can be found occasionally; they must be found more or less across the board. And while the project of changing others' temperaments for the better – that is, for the more utility-generating – need not leave one at a loss for things to do, one cannot respond intelligently to all situations that require decisions by addressing only their pedagogical upshots.

Evidently, the plausibility of utilitarianism depends on the large middle range of cases, and here, I suggest, we will see that the Contoured Presumption of Effectiveness does not hold good. The problem is that large changes in one's welfare are correlated with minor changes in one's utility. Getting admitted to (or rejected by) a prestigious college may make an enormous difference to how well the prospective student's life is going, while making relatively little difference to how she *feels*: after a week or so of celebration or dejection, the applicant will be back on an even keel. The sense of accomplishment in bringing home the washing machine is gone by the next morning, although the contribution the appliance will make to one's well-being is not. (You will very shortly cease to feel much of anything about the fact that you can now just drop your clothes into the machine, instead of spending your afternoons at the laundromat; but, feeling or no feeling, the washing machine continues to wash your clothes and to save you those afternoons.) Having one's aging parent come to live with one may make her life better, even much better, without making her any happier: having complained bitterly about being kept out of the household, she may subsequently complain just as bitterly about the irascibility of her grandchild.

In cases like these, decisions do make a difference to the utilities of those involved, but the difference in utility and the importance of the decision are disproportionate; the incremental utility is evanescent, and quite incapable of supporting the somewhat weighty decision. I have not yet provided an explanation for the phenomenon that shows why this disproportion is and should be normal; for the moment, what matters is that a survey of occasions on which we make decisions of moral significance will show that it is not at all unusual. If that is correct, then utilitarianism must be startlingly revisionist about the scope of morally significant deliberation.

Let me return to the question of how revisionist utilitarians can be about what decisions are morally important or morally significant or morally interesting. I suggested earlier that revisionism cannot go beyond a certain point without simply changing the subject – that is, without ceasing to answer the practical questions for which we turned to moral theorizing in the first place. Now, for my own part, I am all in favor of the

willingness to be persuaded that one's questions are misguided, and interest in them misplaced. But the willingness to be so persuaded cannot be
expected to take utilitarians very far. Large-scale revisionism about what
choices are important ought to wait on being shown that our interests
are misplaced, and that would take an argument. The reason utilitarians
want to employ is that utility is the only thing that matters, and so that
is what the argument would have to demonstrate. Argument about what
matters generally invokes claims about what else matters, so by insisting
that nothing but utility matters, utilitarians have deprived themselves of
the resources needed to assemble such an argument; it is a peculiar feature of the utilitarian view that its competitors are far better equipped to
explain the importance of its pivotal concept than is utilitarianism itself.
So utilitarians are not in a position to insist on replacing our conception
of our practical interests with theirs. And consequently, if I am right about
the ways in which the Presumption of Effectiveness fails, utilitarianism –
that is, the variety of utilitarianism that takes utility to be something
you *feel* – is about as wrong-headed as it is possible for a moral theory
to be.

3

Utilitarianism is false, if the Presumption of Effectiveness is false. But the
evidence so far against the Presumption consists of one briefly reported
study and a handful of anecdotes, and you may be wondering just how
seriously to take the study, or you may be looking around for contrary
anecdotes. However, I do not want to worry too hard about the empirical
question, because the point I am after is not in the first place empirical.
It is not just that most people, most of the time, respond to their circumstances in a way that makes the Presumption of Effectiveness false: it is
that they *should.*

Suppose you are driving in Manhattan and you find a parking place
right in front of the restaurant; you are, quite reasonably, euphoric. But
only for a moment or two; if you are still euphoric three months later,
something has gone very wrong. If, after an appropriate period of mourn-
ing, you find that a friend is not coming out of his depression, you start to
worry; life, after all, goes on. New pleasures fade into the background; it is
one thing, when one has first gotten one's license, to be thrilled at driving
down to the corner grocery store; it is another thing entirely to be just as
thrilled after ten years behind the wheel. If people cannot abandon shat-
tered hopes, or cannot get used to their improved circumstances, we will

think they are not getting something right; in extreme cases, we are likely to be concerned about their mental health. So utilitarianism's problem is not simply an empirically false presupposition, but rather that the moral theory is at odds with our other views as to how it is *appropriate* to feel – and I am willing to take it as a working hypothesis that, one way or another, the requirement explains the falsity of the empirical presupposition.

When good news comes along, we become elated; utility surges. But after a while, even though the news is as good as it ever was, utility fades. And when bad news comes along, utility plummets; but when we have had a little while to adjust, utility rises back to roughly its original level, even though the news has not improved. Evidently, utility does not covary with how well or how badly off one is. Rather, it indicates whether one's circumstances are getting, or have just gotten, better or worse.[8] As is almost always the case in philosophy, the mistaken view has a very large kernel of truth in it: utility *is* very important in practical and in specifically moral reasoning. What utilitarians were wrong about was *how* utility is important. They took it to be a goal, and the sole bearer of value. In fact, however, it plays a very different role in our mental economies. The cognitive function of utility is, I suggest, not to be, or stand in for, the absolute level of one's welfare, but to alert one to changes in it.[9]

There are two points here. The first is that utility is an indicator, not a goal; the difference is exhibited in the way actions and plans appropriately respond to each. A speedometer is normally an indicator: it is appropriate to keep it at 65 by accelerating and braking, but not by nailing the needle to the desired spot on the dial and flooring the gas. Before we go any further, however, the claim that phenomenal utility is an indicator has to be supplemented with a fairly drastic qualification. Human beings have a history of putting indicators to other uses. For instance, our visual representation of our surroundings is in the first place an indicator of what those surroundings are like, but that is an unpromising way to try to make sense of going out to the movies. The traditional category of false pleasures (which are straightforwardly handled in the obvious way by the account we are developing) should be joined by the further category of *fictional* pleasures. I don't have the wherewithal for a satisfactory reconstruction of these, and so here I will put this admittedly important division of the subject to one side.

The second point is that fluctuations in utility tell you that you're doing better or doing worse, but they don't tell you how well, in absolute terms, you're actually doing.[10] And that raises the question of why we would be equipped with an indicator of change in welfare. The frankly speculative answer I want to entertain here turns on a search technique called *hill-climbing*.[11] Imagine yourself standing at some point in a landscape. You want to be as high up as possible, but you don't have a topographical map of the landscape, and (maybe because it's a very foggy day) you can't see the terrain around you. To hill-climb, you identify the highest point within a small radius by taking, first, a step in one direction, then stepping back, then taking a step in another direction, and so on. Once you have identified the highest point within the small circle around you, you step over and stand on that point. You repeat this procedure until there is no point within the small radius that is higher than the point you're standing on.

Now, you can use this technique to solve problems that can be represented as appropriate topographical maps. Think of the space of options: things you are and could be doing, some very close to what you're doing now, and some harder to get to, and so farther away. And think of each location in the plane as having a height that represents how well off you are when you avail yourself of the option the location stands for. As long as you hill-climb, you're changing your situation for the better. Hill-climbing is efficient in that it doesn't demand of you a lot of information that may be hard to come by, such as what the topography of the space you're in looks like overall. It's likely to be computationally inexpensive: it's relatively easy to compare the few nearby options. It also has some important drawbacks, the most well known being that you can get trapped at the top of a relatively low hill; if all you're doing is hill-climbing, you can't go down the hill you're on to climb a higher hill elsewhere.

Human beings are built to hill-climb. (Which is not to say that's *all* they're built to do.) So they need the information this particular search technique uses. Now, in order to hill-climb effectively, you don't need to know what your altitude is (even though you are hill-climbing in order to gain altitude). All you need to know is: which of a few adjacent points is higher than the others? If your strategy for improving your welfare is to hill-climb in the welfare landscape, you don't actually have to know how well you're doing; it's enough to know whether some change you make is a change for the better or for the worse. The only information you require is comparative, and because it's information about nearby locations in the space of options, it's mostly information you can get by sidling over a step or two and seeing if you've gone uphill or not. The role of phenomenal utility in our cognitive economies is to supply that information.[12]

4

I've claimed that phenomenal utility is an indicator, and if that is right, then it is neither the sole nor the primary bearer of value. What matters, in the first place, is what utility is there to help you improve: roughly, how well you're doing. But this may seem to have a consequence which flies in the face of common sense, that pleasure and displeasure or pain are not in themselves good or bad. A speedometer is just an indicator, and so we do not much care about the state of the dial: we care about how fast we are going, and if we think the speedometer is malfunctioning, we ignore it. But when you are in great pain, and the pain indicates no *further* problem, we think your situation can be dramatically improved by alleviating the pain; telling you to ignore the pain is telling you to make the best of a bad situation, not that you just need to remember that your situation is fine as it is. When people's lives are colored by pervasively and inappropriately low hedonic tone, many of us (just how many is suggested by the size of the serotonin-reuptake inhibitor industry) think their lives would be better if their mood improved. At the extremes of idiotic glee and absolutely blue funk, sensitivity to variation in one's welfare may be impaired, but between those extremes it probably is not, and we nevertheless regard those of generally cheerful disposition as luckier than the sourpusses. The account we have under construction will be much easier to swallow if it can accommodate the fact that pleasure seems to just about everyone to be obviously, immediately, and intrinsically a good (and pain and displeasure likewise an evil).[13]

However, we can do better than just accommodate the fact that plea-sure feels good. The indicator account makes that fact out to be more or less inevitable. Imagine a device that provided the information which I have suggested it is the role of phenomenal utility to supply, but which conveyed that information in a way that did not itself feel one way or the other: perhaps an earplug muttering "getting better" and "getting worse" at appropriate moments. Such an indicator could be used by an adult, who already grasps the notion of things going well for him, and already cares that they are. But an infant or small child would not be well-served by such a device, and if all the infant had to go on were the deliverances of the earplug, it would never come to understand the notion of its own welfare at all. Part of learning what it is for things to go well is learning to care about how they are going, and this requires, at the early stages, something about which one cares without first learning to. For indicators with the practical force of pleasure and pain to be possible in creatures with developmental histories like ours, some such indicators must themselves appear obviously good (or evil) on their own. So we should not be surprised to find that pleasure feels good, and that pain feels bad; nothing else would have done the job.

The explanation I have just broached addresses the question of why pleasure *seems* so obviously a good; it does not take a stand on whether it *is*, and I want to leave that question open for now. Think back to an occasion on which you received some very good news. Good news is good in two ways: it is news of something good, but it is also good to *get*. (That is why it is so nice to be the bearer of good tidings.) Getting the good news can be intrinsically valuable (that is, valuable not simply as a means to responding correctly to the news), while being in another way derivatively valuable (its goodness derives from the thing it is news of). Perhaps indicators like pleasure are like good news in this way. If they are, they are valuable or important secondarily, in virtue of something else's being already valuable or important; allowing that phenomenal utility is in this way intrinsically valuable would not be a way back to utilitarianism.

5

Now you may have been inclined to allow me my refutation of utilitarianism, while wondering if the target was not in fact a straw man. After all, the phenomenal variety of utilitarianism that I have attacked took utility to be something *felt*; and this view has, since Bentham, had few philosophical defenders.[14] (Nietzsche thinks that the doctrine of free will "owes its persistence to this charm alone," "that it is refutable"; and it is easy to suspect that something similar is true of the less persuasive forms of utilitarianism.[15]) So recall that what I want us to take away from this exercise is a more important lesson than that an already discredited view has been further discredited. The argument against phenomenal utilitarianism opens out into an account of phenomenal utility on which it registers changes in welfare, and so facilitates hill-climbing; it is one piece of an answer to our question about the use of utility. I now want to proceed to another variety of utilitarianism, one that recommends maximizing the satisfaction of preferences or desires.

Because I am interested in the turn to utility as an expression of the thought that one's stake in something is explained by one's psychology, I want to examine what is perhaps an unusual form of satisfaction-oriented utilitarianism, one that I have never actually seen defended.[16] This view will share with more standard variants the idea that being well off is a matter of having one's preferences (or, equivalently for present purposes, one's desires) satisfied, and that the benefit of having one's desires fulfilled or preferences satisfied is not the *feeling* of satisfaction. Rather, having the desire that *p* makes the truth of *p* good for you, and this kind of goodness-for-you is what makes up your welfare, or well-being, or utility.[17] In keeping with the spirit of the subjectivist approach to utility, the view insists that it is because you have a subjective stake in the objects of your desires or preferences – because you *care* about them — that they matter. But, it continues (and here the view swerves away from more standard variants), nothing in this world comes for free. Caring about something, having a subjective stake in it, involves the commitment of psychological resources, and in the small-finite minds that humans necessarily have, psychological resources are a scarce commodity. As philosophers nowadays mostly use terms like "desire" and "preference," we have too many of each for there to be enough *mind* to go around for all of them – "mind," that is, as in "Do you mind?" Because people cannot have the time or the energy to care about very much, we should expect the desires and preferences in which one has invested one's concern to be rather sparse. Let us call preferences and desires to which such resources have been committed *live*, without trying right now to say too precisely just what that comes to. Then we can say that the form of utilitarianism we are about to consider will take utility to consist in the satisfaction of live desires and preferences.[18]

Now imagine that everything you really want is one day handed to you on a silver platter; suddenly, all your live preferences and desires are satisfied. How long will it take for you to expand your horizons, become more ambitious, and find yourself with as many unsatisfied live desires as you had had before? Or suppose that almost everything you have is taken away from you: desires and preferences whose satisfaction had seemed within reach are suddenly unattainable. How long will it take for you to adjust to the new and narrower confines of your life? In either case, not very long; sooner or later, but probably sooner, you will find yourself back where you started, as far as this notion of utility is concerned.[19]

You might think that, whatever new desires you subsequently acquire, the fact that your past desires have been satisfied is something already chalked up to your credit: they can't take that away from you. And so, as desires or preferences are satisfied, your overall utility increases. But recall that on the extremely subjectivist version of utility we are considering, desires satisfied in the past only matter if we still care about them, and as the limited psychological resources that were invested in those preferences and desires are diverted to new objects, we will inevitably cease to care: one very soon takes one's recent acquisitions and attainments for granted. (When you graduated from high school, it was probably a big deal; but if that was some time back, it probably isn't a big deal anymore.) A past live desire, once satisfied, remains satisfied; but if your subjective stake in it evaporates, we can no longer regard it as part of your present subjective utility.[20] So utility will remain roughly constant, barring temporary fluctuations (and notice that, for the same reason, and allowing for the trickiness of counting such things, the *proportion* of unsatisfied desires and preferences will remain roughly constant also).

What this means is that trying to change an agent's utility – understood, again, in terms of the satisfaction of live desires or preferences – is, in normal circumstances, a Sisyphean task. You may think that you know what you want, and so what it would take to make you happy; but shortly after those wants are satisfied, it will turn out that you now want something else, and that happiness has once again slipped back toward the horizon. And after many such cycles, a life directed toward satisfying desire may start to seem like that of a rat on a treadmill. The Contoured Presumption of Effectiveness fails for this more sophisticated notion of utility as well, and so the corresponding variety of utilitarianism fails also. There is not, the way things ordinarily go, much that you can do to significantly increase a person's utility.[21]

Once again, the claim is not in the first place empirical but normative. The point of desires and of preferences is to guide action. If we are to live, and to live well,[22] then we must act, and act both ambitiously and realistically. So we must have preferences and desires, and they must be ambitious yet realistic preferences and desires.

To say that our preferences and desires must be both ambitious and realistic is to say that it is no accident that they exhibit the responsiveness to circumstance that we have been discussing. One must want what one does not have, or one will not be guided to act. This means that when one's desires are satisfied, one must go on to develop new desires that are appropriate to one's situation. So it is not a merely contingent fact that attempting to satisfy someone's desires is normally a never-ending task. Again, one must want what one believes one has a chance of getting or one will not be guided to act; and one must not want too many different things, on pain of being swamped by competing demands (in which case one will, again, not be guided to act). So we should not be surprised that when the objects of desire move ineluctably out of reach, one's desires adjust themselves to the newly narrow horizons. For *practical* purposes, that is to say, the purposes of practical reasoning, having everything you want, and wanting only things you cannot have, leave you in the same state: paralyzed, and unable to think about what to do next. This is one reason why the capacity to set ourselves new ends, and abandon pointless ones, is the deep feature of practical reasoning that Kant thought it was (though perhaps not in the way Kant thought it was). The thankless nature of the task proposed by this version of utilitarianism points to the way in which treating preference- or desire-satisfaction as a goal is misconceived. To take preferences or desires to be the sole intrinsic bearers of value is to forget what they are *for.*[23]

6

When philosophers and economists realized that phenomenal utility (that is, pleasure, the first of the two forms of utility that we have been considering) would not by itself serve to explain our priorities, discussion by and large turned to satisfaction construals of utility (that is, to preference- and desire-based forms), and pleasure ceased to receive substantial philosophical attention.[24] That was a mistake, or so I will now suggest. Changes in phenomenal utility figure prominently in the processes through which the desires and preferences that anchor satisfaction-oriented forms of utility alter, and to show how this happens, I want to use a fictional but very observant example given by Richard Ford, in his thoughtful novel *Independence Day.*

His narrator and protagonist, Frank Bascombe, is a real estate agent trying to sell a house to a couple looking to buy in Haddam (a renamed Princeton, New Jersey). They have a very clearly specified goal:

What the Markhams were in the market for – as I told them – was absolutely clear and they were dead right to want it: a modest three-bedroom with charm and maybe a few nice touches, though in keeping with the scaled-back, education-first ethic they'd opted for. A house with hardwood floors, crown moldings, a small carved mantel, plain banisters, mullioned windows, perhaps a window seat. A Cape or a converted saltbox set back on a small chunk of land bordering some curmudgeonly old farmer's cornfield or else a little pond or stream. Pre-war, or just after. Slightly out of the way. A lawn with maybe a healthy maple tree, some mature plantings, an attached garage possibly needing improvement. Assumable note or owner-finance, something they could live with. Nothing ostentatious: a sensible home for the recast nuclear family commencing life's third quartile with a kid on board. Something in the 148K area, up to three thousand square feet, close to a middle school, with a walk to the grocery.[25]

But coming to a new situation with desires of this degree of specificity makes it likely that one's desires don't have a lot to do with the choice situation one is in. Once again, the point of desires is to guide choice, and when desires are not realistic, they will fail to perform their cognitive function. In this case, as Ford's real estate agent informs the reader, "houses like that . . . those houses are history. Ancient history."

> The houses I *could* show them all fell significantly below their dream. The current median Haddam-area house goes for 149K, which buys you a builder-design colonial in an almost completed development in not-all-that-nearby Mallards Landing: 1,900 sq ft, including garage, three-bedroom, two-bath, expandable, no fplc, basement or carpets, sited on a 50-by-200 foot lot "clustered" to preserve the theme of open space and in full view of a fiberglass-bottom "pond." All of which cast them into a deep gloom pit and, after three weeks of looking, made them not even willing to haul out of the car and walk through most of the houses where I'd made appointments.

The mismatch between the guiding desire and the choice situation brings about a dramatic drop in hedonic tone (the "deep gloom pit"). Ford's fiction suggests, and I want to suggest as well, that one of the functions of shifts in phenomenal utility is to trigger readjustment of one's preferences and desires, and of one's subjective stake in them. (Over the next fifty pages, we see the Markhams flailing as they try to come by desires appropriate to the choice they've given themselves.) The process of readjustment is complex – in the case Ford depicts, the Markhams' self-images and the stories they have to tell about their lives will need to change – but it will often (and more modestly) involve recalibrating satisficing thresholds.[26] A satisficing strategy is one that aims, not for the very best, but for good enough; having ambitious but realistic aspirations depends, when one is satisficing, on appropriately resetting one's view as to what counts as good enough.[27] Such recalibration is typically initiated by shifts in hedonic tone. Desires and preferences should not displace pleasure in an account of practical reasoning. On the contrary, an interest in how desires and preferences change (and should change) underwrites renewed attention to phenomenal utility.[28]

7

We've now seen arguments against two varieties of utilitarianism, and in each case, the moral theory turned out to be no more plausible than the partial account of mental activity that it presupposed. (Utilitarianism fetishizes one or another kind of mental state – feelings of pleasure, desires, or preferences – by forgetting that these mental items are there to *do* something.) So one way to learn a lesson from the argument I've been developing would be to conclude that if your moral theory is going to have a shot at success, you had better get your philosophy of mind (or your cognitive science) straight first.

But this is not how I think we would do best to take up the anti-utilitarian arguments we've seen. Recall that the claims about the workings of the various mental states turned out to be, not in the first place empirical, but prescriptive. Pleasures *should* be transient. Pains *should* be transient. A state in which your desires have been entirely satisfied should be impossible to attain – or, anyway, to sustain. (And if you find this thought depressing, don't worry, it won't last.)

Now, what is the force of that *should*? Once upon a time, back in the good old days, some logical positivists endorsed the view that certain things could be said either in the "material mode" or in the "formal mode."[29] The insight they had was that there could be statements which, although seeming on the surface to be about completely different kinds of items (for example, numbers and "number-words"), were in fact merely different ways of expressing the same thing. Whether or not these positivists were right about numbers and "number-words," something very much like this is true in the domain of practical reasoning, that is, reasoning about what to do.

Let me take as my illustration of this idea what is probably still the received view regarding practical reasoning: instrumentalism, which claims that all practical reasoning is means-end reasoning. Instrumentalism is expressed in the *formal mode*, as a claim about justification: the only way to justify a goal or action is to show that it is a means to achieving a further goal. But it is also expressed in the *psychological mode*, in the claim that practical reasoning is made up of sequences of desires linked by beliefs, as in this example: I want a hat, and I believe that if I give the clerk behind the counter some money, I will receive a hat; so, other things being equal, I want (or, if I am reasoning correctly, will come to want) to hand over the money. The resulting view, that your mind, or anyway, the bits of it that do all the thinking, is made up only of beliefs and desires, is called "belief-desire psychology."[30]

Belief-desire psychology may sound like a theory about mental inventories that tells us what is there anyway, in much the way that theories in the natural sciences tell us what is there anyway. But we should not be misled: belief-desire psychology is simply one among several expressions of a prescriptive account of practical rationality, and its ontology, merely a projection onto the mind of the inference patterns acknowledged as legitimate by the prescriptive account. If the only form of practical justification you countenance links goals, by way of facts about what goal is a means to what other goal, then when you interpret or describe mental activity as rational, you will find only the psychological stand-ins for goals and the linking facts: you will find only beliefs and desires. Our views about how mental processes work, especially when they turn out on examination to have a prescriptive dimension, are often just views about rationality and justification expressed in the psychological mode.[31]

If views about the workings of one's mental states are typically views, expressed in the psychological mode, about rationality, then we should expect the views we invoked in the course of arguing against different varieties of utilitarianism – about the ways pleasure or hedonic tone, desires or preferences, work (and *should* work) – actually to be views about practical reasoning. We don't have all the pieces of the puzzle on hand, but those pieces we've seen fit together: practical reasoning, correctly performed, involves maintaining an agenda that keeps one an ambitious and realistic agent; change in well-being (indicated by hedonic tone) determines when it is appropriate to add or delete goals (or, as they say in the business world, action items) to or from one's agenda.[32] If that is right, then the real problem with our utilitarian theories is that the practical reasoning required by the moral theory is inconsistent with a background view of practical reasoning that we already accept. This inconsistency is not one that we can overlook. Moral reasoning is practical reasoning applied to moral subject matter; so we must require of our moral theories that they be compatible with our best theories of practical reasoning. The two variants of utilitarianism that we have seen do not pass this test. I suspect that, in this respect, they are not atypical of the available moral theories.

Notes

I'm grateful to Jon Bendor, Sarah Buss, Ruth Chang, Alice Clapman, Allen Coates, Alice Crary, Julia Driver, Christoph Fehige, Daniel Gilbert, Amy Gutmann, Gilbert Harman, Jenann Ismael, Donald Light, Seana Shiffrin, and Eric Wiland for comments on an earlier draft, to Alyssa Bernstein, Jay Bernstein, Lenn Goodman, Amy Johnson, Rachana Kamtekar, Sean Kelsey, Geoff Sayre-McCord, and Peter Singer for helpful discussion, and to audiences at Rutgers, USC, Ben-Gurion University, and a symposium on Practical Reasoning at the 1998 meeting of the American Philosophical Association, Central Division. Work on this paper was supported by fellowships from the National Endowment for the Humanities and the Center for Advanced Study in the Behavioral Sciences; I am grateful for the financial support provided through the Center by the Andrew W. Mellon Foundation.

1. The move from "psychological" to "in virtue of a class of mental states" is evidently optional. The Kantian preference for autonomy over heteronomy expresses the same, or a similar thought about the direction of explanation, but lack of contradiction in the will is not a mental state on a par with desire or preference. Again, advocates of identity-based reasons (the foremost of whom happens also to be a Kantian: Korsgaard, 1996b) take the stake you have in some things to be a matter of your practical identity, for example, of your being a Fiat employee, a skinhead, a Croatian, or an enemy of so-and-so. Having the stake turns out, on such an account, to be a matter of one's psychology, but not of something on a par with a desire or preference.

2. Call a moral theory *utility driven* if it recommends actions or policies on the basis of the difference they make to persons' utilities. Utilitarianism is perhaps the most prominent example of a utility-driven moral theory, but it is not the only one: egoistic hedonism, which recommends maximizing one's own utility, is utility driven, as are theories concerned with the distribution of utility rather than its maximization, for example, those requiring policies to maximize the utility of the worst-off. Theories that replace maximizing with satisficing can count as utility driven as well. Although for expository reasons I will be directing the upcoming argument against one form or another of utilitarianism, it will also cut against utility-driven moral theories that share an understanding of utility with those versions of utilitarianism.

3. While utilitarianism does have a proud history of willingness to overturn received moral views, utilitarians have never been ready to give up the idea that their moral theory was (at least indirectly) relevant to choices of the familiar kinds: Bentham and Mill were social *reformers*. I will return to the question of how deeply revisionist a utilitarian can afford to be in the next section.

4. Mill, 1967–1989, vol. X, p. 214.

5. Brickman, Coates, and Janoff-Bulman, 1978, pp. 920–1. Because the study confined itself to interviewing accident victims within one year of their accidents, it is unclear from the study whether the hedonic effects of the accidents wear off entirely with time. For a recent overview of the field of "hedonic psychology" (formerly called "happiness studies"), see Kahneman, Diener, and Schwarz, 1999.

6. The tendency has from time to time been mentioned in discussions of utilitarianism. Macmillan, 1890, pp. 7–8, remarks on the "vulgar saying, that we can get used to anything as eels get used to being skinned." Or again: "Most boys thoroughly enjoy eating jam tarts. But allow a boy to eat jam tarts at every meal in the day, and he will soon cease to regard them as very delightful." (I'm grateful to Christoph Fehige for drawing this passage to my attention.)

7. For instance, it might be alleged that utility-generating episodes tend to make utility come more easily in the future, by enhancing one's self-esteem, making one more of an optimist, and so on: even if utility comes in short bursts, increasing the frequency and magnitude of the bursts, and changing the

ratio of pleasant to unpleasant episodes, can produce significant alteration in utility over the long term. (That objection deserves to be put more carefully than it usually is; we need to distinguish what you *are* – which is built up over time, and may include such things as one's self-confidence – from ephemeral at-a-time satisfaction.)

This is a good place to consider the more general form of the objection, that my denial of the Presumption of Effectiveness fails to take into account downstream utilities, and that when these are factored in, the differences made to utility will generally prove proportionate to the significance of the decision. Hiring so-and-so will produce just a brief utility spike *now*, but, once on the job, his decisions and actions will affect many other people, and it is *those* effects on utility that account for the significance of the hiring decision.

The objection is unsuccessful for at least two reasons. First, and most familiar, appeal to distant effects is not usually available to the utilitarian, because, as Kant pointed out, no one knows what they are (1785/1981, Ak. 418); the distant and unknown effects generally swamp the known effects. So invoking downstream utilities will lead the utilitarian into the dead end of a moral theory that can (almost) never be applied, and the claim that the differences in utility will prove proportionate to the significance of the decision cannot be convincingly supported.

Second, and more interestingly for our purposes, the appeal to downstream utilities simply pushes the problem we are considering downstream. The decisions the new hire will make are indeed more important than the utility spike he now experiences; but we will again find that their importance cannot be accounted for in terms of the negligible changes in utility that they produce.

8. Plato seems at one point to have held a view similar in some respects to the one I am now developing: that pain indicates change away from, and pleasure change toward, bodily homeostasis; the state of balance that is one's goal feels like nothing at all. See *Philebus* 31bff.

Indicators are of course not always reliable, but I don't want to enter now into the question of how reliable this one is.

9. It follows that there are after all strategies for producing a permanently elevated hedonic tone (Watterson, 1996, p. 40). Evidently, this can be effected by a diet of constant improvement, and situations can be constructed to provide such a diet. The "flow"-inducing tasks described by Csikszentmihalyi (1990, cf. esp. pp. 48ff) provide a series of challenges, each successive challenge harder than the previous, but each obstacle surmountable, and, when surmounted, immediately seen to be surmounted. (Think of the way video games standardly provide levels of difficulty; as soon as you have mastered level six, it's on to the slightly harder level seven.)

Notice that the advocate of "flow" has an answer – but an unsatisfying one – to the charge that, while he can produce largish effects on utility, these do not allow us to make sense of the practical questions we already have. "Flow"-generating activities are completely absorbing, and one's unanswered practical questions may just drop away of their own accord. The compulsive gambler or Nintendo addict, having lost sight of everything beyond the next game, may occupy a perspective from which the Contoured Presumption of Effectiveness is perfectly in order.

In Millgram, 1993, and Millgram, 1997, sec. 6.6, I tried to explain away the diminishing returns of familiar pleasures. I now think that the examples of enduring pleasures that I gave can be accounted for in terms of the increasing levels of, for example, complexity, nuance and challenge that appear as projects and tastes develop, that is, by the presence of a regular diet of improvement. Without improvement, pleasures generally diminish, and this suggests that I was mistaken in treating pleasure as tantamount to a judgment of desirability, as opposed to something like a judgment of improvement.

10. One possibility worth considering is that the indicator is responsive not just to change in well-being, but rate of change: that the connection between utility and welfare is the connection between the first derivative of a function and the value of that function. See Hsee, Abelson, and Salovey, 1991; Hsee and Abelson, 1991.

11. For a standard, if dated, introduction, see Winston, 1977, pp. 93–8.

12. Whether hill-climbing is an appropriate technique depends, among other things, on whether the space of options has the requisite nearness or adjacency relations. I suggested thinking of the distance of the options from one another as how difficult it is to get there from here. Sidling around to determine which of several easily reachable points in a landscape is the highest is a reasonable strategy if it's easy to undo the last step, that is, if the distance from *A* to *B* is the same as the distance from *B* to *A*. But of course that's often not true: it can be very easy to take steps that it's very hard to undo.

In Millgram, 1999, I argued that the fact that many moral reactions extinguish over time is a problem for secondary quality accounts of moral values; the moral significance of a situation, after all, is not supposed to evaporate simply because we get used to it. (Harman, 1982, p. 128, makes a related point against Brandt's use of "cognitive psychotherapy" as a test of the rationality of desire; I'm grateful to Christoph Fehige for bringing this to my attention.) But the point evidently has to be hedged; we can treat a rapidly extinguished response as constitutive of a stable secondary quality provided we can see it as an indicator of change in the secondary quality. I think that a secondary-quality treatment of objective welfare along these lines should not be too hastily ruled out, but I doubt that many of the so-called moral values will be amenable to this kind of reconstruction.

13. The indicator account of phenomenal utility has no problem making room for the instrumental importance of pleasure and displeasure. The sensitivity of one's hedonic tone to circumstances may be important, in the way that other well-functioning indicators are important: because how fast you're going matters, that the speedometer is working also matters. Notice that this can produce situations in which hedonic valence fails to match the direction of change in one's welfare. An example due to Allen Coates: in discovering that one's marriage had been a sham, one feels worse, because one's hedonic indicator is now reflecting how bad things really are, but one is arguably doing better, because recoupling one's various indicators to the world is the first step toward improving one's situation.

The account can also allow that even if we are primarily interested in changes in our welfare because changes affect the absolute level of welfare, the changes themselves might come to be valuable. Speedometers indicate not distance traveled, but speed, the first derivative of distance with respect to time. Our primary or first interest in speed, and so in the speedometer, is in distance traveled: "Are we there yet?" "When will we be there?" But we can come to have secondary interests in speed proper: for the flow of traffic to be coordinated, vehicles must move at approximately the same speed; driving too fast will get you a ticket; and some people just like driving fast.

14. There are exceptions, e.g., Katz, 1986.

15. Nietzsche, 1886/1966, sec. 18.

16. If I am right, however, in thinking that this view best captures the spirit of the subjectivist approach to utility, it is likely to be relevant to the assessment of other, actually articulated satisfaction-based conceptions of utility.

17. Someone who holds this view may hold that satisfaction of a preference or desire is a contribution to an individual's utility, whether or not the individual knows the preference or desire to have been satisfied. As we will shortly see, knowledge of satisfaction is by no means irrelevant to the way utility of this kind functions.

18. There's a widely used technical notion of utility on which the utilities of outcomes are constructed from the agent's preferences, and I need to emphasize that this is not the type of utility we are now starting to examine. For one thing, Expected Utility Theory requires preferences that are, from the perspective of the view we have on the table, extravagantly numerous: over all outcomes, taken pairwise, and also over probability mixtures of outcomes. For the canonical exposition of EU Theory, see Luce and Raiffa, 1957, ch. 2.

    Notice that on the live-preference-satisfaction view we are considering, there are two ways in which one may have a stake in the means to further things about which one cares. They may be of import to one, although one has not come to have live desires for them, as means or instruments; alternatively, one may have invested psychological resources in the now-live instrumentally derived desires.

19. I have found that a very common response to this claim is incredulity, cited together with one instance or another of an event that either has made all the difference (moving to California, land of good weather, has come up more than once), or that would make all the difference if it happened. If you have reactions of this kind, I am going to ask something rather difficult of you: to discount them. The reason is that it turns out that people are very bad both at forecasting affect and at remembering how well they felt. To use the example I was given by someone who was convinced that moving to sunny California had made her life much happier than it had been: a study by Kahneman and Schkade "found no difference in self-reported well-being between students at California and midwestern universities, despite large differences in satisfaction with their respective climates... [but] students predicted large differences across regions in both overall well-being and in satisfaction with the climate" (Lowenstein and Schkade, 1999, pp. 89–90). (For a disconcerting example of unreliable hedonic memory,

see Kahneman et al., 1993. For current work on affective forecasting, see Gilbert et al., 1998, Gilbert and Wilson, 2000.) Certainty in how one would feel, or in how one did feel, is, it turns out, quite often misplaced.

I am of course not the first to have noticed that desires and preferences change in response to changes in the availability of their objects. See, e.g., Elster, 1983.

20. One may, and this is very important, have a subjective stake in something counterfactually: although I have taken my house completely for granted for a long while, if losing it were to become a live option, my desire to keep the house would be enlivened on the spot. (I'm grateful to David Lewis for this example.) One's desires and preferences may be reenlivened when the prospect of losing their objects is made vivid, and one once again comes to care; but this does not mean that one cared all along.

21. There is a related reason for the failure of still another form of utilitarianism, one that demands the satisfaction not of *actual* but of *informed* desires or preferences. Informed-preference utilitarianism is motivated by the idea that what one now wants may turn out to be disappointing when one finally gets it, and so actual preferences or desires must be corrected before they can be used as a guide to action; the standard deployed is the preferences and desires the agent would have in an appropriately idealized situation. Various idealizations have been suggested at one time or another: being better informed, calm and collected, or a beneficiary of "cognitive psychotherapy." But since what we really want to know is what the object of the desire will be like, *to the agent,* when it is obtained, the standard idealizations are really attempts to introduce information you're generally not in a position to have until you've got the object of your desire in hand. Often, the only way to know what things are like is to have tried them out, and so the *right* appeal has to be to the preferences and desires of a counterfactual version of oneself who *has* had them satisfied. The right choice is the choice that would be made by a version of you that has already made the choice both ways, and seen how each comes out; that version's word is the final word.

Now what will that final word be? What would an agent feel about the satisfaction of some candidate desire, given that the desire has already been satisfied? We are seeing it to be a deep fact about the mental processes which keep our supply of motivating states replenished that what we have attained typically ceases to be desired by us: when a desire is satisfied, our attention turns to a different, perhaps newly formed desire, because this desire is able to guide action and the satisfied desire is not. So when the candidate desire is satisfied, interest will fade for that very reason, and we will come to prefer something else – something that we perhaps do not yet want and that we as yet have no reason to pursue. This means that appeal to counterfactually informed desires will give us systematically incorrect results: it will tend to tell us *not* to pursue what now matters to us, in favor of what might someday (but does not – and should not – yet) matter to us. And this means that a utilitarianism of informed desires and preferences, the point of which is to give us what we *really* (rather than what we *actually*) want, will, for the most part, give us something we don't really want at all.

That said, there are many variants of informed-desire theory, and not all of them are directly addressed by this point.

22. A sociobiologist or evolutionary psychologist might add, and if we are to have a good chance of leaving our genes to the next generation. When asking what desires, preferences, and so on are for it is very easy to come up with an answer like: increasing reproductive success. But this is evidently too fast an answer. The point of our earlier discussion of phenomenal utility was that we should be careful to avoid mistaking the indicator for the item of interest. A similar caution is in place when we are examining changing gene distributions in a population: is *this* the item of interest, or is it rather a device that regulates, more or less effectively, the items of interest?

23. There is an analogous point to be made here about democratic politics. I have sometimes heard it said that the point of a democratic government is to satisfy the preferences of the citizenry, the implication being that in an ideally functioning democratic state, the preferences of the citizenry would be almost always satisfied. But this mistakes the function of the voting populace's preferences in a democratic regime. In a healthy democratic polity, the government gets kicked out fairly regularly, and, during its stint as the opposition, is forced to come up with new agendas, new leaders, and new ideals. For this to be possible, voters must *develop* unsatisfied preferences when the party in power is satisfying the preferences they already had. In a well-functioning democracy, a largish fraction of the voters are *dissatisfied* with their government, and it is practically impossible to raise the satisfaction level over the long term.

24. The transition was not without its lurches; for a partial history, see Cooter and Rappoport, 1984.

25. Ford, 1995, pp. 38–9. Note the contrast between this very realistic and rich specification of a desire, and the oh-so-thin typical philosopher's example!

26. Of course, there may be other ways people adjust their preferences, not involving thresholds; I don't want to insist that this is always what is going on.

27. Satisficing was originally introduced as a second-order maximizing strategy, one that took computational and information costs into account (Simon, 1957, chs. 14, 15). But there is a deeper reason for adopting it. It has been pointed out (by, e.g., Landesman, 1995; Fehige, 1994) that maximizing strategies make no sense when one's choice sets do not have maximal elements. Now, if you think about it for a moment, this is, for all practical purposes, almost always one's situation; a little looking around will, surprisingly often, turn up an alternative better than those already under consideration.

    For an overview of an older related literature, see Starbuck, 1963.

28. The connection we have just made may change the way we see some of the available accounts of pleasure. Brandt's view, for instance, "that for an experience to be pleasant is for it to make a person want its continuation" (1979, p. 38), is evidently – although not simply wrong – badly off-base. Part of what pleasure does is to tell you to keep doing what you're doing; but another primary role of pleasure is to *extinguish*, rather than prolong, desire.

29. See, e.g., Carnap, 1937, sec. 74.

30. Instrumentalism can also be expressed in the *material mode*, as the "fact-value distinction," or one version of it, and in the *technical mode*, as one very widespread way of endorsing and interpreting the apparatus of decision theory.

    Let me qualify my analogy to the logical positivists' "modes." The logical positivists rendered their claim of equivalence between items expressed in different modes as the claim that it is possible to translate from one mode to another. I am not making this claim, but I do not think it necessary. Jack loves Jill: he may send her flowers, or he may send her chocolates, or he may send her love letters. Flowers cannot be *translated* into chocolates, or chocolates into love letters, but we understand what is being claimed when we say that these are different ways of expressing the same thing.

31. If I am right in thinking that belief-desire psychology, instrumentalism stated in terms of goals, the (or a) fact-value distinction, and a very common interpretation of Expected Utility Theory are all just different ways of expressing the same view, related to each other as were the positivists' modes, then there is a very important consequence for debates about instrumentalism: using any one of these as a premise from which to prove the other is an argument on a par with stating one's claim in English, repeating it in Dutch, and finally reiterating it in German. That is to say, putative arguments of this form are not in fact *arguments* at all. Instances of the misguided would-be argument pattern include Smith, 1987, and Lewis, 1988.

32. As it happens, this fragmentary view of practical reasoning is evidently not instrumentalist, so if a mental ontology that includes desires is in fact an expression of an instrumentalist theory of practical reasoning, then, although I have been conducting the discussion in the accepted idiom of desires, this should be regarded as a temporary concession to current usage, ultimately to be abandoned.

2

Mill's Proof of the Principle of Utility

In a famous, or infamous, paragraph or so early on in Chapter 4 of *Utilitarianism*, Mill provides his argument for the Principle of Utility. I will first quote the passage at some length, and rehearse two very familiar objections to it. Then I will go on to say what I intend to do with the material I will have introduced.

1

The utilitarian doctrine is, that happiness is desirable, and the only thing desirable, as an end; all other things being only desirable as means to that end. What ought to be required of this doctrine – what conditions is it requisite that the doctrine should fulfil – to make good its claim to be believed?

The only proof capable of being given that an object is visible, is that people actually see it. The only proof that a sound is audible, is that people hear it: and so of the other sources of our experience. In like manner, I apprehend, the sole evidence it is possible to produce that anything is desirable, is that people do actually desire it. If the end which the utilitarian doctrine proposes to itself were not, in theory and in practice, acknowledged to be an end, nothing could ever convince any person that it was so. No reason can be given why the general happiness is desirable except that each person, so far as he believes it to be attainable, desires his own happiness. This, however, being a fact, we have not only all the proof which the case admits of, but all which it is possible to require, that happiness is a good: that each person's happiness is a good to that person, and the general happiness, therefore, a good to the aggregate of all persons. (234/4:2–3)[1]

Almost from the moment it went into print, the passage that I have just reproduced was notorious for the two fallacies it was alleged to contain, one for each of the two stretches of argument that make it up.[2] The first stretch of argument (which is what I will call it from here on in) moves from the premise that each person desires his own happiness to the conclusion that each person's happiness is desirable for him. The second stretch of argument moves from the conclusion of the previous stretch, that each person's happiness is desirable for him, to the further conclusion, that "the general happiness . . . [is] a good to the aggregate of all persons."

The first stretch of argument consists, more or less, of an explanation of the legitimacy of the transition from its premise to its conclusion; the explanation adduces analogous arguments that are clearly in order. You show that something is visible by showing that it is seen; you show that something is audible by showing that it is heard. Similarly, you show that something is desirable by showing that it is desired. It is standardly pointed out, however, that Mill's use of his model arguments seems to turn on an equivocation. "Audible" means "can be heard," and "visible" means "can be seen." But "desirable," in the sense required by the argument's conclusion, does not mean "*can* be desired," but something along the lines of "*should* be desired" or "*worth* desiring." The first stretch of argument is apparently supported by no more than a bad pun.

The second stretch of argument looks just as bad, on a par with taking what is good for each of Boeing's workers – say, a pay hike – to be good for Boeing, only with the added obstacle that "the aggregate of all persons" is not a corporate person in the way that Boeing is, and so there is no clear sense in which something can be good for it.

I am going to demonstrate that each stretch of argument is, not fallacious, but deductively valid. I will show that the conclusion of Mill's argument has been badly misunderstood. And, in the course of so doing, I will show that *Utilitarianism* is a much more tightly constructed text than it is generally taken for.

The exercise is intended to be not merely of textual or historical interest. I mean, first, to use the passage to investigate the relations between theories of practical reasoning and moral or ethical theories. Practical reasoning is reasoning aimed at figuring out what to do; a theory of practical reasoning is accordingly a theory of *how* one should go about figuring out what to do. A moral or ethical theory (I will use these terms interchangeably here) is, on one fairly standard construction of the notion, a general and systematic theory of *what* one should do; that is, it can be thought of as a compendium or summary of the results of practical reasoning. If that is right, we might expect philosophers' theories of practical reasoning to determine the architecture of their moral theories. In the course of re-constructing Mill's arguments, we will see that he does not disappoint us on this score: Mill's utilitarianism drops directly out of his instrumentalist theory of practical reasoning. To be sure, Mill's is only a single case. But making out the claim regarding Mill will lend plausibility and substance to the more general suggestion regarding the dependence of substantive moral theory on the theory of practical reasoning. If taken up, this suggestion would motivate a shift in focus in ethics, away from the moral intuitions which are today routinely treated as the touchstone of moral theorizing, and toward the views of practical reasoning that underwrite particular substantive moral or ethical theories.

Second, while I have said that I will show each stretch of argument to be deductively valid, I do not think that they are unproblematic when put side by side. They do not in fact sit at all well together, and responsibility for the incoherence of the argument that they jointly constitute rests, I will argue, with an incoherence in the underlying theory of practical reasoning. Now the instrumentalist account of practical reasoning that I will attribute to Mill is a very close relative of views still widely accepted today. So the incoherence that our discussion of Mill will expose in the instrumentalist theory is of current philosophical interest. Moreover, if Mill's reasons are still among the best reasons we have for accepting utilitarianism, and if they turn out to invoke an incoherent account of practical reasoning, we will have a reason for balking at utilitarianism. To the extent that utilitarianism is still a live moral theory, this result is also of current philosophical interest.

Finally, I will consider how Mill found himself saddled with the in-strumentalist theory that was the source of the difficulty I will identify in his argument. The explanation I will offer, a failure of nerve in Mill's attempt at a thoroughgoing empiricism, can serve as an object lesson for contemporary philosophy of an empiricist bent.

2

If, as I have suggested, philosophers have misread Mill's arguments for over a century, there are reasons. One is Mill's practice, necessary in an age when philosophy was much less professionalized than it now is, of writing prose that could be read and at least partially appreciated by an intelligent lay audience (and in particular by authors of public policy whom Mill hoped to influence).[3] The elegance of Mill's writing has ob-scured the way in which he deploys a technical philosophical vocabulary.[4]

By way of example, consider the glosses Mill provides for the words attached to the utilitarian conception of the good. In the course of explaining what the Principle of Utility is supposed to amount to, Mill tells us that "by happiness is *intended* pleasure" (210/2:2).[5] Shortly before, he has stated that "every writer ... who maintained the theory of utility, *meant by it* ... pleasure ... " (209/2:1).[6] And elsewhere, as one might by now expect, he uses "utility" as a synonym for "happiness," as in, "a perfectly just conception of Utility or Happiness" (213/2:9). Mill overtly introduces "utility," "happiness," and "pleasure" as synonymous terms.

He is equally explicit in connecting these terms, almost as closely, to the notion of desiring. "Desiring a thing and finding it pleasant ... are ... *in strictness of language,* two different modes of *naming* the same psychological fact" (237/4:10, my emphasis). "Almost as closely," because there is an important distinction to be made between items desired only as means to satisfying further desires, and items desired on their own account: the terminological identity is meant to apply only to the latter. The restriction of the scope of the identification to things desired on their own account is important, and I will return to it shortly. With this restriction in place, "desired" and "found pleasant" are also synonymous terms, and consequently, "to desire anything, except in proportion as the idea of it is pleasant, is a physical and *metaphysical* impossibility" (238/4:10, my emphasis).

If the object of desire is, as a matter of mere nomenclature, pleasure, and if "pleasure" is just a synonym for "happiness," then happiness should be, again as a matter of mere nomenclature, the object, and the sole object, of desire.[7] And so it is: Mill follows the argument we are trying to unravel with a further argument, purporting to show that people desire only happiness. The argument proceeds by insisting that "whatever is desired otherwise than as a means to some end beyond itself ... is desired as itself a part of happiness" (237/4:8); inspecting the argument shows the point to be that, if something is desired (again, with the scope of the claim restricted to desires whose objects are not merely desired as means to further ends), it thereby *counts* as part of happiness.

With this, we have arrived at a view as to the status of the premise of the first stretch of Mill's argument, that each person desires his own happiness. The premise is analytic, true by virtue of the meanings of the words. (As is the further claim, that people desire only happiness noninstrumentally.) It means no more and no less than: people desire what they desire. This should be puzzling; it is hard to see how any substantive conclusion that Mill wishes to draw could be derived from an empty tautology, and it might also seem that this reading of the premise does not match the advertising. Mill, after all, describes the claim that people desire only happiness as "a question of fact and experience, dependent, like all similar questions, upon evidence" (237/4:10). I will return to the puzzles later on; for the present, I want to let this reading of the premise stand, and note only that it allows us to shelve, at any rate temporarily, doubts we may have had about the premise's truth. With those doubts out of the way, we can go on to consider the validity of the first stretch of Mill's "proof."

3

Mill introduces his argument by stating "that questions of ultimate ends do not admit of proof, in the ordinary acceptation of the term" (234/4:1). This passage is commonly used as an excuse for holding Mill to lower standards of argumentation than usual; if an interpretation of the argument makes it come out loose, or shoddy, or invalid, or simply less than an argument, the interpretation can be defended by pointing out that it was not meant to be a *real* argument, anyway.[8] But another look at the passage shows it to be a reminder of an earlier discussion: "*it has already been remarked*, that questions of ultimate ends do not admit of proof, in the ordinary acceptation of the term"; this is in virtue of features that they share, as "the first premises . . . of our conduct," with "the first premises of our knowledge" (234/4:1). So before we decide that Mill is telling us that we are about to get handwaving instead of an argument, we need to look back at this earlier discussion, spell out the shared features, and see exactly why it is they preclude "proof." Now in Chapter 1, Mill tells us that "such proof as [the Utilitarian or Happiness theory] is susceptible of . . . cannot be proof in the ordinary and popular meaning of the term" (207/1:5). This is evidently the earlier discussion to which Mill is referring, and it is here we should look to fill out the analogy between the first premises of knowledge and the first premises of conduct on which the inference from desire to desirability is supposed to turn.

Description of something as a "first premise" implies a pattern of inference in which it occupies this position. So what we need, first of all, from this earlier discussion is the pattern of inference in which this characterization has its home. Mill obligingly identifies it for us immediately after the passage I have just quoted: "Whatever can be proved to be good, must be so by being shown to be a means to something admitted to be good without proof." (207–8/1:5). A contemporary way of putting Mill's view might be to say that all practical reasoning is means-end reasoning; or, to use another bit of current vocabulary, that Mill is an instrumentalist.[9]

We can now make out the analogy Mill has in mind, between the "first premises" of our knowledge and of our conduct. On the instrumentalist view, a practical justification consists in showing that a proposed end is a means to a further end. (More Millian terminology: "Questions about ends are, *in other words*, questions about what things are desirable" (234/4:2, my emphasis).) That further end may be justified in turn, that is, shown to be desirable, by showing it to be a means to a still further end. Iterating justifications in this way induces larger patterns of justification that can fall into three general types: chains of justification can continue backwards forever; they can contain cycles; or they can terminate in ends that are not themselves further justified.

The choice between these patterns should sound familiar; it was certainly familiar to Mill. Beliefs can be justified by further beliefs, and when they are, it is usually thought, the same choices arise: between an infinite regress, circularity (so called if you don't like it) or coherence (so called if you do), and foundational beliefs, that is, beliefs that terminate chains of justification and are not themselves further justified. In a survey of fallacies in *A System of Logic*, Mill rejects the first two options, for reasons that are general enough to apply to practical justifications as well: on the one hand, "there cannot be an infinite series of proof, a chain suspended from nothing" (VIII:746); on the other, "Reasoning in a Circle" is in Mill's view simply a "more complex and not uncommon variety of" "Petitio Principii, or begging the question" (VIII:820). Mill opts for foundationalism, the view that there are "propositions which may reasonably be received without proof" (VIII:746).

I have so far identified the class of foundational beliefs, and the class of foundational ends, simply in terms of structural features of the patterns of justifications in which they appear: foundational beliefs are those beliefs that are not further justified; foundational ends are those ends that are not merely means to further ends. But it is typical of philosophizing in epistemology and ethics to look for a further and independent way of identifying these classes, for example, by taking them to be, or to be associated with, an especially immediate *feeling.* Not surprisingly, given the tradition of British Empiricism in which Mill stood, he took the foundational beliefs to correspond to "sensations."[10] Mill similarly takes the foundational ends to be objects of especially immediate feeling, and it is this presumption that we may suppose licenses Mill's introduction of vocabulary that, we saw, identifies the objects of (noninstrumental) desires with pleasure and happiness, states naturally described as states of feeling.

Now consider what attempts at justification look like at terminal and nonterminal locations in the respective foundationalist structures we have just described. A belief that is not simply the correlate of a sensation ought to come with a further justification: other propositions that you believe. So when someone asks you why you believe it, you can, if the belief is not unjustified, adduce these further propositions. But when you are asked why you hold a terminal belief (that is, a belief that is simply the correlate of a sensation), there is no further proposition to adduce. All you can do is reiterate your claim to be sensing what you are sensing, or feeling (since Mill takes sensation to be a species of feeling) what you are feeling.[11]

This is the point of Mill's remark that "the only proof capable of being given that an object is visible, is that people actually see it." Philosophers have misread the passage by overemphasizing the modal dimension of "visible" (and, in the following sentence, of "audible"), taking "visible" to mean "*capable* of being seen." This is a mistake. "Visible" here means, if you like, "can be seen"; but only in the sense in which a pilot might report that he can see the target: he *sees* the target. "Audible" is likewise meant in a similar sense, the sense in which the petrified victim in the monster movie whispers, "It's audible now – I can hear it moving down below." This means, not that in some other possible world, the monster is heard moving down below, nor that in the future, with some extra effort, the monster might be heard, but that in *this*, actual world, the monster is *now* heard moving down below. At the terminus of the chain of justification, when we have gotten back to the sensations, the only "proof" that an object is visible, that is, *is seen*, is to gesture once again at its being seen. The only "proof" that an object is audible, that is, *is heard*, is to gesture at its being heard.

This is Mill's model for "desire as proof of desirability."[12] At a non-terminal location in a chain of practical justification, the end occupying that location and the justification for it are distinct; whether something is desired and whether it is desirable are two different questions. Asked why you want to do such and such, you can adduce the further ends to which it is a means. But at the terminus of the chain, when we have come back to the feeling of pleasure or happiness, or the desire whose satisfaction is that feeling, there is nothing further to be said. All there is to the desirability of the object of the desire is that it is desired, and all there is left, at the end of the chain, for "desirable" to *mean* is "desired."

We are now in a position to give the first of Mill's two reasons for withholding the title of "proof" from his argument for the Principle of Utility. Recall again that Mill was also the author of *A System of Logic*: "The proper subject... of Logic is Proof" (VII:157), and so we should not be surprised to find that "proof" is, in Mill, a technical term.[13] Proof is inference, the movement from evidence to conclusion: "We say of a fact or statement, that it is proved, when we believe its truth by reason of some other fact or statement from which it is said to *follow*." (VII:158)

> In so far as belief professes to be founded on proof, the office of logic is to supply a test of ascertaining whether or not the belief is well grounded. With the claims which any proposition has to belief on the evidence of consciousness, that is, without evidence in the proper sense of the word, logic has nothing to do. (VII:9)

Sensations, and the beliefs that correspond to them, are not inferred, and so when we get back to sensations, we have left the domain of properly so-called "proof." Likewise, the "first principles" of conduct are ultimate ends, desires that are, for the instrumentalist, ex hypothesi not inferred from further premises. The only question that arises regarding these desires is whether one actually has them, and that is a matter of "consciousness" or "intuition." Since they are not inferred, they too lie outside the domain of proof.

Let's return from this lengthy excursion to the first stretch of Mill's argument. Its conclusion was that each person's happiness is desirable for that person. Let us keep in place Mill's restriction to ends that are not desired merely as means to further ends, but on their own account. Then happiness, recall, is, simply as a matter of terminology, what one desires. Again, with the restriction in place – that is, when we are at the termini of the agent's chains of means-end justification – "desirable" just means "desired": there is nothing else left for it to mean. So the conclusion of the argument just means that what one desires (noninstrumentally), one (noninstrumentally) desires. Recall further that the premise of the argument turned out to mean only that each person desires what he desires. We can now see why the first stretch of argument is so short: the inference rule being used is $p \rightarrow p$. And it is evidently not fallacious after all, contrary to the views of Moore, Sidgwick, and many others: if *any* argument is deductively valid, it is this one.[14]

4

Before moving on to the second stretch of Mill's argument, we need to pause briefly to consider what we are to make of the first. The stretch of argument we have been looking at consists entirely in the repetition of the trivial truth that people want what they want, and seems to be a matter of laying out a series of verbal equivalences. This might still seem hard to believe, but any residual incredulity can be met by Mill's own redescription of his thesis: "what is the principle of utility," he asks, "if it be not that 'happiness' and 'desirable' are synonymous terms?" (258n/5:38n) Still, if that is all there is to the argument, what is it doing here? How could Mill, normally so impatient with "reasoning [that] consists in the mere substitution of one set of arbitrary signs for another," have thought it to be worth presenting?[15]

We can begin by giving the second reason that Mill withholds the title of "proof" from this stretch of argument. Commentators have generally assumed that if Mill is unwilling to call his argument a proof, he must mean at least that the argument is not deductively valid.[16] But to take Mill this way is to get him exactly backwards. With the stipulated meanings of the words put in place, the first stretch of Mill's argument turns out to be the repetition of a tautology. Now, in *A System of Logic*, Mill "exclude[s] from the province of Reasoning or Inference properly so called, the cases in which the progression from one truth to another is only apparent, the logical consequent being a mere repetition of the logical antecedent."[17] Proof is inference, and to count as an inference, Mill holds, there must be more to the conclusion than to the premises. So neither a tautology nor its repetition can count as a proof. This is not, it needs to be emphasized, a minor or dispensable Millian doctrine. Mill was embarked on the radical empiricist project of showing that there is *no such thing* as deductive inference; it is one of the more important burdens of the *System* to argue that all inference (and consequently all proof) is inductive.[18] Because the position is so alien to contemporary sensibilities, commentators tend to leave it behind when they read Mill's political and ethical writings; as a result, they badly misinterpret the passage we are reconstructing. Mill is denying that his argument is a "proof," *not* because it is not deductively valid, but precisely because it *is*.

We have two reasons on the table for Mill's first stretch of argument not being a proof. One is its subject matter; ultimate ends are a category of items picked out as beyond the reach of inference or proof. The other is the argument's form: the argument is (we would say) deductively valid and (Mill would have insisted) merely "apparent, not real" (VII:158). We can now see that the subject matter explains the form. When inference is no longer available, all Mill can do is remind us of something we already know, "not proving the proposition, but only appealing to another mode of wording it, which may or may not be more readily comprehensible by the hearer."[19] Mill is not in a position to argue that happiness is what we are really after, but he can put it to his readers in a way that will remind the readers that what is at stake for them is that they get what they want, and that this is what they call "happiness." "If the end which the utilitarian doctrine proposes to itself were not, in theory and in practice, acknowledged to be an end, nothing could ever convince any person that it was so" (234/4:3). Now if what Mill is trying to elicit is an acknowledgement of what the reader already has as an end, Mill's logical views make syllogistic deduction an appropriate vehicle. Syllogisms are a means of "deciphering our own notes" (VII:187), and the point of deductively valid "argument" is to remind us to what we are already committed.[20]

What is doing the work in Mill's argument? The first stretch of argument reduces to a series of interlocking definitions, and interlocking definitions of themselves only produce empty tautologies. Now, as Mill himself remarked, "most questions of naming have questions of fact lying underneath them."[21] We have already seen one instance of this phenomenon, in the view that feelings, in Mill's sense, terminate chains of justification; this allowed Mill to choose terminology that identified pleasure, happiness, and the objects of noninstrumental desire. I want to suggest that Mill's interlocking definitions are underwritten by his instrumentalist understanding of practical reasoning, and that this instrumentalism is the motor of the first stretch of argument, and of Mill's utilitarianism more broadly.

This is an occasion to say more precisely what I mean by "instrumentalism." I am using it as the label for the still widely shared view that there is only one kind of practical inference, that which takes you from an end to the means to that end; or, in psychological vocabulary, that practical reasoning consists in moving from a desire for one object to a desire for a way of bringing about or attaining that object. Grant that justifying an end amounts to recapitulating an inference by which that end could be arrived at. Every instrumentalist inference proceeds from a desire. So instrumentalism guarantees that when a chain of practical justifications is followed back to its terminus, there will be a desire at the terminus.

It is this that licenses "desire as proof of desirability." Suppose for a moment that instrumentalism were false, and that practical inferences could proceed from premises that were not desires. Then "desire as proof of desirability" would have to be given up, and replaced with the much less suggestive "whatever premises are used to demonstrate desirability are, taken jointly, proof of desirability." The identification of those premises with a class of feelings that cannot be argued about, but simply gestured at, would be suddenly implausible. "Happiness" would no longer be a reasonable label for the aggregate of those premises. Mill's precision-tooled vocabulary would become unusable, and his argument would cease to make sense. Instrumentalism is the substantive premise lying beneath the first stretch of argument, and expressed through the terminological stipulations that make it up.

Many philosophers think that there must be a close and intrinsic connection between rational motivation and what we can for the moment call the Good. Instrumentalism makes it hard to see the dependence as running from the Good to the motivation: if you don't happen to have the right desires, the knowledge that such and such is the Good will not amount to a reason to act. So it is natural to reverse the direction of dependence: the Good is analyzed as a construction out of one's preferences or desires or ultimate ends – that is, as something very much like Mill's sophisticated notion of utility. So we should expect to find the philosophical motivation for utilitarianism and its relatives to be instrumentalism, in cases other than Mill's.

5

It's time to turn our attention to the second stretch of Mill's argument: the move from "each person's happiness is a good to that person" to "the general happiness, therefore, [is] a good to the aggregate of all persons" (234/4:3). The objection, recall, was that the conclusion just doesn't seem to follow from the premise. Rather than repeat my phrasing of the complaint, I'll let Sidgwick give his version:

> even if we grant that what is actually desired may legitimately be inferred to be . . . desirable . . . an aggregate of actual desires, each directed towards a different part of the general happiness, does not constitute an actual desire for the general happiness, existing in any individual; and Mill would certainly not contend that a desire which does not exist in any individual can possibly exist in an aggregate of individuals. There being therefore no actual desire – so far as this reasoning goes – for the general happiness, the proposition that the general happiness is desirable cannot be in this way established: so that there is a gap in the expressed argument. . .[22]

If the gap is genuine, a further premise will be needed to fill it. (Sidgwick volunteered "the intuition of Rational Benevolence.") But it is worth noticing that Mill himself had heard similar complaints, and thought there was no gap. Here is Mill responding to a criticism of Spencer's that was evidently very close to Sidgwick's:

[Spencer] says . . . the principle of utility presupposes the anterior principle, that everyone has an equal right to happiness. It may be more correctly described as supposing that equal amounts of happiness are equally desirable, whether felt by the same or different persons. This, however, is not a *pre*supposition; not a premise needful to support the principle of utility, but the very principle itself . . . (258n/5:35n)

This is an obscure passage, and it is still too early to try to say what it means; it is clear enough, however, that Mill does not agree that there is a missing premise. So we should try to find an interpretation of the argument on which all the pieces are in place. I propose to do that in what may seem like an especially roundabout way, by returning to the model of practical reasoning that, I claimed a moment ago, drives the first stretch of Mill's argument.

I introduced instrumentalism as the doctrine that all practical reasoning consists in finding means to ends, or, equivalently, finding ways to satisfy the desires one has. But that is simply not enough to count as a complete theory of practical reasoning. First of all, this very minimal instrumentalist theory, or rather, theory fragment, takes no account of a very basic fact of human life, that you can get what you wanted and still be disappointed. (This fact has a less depressing flip side, that you can be pleasantly surprised by something you had not desired.) In Mill's vocabulary, the problem can be located in the ambiguity of the phrase "find pleasant," which, it will be recalled, is introduced as equivalent to "desire": in desiring something you may find – that is, *expect* – it to be pleasant, but that does not mean that when the object of your desire is obtained, it will be found – that is, *turn out* – to be pleasant. The possibility of having the thought that you were wrong about what you had wanted has got to be accommodated in one way or another.

Second, the theory fragment says nothing at all about choice in the face of competing desires. Almost every decision involves competing priorities, and so a putative theory of practical reasoning that failed to speak to the issue at all would not be much of a theory of practical reasoning: it would not explain how you figure out what to do.[23] So the minimal theory fragment must come supplemented in a way that enables it to address these requirements.

Instrumentalism is an exclusionary view: *only* means-end reasoning counts as practical inference. So the supplement must consist not of further rules of inference, but of a penumbra, around the one legitimate rule, of claims about the material to which it might apply. The Benthamite penumbra consisted in the view that pleasures could be felt to be stronger or weaker; that the stronger pleasure was to be preferred; and that pleasure itself, as opposed to the more or less reliable means through which it might be obtained, would never disappoint. This is not the place to reconstruct Mill's reasons for rejecting Bentham's views; suffice it for now that Mill found implausible the notion that pleasures could differ only in strength: "Neither pains nor pleasures are homogeneous, and pain is always heterogeous with pleasure" (213/2:8). Mill's more sophisticated alternative is presented in Chapter 2 of *Utilitarianism,* in the course of a discussion whose ostensible purpose is to meet the objection that utilitarianism is a moral theory unable to accommodate our interests in the finer things in life. The relevant passages are these:

Of two pleasures, if there be one to which all or almost all who have experience of both give a decided preference . . . that is the more desirable pleasure. (211/2:5)[24]

From this verdict of the only competent judges, I apprehend there can be no appeal. On a question which is the best worth having of two pleasures, or which of two modes of existence is the most grateful to the feelings . . . the judgment of those who are qualified by knowledge of both, or, if they differ, that of the majority among them, must be admitted as final. And there needs be the less hesitation to accept this judgment respecting the quality of pleasures, since there is no other tribunal to be referred to even on the question of quantity. What means are there of determining which is the acutest of two pains, or the intensest of two pleasurable sensations, except the general suffrage of those who are familiar with both?

What is there to decide whether a particular pleasure is worth purchasing at the cost of a particular pain, except the feelings and judgement of the experienced? (213/2:8)

the test of quality, and the rule for measuring it against quantity, [is] the preference felt by those who, in their opportunities of experience, to which must be added their habits of self-consciousness and self-observation, are best furnished with the means of comparison. (214/2:10)

Mill's proposal, often referred to as the "decided preference criterion," addresses the second lacuna in the instrumentalist theory fragment directly: competing desires are to be referred to the preferences, over their objects, of the majority of the experienced. And the first lacuna is indirectly addressed; if we think of what will be a disappointing object of desire as in competition with the contrasting state of not having it, the preference over these options can be corrected by appealing to the preferences of the already disappointed.

Mill is providing a logically decisive criterion of desirability. It is "final," a "verdict... [from which] there can be no appeal"; "there is no other tribunal." The experientially privileged (as I will call them henceforth) are not being used as reliable witnesses of some independent matter of fact; no matter how reliable, it is always possible that all the witnesses are wrong; but Mill's experientially privileged judges are infallible. (The metaphor is instructive: a judicial verdict constitutes the legal fact.) Like a contemporary decision theorist, Mill is not taking the utilities to be reflected (possibly inaccurately) in the preferences; rather, he is taking them to be constructions from the preferences.[25]

Contemporary instrumentalists need to supplement the instrumentalist theory fragment, for the same reasons that Mill must, and it's worth pausing to point out the similarities and the differences in their respective solutions to the problem. Brandt, in this regard an entirely typical moral philosopher of the last generation, calls "a person's desire, aversion, or pleasure 'rational' if it *would* survive or be produced by" a process he labels "cognitive psychotherapy." Rawls defines "a person's plan of life [as] rational if" it satisfies two conditions, one of which is that it "*would* be chosen by him with full deliberative rationality, that is, with full awareness of the relevant facts and after a careful consideration of the consequences."[26] As these examples suggest, the fashionable way of doing these things nowadays is to invoke a counterfactual self: what is decisive is what a better-informed, more carefully deliberative, and otherwise improved version of yourself *would* think or want. Mill manages to avoid the many problems that come with relying on counterfactual selves by appealing to the *actual* preferences of a majority of (*other*) people.[27,28] But the devices have a good deal in common. Each uses suitably chosen persons as what engineers call a black box. We can vary the box's inputs, and see what outputs it produces. We are instructed to use the outputs in a certain manner. But we are given no account whatsoever of what goes on inside the box. I will return to this point shortly; but it is now time, finally, to reconstruct the second stretch of Mill's proof of the Principle of Utility.

6

Mill's object is to show that the general happiness is desirable to everybody (or, "to the aggregate of all persons" – a turn of phrase I'll gloss a few steps down the road). Consider a particular person, say John Doe. The problem was that the desires he currently has do not necessarily involve a desire for the general happiness, and that even if Doe does have such a desire, it might be insufficiently weighty in his scheme of things. But we now have a technique for correcting desires, and for showing that something that someone does not in fact desire may be desirable for him nonetheless. If an overriding preference for the general happiness can be shown to be the preference of the majority of the experientially privileged, then it will have turned out to be desirable for John Doe, even if John Doe himself does not actually desire it.[29] And since John Doe is simply an arbitrary person, to show that the general happiness is desirable for John Doe is to have shown it to be desirable for everybody.

A first glance at the experientially privileged might make this seem an unpromising strategy. For present purposes, the relevant group can be taken to be, very roughly, people who have both experienced an improvement in the general happiness at some cost to themselves, and, on some other occasion, experienced an improvement in their own happiness at the expense of the general happiness. When we look around at such people, it is hard to say offhand that one preference predominates; and certainly the cynical among us will suspect that those with the egoistic preference are bound to outvote the altruists.

But when votes don't go the way you like, there's a standard solution: gerrymander the voting districts. Mill, the radical utilitarian activist, would have thought of the response in more noble-sounding terms; the obstacle to enacting the utilitarian political program, he was convinced, was the restriction of the franchise, and the first item on the agenda was always to distribute the right to vote more broadly. What populations should we survey, when we are looking for the experientially privileged? All those now living, certainly; but there is no obvious principled reason for excluding the judgments of persons past and future, and if there is no reason to exclude them, they must be taken account of as well; the group to be surveyed is, in Mill's phrase, "the aggregate of all persons" (234/4:3).[30] This bit of redistricting has the potential drastically to alter the outcome of any poll: the human race has had a short and underpopulated past, and Mill would have expected it to have a long and populous future. So the votes of the future experientially privileged will outweigh the votes of their predecessors; what the future sees to be desirable, will (by the decided preference criterion) *be* desirable. So we need to determine what the experientially privileged of the future will prefer.

Mill himself raises the problem we have been trying to solve for him: "why am I bound to promote the general happiness? If my own happiness lies in something else, why may I not give that the preference?" (227/3:1) The occasion for asking the question is his discussion of "The Ultimate

Sanction of the Principle of Utility," in Chapter 3 of *Utilitarianism.* Chapter 3 is conventionally taken to have nothing to do with the subsequent "proof" in Chapter 4: the former, it is said, deals with questions of motivation, while the latter has to do with questions of justification, and the consequentialist form of Mill's theory makes these entirely separate questions. As we are already in a position to see, however, the criterion of desirability introduced in Chapter 2 entails that these are not separate questions, after all. And as we should by now expect, Chapter 3 contains the last missing premise: Mill's view, and the argument for it, as to what the experientially privileged of the future will prefer with regard to the general happiness.

The chapter contains a number of intertwined arguments, and in the interest of brevity I will here pick out just one strand. Because each individual has an interest in *others'* altruism, individuals, whether or not altruistic themselves, will, "in proportion to the amount of general intelligence" (228/3:3), support measures that will induce utilitarian attitudes in their fellows:

whatever amount of this feeling [for the good of others] a person has, he is urged by the strongest motives . . . of interest . . . to the utmost of his power to encourage it in others; and even if he has none of it himself, he is as greatly interested as any one else that others should have it. Consequently, the smallest germs of the feeling are laid hold of and nourished by . . . the influences of education; and a complete web of corroborative association is woven round it, by the powerful agency of external sanctions.

. . . the influences are constantly on the increase, which tend to generate in each individual a feeling of unity with all the rest; which feeling, if perfect, would make him never think of, or desire, any beneficial condition for himself, in the benefits of which they are not included. If we now suppose this feeling of unity to be taught as a religion, and the whole force of education, of institutions, and of opinion, directed, as it once was in the case of religion, to make every person grow up from infancy surrounded on all sides both by the profession and by the practice of it, I think that no one, who can realize this conception, will feel any misgiving about the sufficiency of the ultimate sanction for the Happiness morality. (232/3:9)[31]

Sooner or later, Mill thinks, self-interested motives make it almost inevitable that institutions guaranteeing a society of natural utilitarians be put in place. The persons created by these institutions will prefer the general happiness to any other alternative.[32] Because these institutions will be stable, the persons shaped by them will outnumber those living in previous historical periods. The preferences of the majority of the experientially privileged are decisive with respect to desirability of the objects of one's desires.[33] And consequently, the general happiness is desirable for each individual, no matter what his desires, and so is desirable for everyone. The second stretch of Mill's argument is deductively valid as well.

7

Before considering how well the two stretches of Mill's argument sit together, I want to make a couple of remarks about the stretch of argument that we have just seen.

First, the argument is valid, that is, its conclusions follow from its premises. But it is not, I think, sound. It was reasonable in Mill's day to believe that entire populations could be made over into the natural adherents of any ideology whatsoever. In addition to the considerations we have just laid out, Mill had a number of other reasons for thinking that utilitarian indoctrination would be possible. Some are mentioned in the same chapter: for example, the receptiveness of normal individuals to a humane ideology appealing to the sympathetic feelings naturally present, it was thought, in them. Others, such as his associationist psychology, are left in the background. But Mill's reasons are now beside the point: today we know better. The twentieth century was a large scale test of the effectiveness of ideological indoctrination, and it has turned out not to work. Mill thought that Comte had "superabundantly shown the possibility of giving to the service of humanity . . . the psychical power and the social efficacy of a religion" (232/3:9). But Mill and Comte were, as a matter of empirical fact, mistaken.[34]

Contemporary moral philosophers will tend to find the use of an empirical premise of this kind unsettling: if we have gotten the argument right, evaluative issues, such as whether the general happiness is a good, or the most important good, are *contingent*. This is easily overlooked when we are considering the long-term social processes that Mill thought would result in a society of utilitarians. But the desirability of the general happiness depends not just on the sociological laws that make those processes seem inevitable; there must be a sufficiently long run in which they are able to do their work. If human history is prematurely truncated by natural catastrophe, then utilitarianism will be made false: an asteroid striking the earth can, on this view, destroy not only things of value, but the values themselves.[35] Assessing the plausibility of this view is a topic for some other occasion; for now, it suffices that this upshot is not a reason to think we have misread Mill. Mill's official view is that *no* body of theory – logic and the mathematical sciences included – is a priori true or necessary;[36]

so moral facts should be no less contingent than any other facts. Whether Mill managed to live up to his official view is a question that I will address when the time comes.

Second, the conclusion of Mill's argument was that the general happiness is "a good to the aggregate of all persons" (234/4:3). And we saw Sidgwick, not atypically, trying to read Mill as meaning that the general happiness is desirable for the aggregate: that it is a good of, as it were, the collective entity made up of all persons. But this, we can now see, is to misconstrue the sentence, and in particular, to mistake the force of the preposition. Mill is not committed to anything along the lines of a collective good. The "aggregate of all persons" is not some metaphysically dubious creature whose good the general happiness is, but the population from which the experientially privileged who provide the test of desirability are drawn. "The general happiness [is] . . . a good *to* the aggregate of all persons" means, roughly: among all persons, those capable of judging from experience, or at any rate a majority of them, find (or will find) the general happiness to be a good.[37,38]

Before proceeding to its problems, let me pause to recapitulate the merits of the argument as I have reconstructed it. It is deductively valid. That it is deductively valid explains Mill's unwillingness to call it a proof, and does so without uncharitably construing Mill as attempting to excuse his own sloppiness in advance. The premises of the argument are contributed by the previous chapters of *Utilitarianism*; on the reading just advanced, the book is a single argument, each carefully machined component of which is necessary for the conclusion finally drawn in Chapter 4. And that conclusion proves to be metaphysically sane, in not presupposing the existence of collective social organisms with desires and interests.

If the reading I have given is on target, the text proves to be much more tightly written, and in some ways much more difficult to swallow, than it is usually taken to be. Mill is often pressed into service as the spokesman of a vague and well-meaning lowest common denominator of liberalism. But *Utilitarianism* is not a quotable collection of inoffensive platitudes. It is philosophical writing of the most muscular kind.

8

We have seen that Mill's argument is valid, but it is not for that reason unproblematic. Its problems are worth exploring, and it is now time to take a closer look at them.

The first stretch of Mill's argument was driven by the common core of instrumentalist accounts of practical reason: the view, which I earlier pointed out is somewhat less than a theory of practical reasoning, that all practical inference is means-end inference. Since any chain of practical inferences will terminate in a desire that one just *has*, and since, at the end of the chain, there is no further argument to be given for the desirability of the final end, desirability can be identified with being desired. This identification underwrites Mill's treatment of felt desire "proving" desirability on the model of felt sensation "proving" the basic premises of one's system of beliefs.

The second stretch of Mill's argument exploits a device introduced to handle the shortcomings of the theory fragment that is the common core. These shortcomings, recall, were that the desires one actually has cannot be made the measure of desirability after all, due to the possibility of disappointment, and that the need to choose between competing desires must be accommodated in one's theory of practical reasoning. The device Mill uses, a standard made up of the preferences of other more experienced persons, adheres to the letter of the instrumentalist common core, in that it does not require any further forms of practical inference, over and above means-end reasoning. The inputs to one's practical inferences are indeed being corrected, but not inferentially. The corrected preferences are generated by a black box, a device whose inner workings are invisible and irrelevant.

The problem, at the level of the underlying account of practical reasoning, is this. An instrumentalist theorist who has gotten to this point is not in a position to justify the use (or choice of) a black box; he cannot say why what it produces are *corrected* preferences. For suppose there were an argument that showed the method employing the black box to be a method of correction. That argument could with minimal effort be turned into an argument that the desires or preferences produced by the method were *correct*. But that argument would be an instance of practical reasoning; that practical reasoning would be noninstrumental; and so acknowledging it would mean abandoning the instrumentalist common core.[39] The incoherence is, as far as I can see, inescapable: the problem is a problem not only for Mill, but for contemporary instrumentalists who appeal to counterfactually informed desires. Any instrumentalist must use some such device; but justifying the device means abandoning instrumentalism. Instrumentalism is consequently an insupportable view of practical reasoning.[40]

The incoherence near the surface of Mill's argument can be summarized as follows. The first stretch of the argument makes sense on the supposition that, once you have gotten through the instrumental justifications, there is nothing to be said for an object of desire being desirable, other than that you desire it. The second stretch of argument makes sense on the supposition that there *is* something more to be said about whether an object of desire is desirable, namely, that certain other people, better situated than you are, desire it (or that they don't). Mill is careful to avoid actual contradiction; the decided preference criterion can be inserted parenthetically at the appropriate points in the first stretch of argument without aborting it.[41] But the two stretches of argument cannot both make sense together.

This near-surface incoherence is, we now see, the immediate expression of a similarly shaped incoherence in the underlying view of practical reasoning. Instrumentalism is the engine of Mill's utilitarianism, and instrumentalism is not a sustainable view of practical rationality. Mill's ingenious proof of the Principle of Utility does not commit the crude mistakes for which it is known. It commits instead a deep and philosophically interesting mistake, and one from which we have much to learn.

9

I have argued that Mill's instrumentalism gets him into trouble; so we now need to explain Mill's being an instrumentalist. I'll begin by explaining why an explanation is called for.

Instrumentalism, once again, is the view that all practical inference is means-end inference. So it is a view about what patterns of inference are legitimate, which is to say that it is a logical thesis, in Mill's sense of "Logic." Now Mill was not in the business of accepting received views about inference just because they were received: his *System of Logic*, I have already mentioned, argued for the heretical view that deductive inference is not actually inference at all. Mill was not shy when it came to arguing for philosophical views that he needed. So if instrumentalism is a view in Logic, if it is explicitly acknowledged, and if it is doing the work for him that I have argued it is, then Mill, of all people, should be providing us with an argument for it.

But the expected argument is conspicuously lacking. The closest Mill comes is a discussion which perhaps can be made to speak to a puzzle we have had on the queue for a while. Recall that I suggested that, on

Mill's view, the claim that people desire their own happiness amounts to a tautology, roughly, that people desire what they desire; Mill, however, describes the claim, not as true by terminological stipulation, but as "psychologically true" (237/4:9). Now this might of course simply be a reflexive expression of Mill's doctrine that the truth of *any* claim is an empirical question, but there is likely to be more to it than that: tautologies need not "unmeaning" if they bring to the fore the presuppositions that make the vocabulary in them usable.[42]

For Mill's psychological views, the best source is his father's *Analysis of the Phenomena of the Human Mind* (1878), to which the younger Mill, as editor of a second edition, added extensive commentary. That commentary consists quite often of rather blunt correction; we may take it that where the editor's notes do not indicate disagreement or qualification the views expressed are John Stuart Mill's as well. So we should look to the *Analysis* for the question of psychological fact that Mill takes to lie beneath the questions of naming.[43] Now what remains, in "people desire what they desire," to be underwritten by experimental psychology, is the non-redundant assertion that people *desire*: that human beings are wanting creatures. And the *Analysis* does indeed contain an extended exposition of just this view. Desires are analyzed (as ideas of pleasure); commonplace desires (e.g., for "Wealth, Power, and Dignity") are accounted for; and their role in producing action is explained.[44]

That human beings are desiring creatures, and that their desires move them to action, is not itself an argument for instrumentalism. Mill was quite clear that inference is a normative notion: it has to do, not with what one does, but with what one *should* do. The *Analysis* does contain an associationist reconstruction of the psychological movements involved in means-end reasoning; and it defines the Will in such a way that "in all cases in which the action is said to be Willed, it is desired, as a means to an end."[45] But there is no argument to the effect that associations that proceed in these ways (and only in these ways) are *correct*, and the *Analysis* similarly reconstructs other patterns of association that clearly are not understood inferentially, for example, "proneness to sympathize with the Rich and Great."[46] Mill's psychological views go a great distance toward explaining why he chose the terminology he did, and why he regarded it as expressing interesting empirical facts; but it does not help at all in providing Mill with grounds for his instrumentalist take on practical reasoning.

Beyond these considerations, Mill's corpus contains no treatment of the problem whatsoever.[47] One possible explanation is that the thought that practical inference might have a place in an exhaustive treatment of the theory of inference eluded him, because "Logic," as Mill conceived it, "is the entire theory of the ascertainment of reasoned or inferred truth" (VII:206) – and practical inference is naturally seen as having something other than truth as its formal object. Since what we are trying to explain is Mill's silence on the matter, any line we take will be going out on a limb. But as long as we are being speculative, there is a way of playing out this possibility that I would like to explore.

Let us consider for a moment what a Millian investigation of the forms of practical inference would have looked like. Mill had definite views about how to argue about logic: it is an empirical science, and one establishes what the correct forms of inference are inductively.[48] To show that a candidate pattern of inference is legitimate, that is, is a pattern of *inference*, is to show, among other things,[49] that it works; and the demonstration must be an induction from particular instances.

Now verification of this kind ultimately comes down to observation of particular cases.[50] Assessing the effectiveness of a particular inference will involve assessing the starting points and terminus of that inference. You must determine that, for instance, the premises of an argument being inspected were true, and the conclusion was also true; and doing this will require observing matters of particular fact. So the empirical investigation of inference requires the ability to make observations in the pertinent domain. Were the putative inferences to be practical, that would mean making observations whose content was practical; that is to say, some statements along the lines of "Such and such is desirable" would have to count as *observations*.

Mill was a British Empiricist – the fourth of the great British Empiricists, and the most thoroughly radical. Even Hume had allowed logic to be a priori; Mill was determined to be empiricist about logic as well. But even Mill was not an empiricist to the end. Like his predecessors, he took the class of basic observations for granted: they were sensations, the descendents of (most recently) Humean "impressions of sensation."[51] Because he was not empiricist enough to allow what an observation is to be an empirical question, there was no room in his systematic view for practical observation. Without practical observation, there was no room for the empirical investigation of practical inference. And so, despite his avowed empiricism about logic, Mill allowed himself to treat his views about practical inference as true a priori.

Mill has recently gotten a certain amount of publicity for having taken an empiricist approach in moral matters.[52] But, if I am right, the publicity is unwarranted: it was precisely here that Mill chickened out. Mill is able to let what people want be a matter of experience;[53] and finding out how to get what one wants is of course a matter of experience. But that what *matters* is people getting what they want is not a matter of experience, because Mill is barred from understanding the preferences of the experientially privileged as observations. This restriction is on display in two particularly prominent places. The first is the infallibility of the collective preferences of the experientially privileged. Mill cannot be providing an empirical test for distinguishing higher from lower pleasures, because empirical methods are fallible. Second, the processes described in Chapter 3 of *Utilitarianism*, through which the preferences of the majority of the experientially privileged are to be brought into line, are too clearly manipulative to allow the resulting preferences to be understood as observations. The citizens of Mill's Brave New World are being *conditioned*. The resulting preferences depend on the social pressures that drive the processes of conditioning, and not, in any way appropriate to observation, on the preferences' objects.

And so we have come to the final moral I wish to draw from the story I have now finished recounting. We have already seen that Mill's utilitarianism is very closely tied to his instrumentalism; that his argument for the Principle of Utility, while tight, is deeply incoherent; that the incoherence stems from an incoherence in instrumentalism; and that Mill's instrumentalism turns out to have been an island of apriorism in an otherwise empiricist project. It is tempting to think that if Mill had been willing to look to experience at this point also, his theory of practical reasoning, and consequently his moral theory, would have turned out quite differently – and perhaps less incoherently. So the final moral is that if you're going to be empiricist, be empiricist all the way: about practical reasoning, and about observation.

Notes

Thanks to Alyssa Bernstein, Sarah Buss, Roger Crisp, and Gideon Yaffe for commenting on earlier drafts of this paper. I'm also grateful to Brian Hirsch, Brian Lee, Christian Piller, Debra Satz, Candace Vogler, and audiences at Vanderbilt University, Carnegie Mellon University, Reed College, Ohio State University, Stanford University, UC/Davis, the University of Miami, Arizona State University, Wake Forest University, Syracuse University, the University of Illinois at Chicago, the University of Florida at Gainesville, and the University of Utah for helpful discussion. An ancestor of this material benefited from comments from Hilary Bok, Alice Crary, Christoph Fehige, Bill Haines, Robert Nozick, Hilary Putnam, and Tim Scanlon.

1. References to *Utilitarianism* are by page number in the standard edition of John Stuart Mill's *Collected Works* (1967–1989, Vol. X), followed by chapter and paragraph for the convenience of readers to whom the standard edition is not easily accessible; so the reference above is to p. 234, Chapter 4, paragraphs 2 and 3. Other references in the text will be to the standard edition by volume and page number alone.

   The quoted passage is presented as only half of the argument: it is supposed to show that happiness is desirable, but not yet that happiness is the only thing desirable. It will turn out, however, that the apparent division of labor between the two halves of the argument is at least misleading.

2. For a discussion of the early history of such criticism, see Gerard, 1997.

3. I'm grateful to John Rawls for emphasizing to me Mill's interest in reaching the politicians.

4. Compare Skorupski's recent description of *Utilitarianism*: "It is written for the general reader. It is not a technical treatise of philosophy, like the *System of Logic*; neither is it a carefully polished piece of political argument, as *On Liberty* is." (1989, p. 283). Skorupski takes the second sentence to follow from, or at any rate, to be of a piece with, the first. This, I will show, is a mistake. *Utilitarianism* is written for the general reader, *and* it is a "technical treatise of philosophy."

   This attempt to write for both audiences at the same time is not unique. The Preface to Mill's *Principles of Political Economy* concludes with the following announcement: "although [the writer's] object is practical, and as far as the nature of the subject admits, popular, he has not attempted to purchase either of those advantages by the sacrifice of strict scientific reasoning. Though he desires that his treatise should be more than a mere exposition of the abstract doctrines of Political Economy, he is also desirous that such an exposition should be found in it." (II:xcii)

5. My emphasis. As per usual, Mill adds a clause about the absence of pain; to keep the writing manageable, I'm going to suppress this rider from here on in.

6. Again, my emphasis. Mill is being disingenuous here: as he well knew, in the writing of earlier British moral philosophers, such as David Hume and Adam Smith, "utility" had meant something very different, and the misunderstanding Mill is trying to correct was in fact quite natural. See Sayre-McCord, 1996.

7. I should perhaps note that I am not here taking over Mill's technical sense of "nomenclature" (VIII:704–5).

8. Even as astute a reader of Mill as Skorupski falls into this trap; see note 16.

9. Mill's instrumentalism seems to have been inherited. In an editorial footnote, he approvingly quotes his father's "Fragment on Mackintosh": "all action, as Aristotle says, (and all mankind agree with him) is for an end. Actions are essentially means" (Mill, 1878, vol. 2, p. 262n).

   For a display of instrumentalism in the younger Mill's own writing, see the last chapter of the *System of Logic*, evidently intended by Mill as stage-setting for *Utilitarianism* (cf. VIII:951n), where Mill describes the relations between Science and Art. "Art" is Mill's label for the domain of practice and action, the area of which "the imperative mood is . . . characteristic" (VIII:943). Instrumental reasoning is not only the sole form of reasoning mentioned in the course of Mill's discussion; it is held entirely responsible for the structure of the domain. Art supplies ends, and the role of Science is to determine the means to those ends. Not surprisingly, Mill ends up identifying "the general principles of . . . Teleology, or the Doctrine of Ends" with "the principles of Practical Reason" (VIII:949–50).

There is, however, a caveat required here: while Mill's official doctrine remained unflinchingly instrumentalist until the day of his death, Vogler has pointed out that in his own argumentative practice he helped himself to other and richer forms of practical reasoning. What is more, he produced a striking indictment of instrumentalism in his retrospective diagnosis of his "mental crisis": in a strange and touching passage in his *Autobiography*, Mill argued that if you are an instrumentalist, you ought to find life unlivable (I:141–3). For discussion, see Vogler, 2001b, ch. 3.

10. "The truths known by intuition," he says, "are the original premises from which all others are inferred" – and by "intuition" Mill does not mean what a late twentieth-century philosopher would: he uses the word as a synonym for "consciousness," that is, for "what one sees and feels" (VII:6–7).

11. It might be thought that, at the terminus of the chain of justification, belief, feeling, and justification all collapse into one. But Mill does in fact continue to distinguish the feeling from the belief, for reasons having to do with the role of general terms in observation. These issues can be put aside here.

12. The phrase is borrowed from Kretzmann, 1971.

13. As far as the point at hand goes, Mill's use of "proof" as a technical term matches, and justifies his invoking, "the ordinary and popular meaning of the term" (207/1:5). But there is a further point, which we will soon come to, that stretches what is today the ordinary meaning a good deal.

14. Deductive validity notwithstanding, there are a couple of difficulties that are worth highlighting. In working the finger-exercise version of the first stretch of argument, the claim that happiness is the aggregate of the objects of noninstrumental desire is going to play a pivotal role, and the question is how we come by it. There seem to be two ways of getting there. The first is to read it off the subsequent argument, by noticing that Mill takes being an object of noninstrumental desire to be equivalent to being a component of happiness. But if this is what Mill is doing, then he seems to be entirely ignoring questions of the *organization* of the parts of a person's happiness into a whole. And I think that this is a genuine problem in Mill's view.

The second way of getting the pivotal claim is to use the verbal equivalence of "happiness" and "pleasure," and then that of "desiring a thing" and "finding it pleasant." The problem here is that pleasure has to come out being the *object* of desire; but as we ordinarily use the words, to find something pleasant is not the same as that thing's *being* pleasure. By our lights, there seems to be a slide from treating pleasure as a propositional attitude, to treating pleasure as the object of the attitude. Now, by the end of the passage that introduces the equivalence, it is clear that Mill takes himself to have introduced the terms in a way that bridges the apparent gap:

having said that "to desire anything, except in proportion as the idea of it is pleasant, is a physical and metaphysical impossibility," he then says, by way of repetition, "that desire can [not] possibly be directed to anything ultimately except pleasure." But why would Mill want to use his words this way? I will towards the end of the argument return to the question of what substantive view underlies this aspect of Mill's vocabulary.

15. VII:176; compare VIII:760–1.
16. For instance: "Mill stands accused of committing glaring logical blunders. . . . such accusations . . . are not justified. . . . he explicitly states that a *proof*, in the commonly understood sense of the word, of the Utility Principle . . . cannot be given. So he is not claiming to present a deductively valid argument – which is what one must assume him to be doing to pin on him the familiar fallacies" (Skorupski, 1989, pp. 285–6).
17. VII:162; the full discussion appears in the previous section, at VII:158–62. See note 49.
18. VII:186–93. This may also seem hard to believe; after all, Mill would not have denied, of a syllogism such as "All men are mortal; the Duke of Wellington is a man; so the Duke of Wellington is mortal," that when the major premise is true, all its instances are true also. However, we now have a widely familiar analog of syllogistic reasoning as Mill understands it, and highlighting the analogy may make Mill's claim seem more reasonable.

Think of the file compression utility (e.g., Zip or Compress) on your computer. When you compress and reexpand a file, you do not think of yourself as deriving new results, but as merely reformatting the file for more convenient storage or access. Now, in Mill's view, the actual inference to the Duke of Wellington's mortality is from particulars to particulars: from "A was a man, and he died," and "B was a man, and he died too," and so on, and "The Duke of Wellington is a man," to "The Duke of Wellington will die." The major premise of our sample syllogism is not part of the inference proper, but is rather a way of *storing* the observed evidence in a way that makes it easy to keep track of and use; the syllogism is a method of *extracting* already available information, not of inferring new information.

19. VII:158–9; compare VII:66, or again, the *Analysis*: "We can afford . . . no aid to the reader in distinguishing [a pleasurable or painful sensation], otherwise than by using such expressions as seem calculated to fix his attention upon it" (1878, vol. 2, p. 190).
20. So while Mill did not think that deduction was properly understood as inference, he did not deny, but rather insisted on, the heuristic importance of deduction, and syllogistic deduction in particular. See, e.g., VII:196–9; VIII:665.
21. VII:15n; this quotation is from the 1856 edition of the *System of Logic*, and was omitted in subsequent editions. Compare his criticism, at VII:93–7, of views of naming on which all truth comes out merely verbal, and his discussion "Of Propositions Merely Verbal," where he claims that "when any important consequences seem to follow . . . from a proposition involved in the meaning of a name, what they really flow from is the tacit assumption of the real existence of the objects so named" (VII:113).

22. Sidgwick, 1907/1981, p. 388.
23. Mill registers his awareness of this demand at VIII:951.
24. The omitted phrase is a qualification designed to avoid circularity in the establishment of a specifically moral criterion. This omission is repeated in the next passage.

    The passage is introduced as an explanation of difference in quality in pleasures, as opposed to quantity. But since, as we will see in a moment, quantitative comparisons work no differently, we can disregard the apparent restriction in scope.
25. Mill does differ from contemporary decision theorists in how he thinks of preferences. The current economist's notion of preference ties it very closely to overt behavior: preference is "revealed" in choice. Mill's notion of preference is closer to that of a comparative evaluation: one such preference is described as "a full appreciation of the intrinsic superiority of the higher [pleasure]." The description appears in the course of Mill's acknowledgement that "the influence of temptation" and "infirmity of character" may produce the opposite "election" (212/2:7) – "election" being much nearer to what we would call "preference" today.
26. Brandt, 1979, p. 113, Rawls, 1971, pp. 408–9, and also pp. 417, 421–2; emphases mine.
27. Mill's take on what these problems are is sufficiently nonstandard to be worth spelling out. First, appeal to the preferences of counterfactual selves involves making psychological predictions (about what you would prefer if . . .). But psychological laws fall into two categories. On the one hand, there are what Mill calls "Empirical Laws," that is, uniformities that are observed to hold, but whose underlying reasons are not understood. Mill holds that these cannot be relied upon "beyond the limits of actual experience"; varying the "collocations" (Mill's term for initial conditions) may disrupt the uniformity (VII:516, 519, 548; for "collocation," VII:465). But assessing the truth of a psychological counterfactual normally involves "varying" the collocations "from those which have actually been observed" (VII:516). So Empirical Laws cannot be relied upon to assess psychological counterfactuals. On the other hand, there are psychological predictions derived from the fundamental laws of the human mind. These are ironclad, but, unfortunately, they cannot normally be applied. What people will do in response to given stimuli is a matter of their characters; their characters are shaped by their entire histories; and we cannot observe these histories (VII:865). Consequently, a criterion that appealed to psychological counterfactuals would be unusable: there is simply no way to determine what you would prefer, if . . .

    Mill's second problem is that there are many counterfactual selves – some dulled, some especially nasty, some overly tremulous, etc. – whose judgments are going to have to be ruled out as defective. It's hard to believe that this can be done without importing into the selection of counterfactual selves the full and robust set of evaluations that the use of the counterfactual selves was meant to certify. But if this is what is going on, this use of counterfactual selves is viciously circular: "to explain away the numerous instances of divergence from their assumed [moral] standard, by representing them as cases in which the perceptions are unhealthy" is "a striking instance of reasoning in a circle" (VIII:826).

Notice that this is also a reason for not looking to the preferences of a carefully chosen coterie of right-thinking persons: appealing to the judgments of the *phronimoi* will not do. This is why Mill usually requires only experience of the options being compared. And I am accordingly inclined to think that his sole mention of "habits of self-consciousness and self-observation" is a slip on Mill's part.

28. A quick textual point, for those who are used to reading the passages in question as invoking counterfactuals. In English, counterfactuals are generally (although not necessarily) signalled by the subjunctive mood. These passages, amounting to about a full page of text, contain not even a single subjunctive, and the explanation cannot be stylistic: Mill's discussion of "Permanent Possibilities of Sensation" uses the subjunctive without hesitation (e.g., IX:184).

29. If this sounds implausible – why should I care about what other people prefer, if their preferences turn out not to match mine? – notice that the currently popular counterfactual technique has the same problem. Why should I care about what a counterfactual self would prefer, if his preferences turn out not to match mine?

The difficulty is, however, perhaps especially acute for Mill, who in *On Liberty* had pointed out that others' experience may be an "unsuitable" guide if one has an "uncustomary" character, that "human beings are not... undistinguishably alike," "that people have diversities of taste,... [and] different conditions for their spiritual development," and that there "are... differences among human beings in their sources of pleasure, their susceptibilities of pain, and the operation on them of different physical and moral agencies" (XVIII:262, 270).

I will get around to discussing the more general version of this problem in due course.

30. Kretzmann notices and highlights this move, but worries that he has "extended [Mill] and even departed from him" (1971, p. 241). One other worry that might arise at this point is whether the decided preference criterion is really usable: do we have to wait until all the votes are in before we can make up our minds? Notice, however, that this problem is very like another that utilitarianism already has. When assessing an action or rule, how far into the future do we need to look for the effects it will have on overall utility? The in-principle answer is, of course, to the end of time; but that cannot be the normal procedure.

31. Mill has just given a prediction of the future state of society. Now we saw that Mill does not think that individual psychologies are predictable (see note 27). But he thinks that problems of individual psychological prediction can be sidestepped when large groups of people are being studied. The social scientist "can get on well enough with approximate generalizations on human nature, since what is true approximately of all individuals is true absolutely of all masses" (VII:603). Mill had been impressed by the new science of statistics (VIII:932), and was quite willing to believe that even if you could

not predict the counterfactual preferences of individuals, under certain circumstances predicting the preferences of the majority of the experientially privileged was well within the realm of possibility (VIII:846f; cf. VIII:873, 890).

In that case, the reader might be wondering, why not appeal to the counterfactual preferences of the experientially privileged as a group? Why the reliance on actual preferences? Mill does not actually discuss this option, but he would have had reasons for not availing himself of it. First of all, the desired social science (the science of character, which Mill dubbed "Ethology") was never more than a gleam in his eye; barring special circumstances, such as the argument we now have on hand, we don't for the present have any way of predicting the preferences of a group. Second, prediction in the social sciences has its limits, and of precise predictions of the history of society, extended arbitrarily far into the future (similar to those we have come to expect from astronomy), Mill thought, "there is . . . no hope"(VIII:877). Small errors snowball, and so the predictions of a "Deductive" science like Ethology would need to be continually checked against and corrected by observation – in this case, observation of the actual preferences of the experientially privileged. Since the actual preferences are not, on Mill's account of the social sciences, dispensable, he may have preferred to cut out, as so much wasted motion, the detour through counterfactuals.

32. Mill sometimes suggests that the economic arrangements of the future will also work to mute the conflict between the alternatives; e.g., in the *Principles of Political Economy*, he speaks of a time when "civilization and improvement have so far advanced, that what is a benefit to the whole shall be a benefit to each individual composing it," having in mind in this case the more equitable distribution of gains in productivity (III:768).

33. There's a nicety here that deserves pointing out. The criterion of desirability introduced in Chapter 2 avoids circularity by specifying that the preferences consulted shall be those given "irrespective of any feeling of moral obligation to prefer" one item rather than another (211/2:5). (See note 24.) In order to prevent this condition from excluding the preferences of the acculturated utilitarian majority for the general happiness over all else, Mill argues that the "strengthening of social ties . . . leads [each individual] to identify his *feelings* more and more with [others'] good . . . He comes, as though instinctively, to be conscious of himself as a being who *of course* pays regard to others. The good of others becomes to him a thing naturally and necessarily to be attended to . . . "(231f/3:9, Mill's emphasis). Future utilitarians, thinks Mill, will not want one thing but feel constrained by the moral law to prefer another. Their desire for the general happiness will be a native preference, one that can thus serve as grist for the "decided preference" criterion.

34. For a lengthier and much more thorough rendition of Mill's views on this point, see his essay "Auguste Comte and Positivism" (X:263–368).

35. There is in fact a more likely way for the contingency of value to exhibit itself, and one which I suspect worried Mill a good deal. If A's being preferable to B is a matter of the majority of the experientially privileged preferring A to B, then A's being preferable to B depends on there being individuals

having experience of the different options: if there are no such individuals, or perhaps not enough of them, then there is no fact of the matter as to which is preferable. The applicability of the decided preference criterion requires that there be people who try things out – who conduct, in Mill's phrase, "experiments of living" (XVIII:261) – and I am inclined to think that this was one of Mill's reasons for insisting so strongly on the liberty to try things out. (Notice the awkward tradeoff: in order for there to be a standard of preferability, people have to, and hence have to be *encouraged* to (XVIII:269), do what will prove to be the *in*correct thing.)

36. See VII:227, 231, 237–61, 277.

37. The sentence can be read on the model of sentences like: "*To* the scientific community, the theory of relativity is true." Norman Kretzmann takes Mill's argument to lean in a pragmatist direction (1971, p. 239), and it is in this vicinity that I find his suggestion most evocative.

38. At this point we are able to say what Mill has in mind in his response to Spencer. That "the truths of arithmetic are applicable to the valuation of happiness" (258n/5:35n) is to be read off the preferences of the experientially privileged. (They are not always applicable: higher and lower pleasures are incommensurable, and this fact is also to be read off the preferences of the experientially privileged.) The processes that will make future persons into natural utilitarians will, Mill further argues, also create persons who take it for granted "that the interests of all are to be regarded equally" (231/3:9).

39. It might look like there are a couple of places to get off the boat here: you might object that the reasoning in question isn't actually practical, or, alternatively, that, although practical, it is merely means-end reasoning. But while one can always get out of the boat, it turns out that, in this case, there's no pier handy to step onto.

Notice, first, that the two objections are not as different in spirit as they might at first glance seem to be. Since the reasoning was identified as practical by identifying its conclusion as practical, the first objection requires insisting that that conclusion does not give the agent a reason for action. Now this latter thought is normally underwritten by the idea that sentences like "I ought to do this" or "This is the correct preference" do not express reasons for action because they do not express desires. But the requirement that reasons for action be desires is in turn normally underwritten by instrumentalism.

Because the point of correcting the agent's preferences was to pick out reasons for action, let's abandon the first objection in favor of the second: the reasoning is conceded to be practical, but is entirely means-end, that is, correcting one's preferences is shown to be a way of satisfying some further desire. But now the reasoning so construed faces an uncomfortable dilemma. Either the desires from which it proceeds are corrected, or they are not. If they are uncorrected, then we have the appearance of a pragmatic contradiction: the conclusion of the reasoning, recall, was that one should use in one's practical reasoning, not one's uncorrected, but *corrected* desires or preferences. If, on the other hand, they are corrected, then we have the question blatantly begged. To see that, consider the different "black box" that corrects your preferences to mine. Asked why you should regard my preferences as those you should act on, rather than your own, I would not convince you by answering: because I would prefer it.

40. The point is not that appeals to informed desires are in principle dispensible: taking the argument in that direction would bring us around to a conclusion I would not wish to endorse, that there are no properties that can be understood only via the reactions of their perceivers. (Such properties have traditionally been called "secondary qualities.") The point is, rather, that the explanation for taking the perception of some secondary quality to provide a reason for action will involve a noninstrumental pattern of practical inference.

41. Very quickly: To desire something, noninstrumentally, is to find the idea of it pleasurable, that is, to expect it to be pleasurable; and since the "decided preference criterion" is being used as a way of correcting desires so their objects *are* found pleasurable, we can read "desired" as "desired, subject to correction by the judgments of the experientially privileged." Happiness means pleasure, and so now means something like: the aggregate of the objects of one's desires, as corrected by the preferences of the experientially privileged. So the premise of the stretch of argument that we are now marvering comes out as: the objects of desires corrected by the preferences of the experientially privileged are desired, when those desires are corrected by the preferences of the experientially privileged. Once again, the premise of the argument is a tautology. Now one's noninstrumental desires, corrected by the preferences of the experientially privileged, are what is desirable (by the "decided preference criterion"). So the conclusion, that each person's happiness is desirable for him, comes out meaning: the objects of one's desires, as corrected by the preferences of the experientially privileged (that is, when attained, happiness), are the objects of one's desires, as corrected by the preferences of the experientially privileged (that is, what is desirable). The conclusion is also, once again, a tautology; and is, once again, the premise of the argument repeated.

42. IX:468–9; the passage provides two examples.

43. See note 21.

44. Mill, 1878, vol. 2, pp. 191–2, for the analysis; notice the younger Mill's modification to the definition in the editorial footnote at pp. 194–5. For the desires for wealth, etc., see pp. 207–14. For the role of desires in action, see pp. 256–9, 262n–4, 327–403.

     We can now tie up another loose end: the analysis of desire accounts for what we would see as the terminological slide that I highlighted in note 14. Like his son, James Mill identifies, as a matter of terminology, pleasure (or, more carefully, the representation of pleasure) with desire: "The terms . . . 'idea of pleasure,' and 'desire,' are but two names; the thing named, the state of consciousness, is one and the same" (pp. 191–2; cf. p. 327). A desire just is an idea of the sensation of pleasure, which idea may be associated with other ideas, most prominently, of causes of the sensation. It follows that understanding desires as (what we would nowadays call) propositional attitudes, that is, attitudes whose objects are as it were logically integral to the mental state, is a *mistake*: "when the word desire is applied to the cause of a sensation...it is employed in a figurative, or metaphorical, not in a direct sense" (p. 351). What we would call the objects of desire are actually just the causes of the real objects, pain and pleasure: "The illusion is merely that of a very close association" (p. 192). This view, quite startling by today's lights, accounts for Mill's treating the moves from desiring *x*, to finding *x* pleasurable, to desiring pleasure (which happens to be associated with *x*) as traversing a series of innocuous synonymies.

45. Mill, 1878, vol. 2, pp. 357n, 378.

46. Mill, 1878, vol. 2, pp. 209–11.

47. To be sure, one can see how the fact that human beings are desiring creatures might be made the starting point of an argument for the view we are considering. But the argument is not in Mill, and the mode of argument, as we will see in a moment, would not be one that Mill could admit.

48. See VII:567–77; also VII:306–14; VIII:833.

49. Foremost among further criteria that need to be satisfied in order for a mental transition to amount to an inference is, recall, that "the conclusion is...wider than the premises from which it is drawn" (VII:288). Mill never seems to have asked whether means-end reasoning, which he endorses, satisfies this condition, and it is unclear to me, in view of his discussion of parallel questions, how he could have given a satisfactory answer.

50. See, e.g., VII:193.

51. Even though sense-data are now out of style, taking a class of basic observations for granted is not. A familiar recent example is van Fraassen's identification of observation with "what the unaided eye discerns" (1980, p. 59; see also pp. 16 ff, 56 ff, 214); for criticism, see essays in Churchland and Hooker, 1985.

52. Anderson, for instance, adduces under this heading Mill's diagnosis of his nervous breakdown as an "experiment in living" (1991). I think that it can be so understood, but not the way Anderson would like to: Mill himself was surprisingly unsuccessful in learning the lessons of his breakdown and partial recovery. He was never able to provide a satisfactory account of the importance in his own life of Romantic poetry; willing to surrender neither his instrumentalism nor his associationism, he was forced to treat the resistance of associations formed under the influence of poetry to analytical corrosion as a brute psychological fact. And while Mill is quite clear about his own motivational structure up until his breakdown, his view of himself after his recovery fails, quite strikingly, to match the ways he thought, felt, and lived. I hope to discuss these issues further elsewhere.

There is another confusion in Anderson's paper that is common enough to be worth remark. Anderson thinks that "Mill's emphasis on the intrinsic desirability of gratifying the [higher] sentiments strongly suggests that he believed that dignity, beauty, honor, and so forth are values distinct from pleasure," and she takes Mill to be departing from "the basic premise of ethical hedonism, that pleasure is the sole respect in which things can be intrinsically valuable." She concludes that "Mill's conception of the good is not hedonistic but pluralistic and hierarchical."

But this is just to lose track of Mill's terminology. For something to be desirable is, as we have seen, just to be desired (noninstrumentally, and subject to the correction of the experientially privileged); this is, merely as a matter of nomenclature, to be found pleasurable. Consequently, being pleasurable, in Mill's sense, is not a *respect* in which things can be found desirable. And if we tie the word "hedonism" to Mill's word "pleasure," whether Mill's conception of the good is "pluralistic and hierarchical" has nothing whatsoever to do with whether it is "hedonistic."

53. That people want happiness is, we have seen, a verbal matter, and not a matter of experience at all. But for that reason, happiness is not a substantive account of what is wanted; the substantive account is to be given by empirical investigation of what people, and their experientially privileged stand-ins, actually desire.

3

Does the Categorical Imperative Give Rise to
a Contradiction in the Will?

The *Brave New World* style utilitarian dystopia is a familiar feature of the cultural landscape;[1] Kantian dystopias are harder to come by, perhaps because, until Rawls, Kantian morality presented itself as a primarily personal rather than political program. This asymmetry is peculiar for formal reasons, because one phase of the deliberative process on which Kant insists is to ask what the world at large would be like if everyone did whatever it is one is thinking of doing. I do not propose to write a Kantian *Brave New World* myself, but I am going to ask, of what these days is called the "CI-procedure," what would happen if everybody followed it. I will argue that if the CI-procedure works as advertised, it exposes a practical incoherence in the commitment to having it govern one's actions: in the Kantian vocabulary that goes with the territory, that the Categorical Imperative gives rise to a contradiction in the will. (Less formally, that it is self-refuting.)

My target will be a recently influential interpretation of Kant, due primarily to John Rawls and a number of his students, most prominently Onora O'Neill, Christine Korsgaard, and Barbara Herman, a group I will for convenience refer to as the New Kantians.[2] Although it does draw on earlier interpretive work, this body of writing is relatively self-contained, and manageable in a way that the Kant literature as a whole no longer is. I don't myself wish to take a stand on whether the New Kantian reading is exegetically correct; it suffices for present purposes that it has proven itself interesting, plausible, and powerful enough to have moved Kantian moral philosophy back from the marginalized position it occupied a little over a quarter-century ago to the center of contemporary ethics.

I will begin by rehearsing the CI-procedure and the theory that accompanies it; the reader is warned that the setup will take more time than is usual in papers of this kind. Kant himself used the label "Categorical Imperative" to mark three ideas that he thought were at bottom the same: the practical priority of universalizability, of respect for persons, and of autonomy. They are, however, at any rate on the surface, rather different, and in order to sidestep the issue of whether the different versions of the Categorical Imperative are in fact equivalent, I will be focusing only on the first, viz., on Kant's insistence that one act only according to maxims of which one can at the same time will that they become universal laws.[3] So the first task on our agenda will be describing how the New Kantians reconstruct that demand.

1

The first formulation of the Categorical Imperative supplies a test for the permissibility of a proposed action. The New Kantians render this test procedurally, and have come to call it the *CI-procedure*.[4] When it occurs to you to do something, you are to

1. Identify the *maxim* of the action.

   The maxim is the "subjective principle of volition" (G 400n) that underlies the action. It captures your understanding of the action and of why you are proposing to perform it. The New Kantian account depicts maxims as having something like a logical form:

   In circumstances C, to do A, because P.

   Here A is a description of the type of action; C specifies the occasions that are to trigger actions of type A; and P specifies the point of the action.[5]

2. Consider the maxim universalized, that is, imagine a world (a "perturbed social world," in Rawls's phrase) in which everyone in your circumstances (i.e., in circumstances that share with the one at hand the features you understand to be relevant) does what you are proposing to do. If you *can't* do this – if such a world is literally inconceivable – or if the intention expressed in your maxim is bound to be frustrated in such a world, then your maxim fails the *contradiction in conception* test.[6]

   Each of the elements of a maxim plays a role in the New Kantian reconstruction of the CI-procedure. C and A are the clauses of the rule that is always acted on in the perturbed social world. By specifying the intended achievement, P gives content to the notion of a frustrated plan of action; if P is frustrated by executing the plan, then the plan is self-frustrating.

3. Ask whether there are intentions that you are bound to have simply in virtue of being a human agent, but that cannot be successfully executed if your maxim is universalized.

   If there are, your maxim fails the *contradiction in the will* test.

4. If your maxim passes both tests, you may go ahead and perform the action; if it does not, acting on your maxim is prohibited.

What this comes to is best made clear by example, but before I get to that, a couple of clarificatory remarks. First, although I have described the procedure as something you pause to execute before going ahead with an action you have in mind, the Kantian requirement is of course not that you stand around muttering to yourself before you do anything. The procedure is meant as a rational reconstruction of the deliberative background to a decision properly arrived at, in pretty much the way that Aristotelian practical syllogisms are meant to reconstruct a somewhat different kind of deliberative background to action (Rawls, 2000, p. 218).

Second, the New Kantians understand the point of the CI-procedure to be practical consistency.[7] The idea is that self-frustrating plans of action are the analogs, in practical reasoning, of the kind of incoherence that contradictory beliefs amount to in theoretical reasoning. Uncontroversial models for such self-frustration can be found in means-end incoherence, as when you decide to go to New York, but tear up the ticket that would get you there, or (to borrow an example from Garry Trudeau, 1996, 104) when someone decides he should have gone to medical school, but that dropping out of high school was definitely the right choice. You cannot coherently intend a self-frustrating plan of action, and the CI-procedure is presented as a way of checking whether what you are proposing is something that you can coherently intend. It is not (as such illustrious readers as John Stuart Mill have believed) a way of checking whether the results of everybody acting as you propose would be to your liking. In the postscript to this chapter, I will return to the question of *why* intentions that fail the CI-procedure are supposed to be on a par with self-frustrating plans; for now, we need to bear in mind that courses of action with genuinely awful consequences can pass the CI-procedure, which is to say that it is a deeply nonconsequentialist way of thinking about what to do. The question is: "*Can* you (not: *do* you) will that everybody do as you are proposing to do yourself?"

Kant illustrates his proposal with four examples, and because it is important for the subsequent argument to have the moves clearly laid out, I will walk through four examples as well, construing them as the New Kantians do. However, Kant's treatment of suicide is hard to bring into line with the New Kantian reading (and in fact it is not easy to see how suicide is an appropriate example of Kant's claims on just about anybody's reading). Because we do not want to skimp on exemplary contradiction in the will arguments before proceeding to develop our own, I will substitute an alternative, the recent New Kantian argument against violence.

Lying. Suppose your maxim is: to lie about whether you can and will pay back your creditor, whenever you need a loan that you're not in a position to repay – the point of your action being, of course, to get the money. If we think about a world in which everybody lied in these circumstances, we realize that in that world your plan of action could not possibly be effective; no creditor would believe you, and the lie would not work. Willing both a world in which everybody does as you do, and that your lie be effective, is something very much like adopting a self-frustrating plan. (Though, again, we haven't said why you have to be committed to both sides of the "plan.") Therefore, lies of this type are strictly impermissible. Restrictions generated by failure at the contradiction in conception stage are "perfect duties"; there are no exceptions to the prohibition on acting on this maxim.[8]

Before moving on to the next example, I want, for reasons that will be apparent in the sequel, to give this one a little more discussion than it usually gets. Kant's argument seems to depend on an empirical premise – that a *practice* of lying will undercut its own effectiveness – that is obviously often false.[9] Airlines, for instance, routinely publish schedules that they know they cannot meet; their maxim is, roughly, "When it will allow us to utilize our capital more efficiently, we will announce schedules we can't possibly stick to, in order to increase revenue." But (as you can confirm by looking around, the next time you are in an airport) passengers have not ceased to believe the schedules: they are surprised and upset when their flights are delayed, they have plans made around their flights' scheduled arrival times, and they are completely unprepared when they turn out to have missed their connection.[10] As a matter of psychological fact, people simply do not behave in the way that Kant's argument says they do. There are two ways we might approach this problem, and I just want to indicate what the Kantian's choice is. He can treat the premise as empirical, and reshape his moral arguments around whatever the psychological facts turn out to be. Or, and I am myself inclined to think that this option is the more Kantian in spirit, he can treat it as prescriptive: Kant is on about how people are *supposed* to reason, and not about how they actually do. A rational agent *should* stop believing when it is obvious that there is a practice of lying; and we are to draw our moral conclusions on that basis rather than the empirical one.[11]

Mutual Aid. Suppose one of your maxims is: when someone needs a hand, not to help out, because you have other things to do with your time. Now, a world in which no one helps anyone else is (at first glance) conceivable.[12] But such a world would frustrate, not perhaps the intention expressed in the maxim, but a practical commitment you are bound to have to your own agency. In the Kantian picture, to be a rational agent is to be a creature that deliberates about, settles on, and then pursues its own ends. You have no way of knowing, now, what ends you will settle on down the road.[13] But you do know, humans being what they are, that if people are going to be agents worth the name, they will adopt projects that they cannot manage entirely on their own; and what is more, that the need for assistance crops up frequently enough in situations where there are no formal arrangements for assuring and compensating it. I decide to move my kitchen table, and so I have to get someone to lift the other end. I am lost, and since what I am is *lost,* the person from whom I have to ask directions is someone I do not already have anything like a contractual relationship with: I will have to ask a stranger for a favor. A world in which no one helps out will be a world in which the pursuit of your ends will predictably (often but not necessarily always) run aground. To will such a world is to will a world in which your agency is routinely frustrated, and your stake in your own agency is such that this would amount to a contradiction in your will. The "maxim of indifference" must be rejected.

Development of Talents. "Talent" is here a misleadingly hifalutin word for the specialized skills of one kind or another that pursuing your ends is almost bound to require. There are many projects that you might reasonably adopt that would require driving to bring them off, and so being able to drive counts as a "talent" in the appropriate sense. It is an empirical but unavoidable fact about human agency that you yourself cannot be expected to have all the necessary skills; social arrangements built around the division of labor make it reasonable to expect that suitable resources of this kind will be available at the appropriate stages of your project. A world in which no one takes opportunities to develop their talents is, at first glance, anyway, conceivable.[14] But in such a world, those capacities

are unavailable to you as resources, and your stake in your own agency –
in the New Kantian reading, a kind of necessary end – is bound to be
frustrated. Therefore, you cannot will a world in which the maxim we are
considering is universalized, and the maxim must be rejected.[15]

Because Kant holds that the contradiction in the last two cases is in the
will, rather than in conception – in the New Kantian reading, that the
plan of action is not itself self-frustrating, but that when it is taken together with other ends that you necessarily have, these are jointly mutually
frustrating – he holds that it gives rise to "imperfect duties." You obviously
cannot develop all the useful specialized skills and capacities; you obviously cannot help out every time someone needs it. The argument is
supposed to show that you have to help *sometimes*, and that you have to
develop *some* skill set; but just when to help and when not to is left up to
you, and which talents to develop is also left up to you.[16]

Violence. Suppose your maxim is to take violent means, and in particular
to kill, when that will promote your interests and projects. Being a victim of violence generally, and being killed in particular, tends to interrupt
one's plan of action. (There are odd exceptions, for example, when being
bludgeoned to death is actually part of your plan.[17]) In a world in which
everyone acted on this maxim, your agency in general would be ineffective
because interrupted, and whatever project you are currently pursuing via
the maxim would be interruptable.[18] That your current project be interrupted (or anyway interruptable by anyone else in pursuit of their ends),
or that your agency generally be aborted or abortive, is not something you
can coherently will. The violence-endorsing maxim must be rejected.[19]

Notice a few features of New Kantian applications of the CI-procedure
that turn on contradiction in the will (that is, of the latter three examples). First, they exploit deep facts about specifically human agency –
about the range of ends that it is reasonable to expect humans to adopt,
about the inability of human beings to do everything for themselves, or
to acquire all the skills their projects are likely to need, and about the
vulnerability of human agency to violent interruption. These are facts
about people, not necessary features of agency. There might be creatures
of whom none of this is true, creatures whose individual capabilities, skill
sets, and robustness extend well beyond the range of their reasonably
adopted ends, rather than falling short of it. If we were characters from
Road Runner, the New Kantian argument against violence would not go
through: when Wile E. Coyote is crushed under a falling rock, he emerges

slightly crumpled, but still ready to order the next Acme product. Second, the argument does not suppose that *all* conceivable projects, or even the projects you have actually undertaken, will be aborted if others do not come to your aid, etc.[20] If the argument is to work, the requirement must be rather that the world of the universalized maxim pose *enough* of an impediment to the range of projects that a rational deliberator – a creature that sets its own ends – might well adopt. And third, what drives the argument in each case is your stake in your own effective agency, which makes it impossible for you to coherently endorse a commitment to arrangements that would very broadly undermine it.

2

New Kantians are committed to actions coming in all sizes and levels of abstraction. And refrainings and omissions can count as actions, provided that they are governed by one's intent in the same way that more obvious actions are.[21] It follows that governing one's activity by the CI-procedure – that is, not performing an action if its maxim does not pass the CI-procedure – is, anyway when one is "acting from the moral law," itself an action or plan of action. Like other actions, it can be the dictate of many possible maxims, but a maxim in line with the spirit of (New) Kantian moral theory would be:

> When I am making up my mind what to do, I will act only on maxims that pass the CI-procedure, so as to make (morally or rationally) permissible decisions.

Call this the *CI-maxim*; Kantians are committed to requiring of agents that something along the lines of the CI-maxim capture their volitional stance.[22]

New Kantian moral theory imposes the CI-procedure as a test that all of one's maxims must pass. The CI-maxim, which expresses the willingness to adopt this constraint, is itself a maxim. Therefore, proceeding on the basis of the CI-maxim must be contingent on its passing the CI-procedure.[23]

The point here is *not* that the CI-procedure has to show that the CI-procedure is mandatory; to establish that, one would proceed by testing a maxim containing the clause, "... not to act on the CI...", which is not what I propose to do. The thought is rather that because the CI-procedure tests the maxims you bring to it for practical consistency, you do not want a maxim to fail – even if you think of it as foundational.[24]

(Compare: in a foundationalist epistemological structure, we may exempt its foundational elements from having justifications, but we would still have cause for complaint if their contents turned out to have the form $p \wedge \sim p$.)

I will now walk through the application of the CI-procedure to the CI-maxim; as previously announced, I will be attempting to show that the CI-maxim fails at the contradiction in the will stage of the procedure. We have just completed the initial step of the procedure, that is, identifying the maxim that it is going to be run on. The next step is to represent the perturbed social world in which the maxim is universalized. In the case of the CI-maxim, this is a world in which all agents treat the CI-procedure as a constraint on their actions. That is, they act only when they could will the maxim of their action to be universalized.

In willing that everyone always act in the way you are proposing, "as if the maxim of your action were to become through your will a universal law of nature" (G 421), you are willing that you act yourself in the way you are proposing, as though governed by "a universal law of nature"; after all, "everyone" includes yourself. That is, accepting the CI-maxim involves, in your own case, understanding your actions as governed by, or as the deliverances of, lawlike policies. (I am not just bearing down hard on something Kant happened to say; I will in due course argue that the CI-procedure can work only if its inputs are lawlike policies.) For a policy to be lawlike is for it to have no exceptions. So the perturbed social world is one in which, when anyone acts, he understands himself to be acting from a universal and so exceptionless policy that governs his action.

Of course we are not supposing that agents in the perturbed social world act on the *same* policies (except for the policy expressed by the CI-maxim). Agents in that world do will that others act on the same policies as themselves. But "willing" has, in one's own case, consequences it does not have in others'. When I will that I act from a policy or according to a law, that has the effect of commiting me to act (it amounts to an intention to act) in accordance with the policy. But when I "will" that others act in accord with my policy, that need have no consequences for whether they do: most other people are not subject to my will. I also do not think we need to imagine that agents do not change their policies from time to time. They may decide that a previous policy was mistaken, and is to be replaced. What *is* required is that in so doing they understand themselves to have discarded one universal, exceptionless policy and to have replaced it with another. Kant has sometimes been accused of having a moral theory that generates exceptionless rules (that everybody has to abide by); that was a misperception of a different feature of the view, which is that it *operates on* exceptionless rules (but different ones for different agents at different times).[25]

What this means is that the perturbed social world of the universalized CI-maxim is one in which requests for exceptions to people's policies will be uniformly denied. We will have to proceed carefully here, making sure as the argument develops that we know just what this means. But meantime, notice that we are still on Kant's home turf. Kant diagnoses the immoral person as wanting to make an exception for himself (G 424); but if making an exception for oneself on one's own behalf is illegitimate, surely demanding that others make an exception for one must be illegitimate, too.

Now I want to advance the following claim: that successful agency requires exceptions from others' policies, in just the way that successful agency requires assistance from others, in just the way that it requires immunity from violence, and in just the way it requires the availability of a rich set of skills all of which one cannot have acquired oneself.[26] If this is correct (and if the Kantian model arguments for mutual aid and the like work as advertised), then, by parity of argument, the CI-maxim gives rise to a contradiction in the will: one's stake in one's own agency is such that one cannot endorse having it undermined by being deprived of the exceptions that are its precondition. And if that is in turn correct, then it is forbidden to act on the CI-maxim, and Kantian moral theory is (at least in its New Kantian rendition, and stating the conclusion informally) self-refuting.

Even though the analogous claims in the New Kantian model arguments are not taken to need support, I am going to argue for this one. I will proceed first by giving examples of the kind of case I have in mind. Then I will give an argument meant to explain why cases of this kind are common enough to be an empirical but deep fact about human agency. Finally, I will take up the New Kantian's stock objection to treating the cases as my argument requires – that is, to treating them as bona fide exceptions – and give two counterarguments to it.

Parking in Milan. I'll change a real-life story around a little bit to get my first, very small-scale example. When I was visiting friends in Milan, I needed to run my bags up to their apartment before returning the rental car. I found myself on a one-way and heavily trafficked street, with no on-street parking, and a barrier to keep cars off the sidewalk, which meant that I needed a small exception (the kind that involves blinking hazard lights) to the rule that governed the building's parking lot: only cars with permits. As it happened, the guard staffing the lot wasn't handing out exceptions, and my plans for the day had to be rewritten on the fly.

Trouble in High School. A former colleague of mine reports having been *very* bored in high school, and admits to frequently skipping classes . . . so frequently, in fact, that she ought to have been kicked out of school. She never *asked* for an exception to the rule that gets you expelled for skipping class, but an exception was made: one to which she owes her college education, and so her current job, and so, indirectly, much of the shape of her current life. In this example, the effect of not having an exception made for one is rather more dramatic than in the first.

The Tardy Contributor. A fellow academic who was editing a *Festschrift* had set a hard deadline for the invited papers. One of the authors circulated a draft of his paper, and shortly before the deadline discovered a problem requiring major revisions. The editor granted an exception to the deadline; without it, the author would have had to withdraw the paper, which would have hurt the *Festschrift*, the feelings of its subject, and the author himself, who would have been hard put to find another venue for the commissioned piece.

Cases like these are recognizable enough (although we still need to take up the question of how they are to be interpreted). But are they common enough to make the availability of exceptions a precondition for successful agency? If the need for exceptions is only exceptional, it will not support the argument we are developing against universalizing the CI-procedure. So I will now argue that exceptions will be needed on an ongoing basis.

Let's begin with a fact used by other Kantian arguments that we've already reviewed: that human agency is dependent on the cooperation of others. Human projects are vulnerable, the kind of projects that human rational deliberators reasonably adopt will outrun the resources that an agent can muster on his own, and they will do so frequently enough to make cooperation a *sine qua non*. Once again, this is not being introduced as a necessary truth about agency. For all we know, there could be agents who were successful lone wolves, either because projects that wolves take on fall into a narrower range than do ours, or because wolves are much more resourceful than we are.

The behavior of others is a very large part of the environment in which we pursue our ends, and much of that behavior is policy directed or rule governed in any case; *ex hypothesi*, in the world of the universalized

CI-maxim, *all* of it is. So the contribution that others make to our projects will (mostly, in the actual world, and entirely, in the perturbed social world we are considering) come under the heading of rules or policies in force. So you will be able effectively to pursue your projects (without getting exceptions to the rules) only if policy- and rule-governed behavior gives you the cooperation you need. So we need to ask how likely that is.

It is obvious that your projects have to be chosen largely in ignorance of others' rules and policies. For one thing, most people's policies are unannounced. And perhaps more importantly, even if they were announced, no one could keep track of more than a handful of them. This is a special case of another empirical claim used in the Kantian argument for developing one's talents: that people can't develop all the capacities or skills they will need. The skill in this case is that of knowing what the rules of the game are; lawyers are a class of professionals who specialize in developing that skill for a smallish subset of the official rules of the game, and becoming competent in just such a small subset turns out to be a full-time occupation. In special cases, you may consult a specialist – a lawyer or accountant – before embarking on a project, but most of the time, that's just not feasible. Because it is typical of interesting or important projects that one doesn't know just how they will unfold, one doesn't even know whose rules one will run into along the way. (This is true of not-so-interesting projects as well; in the parking example, I did not know, when I made my travel plans, that I would have a problem leaving the car on the street.) As an agent, you choose your direction with only the sketchiest sense of what the other relevant agents' policies are likely to be.

It is as obvious that both individuals and institutions have to formulate their policies and rules in ignorance, for the most part, of *your* ends. It is not just that it wouldn't be logistically feasible to keep track of everyone's ends. In the Kantian picture of rational agency, the central feature of such agency is that you can formulate and adopt new ends. You yourself can't predict what your own ends will be down the road (recall that the New Kantian arguments for mutual aid and for developing one's talents rely on this fact); a fortiori, others cannot predict what your ends will be either, when they are considering what rules to adopt.

Since each set of decisions – about what rules and policies others adopt, and about what ends and projects you adopt – is made in ignorance of the other, the chances of their being suitably coordinated are very small indeed. Overall, we should not expect that others' policies will, as they are, deliver the cooperation that your projects (and you) need from them. Therefore, a condition on the successful exercise of your own agency is that others make exceptions for you. It is not for nothing that unions use work-to-rule as a threat.[27]

Let me pause to address a handful of worries. First, you may be worrying that parking problems and their ilk are too small to drive a criticism of Kantian morality. I certainly agree that we should not reject Kantian moral theory because on some occasion I could not find a place to park, but the smallness of such examples is meant to serve as an icon for what the world of human agency is really like. The pervasiveness of such small problems means that, although one can probably do without an exception in this or that particular case, doing without exceptions in all of them will make one's remaining agency not worthy of the name.[28]

Second, you may also be worrying that the examples are not *moral*, or that the exceptions in my examples are undeserved. But the Kantian argument (on its New Kantian reading) is supposed to be driven by one's own stake in one's agency, and so that is what matters for the argument, not whether the subject matter strikes one as moral, and not what one does or does not deserve. Objections turning on desert and on what is and is not moral get the order of explanation backwards, because one of the great strengths of Kantian theory is that it purports to provide a criterion for inclusion in the subject matter of morality: to appeal to one's independent and prior view of what is a moral issue and what morality requires is to beg at least one of Kant's questions.

Third, the argument I have been developing, like other arguments for imperfect duties, requires one to make judgment calls about *how often* a given type of situation arises. My own judgment call is that the relevant situations really do arise often enough for your agency to depend on exceptions granted by others (and, although I have not emphasized this side of the argument, exceptions to your own policies granted by yourself – think of a landlord granting himself an exception to a self-imposed rule that prohibits him from renting to dog owners). But if you have not been convinced, recall that the argument is modelled on the Kantian arguments for mutual aid and for the development of one's talents; it will suffice for present purposes if one needs exceptions from others to roughly the same extent that one needs assistance from others. This is much harder to gainsay: after all, one can go days or weeks at a time without needing to ask for anyone's help. That is, the fallback claim is that if the model New Kantian contradiction in the will arguments work, so does this one.

In any case, this line of resistance has an analog discussed by Kant, who remarks that a well-off individual is likely to be happy to forgo the promise of mutual aid.[29] I have noticed that those who think we do not need exceptions as often as all that tend to be the high-SES academics; that is, there is a recognizable class bias to the objection. What is more, even observations that cut across class lines may understate the overall need for exceptions, because some regions (think First World economies) accumulate exceptions at the expense of faraway and less-developed parts of the world. (If the global ecosystem can't handle an SUV for everyone, and if Americans predominantly drive SUVs, then Americans are collectively taking an exception.) In particular, economic surplus that can make exceptions seem unnecessary is itself a giant, economy-size exception. I expect that the insistence that exceptions are unnecessary often marks a deep sense of entitlement that accompanies their being consumed unnoticed.

Let me field one further worry before moving on. If the perturbed social world of the universalized CI-maxim is one in which people act in accordance with the Categorical Imperative, then they will not lie, will lend a hand more frequently and with greater alacrity than is actually their wont, will have skills that make their assistance more effective than it now is, and so on. That world will be a much kinder and gentler place than ours, and even if exceptions are necessary for agency in our world, perhaps they will not be required in what we might as well call the Kingdom of Ends. But if they are not, then the contradiction in the will we have been pursuing is avoided.

Here we are really being asked to choose between two versions of the CI-maxim, one of which has us take such effects into account (to produce what we can call a highly perturbed social world), and the other of which damps out the effects of the universalized maxim much more quickly (call its product the minimally perturbed social world). Recall that the point of the CI-maxim (expressed in its final clause) is to determine whether some line of action that you are actually contemplating is permissible. But the highly perturbed social world is too distant from the actual world to allow you to assess the actions you must in fact consider. Suppose that the maxim you are contemplating is: to fill up your tank when you pass a gas station, so as not to run out of gas. Cars predictably kill and maim some nonnegligible percentage of their passengers, so in a Kantian choice of transportation system, automobiles would be prohibited; in the Kingdom of Ends, there are no cars. So you cannot turn to the Kingdom of Ends to answer questions about when to tank up. Appealing to the highly perturbing version of the CI-maxim to determine what to do is adopting what is normally a self-frustrating plan of action: it amounts either to a contradiction in conception, or something on a par with one.

3

Until this point in the argument, New Kantians will find it easy to be concessive. It is hard not to allow that there are many cases where one needs what the man in the street calls an exception to the rule. But Kantians will have a complaint to register about the interpretation I have been putting on them: that they are exceptions in one sense, but not in another (and in particular, not in the sense my argument requires). Korsgaard has put the response in print, and so I will use her as my stalking horse; however, it is important to bear in mind that I am taking up her discussion not just as an objection one could make to my argument, but as an instance of an objection New Kantians *have* to make: this is a forced move.

Korsgaard agrees that

there's no general reason to suppose we can think of everything in advance. When we adopt a maxim as a universal law, we know there might be cases, cases we haven't thought of, which would show us that it is not universal after all. *In that sense we can allow for exceptions.*[30]

The way she tries to accommodate this very pervasive fact is to allow that one's principles "be willed as . . . provisionally universal," which is to say that we are to "think [a principle] applies to every case of a certain sort, unless there is some good reason why not." She invokes the Kantian comparison to causal laws, and reminds us that when we make causal claims, we usually invoke causal principles that hold only "all else equal." When we find an exception to a natural law, "we look for an explanation. Something must have made this case different: one of its background conditions was not met."

Here the important point is that the explanation must itself have universal (or provisionally universal) force. For this reason, exceptions can be incorporated into laws that are universal in form; and this requirement (or the analogous requirement, since maxims really do differ from natural laws) in the practical case runs as follows:

if a principle was provisionally universal, and we encounter an exceptional case, we must now go back and revise it, bringing it a little closer to the absolute universality to which provisional universality essentially aspires.

That is (and adjusting the terminology to bring it into line with the discussion so far), while (New) Kantians can allow that you may encounter cases that, you will agree, aren't properly handled by whatever universally shaped maxim you had adopted, what you are to do is not, strictly speaking, to grant an exception, but to replace your old maxim with a new one that handles the "exception," as it really ought to have been treated by the rule in the first place.[31]

This might be done by tacking the exception onto the maxim, as an extra clause, so to speak (one you might not bother to mention the next time you state your maxim, but which is now understood to be part of it). Or you might reformulate the rule as a whole, so that separate mention of the class of exceptions wouldn't be needed. There are many ways, some more and some less elegant, by which this might be accomplished.[32] What they share is an adjustment in the contours of your practical commitments, and what matters is that while this adjustment may be very sensitive to, and picky about, details, it too is universal in form: you are now committed to handling other similar cases in the same way.

Now Korsgaard thinks that "the difference between regarding a principle as universal, and regarding it as provisionally universal, is marginal." This, I am going to argue, is a mistake; the difference makes all the difference in the world, and especially in the world of the universalized CI-maxim. There are two things to notice here: first, that making an exception and building an exception-shaped twiddle into a rule work differently in the social world; and, second, that the commitment to revise one's maxim in such cases is itself a maxim, and has to be checked against the CI-procedure as well.

4

Recall the Kantian argument against lying: if lying in given circumstances was a practice, everyone would know that it was, and they would adjust their behavior in the light of that knowledge. (That is, no one would believe your lies, and you would never get that loan.) More generally, when working our way through the CI-procedure, we have to assume that others are going to adjust their plans of action in light of what the rules are. Recall that I left open the question of whether this was to be regarded as an empirical fact, to be retained in the world of a universalized maxim, or a prescriptive constraint – a matter of how Kantian moral theory requires us to think about our fellow persons. I do not want to resolve this question now, so I will try to use cases for which both versions of the constraint are plausible.

It follows that there is a difference between a genuine exception, and an adjustment to a rule that accommodates a previously unnoticed class of cases: when thinking about the latter, Kantian theory requires us to consider how people will adjust their plans in light of the modified rule. (People who grant exceptions sometimes worry about setting precedents; another way to characterize the effect that now has to be taken into account is that Kantian exceptions *always* set precedents.) Let's return to our previous cases:

Parking in Milan Revisited. If everyone who needed to were allowed to leave his car in the lot with his blinkers on, people would soon notice this option and start planning around it. They would count on being able to dash upstairs to make a phone call, or to deliver flowers, or whatever; and so they would plan on making that phone call or delivering the flowers. The parking lot would very quickly be full of briefly parked cars. The primary users of the lot would not be able to get in and out, and the visitor who needed an exception to the rule would generally find all the free spaces already taken. That is, what I needed to make my day work was an *exception*, and not an adjusted rule.

Trouble in High School Revisited. If it became the rule, roughly, that promising and bright high school students got to skip class with impunity, they would soon realize that. An important incentive for attending classes would disappear, better students would stop coming to class, less promising students would be transformed into resentful second-class citizens, and the effect would be, not to help out bright and promising students (the intent of the original exception), but to undermine their academic performance. Again, what is needed is an exception, rather than a modification to the rule.

The Tardy Contributor Revisited. Likewise, if it were discovered that deadlines could be broken, contributors would quickly realize this. And in fact they have; some authors routinely overbook themselves, knowing that deadlines do not have to be taken seriously. (If you're in the business, I don't need to tell you who the egregious abusers are.) Any volume with a sizable number of contributors is bound to have one or more such authors, and since other authors know that the volume will be delayed, they too plan on dawdling. Since no one really believes the volume will have a timely appearance, authors reserve their best efforts for other venues. The point of granting the original exception was to facilitate the appearance of a strong and timely collection; precisely this point is undermined by universalizing the exception. Again, what is needed is an exception, rather than a modification to the rule.

More generally, because rational agents adjust their plans to take account of changes in the rules (because they, quite correctly, come to *count* on the new rules), institutionalizing exceptions – writing them into the rules in the way that Kantian moral theory requires – tends to have perverse results. The results are perverse in the ordinary sense, that of giving rise to baroque and unwanted side effects (think of the tax code, to take a bureaucratic example); but they are also perverse in a technical and Kantian sense, that of undercutting the connection between the exception and its originally intended effect. Usually, granting an exception while institutionalizing exceptions of that kind amounts to what is, by Kantian lights, a self-frustrating plan of action.

There are of course two sorts of cases: those in which universalizing an exception undermines the point of granting such an exception, and those in which it does not. New Kantian arguments for imperfect duties turn on judgment calls (about how much of an impediment to agency a given social phenomenon will turn out to be); my sense of the territory here is that you can't get by just on the latter sort of exceptions. But once again, if your sense of the territory differs, the backup claim is that such undermining happens to roughly the extent that you turn out to need help (and skilled help) from other people – that is, that if the New Kantian model arguments work, so does this one.

5

Our first objection to treating maxims as "provisionally universal" was that there is a substantive difference between exceptions and changes in the rules, and often agents need the former rather than the latter. Our second objection is located on the side of the person dispensing exceptions, rather than on the side of the recipient. Kantian strategies need to be subjected to the Kantian consistency test. Accordingly, consider the following second-order maxim:

> When I run into a case that my (first-order) maxim does not handle properly, I will revise my (first-order) maxim to incorporate the exception, so as to be able to act on rules that I understand to be "provisionally universal."

Call this the *Revision Maxim*. If a Kantian is to find the Revision Maxim acceptable, it must pass the CI-procedure; but there is a quick argument to show that it does not.

I have for expository convenience been speaking of agents adjusting themselves to changes in the rules, and recent Kantians may have found that turn of phrase worrisome; what we are supposed to be imagining is not a response to change, but the steady-state social world of which the contrary-to-fact alteration is a permanent feature. (See, for example, Rawls, 2000, pp. 171–2.) Now in the steady-state world where agents follow the Revision Maxim, most of their maxims will *already* be much revised. That is to say, they will be very complicated (in something like the way the legal code or the tax code is complicated). But it is a deep empirical fact about human beings – a fact on a par with their vulnerability and the limitations on how many useful skills they can acquire – that they are not very good, cognitively, at handling this kind of complexity and detail. It is very easy to swamp human cognitive resources, and in a world in which one's maxims have had many exceptions appended to or integrated into them, they will be too complex to think with.

First, it will not be realistic to demand of agents that they be sensitive to whether their maxims are universalizable, because that will usually be too complicated a question for them to answer. The perturbed social world of the CI-procedure is a complex abstract object, and you can think of it as being a little like a chessboard. Just as it is very easy to produce boards that are hard to see your way through (the starting state of the board is hard for anyone, including grandmasters and IBM's Deep Blue; that's why people *play* chess), so it is easy to produce perturbed social worlds it's hard to see your way through. Adding detail to rules makes it harder to see, and see one's way through, the structure of the perturbed social worlds they generate. (Compare the way the tax code evolves: policy makers fail to see that a provision they are introducing will create new loopholes, and that these will be exploited to the hilt; they then need to add further provisions, which in turn create further loopholes; and so on. If human beings could generally see what the perturbed social world of a relatively complex rule looked like, they would be able to do so when the subject was taxation, and the tax code would not have the daunting patch-on-top-of-patch look that it does.) The point of the Revision Maxim is to allow one to act on rules that are universalizable; but in the world of the universalized Revision Maxim, one often cannot tell whether the maxim one proposes to act on is universalizable.[33]

Second, as maxims get more complicated, it becomes harder to see what actions they demand. (Think again of the tax code; who among us, accountants included, knows what taxes we should really be paying? If human beings could see what very complicated rules require, they could do it when the subject was taxes.) Again, the point of the Revision Maxim is to allow one to act on rules that are universalizable; but in the world of the universalized Revision Maxim, one often cannot so much as tell what one's rule requires that one do. If this is right, the Revision Maxim fails the CI-procedure (twice over) at the contradiction in conception stage.[34]

Kant himself seems not to have appreciated the problem here; he apparently thought that making out the demands of the Categorical Imperative, first formulation, was within the reach of even the simplest intelligence. Kant has not been alone. Widespread awareness of complexity as an obstacle to problem solving dates only to the 1960s, and even now the idea has just barely become respectable within economics and political science.[35] For instance, with occasional exceptions such as Hayek, the insuperable difficulties of managing centrally planned economies were overlooked until very late in the twentieth century (and it is suggestive that the construction of a Soviet-style Five Year Plan bears a family resemblance to the mapping out of perturbed social worlds that we are now contemplating).[36] If the realization that it is often not cognitively possible to solve problems about complicated social structures is still being assimilated in the social sciences, we should not blame Kant for not having noticed it.

You may be inclined to think that the complexity of the perturbed social worlds generated by the CI-procedure cannot be as intractable as all that. After all, there are domains – such as producing syntactically correct speech – that seem to be quite complex and in which humans do quite well.[37] And you may be wondering whether perhaps the CI-procedure belongs in such a domain. To see why this is unlikely, contrast the almost effortless production of sentence after grammatical sentence (that gives the Chomskian hypothesis of a special-purpose hardwired grammar module whatever plausibility it has) with the paucity of worked examples of the CI-procedure. Earlier on, I added the New Kantian argument against violence to the three examples that canonically accompany presentations of the Categorical Imperative. Despite the fact that violence is a very basic moral issue, it took Kantians some two hundred years to come up with the argument, and it is treated, in the New Kantian literature, as a noteworthy achievement; it is, in any case, one of the very few new applications of the CI-procedure. If humans came to the problem space generated by the CI-procedure possessing anything like their innate competence with the syntax of natural languages, then the solved problems would not be nearly so few and far between, and this particular application would have been merely one more of a practically endless stream of them.

Even if treating maxims as provisionally universal is unworkable, it might still be tempting to think that the pressure for exceptions can be relieved, in a way Kantians would welcome, by building generic exception clauses of one kind or another into the contents of maxims themselves. (For instance, "...unless an emergency comes up," or "...other things being equal," or "...unless an exception is needed.") An argument of the kind we have just assembled disposes of these proposals. When it comes to "other things equal," there are indefinitely many such cases that might come up, we cannot estimate their frequency, and they do not lend themselves to being neatly classified in advance. So when maxims contain such clauses, it is impossible to tell what their perturbed social worlds will look like. For maxims that have had their contents blurred in this way, the CI-procedure does not give definite results. The point of adopting a second-order maxim that dictates generic exception clauses in one's first-order maxims would be to rescue the CI-procedure. So such a maxim founders on a contradiction in conception. This is why agents' maxims have to be treated as laying down exceptionless policies.

To recap: First, modified rules differ from genuine exceptions, and they tend to be self-frustrating when universalized. Second, acting on the Revision Maxim is what New Kantian moral theory requires of agents who make exceptions, and the Revision Maxim fails the CI-procedure. This means that New Kantian moral theory cannot accommodate the need for exceptions. If Kantians cannot after all make exceptions, and if, as I have argued, exceptions are a necessary precondition for successful agency worth the name, then the CI-maxim does indeed give rise to a contradiction in the will.

6

Before concluding, I want to take up two related objections to the argument we now have on the table. These try to abort it by circumscribing the application of the concept of a maxim. To frame the objections, I am going to take a moment to introduce another element of the New Kantian picture, which I will call *maxim hierarchies*.

The third clause of a maxim, as the New Kantians construe it, specifies the end or point of one's action: to revert to an earlier example, "when I pass a gas station, to top off my tank, *so as not to run out of gas*." Now that point can in general be understood as a further action or plan of action; the intent of that further plan of action can in turn be rendered by a maxim; and that further maxim will itself specify a further point: perhaps, "when I am driving a car, not to let myself run out of gas, *in order to keep my car a reliable means of transportation*." And likewise, that further point can be unfolded into a still further maxim: maybe, "when I am in a location that does not have convenient and dependable public transit, to keep my car a reliable means of transportation, *so that I can get where I need to go, when I need to be there.*" Maxims that appear at the upper reaches of such hierarchies tend to specify more abstract and more general policies (and I'll sometimes talk about them as dictating "larger" actions, because they contain the actions specified by their inferiors in their hierarchies as subplans or components).[38] Such hierarchies turn up in the exposition of most New Kantian positions,[39] and they give a claim I made earlier the status of an observation: what counts, for present purposes, as action does not have to look *busy*; in particular, suitably governed omissions or refrainings can count as actions. In order to keep my car a reliable means of transportation, I don't strip the gears. (And so I don't shift directly from fifth to first; I don't shift into reverse while I'm speeding down the highway; and so on.) Not stripping the gears occupies a place in (another branch of) my maxim hierarchy, even though it, and many of the actions below it, are things I *don't* do. (Recall, under this heading, that testing a general policy of *not* helping was the Kantian way of arguing for a duty of mutual aid.) For the purposes of practical reasoning, deliberatively governed plans of inaction are plans of action, too.

Now we can state the objections. First, at the upper reaches of such a hierarchy of intentions, there is a glass ceiling above which the policies are not to be considered maxims. In particular, being guided by the CI-procedure need not be a maxim, and so such a policy does not itself need to be tested using the CI-procedure. But if we exempt what we were calling the CI-maxim (and similarly general or abstract policies, such as the Revision Maxim) from passing the CI-procedure, then the argument we have just finished constructing will not go through. Since maxims were introduced as generic representations of the contents of intentions or volitions, this amounts to saying that, while you are to act in conformity with the dictates of the CI-procedure, this is not to be taken for a further intention on your part: in an older Kantian locution, you are to act *in accord with,* but not *from,* the moral law. Call this the *Upper Glass Ceiling Objection.*

The Upper Glass Ceiling Objection does not sound much like Kant, who *is* very concerned that one act, not merely in accord with, but out of respect for the moral law; Kant explicitly characterizes as a maxim an extremely general and abstract policy, "that I should follow such a law even if all my inclinations are thereby thwarted" (G 400); he also worries about how maxim hierarchies are going to top out, treating the Categorical Imperative as one of the possible basic postures an agent might assume.[40] So the Upper Glass Ceiling Objection would have to be understood not as an explication of Kant, but as an amendment to him. Now, the CI-procedure is motivated by the idea that it is important to assess, not your actions on their own, but why you do them; if you did not think that what mattered was the practical consistency of the volition, rather than the outcome effected by the volition, there would be no point to deploying the CI-procedure in the first place. So it's hard to see why someone who cared only about conformity of reasons and rationality to some template would end up requiring *this* pattern to be conformed to in one's mode of producing action. That is, the move made by the Upper Glass Ceiling Objection is evidently motivated not by considerations that have their home in the (New) Kantian way of seeing things, but as an ad hoc response to the problem posed by our argument. Of course, that is not yet reason enough to dismiss it.

Second, it will be suggested that what we find at the lower reaches of the hierarchy are not, properly speaking, maxims. Only suitably general principles, such as those mandating or prohibiting lying, are subject to test by the CI-procedure; "specific intentions" are not,[41] and so need not be exceptionless. Since the argument we have been constructing turns on the pervasiveness of needed but unavailable exceptions, if a glass ceiling below which maxims are not to be found is set suitably high, then the argument will not go through. Call this the *Lower Glass Ceiling Objection.*

The Lower Glass Ceiling Objection requires a Kantian willing to make a difficult sacrifice. Hegel complained that Kantian universalizability was too formal a device actually to produce substantive results, and the New Kantian tradition takes visible pride in having shown how a recognizably Kantian rendering of the Categorical Imperative can indeed produce conclusions as concrete as those we have reviewed. But the further up the Lower Glass Ceiling is set, the fewer substantive results there will be. Moreover, this New Kantian rejoinder puts a great deal of pressure on the notion of a maxim. If maxims are not simply a way to capture the form of any intentional action whatsoever, we need to be told what they are. And looking more closely at this lacuna gives us a decisive response to both the Upper and Lower Glass Ceiling Objections.

Recall the structure of Kantian imperfect duties. No one can help everyone who needs it, and there is no way of marking off just those cases in which you really have to help out from those in which you don't. So it is up to you to decide when to help out; in the end, when to help is your judgment call. Now, it is not as though we have a principled way to place what I was calling the Upper and Lower Glass Ceilings; after all, what is the hard and fast difference between maxims, more specific intentions, and more general policies? The CI-procedure applies only to what counts as a maxim, so the Glass Ceiling objections give the moral law the structure of an imperfect duty: they entail granting to agents the discretion to decide when to invoke the CI-procedure as a constraint on their actions. (So one might insist, entirely legitimately, that lying was permissible because, in one's own judgment, the intention to lie was either too specific or too general to count as a maxim.) The effect would be to erase the distinction between perfect and imperfect duties from New Kantian moral theory. I am confident that the New Kantians would regard that consequence as unwelcome and unacceptable.[42]

New Kantians tend to allow that maxims can be very general and abstract.[43] But some New Kantians already think that intentions at the lower regions of the hierarchy cannot in any case count as maxims. So is my objection to Lower Glass Ceilings uncharitable?[44] In my view, New Kantians face a hard choice, and here is how I think it looks.

When running a maxim through the CI-procedure produces a startling result, there is an unfortunate inclination on the part of Kantian theorists to try to block the result by insisting that the input was not really a maxim in the first place.[45] I am for my own part disappointed by how frequently that inclination wins out. Kantian theory is deep and interesting only when it is taken seriously, and I have found that facing up to the startling result is usually theoretically fruitful. Just for instance, the maxim, "I will buy clockwork trains but not sell them," does not universalize: if no one sells the trains, no one will be able to buy them (Nell, 1975, p. 76). The moral really is that *that* intention is impermissible. (Morality requires more carefully conditionalized maxims, perhaps ones that are explicitly sensitive to the idea that being a toy collector is only one of the many social roles you might contingently occupy.) Or again, it's a standard classroom example that maxims like "I will turn up at Times Square tomorrow" don't universalize. (There's not enough room for everyone.) The moral here is that introducing proper names into maxims produces contradictions in conception. Or again, Herman's example of a "puzzle maxim" that must be "set aside" is, "To always be first through the door." I disagree: the fact that this maxim is not universalizable is a very good candidate explanation for the fact that this sort of pushiness is, while not a big deal, nonetheless *rude*. That is, one option for the New Kantians (and the one that seems to me likeliest to produce richer results) is not to give up so easily on the intentions at the bottom of the hierarchy (but this means giving up on the Lower Glass Ceiling Objection).

A second option is to find a principled way of distinguishing the maxims to which the CI-procedure applies from the more concrete intentions to which it does not. This seems less promising to me. One reason is that no one who has tried to introduce the distinction has made much headway at cleanly articulating it. Another is that the New Kantian tradition has seen the CI-procedure as a test of practical consistency. That way of motivating the CI-procedure makes sense when its range of application is intention, generically understood. But what kind of distinction could support a narrower notion of consistency? And why should practical consistency be required only of some special type of intention?[46]

The third option is to allow perfect duties to vanish from New Kantian moral theory, and the centrality to the tradition of the perfect duties makes this tantamount to altering the content of Kantian moral theory almost beyond recognition. But if New Kantians cannot afford glass ceilings, then they are committed to maxims coming in all degrees of generality and abstraction. The New Kantian position may require that maxims share a shape – the logical form that is used to express the content of an intention that comes up to snuff – but their shape cannot constrain the level of abstractness of the maxim's content. And this is (one more reason) why I have been using the looser "point" to describe what the third slot of New Kantian maxims expresses; some people are finicky about the term "end," and prefer to use it only for fairly concrete aims with definite termination points. But this notion of end is much narrower than what maxims must be able to capture.

7

What lesson should we draw from the argument that we have just concluded? Not the easy one, that we should give up on New Kantian moral theory. True, if contradiction in the will arguments establish imperfect duties, it looks as though we have exhibited a Kantian imperfect duty to *violate* the Categorical Imperative, and so that part of the position will have to go. But New Kantian moral theory would not have gotten nearly the attention it has if it were so intellectually impoverished as to be a one-idea view. I mentioned at the outset two other ideas traditionally identified with Kant (the requirement that persons be treated as "ends in themselves," and the importance of autonomy), but there are many more: just for instance, the conception of personhood as a practical rather than a metaphysical status, ingenious arguments against instrumentalist accounts of practical reasoning, and the suggestion that actions are to be thought of as moves in the only game in town. (See Korsgaard, 1996a, chs. 13, 11; Schapiro, 2001.) Showing that one of the ideas in the Kantian portfolio is unworkable leaves a valuable and still-diversified grouping of philosophical assets. (And in fact some New Kantians have, over the past decades, come to rest more weight on the so-called Formula of Humanity in particular.)

It is also too early to go looking for constructive lessons about practical reasoning and morality – the kind of lessons that would help us frame improved accounts of one or the other. We ought first to develop a deeper diagnosis of what has gone wrong with the Categorical Imperative, first formulation; but to come by that, we will need a better handle on the philosophical motivations of the New Kantian position than we now have, starting with an explanation of why an agent wills the universalization of his maxim (so that the contradictions exhibited by the CI-procedure are contradictions *in* the agent's will). I do not think this question can be successfully pursued without turning from the New Kantians back to Kant himself, and that is an undertaking for another time and place. (I append some preliminary discussion in a postscript to this chapter.)

So allow me to suggest an interim and methodological lesson. When you are working up your philosophical theory, always stop to check what happens when you apply that theory to itself. Sometimes that operation will not so much as make sense. Sometimes the result will be fast and reassuring. But sometimes, as we have just seen, it will not, and so the test of reflexive application is not one that you can afford to neglect.

POSTSCRIPT

The CI-procedure is both a theory of practical reasoning and the central element of a revived Kantian moral theory. If the Categorical Imperative does, as I have argued, give rise to a contradiction in the will, and if we want to draw lessons from that fact which will help us in developing better theories of practical reasoning, and so better moral theories, we need to figure out what it was doing there in the first place. I am going to make some suggestions about where to look for the philosophical motivations of the universalizability formulation of the Categorical Imperative. By philosophical motivations I do not mean the reasons for it that Kantians have given and would endorse, but, as it were, proto-reasons that are not, in either sense of the word, well articulated. It hardly needs to be said that such an investigation will be a good deal more speculative than the argument we have just concluded.

The CI-procedure is supposed to be a consistency or coherence test for a proposed plan of action.[47] The maxims that get run through the CI-Procedure are not normally means-end incoherent; when you propose, say, to lie as a way of getting the money, to lie is precisely to take the means to your end. So why think of universalizability as a *consistency* condition on one's maxims? This question is the most direct entry point into our diagnostic problem, but it takes us into the territory of Kant's notoriously puzzling theory of freedom. Because the doctrines going under that heading are, in my view, often misread, let's pause to frame them, by recalling a bit of history which seems to have been quite unaccountably forgotten by the community of Kant scholars.

With the decline of European monarchism, we have lost the curious legal fiction that kings had two bodies, one of which was the so-called "body natural" (what we would now think of as the king's body, plain and simple), and the other, his "body politic" (a phrase we still retain), that is, his realm. (The body politic of the King of France was France, and he might – as in *Lear* – actually be referred to as "France.") These bodies were held to be identical, in the same mysterious way that the persons of the Catholic Trinity were (and still are) held to be identical. This bizarre-sounding doctrine had a very practical point, viz., to prevent the country, which was legally the king's personal property, from going into probate on his death (and perhaps being divided up among the heirs). So while the king's body natural died, his body politic, which was (anyhow potentially) immortal, continued on. This is what the cry, "The King is dead, long live the King," meant: his body natural has died, but his body politic persists.[48]

The two-bodies doctrine has been all but forgotten, but in Kant's time any halfway educated person would have known about it (remember that cry, "The King is dead!"), and Kant was much better than halfway educated; he was in fact quite knowledgeable about the law.[49] What is today perhaps the most puzzling aspect of Kant's theory of freedom is the idea that people have two selves: one belonging to the world of appearances or phenomena, and subject to the laws of nature; the other to the intelligible world, and subject to the laws of freedom. But it would have been obvious to Kant's contemporaries that the two-selves doctrine was modelled on the two-bodies doctrine: in a kingdom, the sovereign has two bodies, and in the kingdom of ends, where everyone is a sovereign, *everyone* has two bodies. Like the two-bodies doctrine, or like the modern corporation (which is descended both etymologically and functionally from the two-bodies doctrine), the two-selves doctrine has a primarily *practical* point. Just as the legal device of the corporation allows us to distinguish the personal obligations and liabilities of Mr Turner from those of Turner Broadcasting, so (to make do with no more than a gesture) the device of the intelligible self allows us to distinguish the demands of practical reason from those of theoretical reason.

For present purposes, the important feature of the two-bodies doctrine is this: it was (and everybody knew that it was) a *legal fiction*. It may have had the *look* of metaphysics, but pursuing the metaphysical questions that would occur to someone who took it for real metaphysics – what is the criterion of identity? how can we square the identity with the differing spatial and temporal extensions of the two bodies? and so on – would show only that one did not get the point of the legal device. The two-selves doctrine is modelled on the two-bodies doctrine in this respect also, and we can analogously call it a *philosophical fiction*. Pursuing the metaphysical questions that would occur to someone who took it for real metaphysics – why (by Kant's lights) isn't the insistence on the intelligible self a paralogism? how can the self that performs the reasoning about what to do be atemporal? and so on – would show only that one did not get the point of the philosophical fiction.

Three quick preemptive points. First, to deploy a legal fiction is not necessarily to act as though it were true. (Acting as if France were identical with the King of France would, I suppose, preclude ploughing the fields, which no one took the two-bodies doctrine to entail.) So to deploy a philosophical fiction need not entail acting as though it were true, either. The guidance it provides is less direct than that.

Second, if philosophers have forgotten about the two-bodies doctrine, and its bearing on the two-selves doctrine, that is because Kant does not explicitly remind us of it. But then why doesn't he tell us straight out that the two-selves doctrine *is* a philosophical fiction? (He had a vocabulary in which to do so: he could have called it a Postulate of Pure Practical Reason, or, per the Canon of Pure Reason, a "belief" [*Glaube*; A820/B848–A831/B859].) It's hard to be sure, but recall that his failure to do so is not unprecedented; other Kantian borrowings from the legal repertoire go unannounced.[50] And because such an explicit announcement would have entailed stating outright that the two-bodies doctrine was indeed a legal fiction, Kant may have chosen to follow frequent Enlightenment practice: to step lightly by allowing it to remain unmentioned but understood. It just would not have done, in an age where the institutions of official censorship remained in place, to be too overt about such matters.[51]

Third, let me emphasize that I am not suggesting that the whole of Kant's Transcendental Idealism falls under this rubric. On the contrary: the two-selves doctrine assumes the status of (something on the order of) a legal fiction because it is an add-on, one that fits awkwardly with the more central parts of his system.

Bearing all that in mind, let's assemble an argument for the universalizability criterion out of some pieces of Kantian theory.

"Willing" is an archaic philosophical concept that does not have a current exact equivalent, but "intending" comes close enough for government work. It is frequently remarked of intentions that their content has a reflexive component: part of the intention to ϕ is that one's ϕing be caused by that very intention.[52] (This distinguishes intending to ϕ from merely wanting or wishing to ϕ.) Now when one takes oneself to be acting for reasons, a further part of the content of one's intention will be that it really is responsive to those reasons: that it is not merely the case that one has the reasons and that, by coincidence, one also intends to do the action that the reasons support. That is, one's intention is in part that it be *caused* by those reasons. Putting these back to back, we have the idea that one is tacitly intending, when one intends oneself to be acting for reasons, that the action be caused by those reasons. This is what Kant has in mind when he tells us that "the will is a kind of causality belonging to living things insofar as they are rational."[53]

What this tacit intention commits one to, in the Kantian system, is spelled out by Kant's account of causation. If x causes y, then there must be an exceptionless law under which x and y fall, requiring items of the relevant type under which x falls to be followed by items of the relevant type under which y falls: "The concept of causality involves that of laws according to which something that we call cause must entail something else – namely, the effect" (G 446).

Since, in intending to act for a reason, you are committing yourself to a causal connection between your reasons and your action, and since the causal connection would involve an exceptionless law connecting such reasons and such actions, part of what you are "willing" – part of the way you would have things be, whether you are aware of it or not – is that circumstances that function as your reasons and cause your actions produce those actions as effects, in the same way, *whenever anybody is in them*.[54] This is why to find that the world in which your maxim is universalized cannot be conceived, or that such a world would frustrate the line of action specified by your maxim, or that such a world would frustrate another practical commitment that you as an agent inevitably have, is to demonstrate a contradiction in *your* will.

Although the components of the argument I have just sketched are lying around in plain view, Kant himself never got around to putting them end to end, and I will accordingly call it the *Missing Argument.* One explanation for the Missing Argument's absence is that it is a *bad* argument, and if we are going to use it to understand what is motivating the CI-procedure, we will have to find a way of putting that reaction to one side.

The Missing Argument makes one's theory of rationality (and so the moral theory derived from it) less dependent on one's "intuitions" about what is and is not rational (a good thing), but it also seems to make one's theory of rationality more dependent on a number of dubious metaphysical premises (a bad thing). For each premise in the Missing Argument, it is not hard to find a contemporary philosopher who accepts (something like) it, but it would be difficult to find many philosophers who accepted all of them.[55] And if you press the Missing Argument, it seems to get into trouble very quickly. For example, the causes of an action obviously include not just the reasons for it, but an indefinitely wide range of other events, facts, and conditions. Or again, notice how very peculiar it is that Kant, of all philosophers, should take a commitment to the universal causal efficacy of one's reasons inevitably to be an aspect of one's will. Kant was the champion of autonomy, that is, of acting on one's *own* reasons (on laws that one legislates for oneself). But when you decide to act for your own reasons, it turns out that you are also willing that everyone else act for your reasons, too, rather than for theirs.[56] And finally for now, since other people do *not* in fact always act on your reasons, wouldn't it follow that the intention to act for reasons inevitably fails, and that people who think they are acting for reasons are just fooling themselves?

The pivot of the argument is the "category" of causation, which Kant tells us can be "transferred" from its theoretical home (the synthesis of the world of appearances) to the intelligible (and so not synthesized) world (C2 49–50, 54). Now, intelligible causation sounds a little like that old shtetl joke: A sophisticated world traveler explains the telegraph to his provincial audience. He asks them to imagine a very long dog, with its head in Minsk and its tail in Pinsk; when you scratch the dog's head in Minsk, the tail wags in Pinsk, and when you pull the dog's tail in Pinsk, the head barks in Minsk. A telegraph, he tells them, is just like that – only without the dog.[57] Causation, the first *Critique* teaches us, is an artifact of synthesis, and the will, that is, intelligible causation, is just like ordinary causation – only without the synthesis. If intelligible causation is taken as metaphysics, it is *un*intelligible. But it is not metaphysics: intelligible causation is a piece of, and of a piece with, the two selves doctrine, the perspective from which Kant takes the view that "the will is to be the cause of the objects" (C2 44). So we should likewise think of it as a philosophical fiction. That means that there would be no point in exerting pressure on the metaphysical components of the Missing Argument, in just the way that there is no point in exerting pressure on Kant's account of the noumenal self; to complain about bloopers of the sort we itemized a few moments back would show only that one had not gotten the point of the philosophical fiction. Rather, the Missing Argument would serve as the *emblem* of a moral or practical position, and the only real question in the neighborhood is then what practical position the argument could represent. And once the question is put that way, I think there is a fairly obvious answer.

In the Missing Argument, Kant's causal doctrines operate as a stand-in for a variation on the Principle of Sufficient Reason, that is, for the idea that if by adducing R you have given a full and sufficient reason for ϕing on one occasion, then R must be a sufficient reason for ϕing on any other occasion as well. (Conversely, if R is a reason for ϕing on one occasion, but not on another, then R cannot have been the *full* reason in the first place.) Kant's account of causation is built around the Principle of Sufficient Reason,[58] which would make it natural for him to express his justificatory requirement by attributing to agents the tacit commitment to a causal connection between their reasons and their actions. One's reasons are given in the content of one's representations, and this would in turn justify a willingness to think of the exceptionless causal connection as operating at the level of contents. And since all there could be to intelligible causation is inferential dependence, it is a reasonable way to cast what is really a claim about reasons.

In the Jäsche *Logic*, Kant distinguishes the material criterion of truth – whether the cognition agrees with the object to which it is referred – and the formal criteria, which specify "universal logical marks of the agreement of cognition with itself or – what is one and the same – with the universal laws of the understanding and of reason." Since in the practical domain agreement with the object of cognition is not at issue, the formal criteria Kant identifies – the Principle of Contradiction and the Principle of Sufficient Reason – ought together to constitute conditions of adequacy for a practical cognition.[59] The Missing Argument appropriately presents the CI-procedure as a method of verifying that a practical cognition – a maxim – satisfies both formal criteria. In particular, the Categorical Imperative, first formulation, is made out by the argument to be a test for when one's reasons could be sufficient for, that is, justify fully and completely, on their own, the action one is proposing.[60]

The pieces of the Missing Argument are all there in Kant, but the Missing Argument is *missing* – and not because the objections we would bring to bear on it, were it to be read as metaphysics, are an obstacle to deploying it as a philosophical fiction. (If it were assembled, it would appear as part of a doctrine whose function was symbolic and practical, a view from which inconvenient entailments need not be drawn.) When I said earlier that I hoped to track down the motivations for the Kantian universalizability requirement, I distinguished those from the reasons (i.e., the arguments) that Kant and later Kantians actually have given. I am proposing the logical doctrine we have just identified as the proximate motivation for the Categorical Imperative, first formulation (and its later reformulation as the CI-procedure). To say in what sense that claim is to be taken, I want to apply a perhaps unusual description to the Missing Argument, which I will borrow from the lexicon of psychoanalysis.

An unconscious thought or motivation is not to be understood (in the way the popular reception of Freud understands it) as a fully articulated thought that is somehow kept hidden out of its owner's sight. For psychoanalytic practice, thought is unconscious because it is unarticulated, and therefore inarticulate. For instance, an unconscious desire might consist in fragmentary images, patterns of association, bodily behavior such as hysterical paralysis and vomiting, and the like: that is, in proto-cognition which is unavailable to the thinking subject because it lacks the conceptual and propositional structure that would allow it to interlock inferentially with other articulated thoughts. A psychoanalytic interpretation offers to its client a form which the chaotic bits and pieces can fill naturally; if the client accepts the interpretation, the associatively triggered images, unregimented impulses, and so on become the matter of a new proposition, and of a definite propositional attitude. The additional structure then allows the deployment, within the client's regimented conceptual and inferential system, of what had been chaotic bits and pieces. Once that has happened, the owner of the newly formed thought can look at it straight on, assess it, and, more to the point, *think* with it – thus making it properly part of its owner's (conscious) mind. This is why successful psychoanalytic interpretations serve a therapeutic function.[61]

Consider the Principle of Sufficient Reason as an unconscious motivation, in the psychoanalytic sense I have just sketched, for the Categorical Imperative, first formulation. That is, it is a doctrine, with an ensuing train of thought, into which some of the unregimented bits and pieces of Kant's views can be integrated.[62] In attempting to bring the unconscious motivations of Kantian moral philosophy to consciousness, I am practicing what you can if you like call philosophical psychoanalysis; but let me emphasize that the point is not to engage in personal speculation about Kant. If I am interested in the philosophical motivations for the Categorical Imperative, that is because I suspect that they can and do still move us today, even when they do not express themselves as textually orthodox Kantian positions. But it is very implausible that we are moved by hidden aspects of Kant's very likely idiosyncratic personality. If this is psychoanalysis, it is psychoanalysis *of philosophy*, not of this or that practitioner of it.

The point of providing this sort of psychoanalytic interpretation is not to set up a *modus tollens*: to say that the Principle of Sufficient Reason commits you to the CI-procedure; that we have seen the CI-procedure to be self-refuting; and so that we should reject the Principle of Sufficient Reason. That would not be a manageable argument to run; it's too easy to surrender the further premises required to make up the Missing Argument. Rather, it is to motivate a clearheaded and self-aware examination of the Principle of Sufficient Reason, and of whether we are committed to it.

If we end up rejecting the Principle of Sufficient Reason, then the CI-procedure is likely to come to seem an unreasonable constraint to impose on our decisions. The thought we found in the Kantian unconscious was that proper reasons are sufficient reasons: reasons that give the full and complete justification for an action, and whose sufficiency is shown in their being equally full and complete justification for similar actions, on occasions that are similar in the respects specified by the reason. The CI-procedure tests, not that one's reason *is* a full, complete and successful justification for one's action (I imagine that would make the action required), but that it meets the logical conditions for being such a reason (which makes it permitted). Whether or not the reason expressed by your maxim *is* sufficient, if it passes the CI-procedure it is, as far as its logical *shape* goes, a candidate for being a sufficient reason.

But we can now reconsider whether this demand is reasonable. If we take seriously the idea that defeasibility is a basic and ineliminable feature of practical inference, and one that is not usefully modelled in terms of the approach to a deductive ideal, then we need to confront the fact that our practical reasons are *never* (or almost never – there may be exceptions even to that practical rule) sufficient reasons, in the Kantian sense. And if our practical reasons are not ever actually going to *be* sufficient reasons, why should we care if they have the logical shape of a sufficient reason? (If you are never actually going to be the president, why worry about whether you satisfy one or another of the formal preconditions for running for the office?) If there's too much of a disconnect between the advice you give people, and what they can and will do, your advice is practically irrelevant. But advice that isn't practically relevant isn't really advice. (A related but perhaps overstated point is sometimes made with the slogan "Ought implies can.") If the Principle of Sufficient Reason is something that we have to *ignore* in the course of working up the considerations that figure into practical deliberation, then it doesn't belong in our theory of practical reasoning.

That is not a stopping place, but rather a frame for a further investigation. When a patently implausible claim has been identified as the motivation for something on the order of the Categorical Imperative, the ensuing question is, what considerations motivated (and perhaps still motivate) *it*? And is there another and more plausible way to address those further motivations? (What is the Principle of Sufficient Reason, as a constraint on practical reasons, getting *right*?) But I will not begin that investigation here.

Notes

I'm grateful to Lori Alward, Lanier Anderson, Carla Bagnoli, Jon Bendor, Sarah Buss, Alice Clapman, Alice Crary, Don Garrett, Valeria Ottonelli, Ram Neta, Tamar Schapiro, Cindy Stark, and the *Philosophical Review*'s anonymous reviewers for comments on earlier drafts, and to Irene Appelbaum, Jerry Dworkin, Christoph Fehige, Konstanze Feigel, Beatrice Longuenesse, Brenda Lyshaug, Rose Glickman, and audiences at the University of Minnesota, the University of Chicago, the University of New Mexico, the Ludwig-Maximilians-Universität München, the Bellagio Study and Conference Center, the University of Milan, Florida State University, Washington University in St. Louis, UNC/Chapel Hill, Pace University, the Values Institute at the University of San Diego, and Bowling Green State University for helpful discussion. Work on this paper was supported by a fellowship from the Center for Advanced Study in the Behavioral Sciences; I am grateful for the financial support provided through the Center by the Andrew W. Mellon Foundation.

1. Instances include Huxley, 1998, Gunn, 1961, Lukes, 1995, chs. 7–14, and, if I am reading it right, Kubrick, 1971.

2. Rawls, 1989, is an overview that appropriates the position it attributes to
   Kant as a precursor of Rawls's own constructivist political theory; Rawls, 2000,
   makes available his very influential lectures. It should not be assumed that the
   influence was all one-way; over the years, his presentation of Kant assimilated
   much of the work he had delegated to his students.

   Nell, 1975, focuses on laying out the Kantian deliberative procedure, providing a much less terse rendering of the view set out in O'Neill, 1989,
   ch. 5 (and more generally throughout the volume). Korsgaard, 1990, accepts O'Neill's account of the procedure and focuses on motivating it;
   Korsgaard, 1996a, develops a range of Kantian positions around the motivated procedure, and it is now probably the center of gravity of this reading.
   While Herman, 1993, advances the interpretation, it also breaks ranks on a
   number of points, and in Section 6 I will discuss the reasons Herman's views
   diverge from others in the group.

   I will not tie myself too tightly to the nuances of any version of the New
   Kantian view; I mean my sketch of it to represent the shared structure fairly,
   but I do not want to imply that the fine print is attributable to each and
   every instance of the class. I will flag important disagreements as I go, as
   well as descriptions of their view that New Kantians would themselves find
   controversial or prejudicial.

3. From G 421, with grammatical modifications. I will cite Kant's works using
   the following abbreviations, in the translations following the title.

   > G: *Grounding for the Metaphysics of Morals* (1785/1981)
   > A/B: *Critique of Pure Reason*, giving the pagination for the A and B editions
   >   (1781/1787/1998)
   >   C2: *Critique of Practical Reason* (1788/1997)
   >   DV: *Doctrine of Virtue* (*Metaphysics of Morals*, second part) (1797/1994)
   >   R: *Religion within the Boundaries of Mere Reason* (1793/1998)
   >   L: *Logic* (1992)

   With the exception of the first *Critique*, pagination will be that of the standard
   Academy edition of Kant's works (1902–).

   Herman, 1990, pp. 150–1, 188, provides a useful compilation of the different formulations of the Categorical Imperative.

4. Despite the step-by-step presentation and occasional remarks by the authors
   we are considering (Herman, 1993, p. 115, calls it an "algorithm"), the CI-
   procedure is not technically a procedure or algorithm. Procedures can be
   executed mechanically and are guaranteed to terminate; inspecting the steps
   in this one will show that neither is true of it; Rawls, 2000, p. 166, acknowledges
   this point, as does Nell, 1975, p. 73. Rawls's own work progressively distanced
   itself from the idea that the central problems of political theory could be rendered as well-defined exercises in game theory, and I suspect that the "procedure" terminology is a holdover from an earlier stage in his development.

5. Rawls adds a fourth "unless" slot that we can understand to be included in *C*
   (2000, p. 168). Kant and the majority of the New Kantians think of the point
   of the action as its end; Kant in particular holds it to be a formal fact about
   actions that they have identifiable ends (C2 34; DV 382–5). I am being looser

about this partly to accommodate Herman, 1993, p. 221, who quite plausibly insists that the full desirability characterization of an action is to be represented in its maxim, and partly for reasons I will get to in due course.

6. I'm framing the condition disjunctively because it's not always clear or agreed among the New Kantians which disjunct the test pivots on. See Nell, 1975, pp. 69 ff; Herman, 1993, p. 118; Korsgaard, 1996a, ch. 3, esp. sec. 3; Rawls, 2000, p. 169; O'Neill, 1989, p. 96.

7. Herman is something of an exception; see note 46.

8. G 421n, DV 390, 392–4. I don't here want to take up the question of how plausibly the perfect/imperfect distinction can be tied to the step at which the CI-procedure is exited. For a New Kantian review of exegetical controversies having to do with this distinction, see Nell, 1975, ch. 4.

9. The point now is not that a practice that is unsuccessful for this kind of reason will be replaced by a different practice. As a matter of fact, we more or less live in the world Kant describes, where people lie to get loans as a matter of course. That is why loans are not made on the basis of such promises. Mortgage originators do not stay in business by trusting their customers; they make sure there is collateral to foreclose on.

10. Closer to home, letters of recommendation for the academic job market are another case where, for the most part, the discounting doesn't go nearly deep enough. "His dissertation will certainly change the field he is in." "She is the best student who has ever come through our program." "The work he has done as a graduate student would make a successful case for tenure." Sound familiar?

11. Because Kant predates the twentieth-century repudiation of psychologism, claims with prescriptive force are often presented in his work as descriptions of an idealized mind. For some discussion, see Anderson, 2001.

    Presentations of the CI-procedure usually include a gloss to roughly the effect that in constructing your representation of the perturbed social world you are to keep as much as possible of the world as we know it intact. This is analogous to the way we reason about contrary-to-fact conditionals; when asking "What would have happened if *p*?" we imagine as much as possible of the background to remain as is. We have just seen that it is still an open question whether this is the appropriate understanding; however, see also the final objection in Section 2.

12. Is it *really* conceivable? Perhaps not: a feminist objection to Hobbesian state-of-nature arguments is that human beings are too vulnerable actually to grow up or live in such a world (Vogler, 1995).

13. Again, this could be taken as an empirical claim, or as prescriptive, about how your choice has to look "from the practical point of view." (For development of this latter idea, see Bok, 1998.) The prescription can be motivated by a specifically moral thought such as: just as you have to respect others, by leaving them space to adopt a reasonable range of ends, so you have to respect yourself, and not allow that range of ends to be foreclosed. The price of this kind of motivation, however, would be building explicitly moral considerations into the conception of practical rationality at the core of the theory. (I'm grateful to Geoff Sayre-McCord for discussion here.)

14. Again, is it really? It is suggestive that, while Kant seems to have thought that the no-talent maxim guided the way life was lived in the South Pacific, no actual human society has ever operated on this basis.

15. This particular argument may not seem much like Kant's (somewhat obscure) text, but it is a New Kantian way of handling the case; see O'Neill, 1989, p. 99. Kant does remind us that parents try to have their children develop a range of skills that will serve whatever ends they adopt down the road (G 415).

16. For a reconstruction of the argument that there must be "broad obligations," i.e., imperfect duties, see O'Neill, 1989, p. 230. The argument turns on the claim that one does not have available principled ways of delimiting one's obligation more tightly. Kant provides a subsidiary argument to support this observation that is, however, less plausible than the observation itself is: any further argument would establish a different ground of obligation (DV 403; compare A787–8/B815–6).

17. And more generally, as Cindy Stark has reminded me, not all violence is an impediment to agency; *Fight Club* is a recent film whose eponymous institution can serve as an example.

18. Whether this argument is to be understood as invoking a contradiction in conception or a contradiction in the will depends on how contradiction in conception is understood (see note 6), and on whether the former or the latter of these problems is being emphasized. Herman presents it as invoking your stake in your own agency generally, and so as exploiting a contradiction in the will; on that reading, the duty not to avail oneself of violent means would be imperfect. I want to leave to one side here the question of whether we should be happy with an argument that portrays abjuring violence as an imperfect duty; what does matter is that the argument is endorsed by several New Kantians, being treated by them – and this is a point for which I will have a use later on – as something of an accomplishment.

19. Loosely adapted from Herman, 1993, ch. 6; compare Korsgaard, 1996a, pp. 98–100; Nell, 1975, pp. 79–80.

20. Herman (1993, pp. 53–4) gives an argument meant to block the following objection: that you can avoid contradictions in the will by deciding to adopt only projects guaranteed not to require resources provided by mutual aid, others' talents, and so on.

21. I'll provide arguments for these claims, as well as an explication of what is meant by the "size" of an action, in Section 6.

22. There are other possible final clauses for the CI-maxim, for instance, "out of respect for the moral law." That would express the point of the action, but not perhaps an end. (I say "perhaps," because while such respect is not anything like a goal, Kant redescribes respect for persons as treating them as "ends in themselves," and persons are not, except in pathological cases, anything like goals either; possibly the right gloss on Kant's term "end" would make an end of respect for the moral law.) Another alternative final clause might be "to promote the Highest Good"; I take it that the Highest Good is best understood as occupying the role, in Kant's account, of the formal end (but of course not the determining ground) of moral and rational action in

general. For present purposes, however, it does not much matter what the final clause of the CI-maxim is taken to be, because final clauses do work at the contradiction in conception phase of the CI-procedure, and not at the contradiction in the will stage. The argument I am about to construct will not need to demonstrate a contradiction in conception.

23. Taking seriously the requirement that the CI-procedure is self-endorsing conforms to the approach taken by New Kantian metaethics. Korsgaard, for instance, extracts from a historical survey the lesson that self-endorsement is the only possible source of normativity; she subsequently generalizes the first-cut requirement, of a faculty's endorsing itself, to the general endorsement of all of one's faculties by all one's faculties. (Korsgaard, 1996b, pp. 62, 65–6.) On both the less and the more stringent versions of the view, a faculty's flunking itself out should strip the normativity from its pronouncements.

24. *Need* the sort of maxim we have in mind be foundational? Perhaps you have some reason for a proposal as important as: always acting on the moral law. (Respect for persons, or a deep commitment to some set of values; see note 46.) And normally, when you get around to running a maxim through the CI-procedure, you already think the course of action it proposes is a good idea, for some reason or other. But Kant himself seems to have thought that adherence to the Categorical Imperative could have no *further* ground; see note 40. That said, I don't think we have to settle the question here.

25. Compare O'Neill, 1989, pp. 129–30. But how could Kant have held both this view and accorded the importance that he did to imperfect duties? I think there really is a deep tension in his view here, but the parts of it that are on display are formally compatible. The imperfect duties are given as mandatory ends, not as maxims. Acting to promote a mandatory end requires formulating a more structured intention – a maxim – that specifies what, on a specified class of occasions, you will do to promote the end. (The class of occasions you specify may not exhaust the occasions on which you will, in one way or another, act to promote the end; those further occasions will have to be covered by other maxims.) Your maxim will then have to be checked for permissibility, using the universalizability test. For instance, to develop my talents is a mandatory end, but not yet a maxim. When I consider developing my talents by robbing banks, I now have a maxim, but this maxim fails at the contradiction in conception stage of the CI-procedure. (If everybody robbed banks, there would be no banks to rob.) So although I must find ways to develop my talents, I may not do it by robbing banks.

26. Rawls tries to deal with a related objection – that moral restrictions will also get in the way of plans you may have – by appealing to a special class of interests, which he calls "true human needs"; the idea is that these give rise to different kinds of obstacles to agency. (Rawls, 2000, pp. 173–4; such needs are an exegetical adaptation of his own notion of "primary goods.") So note that I am constructing the argument so that there is no plausible difference of this kind to which to appeal.

27. Kant himself had been influenced by the Leibnizian tradition, and so there is some plausibility to a reading of the text on which permissible actions turn out to be unique and so required, and on which Kant's vision of the kingdom

of ends is reminiscent of Leibnizian preestablished harmony. For now, we can say that the New Kantians find this sort of rigorism uncongenial, both because it is not in keeping with the *Zeitgeist*, and because the point of their project is to reclaim Kant as a predecessor to Rawlsian liberalism, a position that tries to maximize, rather than maximally constrict, freedom of action. We will provide a more principled reason for not falling back on rigorism below.

28. Over and above that, you might be worried that your needing an exception shows that you did not have a (by Kantian lights) coherent intention in the first place. But since we cannot anticipate the exceptions our projects will require, insisting that a project is coherently intended only if it will not require exceptions would unacceptably undermine agency.

29. G 423; we can imagine someone wealthy enough to pay for all the help he needs.

30. Korsgaard, 1999, p. 25, my emphasis. Quotations below are from pp. 24–5 of this same paper.

31. Compare Hill, 1992, a paper whose title announces its subject to be a Kantian treatment of exceptions, and which turns out to be an attempt to work up more nuanced reasons for more nuanced – but formally universal and exceptionless – policies. (In this case, "policies that involve taking the lives of terrorists," and possibly bystanders.)

32. One option that has been suggested to me is that the burden be taken up by an Aristotelian sensitivity to when exceptions are called for. (That is, the more complex policy is to be implemented partly as the original, explicitly stated, but less complicated policy, and partly as a disposition to notice the specified classes of exception when they come up; Herman's "rules of moral salience" are a New Kantian attempt to integrate such patterns of attention and recall into the Kantian apparatus.) What matters for present purposes – and the reader should verify this as we walk through the argument – is that how the more complex rule is implemented makes no difference, first, to its social effects, and, second, to the cognitive burden (computational and otherwise) involved in following it.

33. Why can't the problem be solved by integrating the accumulating exceptions into cleanly formulated rules? After all, something like this goes on in the sciences; why not in ethics?

I think that the accretion of detail outpaces our ability to identify simplifying patterns; that's visibly true of such examples as the tax code. It's true in the sciences as well, and some philosophers of science, such as Cartwright (1983), argue that the simplicity of the laws is consequently purchased at the expense of their truth. And there is a further obstacle in ethics. Recall that maxims have to capture the motivations the agent actually has. Those motivations are normally tied to a specific conceptual apparatus. Now what we learn from the history of such simplifications in the sciences is that they are accompanied by fairly radical conceptual shifts. But we can only insist on deploying a new set of concepts in one's maxims if they can summon up corresponding motivational structure. As a matter of sociological fact, change in such concept-embedding motivations is very slow. So once again, we should expect the process of practical simplification to fall ever farther behind the accretion of legitimate exceptions to our rules. (For example, an anti-Semitic maxim will express a motivation tied to the concept "Jew." That means that we can't effect the gestalt or paradigm shifts that would render our maxims less complicated, when those shifts would involve replacing the concept "Jew," if we can't get rid of the anti-Semitism.)

34. You may be inclined to look for more restricted versions of either the CI-maxim or the Revision Maxim; in that case, notice where the strategy lands you. The Kantian account needs machinery to prevent tailored versions of intentions to lie, cheat, and steal from slipping through the CI-procedure. (See note 39 for a terse recapitulation of the problem.) So a restricted version of, say, the Revision Maxim needs to come with a *motivated* account of the machinery, and an argument demonstrating how, in light of that account, proposed revisions to the Revision Maxim are not blocked (even though unacceptable revisions to lying maxims and their ilk are). I don't have a tight argument showing that no such proposal can work – that's because it's hard to have a good enough sense of the range of possible proposals ahead of time – but I have no reason to expect that any will.

35. Bendor, 2003, reviews the history of (and obstacles to) the reception, in political science, of the methodological suggestion that human cognitive limitations need to be taken into account in theory construction.

Computer science has a well-established mathematical subdiscipline that studies computational complexity, and novice computer scientists are taught that intractability is ubiquitous. But it is remarkable that, half a century ago, as distinguished a founder of that discipline as Alan Turing (1950) could be quite certain that a program exhibiting intelligence would run on the hardware available in his day – that is, on what was, by our lights, scarcely a pocket calculator.

36. See, for instance, Hayek, 1989, at pp. 143–4, 149–50, Hayek, 1948, chs. 2, 4, 7–9. Invisible-hand capitalists have taken to gloating over the vindication of Hayek's attack on socialism, but they may well have very similar problems; there is a growing body of evidence that market clearing is often a computationally intractable problem.

We can now give the principled response to the rigorist rejoinder broached in note 27. Even if there is a unique equilibrium point in the game of policy selection (and of course we have no proof that there is), we have no reason to believe that it is computationally accessible. If it is not, then it is not for practical purposes a solution at all. From the standpoint of practical reasoning, a solution that it is in principle impossible to produce is irrelevant.

37. Some domains may look to be complicated, but be question-begging if used as counterexamples. I am arguing that humans have to negotiate their environments by deploying exceptions, rather than complicated rules. So one should not slide from thinking that, say, etiquette looks tricky, to thinking that, because tricky problems have to be handled by complicated rules, it displays a human ability to deploy complicated rules. In fact, etiquette is tricky mostly because exceptions require a good deal of delicacy and judgment.

Recall that the CI-procedure is meant as a rational reconstruction. That means that we do not have to walk through the procedure aloud, before each action, but we must still possess the cognitive abilities needed to underwrite sensitivity to its dictates. Analogously, we do not write out parse trees before we utter sentences, but the grammatical complexity of the sentences we produce is limited by our cognitive capacities.

38. Members of a maxim hierarchy are related to one another roughly as the answers to Anscombe's famous series of "Why?"-questions (1985, sec. 23); for work in the Anscombian tradition that takes up the ways in which "larger" actions embed and justify "smaller" actions, see Vogler, 2002.

39. In Herman, they are prominent as a partial solution to the so-called Problem of Relevant Descriptions. It is a familiar point that whether or not the CI-procedure rules any *actions* (as opposed to maxims) out of order depends on how much flexibility there is in selecting a maxim to test. Actions have indefinitely many descriptions, and one can always find a description of an action that really could be made the rule: lying may not be universalizable, but lying only to the naive and clueless probably is universalizable.

Herman has realized that the requirement that what is checked be the psychologically actual intention underlying the contemplated action, and not just any old description of it, will not produce a recognizably moral pattern of permissions (and, more important from a theoretical point of view, an *orderly* pattern) if agents' psychologies are sufficiently idiosyncratic. If the peculiarly tailored maxim (the one that slips past the CI-procedure) really *does* express your intent, then the CI-procedure will tell you that you can go ahead with it. The problem is not just that the CI-procedure usefully regulates only those with already very standard patterns of motivation, while giving the strange and the psychopathic *carte blanche*. It is that necessary but entirely unaccounted for regimentation of agents' motivational structure has become the engine of the theory. This would amount to failure of the New Kantian theoretical enterprise, and Herman has devoted much thought and ingenuity to forestalling it (1993, esp. ch. 4; ch. 7, sec. 4; ch. 3, sec. 3).

Maxim hierarchies can be used to provide a certain amount of anchoring against the tides of agential idiosyncrasy, because, for any given maxim that itself passes the CI-procedure, one can still test its superiors and inferiors in the hierarchy. (Something like this move can also be found in O'Neill, 1989, p. 87, where "specific intentions" turn out to be "ancillary to more fundamental intentions *or principles* that might indeed have revealed moral unworthiness in the agent.") However, perhaps maxim hierarchies do not solve the Problem of Relevant Descriptions on their own: for all it has been argued, agents could be thoroughly perverse, all the way up their casuistical hierarchies, in a manner that would slip through the CI-procedure.

40. Kant does give a quick argument that looks like it should be working as a reductio, but that he claims instead establishes that "the first subjective ground of the adoption of moral maxims is inscrutable" (R 21, and esp. 21n). The problem is that the ground of the free adoption of a maxim must be sought, not in any incentive of nature, but in a further (freely

adopted) maxim; this generates a regress of maxims; but since humans have small-finite psychologies, they cannot support such a regress; their psychologically available reasons will bottom out, if you keep pressing, in a brute natural fact (typically an impulse or inclination).

In my view the best way to accommodate this tension is not to take refuge in "inscrutability," but to regard the demand that leads to embedding maxims in a hierarchy as just that: a demand, to make the effort to articulate one's motivations further when that is appropriate.

41. The phrase is from O'Neill, 1989, p. 87: "if in welcoming my visitor with a cup of coffee I intentionally select a particular cup, my specific intention clearly cannot be universally acted on." Her distinction between "specific intentions" and "maxims" is intended to get you out of having to have such choices approved by the CI-procedure. See also her note 6 on that page, and 112, n. 2.

42. New Kantians *are* comfortable with judgment calls in the application of maxims; see, e.g., Nell, 1975, p. 37. But they see that as a very different matter, having to do with the fringes of the theory, and not with its overall structure.

43. Herman, 1993, pp. 220–1, allows that "the maxims Kant uses are at all levels of generality" (she thinks her own account of maxims to be "unorthodox"). Korsgaard, 1996b, p. 107, reminds us approvingly that "Kant proposes that we can tell whether our maxims should be laws by attending not to their matter but to their form," to which we can add that the size of a maxim is a matter of its matter and not of its form.

44. O'Neill thinks of maxims as "underlying [practical] principles" (1989, pp. 84–5), to be contrasted with both "aspects of action that are 'below the level of intention,'" and "our more specific intentions"; see pp. 129, 151–2, 158. In her earlier writing, the issue is "the amount of detail about an agent's circumstances and his proposed act which can be included in his maxims" (Nell, 1975, p. 37).

45. Not always: O'Neill suggests getting out of a class of hard cases not by refusing the title of maxim, but by simply waiving the test provided by the CI; Nell, 1975, pp. 76–7. Herman, 1993, p. 225, announces that "each interpreter of the CI must develop ways to set aside the puzzle maxims."

46. In the course of her efforts to address the Problem of Relevant Descriptions, Herman has endorsed reversing the characteristically Kantian priority of deliberative procedure to value, so as to let values underwrite and control the procedure (see Herman, 1993, pp. 153–4, and compare C2 63); and you might think that some such appeal to values could be used to address the difficulties raised by the argument we have been developing. Herman has come to see the CI-procedure as expressing respect for persons (or "ends-in-themselves"), and this alternative way of motivating the CI-procedure allows one to forgo thinking of it as a consistency test. Making that move opens up the possibility of restricting the applicability of the CI-procedure, because an intention or policy (such as the policy of acting in accord with the CI-procedure) will no longer have to be considered practically inconsistent if it fails to pass the CI-procedure. (However, the alternative motivation does

not fix what I claimed above was the decisive rejoinder to the Glass Ceiling objections.)

This is radical surgery on the Kantian position that I hope can in the end be avoided, if only because it would make Kantian moral theory much less deep, and much less interesting, than it has the promise of being. To see how radical, recall the Kantian commitment to autonomy over heteronomy, and recall that whether one is autonomously or heteronomously related to one's evaluations is a matter of how they are accepted, and not a matter of their content. In principle, one's acceptance even of the importance of autonomy, or of the value of persons, could be heteronomous (for instance, if one believed that autonomy was supremely valuable because an authority had said so). Now in Herman's revision of Kant's views, it is the value of persons and of autonomy that come first, and that underwrite allegience to the Categorical Imperative. So Herman is advocating a "Kantian" position on which one is to be heteronomous with respect to one's deepest and morally most central commitments.

47. Not always: New Kantians sometimes write in a way that suggests they think Kant's moral theory to be supported by our pretheoretical sense of what morality requires. (E.g., O'Neill, 1989, p. 94.) They may be encouraged by Kant's own claims to this effect, but it is a rare philosopher, however original his view, who does not help himself to this sort of PR; to take such a pronouncement at face value is to forget how startling and radical Kant's moral views are. Alternatively, it may indicate the extent to which some "moral intuitions" have been reshaped by long exposure to Kantian theory.

48. Kantorowicz, 1957, is the classic treatment. A similar purpose was served by the English device of the crown (the property of which was distinct from the personal property of the king); philosophers will be familiar with the much-reproduced frontispiece of Hobbes's *Leviathan*. Even in the United States, the two-bodies doctrine has left traces in canon law: the concept of corporations sole, a device that makes of the successive occupiers of an ecclesiastical office a corporation able to own property; for an overview, see Gerstenblith, 1995, pp. 454–61.

49. Kant's willingness to help himself philosophically to now obscure legal doctrines has been documented by Henrich, 1975.

50. That Kant adapted concepts from the legal tradition of the Holy Roman Empire – see note 49 – would not count as a scholarly discovery if he had taken the trouble to say so explicitly.

51. For an example of this sort of coyness in another Enlightenment author, take Hume, 1778/1983, vol. iii, p. 436: "in all religions except the true, no man will suffer martyrdom, who would not also inflict it willingly on all that differ from him." Hume was known to his contemporaries as the "great atheist," and although his readers understood that the qualifying clause was meant to be empty, he nevertheless went through the motions of supplying it.

52. See, for instance, Harman, 1976, pp. 442 ff. This condition is understood to be part of the content or object of the intention, not a piece of, as it were, the propositional attitude wrapper. Attempts are sometimes made to analyze intentions as complex desires; in such analyses, the condition that

the intention cause the intended action is introduced as one of the things one wants.

53. G 446. Note that, as I've presented the train of thought, it relies on the contestable assumption that causation is transitive. Note also that we need to understand this claim so that it is compatible with a point recently emphasized by Korsgaard: that in the Kantian way of seeing things, *you* are the cause of your actions.

54. Here is one place where "willing" (at any rate prior to Kant's *Wille/Willkür* distinction) and "intending" diverge: it is another contemporary commonplace about intending that one can only intend what one believes one can effect (Harman, 1976, p. 432). But one can "will" that circumstances of some type be causally connected to actions of another type – in fancy terminology, one can will one's maxim to be universalized – regardless of whether this is something one can effect.

55. For instance, the argument assumes both that causal laws are exceptionless, and that they operate at the level of the contents of the agent's cognitions; Davidson, 1980, accepts the former but not the latter; Fodor, 1994, cf. pp. 3–4, 8, 46, accepts the latter but not the former.

56. Nietzsche makes this point – as per usual, angrily – in *The Gay Science* (1887/1974), sec. 335. (I'm grateful to Lanier Anderson for bringing this passage to my attention.)

57. Joke credit: Warren Goldfarb.

58. Compare, in the first *Critique*, the Second Analogy, and esp. A201/B246 ("Thus the principle of sufficient reason is the ground of possible experience..."), as well as the beginning of the third Antinomy, where in characterizing natural causation Kant is explicit about the requirement that the governing rule must be "without exception" (A444/B472). (Kant proceeds to paraphrase the latter point with what is a variant of traditional formulations of the Principle of Sufficient Reason: "But now the law of nature consists just in this, that nothing happens without a cause sufficiently determined *a priori*" [A446/B474]).

59. L 51–2. I don't mean "cognition" here to translate "*Erkenntnis*," but rather as a generic term for a contentful mental state deployable in inference.

60. There is some uptake of this way of seeing the CI-procedure among the New Kantians (e.g., Herman, 1993, pp. 143–4). The idea that the Principle of Sufficient Reason is implicated in the Categorical Imperative is not a new one; see, for instance, Engstrom, 1986.

On occasion, New Kantian interpreters seem aware that something like the Missing Argument is lurking in the background. (Korsgaard, 1990, ch. 3; however, I don't claim that she would agree with my reconstruction.) When they are, they hasten to look for machinery more congenial to contemporary metaphysics, which might be substituted for it, and much of Korsgaard's recent effort has been channeled in this direction: Korsgaard, 1996b, pp. 136 ff; Korsgaard, 1999.

Kant was aware that often enough we must act on the basis of reasons that are not sufficient. Not taking the self-same reasons to be good enough in some other situation is a stance typical of the imperfect duties: that some people need help is a reason to help them, but it cannot be a sufficient reason, because we quite correctly do not help others who also need help. (It would be impossible to help everyone who needed it.)

61. This exposition follows Jonathan Lear (1998a; 1998b). Note that the uses to which I propose to put this rendition of psychoanalysis don't require that it be standard issue Freudian doctrine, and in fact Lear presents it as psychoanalysis psychoanalyzed, that is, as an interpretation offered to psychoanalysis, of precisely the kind I have just described.

62. Three remarks. First, why describe such a thought as unconscious, with the accompanying suggestion that one already *has* the thought? Therapeutically successful psychoanalytic interpretation typically produces acknowledgments of the form: Yes, that's what I was thinking all along. Such retroactive self-ascriptions are a useful marker of acceptance and uptake, even if we don't have to understand them as literally true.

Second, calling a thought unconscious, in this sense, does not mean that the bits and pieces to be integrated into it have not themselves been conscious. Kant, for instance, was giving explicit attention to one or another version of the Principle of Sufficient Reason as early as the *New Elucidation* (1755/1992).

And third, why is this particular thought unconscious? (Why is the Missing Argument missing?) The default explanation, on the psychoanalytic approach we are appropriating, for the matter of a potential thought remaining inchoate and fragmentary, is that imposing a unified and inferentially tractable form on it takes cognitive resources, that the resources are in short supply, and that one just hasn't gotten around to it. But it would be possible to look into the sort of explanation for its absence that is widely regarded as characteristic of the psychoanalytic school, namely, that a thought is being repressed because it is too dangerous to entertain. I won't pursue that line of thought here, but if one were to do so, one might begin with the following observation: that to turn to the intelligible self is to abjure the elaborate theoretical resources of the first *Critique*, and to be left facing the practical domain almost empty-handed.

4

Reasonably Virtuous

What kind of a person should you be? This question, labelled the "ethical" as opposed to the "moral" question, has become, over the past quarter-century, the focal point of a prominent movement in Anglo-American moral philosophy, one that looks back to Aristotle's *Nicomachean Ethics* for inspiration and origins.[1] The formal answer is that you should be a virtuous person, and so work in this tradition is generically described as "virtue theory" – the substance and disagreements having to do with what virtue is, or, more practically, requires. Virtue theory's shift of focus makes urgent the further question of *why* you should be virtuous (on one or another substantive understanding of the notion): does rationality require virtue, or can you be, as Candace Vogler's provocatively titled book has it, reasonably vicious?[2] I hope here to motivate a different way of thinking about virtue, partly in order to give a new spin to this further question about its rationality.

Let me say very synoptically why I am so unhappy with contemporary treatments of virtue that I feel the need to strike out in a new direction. The record shows that even very intelligent and thoughtful philosophers who try their hand at this topic by and large produce work that uncritically consecrates local preconceptions of the morally admirable. The substantive renditions of virtue hold no surprises about what the virtues *are*, which I take to be a symptom that the kind of theoretical articulation we rely on to keep our premises at arm's length from our conclusions is lacking. If discussion of virtue is going to be philosophically worthwhile, it needs to be rebuilt around a technique able to criticize and correct platitudes, and so able to generate unanticipated and even startling consequences.[3]

Aristotle has been the richest source of inspiration for thought about virtue, and indeed the various approaches with which I am dissatisfied appropriate one or another aspect of his treatment.[4] So I suggest returning to Aristotle and seeing whether there is yet another way to appropriate him. In the service of developing a fresh understanding of virtue, I want to propose a new way of reading the *Nicomachean Ethics* (or the bulk of it, since I will set his description of the contemplative life, in the last book, to one side for the present). I do not claim that it captures Aristotle's own intentions, or reconstructs his train of thought; it is not that he saw his own argument in the way I will describe. Rather, I am about to outline a way of organizing the material in the first nine books, one that will be useful to us as we look for another angle from which to approach the topic of virtue.

1

Aristotle introduces the practical syllogism as the logical device that (in a twentieth-century idiom) rationally reconstructs our practical reasoning (that is, our deliberations about what to do): it is possible in principle to recast the support for choosing a course of action in this form, and in doing so to display the force of the reasons underwriting the choice. A practical syllogism will have a major premise, expressing a general view about what is important or what one wants, a minor premise about a (relatively) particular matter of fact, and a conclusion expressing a resolution to act that is at the level of particularity of the minor premise. For example:

1. I could really do with some coffee.
2. What I'm being offered is a cup of coffee.
3. I'll take it.

In this practical syllogism, (1) is the major premise, expressing a generic desire that could in principle be satisfied by many different cups of coffee; (2), the minor premise, registers an opportunity to have a particular cup of coffee; and (3), the conclusion, is to be thought of as having practical force, and quite possibly as being directly expressed in the indicated action. (The considerations represented by a practical syllogism typically lie behind an action in something like the way a parse tree lies behind an utterance; one need not be a linguist, or be at all articulate about the grammar of one's native language, in order for the grammar to explain the form of the utterance, and one does not have to have taken time out to think about the grammar for one's sentence to be informed by grammatical considerations.) Consider this next practical syllogism:

1. I'd better give up things that make me jittery.
2. Coffee makes me jittery.
3. So I'd better give up coffee.

Here the resolution will become the major premise of more particular practical syllogisms, involving particular cups of coffee, before it is translated into action; although practical in force, its conclusion remains at the level of particularity of the minor premise.[5]

Notice that I have not tried to coerce Aristotle's practical syllogisms into any very uniform format (one which designates its elements as, say, oughts or shoulds or desires); the practical syllogism is essentially an *imprecise* inference pattern. Aristotle famously insists that one should not demand more precision of a subject matter than it will bear (NE 1094b, 1098a25ff); the subject matter he has in mind is ethics, and I will shortly be in a position to suggest that the source of its imprecision is the imprecision of the logical device we are examining. And notice that the imprecision of the practical syllogism is not just a matter of the way it resists overly fastidious attempts at characterizing its components. Practical syllogisms are *defeasible*, that is, even when a bit of reasoning of this form seems to be perfectly in order, it can be defeated by suitable additional information.[6] The first of our sample syllogisms is defeasible by further premises such as: but I've given coffee up; or, the coffee here tastes like muddy dishwater; or, I think this is the cup that Hercule Poirot has put the knockout drops in; or, but I only drink organic fair-trade. That is, any of these additional facts, and indefinitely many others, warrant not drawing the conclusion of this otherwise perfectly satisfactory snippet of inference.

The *Nicomachean Ethics* (again, excepting its final book) is a portrait of the *phronimos*, or practically intelligent man – who Aristotle argues is identical both to the virtuous man and to the happy (or successful or flourishing) man.[7] I propose the following characterization of the *phronimos*: he is the master of the logical device that, according to Aristotle, represents properly performed practical reasoning; that is, he is the master of the practical syllogism. (That practical reasoning plays an important part in Aristotle's conception of virtue is not a new point, but this formulation of its role is, I believe, new.) Aristotle's portrait displays what it takes to deploy this inference pattern competently – and not *just* competently, but sure-footedly and expertly. By way of confining our attention to the cases in which we have a significant interest, let me stipulate that I do not mean merely that the *phronimos* is capable of executing practical syllogisms, whether or not he does much of it. (Viz., I don't mean that the practically intelligent person might be someone who exercised his intelligence only as a weekend hobby.) Rather – call this the *Scope Condition* – we are to understand him to be a person in whose life the practical syllogism plays a pervasive and important role.

If the characterization is right, then it should be possible to derive from it everything that Aristotle tells us about the practically intelligent person. It is in fact almost possible,[8] but I will not defend that large exegetical claim now; it would require a treatise-length reading of the *Nicomachean Ethics*, and I have other tasks on my agenda. Instead, here are a few examples intended to show what the claim comes to.

Consider Aristotle's doctrine of the mean (sometimes called the Goldilocks theory of virtue), that is, the idea that virtues are intermediate states, located between corresponding vices of excess and deficiency (see, e.g., NE 1108b10–15). Recall that practical syllogisms are defeasible, and take as a further example a practical syllogism appropriate to the Greek battlefield:

1. When the hoplites attack, you'd better charge.
2. The hoplites are attacking.
3. Charge!

To be a competent user of this inference pattern requires exhibiting sensitivity to the practical syllogism's defeating conditions: if you don't know when *not* to draw the conclusion, you don't know how to reason with practical syllogisms. And there are two directions in which you might fail to exhibit the proper sensitivity. On the one hand, you might treat *too many* circumstances as defeating conditions, and be prone not to draw the conclusions of such syllogisms when you should. (For example, you might think that the especially menacing way their weapons glint in the sun excuses you from charging.) On the other hand, you could treat *too few* circumstances as defeating conditions, and be prone to drawing the conclusions of such syllogisms even when you shouldn't. (For instance, as in Lord Tennyson's "Charge of the Light Brigade" – although the poet seems to take the cavalry to have had a *correct* grasp of the defeasibility conditions of their practical syllogisms.) The former disposition is cowardice; the latter is rashness; the virtue of courage is the happy medium between these two vices.[9] That is, the way in which virtues can be positioned between contrasting vices is (in part) a matter of what competence with the defeasibility of practical syllogisms looks like, surveyed over appropriate domains of practical syllogisms picked out by shared subject matter.

Or again, take Aristotle's analysis of how virtue lapses into *akrasia* (or weakness of will). When you affirm the premises and conclusion of a practical syllogism, but then fail to implement the conclusion you have drawn, the best explanation is that you did not really affirm the premises after all: rather, you were mouthing them, in something like the way that an actor recites the lines of his script (NE 1147a18–24; cf. 1142a20). The point here is that mastery of the practical syllogism requires being able to take its premises on board not merely as it were by rote, but with the full emotional understanding of their import that will allow you to act on their consequences. The practically intelligent person will be someone for whom this kind of emotional comprehension is a matter of course, and so who will not exhibit akratic patterns of deliberation and action.

Let me gesture at just one further aspect of Aristotle's portrait of virtue, his discussion of friendship.[10] This is perhaps the most sustained treatment of a single topic in the *Nicomachean Ethics*, but it is not so much an analysis of the dispositions or character traits of the virtuous man as a description of his social surround. In order to be virtuous, your friends must be virtuous themselves; virtuous friends inspire you to imitation, call you on your failings, and so on. (This means – though Aristotle does not quite say it – that you need straight-talking rather than wishy-washy friends.) If virtue amounts to mastery of Aristotle's preferred practical logical device, this kind of peer pressure means being corrected by your friends when you get the defeasibility conditions of a practical syllogism wrong, being pressed toward an appropriately robust emotional grip on the practical considerations you are in the course of deploying, and so on. Virtue theory tends to get thought of as stopping at the boundaries of the individual, but if the question is "What has to be true of you in order for you successfully to use the practical syllogism?" part of the answer will be facts that are not so much about you as what is around you. In this case, to be a master of the practical syllogism, you have to have the right kind of social support network, viz., virtuous friends.

To recap, the suggestion is to see the practical syllogism as the explanatory core of Aristotle's picture of virtue, in the following sense: the features of the virtuous person are necessary preconditions for wielding the practical syllogism successfully, and for employing it in the full range of cases to which it is appropriate.[11] An account of virtue begins with a theory about what it is to deliberate correctly, and goes on to ask what a human being must be like if he is to be successfully guided by this theory. Answering that question tells you everything you need to know about virtue.

2

Aristotle's account of practical reasoning is important, and it repays close examination. But it is only one of the many theories of practical reasoning currently in play.[12] We can abstract away from Aristotle's account by identifying virtue as: what a person has to be like if he is to be a master of the inference patterns that rationally reconstruct practical reasoning properly performed – whatever those turn out to be. I want to suggest that this is the most profitable way to think of virtue, and to support that suggestion I want to see what happens when we unplug Aristotle's own theory of practical reasoning, and plug in a succession of alternative theories instead. This sort of survey will of necessity be telegraphic, but it ought to convey a sense of the range of different character portraits that this notion of virtue can generate when we allow the underlying conception of practical reasoning to vary.

Take, first, instrumentalism: the idea that all practical reasoning is means-end reasoning; that your goals or desires are given, and that figuring out what to do is entirely a matter of determining how to achieve those goals or satisfy those desires. For the majority of analytic philosophers, instrumentalism is probably still the default view of practical reasoning;[13] so it is helpful to ask what the instrumentalist portrait of virtue would look like.

First, you can't make any progress on determining the means to your ends unless you know what it is that you want in the first place; that is, a relatively narrow type of self-knowledge is one of the instrumentalist virtues, and people who poke around in the kitchen cupboards looking for they're not quite sure what exhibit, on a small scale, what it's like to lack this virtue. (Many virtues are required by more than one of the theories of practical reasoning in play, and as we traverse them I will use self-knowledge as an illustration of how such commonalities end up looking on slightly closer inspection.) Second, determining the means to your ends is just so much wasted motion unless you actually go through with them, and unless you persist until, well, the very end, so a further instrumentalist virtue is resoluteness.[14] Third, being good at means-end reasoning is in large part being good at coming up with means to your ends, which is to say that resourcefulness is another instrumentalist virtue, one with two contrasting components. On the one hand, the resourceful person has the talent of improvising nonstandard means to his ends out of whatever his circumstances make available.[15] On the other hand, preparedness is a characteristic of the instrumentally effective individual: he makes a point of having at hand a toolkit of relatively generic means. (In societies such as ours, he can read and write, he has a driver's license, a credit card, and favors owed him by people in high places.) He is likeable (which makes others inclined to do what he asks), persuasive, fast on his feet, unencumbered by scruples, and charmingly portrayed by Cary Grant in Howard Hawks's classic film, *His Girl Friday* (1940).

Fourth, in the normal course of things, most of the ends one adopts can be reached not only via sane and straightforward means, but via crazy and pointless ones: if what you want is a pizza, you could order takeout around the corner . . . or you could fly to Paris, where they have pizza, too.[16] The cartoonist Rube Goldberg became known for depicting pointlessly roundabout ways of attaining otherwise plausible goals; his "machines" are funny because they exhibit what is as far as the interests of instrumental rationality are concerned a vice, while remaining technically in conformity with the means-end pattern. Leaving to one side the question of whether doctrinaire instrumentalists are in a position to help themselves to the distinction between sane and crazy means to an end, part of being a competent instrumental reasoner is noticing and choosing the sane rather than the crazy ones. Call the virtue *efficiency*, and call the vice *Rube Goldbergism*.[17]

Fifth, for instrumental reasoning to play an important role in one's life (that is, for the Scope Condition to be satisfied), one must have ends that are largely attainable, that is, ends to which available means can be taken. The spirit of instrumentalism is that while you can be criticized for an inappropriate choice of means, your ultimate ends are neither rational nor irrational, but just the ones you happen to have. Nonetheless, realism – the disposition to have ends that are achievable – turns out to be an instrumentalist virtue, on the approach we are now exploring.

Finally for now, satisfying the Scope Condition (that is, having the instrumental virtues be important enough to be interesting) requires an environment that puts a premium on means-end reasoning. Perhaps extremely traditional societies do not; I have been told that the now-vanished Soviet Union did not. (In the USSR, the means to most available ends had been preselected; you didn't try to figure them out, you just got on line.[18])

3

Proceeding now to a further account of practical reasoning, consider Michael Bratman's planning-oriented theory.[19] On this view, much practical reasoning consists in forming, adopting, filling in, and finally implementing plans. Plans have three relevant defining features. They are stable, that is, once you have adopted a plan, you will not reconsider it unless special circumstances arise. (Because it will take a minor emergency to make me reconsider our cafe appointment, you can plan on meeting me there yourself; plans facilitate coordination, both inter- and intrapersonal.) Plans are normally incomplete when adopted; they get filled in as you go. (When I plan to meet you at the cafe, I do not figure out how I am going to get there; rather, I leave that for later, when I will know where I am going to be coming from.) And plans frame deliberation, restricting the courses of action that I actively consider to those compatible with the plan. (Since I am planning to meet you at the cafe, I can save myself the trouble of wondering whether to go shopping instead.)

First, dispositions having to do with reconsidering one's plans make up the virtue most obviously demanded by practical reasoning of this kind. If you will not reconsider your plans under any circumstances, you will too often end up performing wildly inappropriate actions. But if you reconsider your plans at the drop of a hat, *any* hat, then you forgo the benefits of stable plans entirely. A competent plan-using agent has to get right the range of conditions that trigger reassessment of his plans.[20]

Second, while some steps of some plans are triggered by conditions enumerated in that plan, others are not; the difference is that between a plan to go to the gym on Monday morning at 10:00, on the one hand, and planning to get more exercise by getting in more running, swimming and biking, on the other. Plans with the latter kind of indefiniteness are in practice dropped if you don't find occasions to execute their steps. So a competent plan-using agent will find suitable occasions for taking the untriggered steps, rather than falling victim to procrastination.[21]

Third, given that plans are filled in as you go, you need a sense of what's feasible, one that will discriminate between realistic and unrealistic plans – without your having to see what the details are. (This is nontrivial, as many thesis advisors staring at dissertation proposal drafts will testify; the virtue is that of knowing how much to bite off.) This normally involves the ability to budget time and other resources realistically.[22] Fourth, you need a sense of how much of your plan has to be firmed up now, and what can safely be delegated to your future self. Fifth, since you will normally have more than one plan in progress, you have to be good at coordinating your plans; this will constrain both what plans you adopt, and how you fill them in. Budgeting skills help here also, and sometimes techniques like modularization are appropriate (for example, doing your writing on Tuesdays and your class prep on Wednesdays). Perhaps more interestingly, coordinating your plans with one another on the one hand requires you to have a clear enough idea of what they are (which is to say that self-knowledge is a virtue on the planning theory of practical reasoning as well), but on the other hand, requires you to manage the coordination without having the plans fully filled in (which is to say that there are built-in limits to what there is for self-knowledge to know).

Sixth, notice that while the freewheeling willingness to treat *anything* that will advance one's objectives as a live option is (modulo the need to avoid Rube Goldbergism) a virtue, on the instrumentalist conception of practical reasoning, because plans frame deliberation, it is a vice on the planning conception. The newspaper editor of *His Girl Friday*, for whom it is all in the day's work to have pockets picked, romantic rivals' mothers kidnapped, and counterfeit money planted on unsuspecting insurance salesmen, may be the very model of a modern instrumentalist, but he turns on too many dimes to be a good planner.

And finally, you need social surroundings that support planning: devices like day planners and watches (but perhaps not cell phones, which seem to undermine the stability of plans), collective success in holding natural disaster and social chaos at bay (since planning, and even contingency planning, is only a sensible approach against a background of relative stability), and an environment in which others are also guided by plans, and so provide a relatively stable backdrop for your own plan execution.[23]

4

Next in our list of theories of practical reason, take a recent Kantian rational reconstruction of practical deliberation, the so-called CI-procedure.[24] Let me digress to explain how it is supposed to work, starting off with a little bit of quasi-technical terminology: One, a *maxim* is a three-part representation of a course of action you might perform; it specifies a description of the action, a triggering condition for actions of this description, and an end or point of performing the action. (For instance: When hiring a CEO [triggering condition], make sure to tie his compensation to the company's performance on the stock market [action description], so he'll be motivated to prioritize shareholder value [end or point].) Two, a *perturbed social world* for a particular universalized maxim is a representation of a world in which everyone acts on that maxim – that is, it is the answer to the question, What would happen if everyone did that? (So the perturbed social world for the previous maxim is one in which CEOs get much of their pay in stock options.)

Executing the CI-procedure means testing a proposed course of action for permissibility, as follows. First, you are to identify the maxim that genuinely captures your motivation and intent. Second, you are to ask if the perturbed social world for your maxim is conceivable, and whether it so much as makes sense to proceed on your maxim in such a world. The Lake Wobegon maxim (When raising a child, make sure it is above average, so that you can take parental pride in how much better your child is than other children) fails this test: Garrison Keillor's famous description of the perturbed social world in which "all the children are above average" is incoherent, and were we to waive that problem, it would still be a world in which the point of the maxim is not served by the action it proposes (since you can't be proud of your child being better than the other children by being above average, if they're *all* above average). Third, you are to ask whether you could "will" such a world, where this means, roughly, checking that your own agency would not be radically undercut in the perturbed social world. If a more or less stably valued currency is a background condition of enough successful agency, a hyperinflationary economy cannot be "willed," and if hyperinflation is what you get in the perturbed social world that universalizes some maxim of yours, say one that has you double your prices, then acting on that maxim is prohibited. You may act on your maxim (only) if the associated perturbed social world can be both conceived and willed.

What would the Kantian virtues look like, on the conception of virtue which we are exploring? In his *Tugendlehre*, Kant treated the topic of virtue at length,[25] focusing on the "imperfect duties"; the idea is that you have to use your judgment in deciding how far to take mandatory but open-ended pursuits like helping others and developing your talents. From our point of view, the focus of his treatment is very close to Aristotle's concern with mastering the defeasibility conditions of practical syllogisms; that is, it is peripheral to a conception of deliberation that puts the CI-procedure at its core, and looks like an Aristotelian wing clumsily added onto Kantian architecture. By walking through the steps of the CI-procedure, we can generate virtues more in keeping with the original foundations (or, if you like, the "groundwork").

First, self-knowledge is necessary for deliberation of this kind: you cannot very well check that your maxims universalize if you do not know what they are (and Kant himself used to worry about how difficult self-transparency of this sort really is).[26] Because what have to be tracked are maxims, rather than simply ends, this variety of self-knowledge is more demanding than the instrumentalist's. It did not really matter whether means-end reasoners were able to articulate the class of conditions under which they were willing to take an action, as long as they could see that the right instrumental connection held in the case at hand; but it *does* matter to Kantians.

Second, there is the related ability to notice (and to be motivationally engaged by) the aspects of your circumstances that belong in a sensible maxim; Barbara Herman has discussed this under the heading of "Rules of Moral Salience," and we can call it *moral alertness*. She has also suggested that the way to avoid being alienated from the deliverances of the CI-procedure is to have concerns shaped by a personal history of Kantian deliberation (in a not entirely successful metaphor, by one's "deliberative field"), the desired effect being that the maxims you entertain get rubber-stamped by the CI-procedure.[27]

Third, there is the ability imaginatively to explore the perturbed social world. Kant seems to have underestimated the difficulty of the task, but it is in fact a daunting requirement, and our initial example of a maxim is a convenient illustration. In retrospect (meaning, after a dramatic series of corporate scandals, bankruptcies and Congressional hearings), it seems that when the maxim is generally adopted, the pressure to up stock prices gradually corrupts the practices and institutions that link those prices to the underlying performance of the corporation. Eventually the fraudulent accounting comes to light, the stock prices collapse, and the shareholders end up not with more value but with less. That is, this particular maxim gives rise to a contradiction in conception – which fact was entirely unobvious back in the 1980s, when it seemed like enlightened capitalist management reform. Again, not a few governments – Weimar Germany is a memorable example – have blithely marched down the road to hyperinflation without anticipating the ensuing economic chaos. Thinking through cases of the CI-procedure is hard because one has to anticipate the workings of what sometimes gets called the Law of Unintended Consequences.

The point here is that a perturbed social world – a representation of the world as it would be if everyone hewed to a given maxim – is an abstract object of at least the complexity of a chess board. (Actually, it is far more complex, because so much of the perturbed social world is made up of obscure empirical facts, rather than cleanly announced conventions, because the social milieu has so many more elements than a chessboard, and because the pathways of influence are so multifarious.) The ability to see deep into the board is a talent that anyone who wants to be a strong chess player has to cultivate, and the ability to see deep into the perturbed social world – call it *psychohistorical sensitivity*[28] – is likewise a talent that anyone who wants to be a grandmaster of the CI-procedure will have to cultivate. What will happen, six moves down, if I castle now? is an easier question to answer than, What *would* things be like if – as it's now being widely proposed – stock options were always treated as an expense?

Fourth, because there are many ways an environment can support or undercut your agency, and because your agency can be undercut to one or another degree, in determining whether you can "will" a perturbed social world you need a well-developed sense of how manageable a prospective impediment to agency really is. (Is it intolerable or merely irksome?) Consider the maxim, "When it's easier than not, I will litter, so as to get rid of my trash with the minimum effort." A world in which that maxim is universalized gets in the way of projects such as going for walks in litter-free surroundings, but such projects are clearly not so critical to my agency as to make endorsing the maxim amount to a contradiction in my will.[29]

Like the theories of practical reasoning we have surveyed so far, Kantian virtue requires an appropriate social backdrop. For one thing, satisfying the Scope Condition means living in an environment where the CI-procedure does not filter out all of one's options. For another, the chess analogy suggests that becoming a grandmaster of the CI-procedure will normally require analogs of the institutions used to train strong chess players.

Think some more about the chess players. Kantian virtue is *geeky*, and that means that you wouldn't want everyone to have it. I have nothing against geeks (after all, I'm pretty much a geek myself), but I'm very aware that if the world is going to keep on turning, there have to be a lot of people who aren't geeky (people who aren't like me), doing the many non-geeky things that need to be done. Recall that standard Kantian arguments for the so-called imperfect duties take division of labor very seriously – you have to have other people, with different skill sets, around to help you out – and here we are facing an analogous fact of life, call it *the division of virtues*. It's not just that you wouldn't *want* everyone to be a chess or CI geek: you couldn't *will* it, because that would mean that none of the skills requiring incompatible personality traits would be available for projects you might undertake. So it looks as though you can't universalize a virtue that is a precondition for successful Kantian decision making, which is awfully close to saying that Kantian decision making does not pass the test that it itself imposes.[30]

Now I don't want to claim right now that the problem is irresolvable; that would take more argument than I'm willing to present here. Rather, notice instead what the payoff of demonstrating its irresolvability would be. We are construing virtue as what it takes successfully to implement a theory of practical reasoning. If the portrait of virtue associated with a theory of practical reasoning is incoherent, or (as I am suggesting in this case) incompatible with the theory of practical reasoning itself, then that theory, a theory of how to figure out what to do, is *impractical*, which is to say that it fails in the worst way that such a theory can. That is, the problem I have started sketching for Kantian moral theory shows how virtue ethics, as we are now reconstructing it, can serve as a reality check for theories of practical reasoning.[31]

On the one hand, we have in virtue theory a method of assessing candidate theories of practical reasoning for feasibility. On the other, I've been suggesting that we may be on our way to a notion of virtue that does not depend unduly on our prior and probably untrustworthy intuitions (that is to say, our prejudices) about virtue.[32] The attractive prospect before us is: first to arrive at our conception of how to figure out what to do, in a way that does not depend on our conception of virtue, and then to use that conclusion to determine the correct substantive account of virtue. Our reality check on theories of practical reasoning is formulated so that we can help ourselves to both these strategies at once, without circularity. Notice that the broad outlines of the link between rationality and virtue are already fairly clear. Because the virtues are preconditions of effective practical rationality, one's stake in being virtuous is just one's stake in effective practical reasoning – that is, it is one's interest in and commitment to successful because thoughtful choice.[33] And if we allow the Scope Condition to represent our view that choice is characteristic of human life, in that good choices are a *sine qua non* of almost anything of importance in human life going well, then that stake is large – large enough for it to be entirely understandable that Aristotle came very close to identifying the happy with the practically intelligent life.

5

Practical empiricism is a theory of practical reasoning for which I have argued elsewhere, and so I want to consider the virtues associated with it.[34] A good way to quickly lay out its main ideas is to look at how a natural extension of the Aristotelian picture we started out with ends up becoming overidealized.

Recall that the Aristotelian practical syllogism is first and foremost defeasible, and notice that mastery of its defeasibility conditions amounts to being implicitly aware of the relevance of all of one's other concerns to the practical problem at hand. John McDowell has argued that such knowledge will in turn have to include an understanding of the relevance of the various potentially defeating concerns to each other, and that consequently the application of a practical syllogism is to be guided by a global conception of what matters – in Aristotle's vocabulary, of *eudaemonia*. Aristotle's virtuous man is not only, normally, happy; he also understands what happiness is (and this explains how it is that mastery of a practical inference pattern entails having the right major premises to feed into it).[35]

The practical empiricist criticism is that this is far too ambitious a demand to make of anyone. If many very different things matter and are important (or to put it a different way, if what matters overall is not internally homogenous but variegated and complex), why should we expect that anyone ever grasps all of it? People know their way around the parts of life they are familiar with, and they are unsurprisingly ignorant about those parts they have not yet encountered. All models of virtue are idealized, but the idealization in the Aristotelian depiction is so fantastic that it is hard to see how it could be a useful guide to anyone's actual life.[36]

On the contrasting view that I endorse, you learn as you go, bit by bit. Practical empiricism holds that you learn from experience about what matters, about what is important, what is desirable, what undesirable, what makes things go better for you, and what makes them go worse. Learning from experience entails being able to make observations whose content is intrinsically practical; the cognitive function of such reactions as pleasure, displeasure, pain, frustration, boredom, and interest is to underwrite such observations. (That it feels bad is a signal, one whose content is, more or less, *stop that!*)

Since observations are essentially particular and present, drawing lessons from experience that are going to be useful for the future requires generalizing, that is, using inference patterns that amount to practical versions of induction. For instance, when you notice that selling cars feels easy and *good* and likewise selling headstones, and annuities, and satellite dish contracts, you might conclude, inductively, that being in sales is a good thing. Notice that the content of one sort of pleasure is *competence*: more or less, *I can do this!* And notice that one is arriving at conclusions of the form, "Such and such a *type* of thing is *generally* worthwhile," or, "So-and-so a course of action is *generally* a bad idea." Practical induction is where the major premises of your practical syllogisms come from (or ought to come from), and where you get (or ought to get) the generalizations that allow you to manage practical considerations which press you toward conflicting courses of action.

In short, practical empiricism is about not being sure that you know what you want; instead, it adopts the more openminded view that you need to *find out* what *to* want, and to do so in just the way you find out much else that matters, by empirical investigation. Where Aristotelian ethics demands of you that you apprehend, all at once, what matters overall, practical empiricism takes you to be doing well if you manage to see, in a timely way, the small chunk of the big picture (if there even *is* a big picture) that you actually need next, and here's a for instance. Perhaps you dreaded being a summer associate at a law firm enough to have thanked your lucky stars that it included an externship with a public interest group. And perhaps, to your immense surprise, you find yourself spending your time at the nonprofit wishing that you were back in your office at the law firm. (When this happens, it's not just an accident: law firms supply law students with summer jobs hoping that they will draw inductive conclusions from practical observations about their time there, and join the firm.) If you do draw those conclusions, you may change your mind about what to do when you graduate from law school. Doing so may, if you like, amount to acquiring a piece of the Aristotelian vision of *eudaemonia*, but the point is that you don't need the big-picture vision to make your next choice: what you need is to know what it feels like to be working in your law office versus what it feels like to be working for an NGO.[37]

In sketching the practical empiricist virtues, we have to proceed cautiously, because the arguments for the practical empiricist approach also suggest that the question of what character traits conduce to practical-inductive inference is itself an empirical question. For that reason, I want to start out with what it takes to make practical induction work in an artificial, constrained, but nonetheless real and entirely familiar family of environments – specifically, restaurants. Here we can be fairly confident that our description of the practical-inductive virtues is realistic. Afterwards, I will relax the constraints of the toy environment, and speculate about what the more demanding environments necessitate.

For practical induction to have scope to operate, you need to be trying things out, which in turn means that the social environment allows you to try things out (restaurants provide this by offering you a la carte menus, and the local restaurant scene provides you a relatively slowly changing range of restaurants to explore). Trying things out is normally driven by curiosity and a willingness on your own part to experiment; it also requires tolerance on the part of your social circle for your very small-scale Millian "experiments in living."[38] (Dining is a social occasion, and if your friends won't accompany you to the new restaurant, that is usually a significant impediment to exploring its cuisine; notice the contrast with Aristotelian virtuous friends, who play their role in Aristotelian virtues precisely by being *in*tolerant.) Practical induction requires self-knowledge: an awareness of one's pleasures and displeasures, and more generally of how one feels, accompanied by noticing the circumstances in which the feelings arise. (Not a common accomplishment: most restaurant-goers scarcely notice what they're eating). But the sort of self-knowledge that we saw instrumentalist practical reasoning to demand can get in the way of successful practical induction; it's easy to be so sure you know what you want that it prevents you from learning that it isn't what you *really* want, after all.

If you are to benefit from learning what is important from experience, then you must be willing to leave old concerns behind when something better comes along. This is fine when it comes to restaurants; once we discover that the desserts at some restaurant are not up to the rest of the meal, we change venues for dessert. But there is an entrepreneurial aspect to practical empiricist virtue which can look dishearteningly like unsentimental rootlessness, and which competes with loyalty, commitment, and ties to home. This is an instance of a general point that I will take up in due course: that virtue, on this generic conception of it, may turn out to be the kind of thing that elicits, at any rate at first viewing, not admiration, but a sigh and a shrug.

Practical induction (whether the form it takes is the traditional and caricature-like induction by enumeration, or a more sophisticated version of generalizing from experience) requires repeatability. Now this has three consequences for practical-inductive inference which are evidently manageable in the restaurant domain. First, the more holistic the domain, the less inductively relevant repeatability there is. In the restaurant domain, there is already a certain amount of holism: how you enjoy the sauce depends on what it's on; likewise, how the dessert goes down may depend on how heavy the rest of the meal has been. You can't predict whether the grilled sugar loaf chicories will be successful solely on the basis of whether you enjoyed previous grilled sugar loaf chicories. Still, partly because restaurant menus are so very structured, the holism is quite restrained compared to other domains – a point humorously underlined for aesthetics by Komar and Melamid.[39]

Second, the larger the decision, the less chance you will have to repeat the choice, to see how it comes out if you make it differently, and so on. Restaurant decisions are small scale; because you can go back night after night, you can work your way through the menu, trying out all the items and many of the allowable combinations. But even for restaurants, there are exceptions: Charlie Trotter's is too expensive, the menu changes too frequently, and you wouldn't fully appreciate it if you became a regular. And once you leave the restaurant, real life faces you with big choices, choices you will make only once, or at most a handful of times.

Third, even when it comes to restaurants, there is only a moderate degree of intersubjective constancy. My own tastes may be fairly consistent over time, and so I can rely on my own practical observations; but I cannot rely nearly as much on the Zagat's, which compiles the observations of the restaurant-going public. Science compensates for holism and for the scale problem – for the fact that there are only so many experiments a single scientist can do – by relying on intersubjective constancy; scientific method means being methodical, i.e., waiting for results. That's possible because science is a collective enterprise: you may not be around for the results, but some other scientist will be, and you can help yourself to the results of previous scientists. Such enterprises, however, require high levels of intersubjectivity, and the worry is that many practical domains aren't, as they say, rocket science, or any other kind of science either, and that this technique won't work. I take it that this is why, when liberal societies allow "experiments in living," they do not subject the experimenters to the procedures and reviews that are routinely imposed, in those same societies, on pharmaceutical research. (When I decide to try out a new way to live, I don't have to run my proposal past a human subjects committee; I don't have to show that the "experiment in living" has a control group, is double-blind, etc.) Unlike the results produced by pharmaceutical trials, others' "results" are perhaps inspirational and suggestive; but to know what works for me, I will have to try it out on my own.

What virtues are required when real life outside the restaurant poses large choices, in domains characterized by a high degree of evaluative holism, and by no more than the moderate level of intersubjectivity we are familiar with from eating out? If you need the results of practical induction quickly enough for them to be of use to you, you cannot afford to be methodical about exploring these choices. Instead, you will have to be good at guessing a way of parsing your practical situation – *very* good, since for larger decisions, you will need to guess right on the first few tries. A virtue like this one ought to remind you of the abilities needed to learn the syntax of one's first language, a routine accomplishment that prompts some surprising explanations.[40] A similarly surprising explanation is evidently called for here, if users of practical induction are to have a way between the horns of an uncomfortable dilemma: that of either needing constrained, restaurant-like environments to make it work; or of resigning themselves to doing their practical reasoning badly in just those cases that matter most.

Pending such a surprising explanation, is there a way between the horns of the dilemma? We could say, somewhat defensively, that there is no method of decision making that works well everywhere; the various accounts of practical reasoning do have this in common, that they demand a great deal of individual agents (that's why what they demand can without too much strain be called *virtues*), that agents can't always be expected to live up to those demands ... and that that's all we're likely to get. We could say, also defensively, that we shouldn't pessimistically overestimate the scope of the problem; childraising would not be possible if whatever you did amounted to letting the child make all the deadly and painful mistakes for itself, and in fact you don't reinvent or personally recapitulate all of human history. (Ontogeny can't *really* recapitulate phylogeny, not this way.) We could say that many choices, especially the very large-scale ones, are too unspecific to be, as they are, *wrong*; whether deciding to live in London is a mistake or not depends on how you fill in the details. (I'll take up this sort of specificationist practical reasoning in Section 7.) So practical induction does not have to account for what success we have in making decisions like these. And we could say that since, when it comes to making decisions, people normally get better with practice, and since human life is short, we ought to conclude that practice in making real decisions is best begun as soon as possible. Our institutions of formal schooling have, in the past century or so, become so hypertrophied as to defer the onset of this kind of experience, for an ever-growing proportion of the population, well into adulthood. But if practical induction is a correct characterization of practical reasoning properly performed, this policy is a terrible mistake. For, on the account of virtue we are exploring, our educational institutions provide what is quite literally schooling in vice.

6

This is all very well, I expect traditionalist readers to object, but what does it have to do with *virtue*? When Edward Gibbon attributed the decline and fall of the Roman Empire to the erosion of the republican virtues, he did not mean that Romans became poorer practical reasoners, but rather that, while their "personal valour remained... they no longer possessed that public courage which is nourished by the love of independence, the sense of national honour, the presence of danger, and the habit of command,"[41] or, more briefly, that the Roman character ceased to be conducive to the collective good. Practical reasoning is something done by individuals; virtue is essentially social; and so thinking of virtue as turning on practical reasoning is leaving out the most important aspect of it. Cleanliness, we are told, is next to godliness, but it's hard to see what the socially important property of being well scrubbed has to do with high-quality decision making. And in answering the question, What kind of person should you be? the more traditional theories tell you how to live your *whole* life, not just how to handle the smallish part of it that contributes to deliberative success: they give you a much richer picture of the virtuous man than is on offer here. If aspects of traditional thought about virtue such as these cannot be preserved in my account, then I am not advancing a new approach to virtue, but just changing the subject.

Now first, I doubt that the worry that we are not getting portraits of full lives is on the mark. Just for instance, we saw Bratman's planning view to be fairly tightly circumscribed, as theories of practical reasoning go, but Vogler criticizes planning views on the grounds that the social surroundings required for planning betray the way in which this conception of practical reasoning is class bound.[42] Because it is a familiar kind of person who is equipped to engage in planning across the board – roughly, a member of the Western managerial classes – she concludes that such views are unsatisfactory as general accounts of deliberative rationality. We should conclude instead that this approach to virtue tells you a good deal more about how your life should look than you might have thought at first glance. If even such a relatively minimalist theory of practical reasoning presents us with a recognizable character and lifestyle, we can expect other and more elaborate theories to give us no less.

Second, in my view it is a mark of the theoretical power of the approach that we are going to have to be openminded about what virtue turns out to be, and to take seriously whatever results we get by applying the very abstract account of virtue to what we take to be the correct theory of practical reasoning. We should not expect every theory of practical reasoning to give us *nice* virtues; we should not take it to be an a priori feature of virtue that it benefits others, or that it is pretheoretically attractive.[43] If, as it happens, our theorizing ends up telling us that the virtuous man is a pillar of the community, that he is likeable, that he is someone whose company we would enjoy, and so on, the compliments are worth having only because they are not automatic. And so, because I think that we ought not to sacrifice the leverage the approach gives us, I do not recommend traversing the connection in the other direction, that is, using the relative niceness of the ensuing portraits to make one's choice of a theory of practical reasoning.[44]

I've been claiming that the most influential philosophical analysis of virtue exhibits a certain structure, and that the approach it introduced can be extended by detaching that structure from Aristotle's own theory of practical reasoning, and reconnecting it to alternative such theories. So I am suggesting that extending the approach this way preserves the philosophical role of virtue theory. The complaint, that the results of doing so may not be what we are ordinarily used to calling "virtue," asks us to make a choice: should we follow ordinary usage, or philosophical function? History indicates that sticking with ordinary usage, at the price of sacrificing theoretical structure, will not prove to be all that philosophically useful. The more mediocre ranges of so-called ordinary-language philosophy produced many analyses of one or another not very structured concept. ("When do we say that it's a *chair*?") Those analyses have been largely forgotten, because, whether or not they were successful in their own terms, there was very little that other philosophers could *do* with them.

Philosophical approaches to virtue that too directly tie the virtues to beneficial or approved social outcomes tend to make virtue incomprehensible. Woody Allen's *Zelig* (1983) portrays the bearer of an impossible character trait, the chameleon-like ability to fit in *wherever* one happens to be. Since part of fitting in in Chinatown is speaking Chinese, part of fitting in in Germany is speaking German, and so on, Zelig speaks Chinese in Chinatown, German in Germany, and so on . . . or rather, since he has never learned any of these languages, he imitates speaking Chinese, etc., well enough to fool the native speakers. The comic impossibility reflects the theoretical disadvantages of the too-direct approach. Just as you cannot *simply* have the disposition to say the right thing at the right time, without actually learning particular languages with their particular grammars, and just as you cannot more generally have the disposition to fit in, wherever you happen to be, without actually learning the skills that the particular social locations require, so you cannot have the disposition to do the socially beneficial thing, without having the ability to engage in successful practical reasoning about what to do in one or another particular situation. (Likewise, you cannot *just* have the disposition always to do the *appropriate* or *correct* thing: another way of putting the problem with McDowell's rendering of the virtuous man is that he is an ethical Zelig.)

It would be a fruitless theoretical approach to language to decide that what we are interested in is the ability to say the right thing at the right time, and so we should focus on *that*, rather than on grammar, mastery of which underlies the ability to speak a natural language (and so, incidentally, the ability to say, in one natural language or another, the *wrong* thing at the *wrong* time). If virtue theory is going to be philosophically serviceable, it requires the sort of theoretical articulation that is provided by seeing practical reasoning as its backbone. Letting go of popular preconceptions of virtue, in the way that the theoretical commitment to starting with practical reasoning requires, need not be a bad thing. Not that long ago, the willingness to duel over small points of honor was a popularly acknowledged virtue, but it no longer is; the character traits that merchants have had to cultivate were formerly dishonorable, and are now part of our image of the well-comported individual. Rather than tying ourselves to a focus-group conception of virtue, we should be willing to change what we think of as virtue, as we have done so many times in the past.

7

All that said, there is nevertheless a natural way to connect the approach I am advocating with the social dimension of the ethical tradition. Most treatments of practical reasoning focus on the case in which it is performed by individuals, just because it is so much simpler to start out there. But organizations and other collectives make decisions, too, and we can ask what a person has to be like to be good at collective decision making of one kind or another.[45] What traits make up this kind of personality profile, and so, the virtues of collective practical reasoning, depends, as before, on what collective decision making, properly performed, looks like, that is, on what the right theory of (collective) practical reasoning is. But regardless of how that comes out, we might expect treachery, for instance, to prove a vice: to use Gibbon once more, effective collective decision making does not take place when the decision makers are overly willing to (metaphorically or literally) stab one another in the back. And quite possibly justice, in two of its senses, will turn out to be a virtue: collective decision making works only when individuals abide by the deliverances of its procedures; *pleonexia* – the disposition to grab more than your share – is prone to undermine cooperation among deliberators. (Of course, what stake one has in being a good participant in collective deliberation may be less obvious, or more tenuous, than one's stake in doing one's own personal practical reasoning well.)

What counts as collective virtue will not depend solely on an a priori theory of practical reasoning, and the virtues that support collective practical reasoning will not be everywhere the same, but rather will vary with the institutions that provide the framework for the deliberative process. For example, capitalism comes in more than one variety. Liberal (or stockholder) capitalism is characterized by short-term business relationships, and so the obligations that govern those relationships tend to be exhaustively and explicitly defined by (so-called "sharp-in/sharp-out") contracts. In stakeholder (or Rheinlander or "coordinated") capitalism, business relations are longer term, and incomplete contracting is the norm; the understanding is that when unexpected circumstances arise, the parties to a contract will address those circumstances so as to preserve their stakes in the relationship. Accordingly, in the environment of stakeholder capitalism, having a reputation for being someone with whom you can work things out matters a great deal more than it does in the environment of stockholder capitalism. What counts as deliberatively working things out is different in the two sorts of business environment, and so the different business environments give rise to different virtues of collective deliberation.[46]

Rather than trying to show how one or another theory of practical reasoning can be made to reproduce a set of virtues of which the traditionalist will approve, I want to explore briefly how turning to collective practical deliberation can give us a new perspective on yet another theory of practical reasoning. (Of course, many different theories of practical reasoning lend themselves to social and institutional implementations, not just this one.) Specificationism has it that many of our ends (as well as rules, policies, and so on) are too indefinite to be starting points for means-end reasoning. Before you can start looking around for steps to take, you need first to come up with a further specification of the end, one that is concrete enough to fix what counts as a step toward it. Suppose we have decided that our new political party stands for the common good. That is not yet a platform, and in hashing out a platform we will be specifying a conception of what the common good is, and thus, our common end.[47]

The main problem with launching in on a discussion of what the specificationist virtues would look like is that specificationism is not yet sufficiently specified. By way of sidestepping that problem, let's further specify a *social* procedure for specifying ends, one that academics ought to find familiar. Agencies that support research may want to fund work that is original, promising, agenda-setting, and so on. This kind of end is not specific enough to guide any actual course of research (and if the agency laid out guidelines concrete enough to guide an actual course of research, it would thereby fail to be original, promising, and so on). So such agencies solicit proposals on the part of researchers, and constitute a panel whose task is to select those that are original, promising, and so on. Such a proposal amounts to a concrete specification of the agency's originally indefinite goals, and the selection process amounts to adopting one such specification (hopefully, the best).

Here we can divide up the virtues that figure in this version of specificationist deliberation into proposal-related and selection-related. On the proposal side, we can further divide up the virtues into those related to the content of the proposal, and those related to its packaging. On the packaging side, virtues include the display of professionalism (needed to give the selection panel confidence that the project will be executed as promised), and the ability to present the project in a way that is comprehensible, engaging, and attention-grabbing.

The social nature of the process means that the emphasis is not on applicants coming up with many good ideas; each applicant will only submit one proposal. Rather it lies on applicants developing the proposals they will actually submit, making them stronger, more interesting, and generally making them stand out from the crowd. So perseverance and sticking to it are virtues. The attention that lets you notice ideas, results, subprojects, and so on that can be used to further articulate, enrich, and even merely embroider your proposal is a virtue. On the other hand, so is an ability not to be distracted by ideas for competing proposals; if you brainstorm your way into too many good ideas, you need to be able to abandon most of them. A willingness to renegotiate your project, so as to bring the panelists (and other necessary players) on board turns out to be a virtue as well.[48]

On the side of the reviewers or panelists, since the method relies on panelists knowing, for example, promise when they see it, a good deal of the work is done by *taste*.[49] Taste is in many ways a mysterious matter, but one thing we know about it is that palates go dead fast. So while you will only be a good reviewer if you've had some experience, to be a good reviewer you need the ephemeral virtue of not having had too much.

Openmindedness is a further reviewer's virtue, and notice that because the stick-to-itiveness of successful applicants in developing their ideas normally has partisanship as a concomitant, good applicants do not typically make good reviewers: the virtues of the different roles in this socially distributed form of deliberation are not just different, but to some extent psychologically incompatible.

Finally, notice how this specification of specificationist deliberation makes a very open-ended task more tractable by turning it into a comparison problem. Having the stack of proposals in front of you means that you need to generate a scale or ranking that is suitable to the proposals that are already there. And so a further panelists' virtue is being good at comparisons, and being good at identifying features of the items you are comparing that can be used to specify your initially indefinite end.[50]

8

I have not been arguing for a conclusion, but rather advancing a proposal, and so I will conclude by recapitulating its merits.

The conception of virtue we have been considering is theoretically powerful in that it allows us to engage in genuine argument as to what character traits are virtues. It comes with an explanation of why it is rational to be virtuous, and so makes intelligible our interest in virtue. It allows us to generate portraits of the virtuous character corresponding to the different theories of practical reasoning in play. On the one hand, it allows us to select the correct portrait from among these by choosing the correct theory of practical reasoning; on the other hand, it provides an implementability test for the various theories of practical reasoning, and so advances the debate as to which one of those is the correct one. (Of course, more than one of the accounts of practical reasoning may be correct – not all of them claim exclusivity, and in particular practical empiricism does not – and so we may need to merge the portraits of the corresponding virtues.) And while theoretical power comes at a price, that of not building the traditional image of the virtues as socially beneficial into their definition, essentially social virtues can be delineated by investigating what character traits contribute to the success of collective deliberation. All in all, this seems to me to be a promising approach.[51]

Notes

I'm grateful to Janet Abbate, Lori Alward, Michael Bratman, Pepe Chang, Ursula Coop, Amy Johnson, Jennifer Johnson, John Leslie, Gloria Park, Rachel Shuh, and audiences at Wake Forest University and Oxford University for helpful discussion, as well as to Scott Anderson, Chrisoula Andreou, Carla Bagnoli, Sarah Buss, Alice Clapman, Alice Crary, Julia Driver, Robert Firmage, Steve Gardiner, Don Garrett, Eric Hutton, Gabrielle Juvan, Mitzi Lee, Ron Mallon, Maria Merritt, Matt Pamental, Henry Richardson, Gabriel Richardson Lear, Valerie Tiberius, and Shelley VerSteeg for comments on an earlier draft.

1. I'll refer to it in the running text by NE and Bekker's page and line numbers. The ethical/moral contrast, made current by Bernard Williams (1985), appeals to the respective etymologies of the words "ethos," meaning character, and "morals," related to mores or customs, so picking out rule-oriented views; see also Anscombe, 1997. For recent overviews of virtue theory, see Watson, 1990, Hursthouse, 1999, Copp and Sobel, 2004.

2. Vogler, 2002. That, conversely, virtue requires rationality is by and large but not always taken for granted; for instance, Driver, 2001, objects.

3. Some current approaches promise the sort of theoretical power I am demanding, but then fail to deploy the machinery they claim to put in place. For instance, Thompson, 1995, Thompson, 2004, and Foot, 2001, look to a kind of Aristotelian natural history to tell us what normal, nondefective members of the relevant species (human beings, but the theory is in principle more general) are like and what they do. But *real* natural history of the sort invoked by the methodological framework is lacking: there is no investigation of how the human species occupies its ecological niche (and no evolutionary investigation of how it came to do so); there is no use of the work – in, for instance, evolutionary psychology – that ought to be relevant to this sort of project; there is no *feel* for what such natural histories are like. Descriptions of how species *work*, what their *erga* are, are not usually *pretty* and *sweet*: female black widow spiders eat their mates; in primate species that forage in groups, males kill infants that they take to be not their own children (Hrdy, 1981); in many species of birds, the first-hatched chick will push its sibling eggs out of the nest. So we should not just be handed Foot's pious and unsupported assertion that justice is part of human practical rationality. (Thompson, 2003, does point out that Foot's substantive ethical views are detachable from her metaethics, but as far as I can tell, he neither disavows Foot's substantive ethics nor provides the missing argumentation for it.)

Consequentialist approaches to virtue theory (such as Driver, 2001) exhibit a similar problem. They hold that you tell what the virtues are by looking to the consequences, and that what the consequences are is an empirical question. (This seems to promise the kind of theoretical traction we're looking for.) But consequentialists don't conduct empirical investigations into what consequences ensue on the various character traits, and are nonetheless quite confident as to which character traits are virtues.

When you appeal to results, and it's an empirical question what traits produce the best results, it's not a good idea to assume that you know without actually investigating. Reliabilist virtue epistemology has already turned up these sorts of surprises: when Gigerenzer, Todd, and the ABC Research Group, 1999, investigated what cognitive techniques produced the best results in various theoretical domains, they found that *ignorance* was often the best approach. So we shouldn't assume or expect that anything like what are ordinarily called the virtues will be selected by a consequentialist methodology.

Should we really expect the results the consequentialist needs to be as surprising as all that? Don't we have all of human history to instruct us? So we do, but notice how rarely it is that people can agree on what the lessons of history are; and notice also that in the cases where someone has taken a methodologically careful look, what everyone *knows* to be the lessons of the past turn out all too often not to be well supported at all. (For a popular – but bitter – survey of what this problem looks like in professional psychology, see Dawes, 1994.)

4. The Thompson-Foot idea of ethics as biology is certainly there in Aristotle; the consequentialist approach takes up Aristotle's expectation that virtue will normally reveal itself in a life that is both happy and socially beneficial; and of course intuition-driven virtue theory will remind one of the Aristotelian method of systematizing *endoxa*.

5. There's an important point that I just want to touch on here, which is that Aristotle's practical syllogism shouldn't be identified with plain old means-end reasoning (which I'll get to in the next section). For one thing, means-end reasoning is solely about: what is for what *else*. But, if the claim I am about to advance is correct, the practical syllogism will have to account for Aristotle's "middle level" ends, ends that we have *both* for their own sakes *and* for the sake of something else (namely, *eudaemonia*). (I'm grateful to Henry Richardson for pressing me at this point.) For instance, Aristotle implicitly rehearses the following practical syllogism: One ought to have a happy and well-lived life. A happy and well-lived life involves having friends. So one should have friends. But, as he also points out, one loves one's friend for the friend's own sake, and not for an ulterior motive, that is, not as a means to an end such as one's happiness. So if this practical syllogism is to make sense of friendship, it should not be understood as a straight means-end inference.

6. In the terminology of the AI community, inference deploying practical syllogisms is *nonmonotonic*.

7. For the rendering of *eudaimonia* as success, see Hutchinson, 1995, pp. 199ff; as flourishing, see Cooper, 1986, p. 89, or Putnam, 1981, p. 148.

8. The qualification is meant as follows: I think the large-scale features of Aristotle's virtuous man can be derived from this characterization, as well as many of the more minor features; but a number of incidental traits do not in any obvious way drop out of it. See, for instance, Aristotle's remarks about what the virtuous man is prone to forget, at NE 1124b10–15 and 1125a1–5.

9. Of course, "too many" and "too few" don't here bear a numerical or counting interpretation: keep in mind that there are indefinitely many of either. And more carefully, there are two contrasts on the side of excess, one (rashness) having to do with action, and the other (nameless) vice having to do with lack of fear (NE 1107b1–5); in general, virtues have to do both with actions and with feelings (NE 1106b15–20). There are two ways to integrate Aristotle's points about appropriateness of feeling into my account. I will touch on one in a moment, when I discuss Aristotle's account of *akrasia*; because I will have a use for it later, let me just mention the other. Although feelings are involuntary, they admit of justification; for Aristotle, these justifications have the form of practical syllogisms. (For example, one should be angry when one has been insulted; I have been insulted; so I should be angry.)

    The doctrine of the mean has taken on a life of its own, and turns up even when defeasible practical syllogisms are not in the background. For instance, Kenny, 1992, ch. 4, presents faith as the virtue positioned between the vices of credulity and skepticism.

10. I'll briefly take up another – the fact that the *phronimos* has the *right* major premises for his practical syllogisms – at p. 146, and in note 50.

    For a lengthier reconstruction of Aristotle's actually rather counterintuitive understanding of *philia*, see Millgram, 1987.

11. N.B.: This way of reading Aristotle can be anchored in a (Thompson-Foot) natural-history characterization of humans provided that Aristotle's view of the human *ergon* as "the soul's activity that expresses reason" (NE 1098a5–10; cf. 1103b30–35) is properly rephrased: what humans *do* is perform actions informed by practical syllogisms.

12. For an overview of the field, see Millgram, ed., 2001, ch. 1. MacIntyre, 1999, takes an approach that is quite close in spirit to the one I'm about to recommend, in that he identifies the virtues as preconditions for successful practical reasoning. (See esp. pp. 96, 105, 107, 110–11, 120, 136, 140f, 148, 155–6.) Our accounts differ in the first place in that his avoids relying on the kind of substantive theories of practical inference that I survey below.

13. For a sophisticated defense, see Vogler, 2002, where it is called the "calculative view." (She reserves "instrumentalism" for its psychologistic or mentalistic versions.)

14. The term is borrowed from the discussion in Korsgaard, 1997, p. 232.

15. Aficionados of the 1985–92 ABC television show can think of this as the *MacGyver* virtue: the ability to assemble, out of a piece of lead pipe, a roll of scotch tape, and a few other random-seeming contents of the locked room, a working explosive device.

16. I've seen the point made by John Searle (in a manuscript that is, as far as I know, not destined for publication), and I think it's his example; and I've heard it made by Steve Engstrom.

17. Goldberg, 2000. "Efficiency" fails to highlight the aesthetic dimension of the virtue; notice that Goldberg is able to portray the vice as *comic*. Perhaps Aristotle is trying to capture this in his characterization of how the virtuous man will choose between alternatives, selecting "the one through which it will come to be most easily and most finely [kallista]" (NE 1112b17).

(I'm grateful to Gabriel Richardson Lear for suggesting the point and the passage.)

18. My informant here is David Wolff. Korsgaard, 1990, ch. 3, interestingly suggests that social progress consists largely in removing occasions for means-end reasoning. Vogler, 2002, however, holds the need for instrumental (or, in her vocabulary, "calculative") rationality to be pervasive because actions have instrumental structure; if you are acting, the Scope Condition is trivially satisfied.

19. Bratman, 1987, Bratman, 1999, Bratman, 2001.

20. Several points. First, this is a temporally extended analog of the Aristotelian command of a practical syllogism's defeasibility conditions.

Second, the virtue covers more than just explicit reconsideration. Sometimes one drops one's plans by simply forgetting about them (for example, one's childhood intention to become a fireman), and the virtue we're acknowledging involves having this happen when appropriate.

Third, pressing on this virtue is likely to get us versions of some of the traditional "executive virtues." For instance, temperance or continence – not being too easily distracted by temptations – will be necessary for stable plan execution, as will courage, in those cases where plans need to be executed under dangerous conditions.

Fourth, Curtis Bridgeman has pointed out to me that just how prone to reconsideration you should be depends on which phase of the plan you're in. At the early brainstorming phases, a willingness to subject your plan to top-to-bottom revision is probably a good thing; later on, when you are getting down to the nitty-gritty details, and there is more sunk cost, your plan should be stiffer.

And fifth, notice that the right kind of stability in one's intentions normally presupposes a related sort of stability in one's assessments. Bratman has been working on the question of how stability in one's plans is to be sustained in the face of instability in one's evaluations (1999, chs. 3, 4), but if I am right, that may be the wrong strategy to take.

21. I'm grateful to Michael Bratman for suggesting the virtue.

22. For this last point, I'm grateful to Michelle Hill. See also Cummins, Poirier, and Roth, 2004, which points out that how much time you allocate to the planning process must itself be task-sensitive.

Policies are open-ended relatives of plans; my plan for tomorrow will be over tomorrow, but our joint intention as to how we are going to treat petitions to be exempted from a curriculum requirement may be activated indefinitely many times in the indefinitely distant future. Staying within the spirit of the planning theory means that policies should also be minimally filled in; sufficient unto the day thereof is the determination of what counts as a "comparable course" or a "language contributing to the student's program of research." This means that the planning agent needs an appropriate set of *interpretive* skills and abilities, similar to those applied to the laws by judges (but to be distinguished from the omnipresent forms of judgment emphasized by Wittgensteinians). (I'm grateful to an unpublished – and untitled – manuscript by Paul Teller for this point.)

23. There are many preconditions for a capacity like planning, and we do not normally think of all of them under the rubric of virtues. (Maybe you won't do a good job of developing and executing your plans unless you have had a good night's sleep; but is insomnia a vice?) Some of the contrast is shouldered by our taking for granted some things and not others, but notice that the sort of imperialism we are seeing is shared by almost all of the standard moral theories: what they count as moral or ethical subject matter usually includes a great deal that the ordinary person does not think of that way. (What the standard moral or ethical theories count as their subject matter typically excludes a good deal that the ordinary person thinks of as belonging to it, as well.)

24. This rendering of the first version of the Categorical Imperative is due to John Rawls and a number of his students; see Nell, 1975, O'Neill, 1989, Korsgaard, 1990, Korsgaard, 1996a, Herman, 1990, Rawls, 1989. I wish here to remain agnostic as to how faithful the rendering is to Kant, and also to put to one side the other formulations of the Categorical Imperative.

25. Kant, 1902–, vol. 6, pp. 375–493 (1797/1994, for an English version).

26. Kant, 1785/1981, Ak. 407; see also Kant, 1902–, vol. 6, pp. 441–2, 447.

27. Herman, 1993, chs. 4, 8 (esp. p. 179). Kantians should have a worry that Herman herself has not fully addressed, namely, that the Rules of Moral Salience will constitute a locus of heteronomy in a moral theory devoted to extirpating it: if it is just a brute fact that you notice some things and not others (and take account of them in your maxims), and your noticing these rather than those is needed to get the CI-procedure to work, then the moral theory bottoms out in the brute facts. There is a response that Herman might develop, which is that Rules of Moral Salience have to be generated by the CI-procedure. So, for instance, rules like, "When in polite conversation, ignore your interlocutor's physical deformities, in order to put him at ease," might well *fail* the CI-procedure. (If *everybody* were to pretend the physical deformity wasn't there, it would acquire the status of an unmentionable, therefore horrible fact; its owner would be generally uneasy, and conversations awkward – a contradiction in conception.) Or again, testing a proposed maxim like, "I won't pay any attention to other people's problems," and seeing it to generate a contradiction in the will (if nobody notices your problems, they won't help you out), would give rise to an imperfect duty to keep on the lookout for other people in trouble. To be sure, there is a bootstrapping problem in this neighborhood to be figured out: how do you get the process of acquiring a suitable body of tried and tested Rules of Moral Salience off the ground?

28. After Asimov, 1991; I'm grateful to Amy Johnson for suggesting the name. We can distinguish that ability from a further component, that of actually noticing the "contradictions" in conception and the will. For a fascinating description of what it is like to see deep into a chess board, see de Groot, 1965.

29. Because judgment calls of this kind cannot be executed mechanically, and because *all* impediments to agency obviously cannot be allowed to generate contradictions in the will, a startling result for Kantian moral theory follows: that the duties generated at the final step of the CI-procedure, each of which

is an imperfect duty, collectively have the formal structure of an imperfect duty. That is, just as it is left up to the agents to decide which of the indefinitely many actions that might come under the heading of imperfect duties to perform, so it is left up to the agents to determine which of the indefinitely many would-be imperfect duties are binding on them, that is, are real duties.

30. Why do we need grandmasters of the CI-procedure? Why won't a lower level of adeptness do? My sense is that philosophers underestimate the skill level required to get results that are worth having at all. It is noteworthy that when you ask what would happen were such and such a maxim universalized, you rarely hear the response: Who on earth knows? (I'm grateful to Brad Hooker for reminding me of that fact.) But examples like those we have surveyed suggest that that is very often the *right* answer: even the best and the brightest seem to get it wrong often enough.

31. There is a recently popular line of argument which might seem to constitute an analogous reality check for – and objection to – virtue theories, namely, that virtues are robust character traits (robust in that they're stable across a broad range of social situations); empirical work in social psychology shows that character traits are not in this sense robust; therefore there are no virtues (Doris, 2002). But notice that if virtues are introduced as personality features needed for successful practical reasoning, to show that a personality feature is only stable over a narrow range of situations may tell us that we are not robustly effective practical reasoners, without making the notion of virtue any less useful. Merritt, 2000, suggests compensating for lack of internal robustness by designing compensating environments; this is a suggestion I would be happy to adopt, and one which would put the account of virtue I'm advocating to good use. Or again, we might use a characterization of virtue, developed along the lines I'm suggesting, as a basis for a training program designed to improve our abilities as practical reasoners.

However, we shouldn't be too hasty in buying into the argument Doris is constructing even on the older view of virtue. On the traditional conceptions of virtue, virtue is the product of forms of training that are simply no longer seen in advanced industrialized societies; consequently, with one marginal exception, Doris draws his conclusions using research performed on populations that, by the lights of the ancient Greek and Roman virtue ethicists, are not virtuous. (So of *course* the subjects of the experiments Doris reports don't exhibit stable virtues . . . they haven't been trained. For a recent and philosophically very insightful description of what such training plausibly looks like in nonhuman cases, see Hearne, 1987.) His argument consequently fails to make contact with the historically central discussions of virtue. And for the same reasons, it does not show that training programs aimed at virtues as they are being recharacterized here would be unsuccessful.

32. "May," because we cannot claim these merits if our arguments for our preferred theory of practical reasoning do in fact turn on our intuitions. And recall that it is an important (and much-discussed) feature of Aristotle's own view that you can't determine what counts as a correct inference without using the practically intelligent person as a reference point, so that there

is a circularity built into the foundations of the view. Rationality does not function, in Aristotle's theory, as a criterion for virtue that is independent of the virtues it endorses, and so his account falls short of the kind of theoretical independence we would like to have.

On some popular ways of reading Aristotle, he arrived at his account of virtue by systematizing the body of opinion available in his culture. But isn't that in tension with my taking Aristotle as a model for ways of thinking about virtue that do not simply endorse local preconceptions of it? And if Aristotle *did* move beyond those local preconceptions, and if competing approaches to virtue also model themselves on Aristotle, why should we expect them to prove beholden to the local preconceptions?

It's important not to overestimate the degree to which Aristotle's virtues are just the virtues of the ancient Greeks; his methodology makes his theories responsible to *endoxa* – things people think – but also allows the *endoxa* to undergo reinterpretation, so that what Aristotle has them mean is in the end often quite distant from what the man on the street would have thought he meant by them. And recall that I've already touched on the potential of alternative theoretical approaches for revision, and the ways in which they fumble that potential, in note 3.

33. Two points: First, that's not to say that virtue is merely a *means* to practical rationality; only on an instrumentalist theory of practical rationality *must* a practical stake in something, or a commitment to it, take that form. Second, it's also not to say that the virtue is something *over and above* the capacity to successfully deploy practical argumentation: that having the capacity is not enough, because you also need the appropriate virtue. (Compare: if it takes a couple hundred thousand dollars to buy a particular house, it's not as though having the money is something additional to the ability to buy the house.)

34. See Chapter 1, and Millgram, ed., 2001, pp. 16–17, Millgram, 1997, Millgram, 2004.

35. McDowell, 1998, esp. chs. 4, 5. While McDowell's reading of Aristotle has become, in recent years, fairly standard, it is of course by no means the only available reading.

36. McDowell works his way into his conception of the virtuous agent by objecting to the idea that one's reasons could be codified into a rule; in particular, what can't be codified are the defeasibility conditions of practical syllogisms. He takes himself to have learned the futility of the appeal to rules from Wittgenstein, and more generally, he writes as though Wittgenstein had provided the metaethical theory that would be naturally paired with a substantive ethics derived from Aristotle.

But this pairing is a mistake. In McDowell's picture, the ideally virtuous person is functioning as a standard or anchor for the theory, the reference point with respect to which correctness of character and behavior is to be assessed. (The right thing to do is what the *phronimos* would do; the right *way* to do it is as the virtuous person would.) That is, the *phronimos* is functioning as a *replacement* for the very rules that Wittgenstein tried so persistently to show cannot do such a job. Wittgenstein devoted a great deal of effort to discrediting other such substitutes (think of his treatment of the fallback appeal to perfectly rigid machines). If Wittgenstein has taught us that an anchoring appeal to rules is futile, he has also taught us that the same kind of appeal to other devices – whether impossibly perfect machines or impossibly perfect persons – is also futile.

From Wittgenstein's point of view, the problem with focusing on, say, a yardstick, in order to understand what length is, is that the yardstick distracts you from the complicated mesh of practices in which it is put to use. (It's not as though you understand length better by staring harder and harder at the yardstick.) Likewise, the problem with an exclusive preoccupation with the perfectly virtuous person, from a Wittgensteinian point of view, should be that it distracts you from the complicated mesh of practices in which ascriptions of virtue have their home. (It's not, a Wittgensteinian should think, as though you understand virtue better by staring harder and harder at the *phronimos*.)

37. Henry Richardson has pointed out to me that Aristotelian virtuous persons might still need practical induction, in order to make explicit the implicit conception of *eudaemonia* which they owe to their upbringing. I have been arguing not that Aristotelians have no use for practical induction, but that, since no one could ever be brought up *that* well, we need practical induction for other reasons.

38. See Anderson, 1991, for attribution of this notion to Mill.

39. The artists commissioned a survey that produced, for each country in the survey, a list of features that respondents preferred in a painting; then, for each country, they executed paintings that jointly realized the list of preferred features (Komar and Melamid, 1999). The resulting paintings are very funny, and absolutely hideous – and not necessarily because popular taste in art is bad, since it is quite clear that the respondents would find the (entirely competently executed) paintings hideous, too. Observing that blues and greens in previous paintings were to your taste does not allow you to infer that a subsequent painting will be to your taste because it has blues and greens. Agnieszka Jaworska has pointed out to me that in principle one could paint a very good painting with all the features on the list – even though it's now not at all obvious how – which I take it goes to show that in aesthetics the phenomenon I'm labeling "holism" goes as deep as you like.

40. Chomskians opt for built-in knowledge of a 'Universal Grammar'; Deacon, 1997, more plausibly points out that natural languages are the product of a process very much like natural selection, one that filters elements of a language for learnability.

41. Gibbon, 1906, vol. I, p. 44.

42. Vogler, 2002, pp. 106–7; her primary (though unnamed) target appears to be the Rawlsian notion of a "life plan."

43. For instance, I would be very surprised if instrumentalism supported an account of virtues on which they tended to advance the collective interest; going after whatever goals you happen to have is not, even when the invisible hands don't just twiddle their thumbs, a way of being mutually supportive. I have already remarked that Kantian virtues look geeky, and that the virtues

of practical empiricism can on occasion look a little too ruthless for comfort. Perhaps when Machiavelli describes the Prince's "virtue," he is providing historical precedent for adopting this sort of position.

Other theoretical approaches to virtue for the most part try to explain away antisocial appearances; in my view, that's just not facing up to the consequences of one's theory.

44. As does Foot, 2001. Bear in mind that when you let your conception of morality shape your theory of rationality too directly, talk about reasons and rationality becomes no more than a dialect in which you express your prejudices and preferences. That is, if you happen to approve of so-and-so doing such and such, you'll say things like, so-and-so has reason to do such and such. The actual effect of not maintaining arm's-length distance between your moral theory and your theory of rationality is that a crude form of noncognitivism becomes the substantively correct account of your rationality-related vocabulary.

45. Compare Bratman, 1999, chs. 5–8, which tries to characterize joint intentions in a way that is continuous with his treatment of individuals' plans, as well as Bratman, 2004.

Why focus on collective *deliberation*? After all, most of what we spend our time doing together is not deliberating. But then, most of what we spend our time doing individually isn't deliberating, either, and individual deliberation has enough of a central organizing role to shape a life. That is to say, there's justification for a collective analog of our Scope Condition.

46. See Williamson, 1985, esp. ch. 3, pp. 120-3, and Hall and Soskice, eds., 2001, esp. ch. 1; I'm indebted to John Leslie for the example.

47. For discussion of specificationism, see Chapter 10, and Kolnai, 2001, Wiggins, 2001, Richardson, 1994, Millgram, 1996a.

Perhaps because both practical empiricism and specificationism share the claim that one can deliberate about one's ends, I have occasionally seen the two views conflated; so here is a quick compare and contrast. Recall that practical empiricism turns on the idea that you have to learn what matters from experience, using practical versions of observation and inductive arguments from those observations. Specificationism turns on the compelling thought that your ends might have so little content that it would be premature to go looking for means to them, and so that a preliminary stage of adding content has to be understood as practical reasoning. As far as practical empiricism is concerned, your views about what matters could be already fully specific when they are acquired; this would allow you to skip the specification stage entirely. As far as specificationism is concerned, you could make your ends more concrete without appealing to experience at any point. This means that, in principle, practical empiricism and specificationism are conceptually orthogonal to one another. My own view is that some version of each is probably correct; for a brief treatment of the bearing of practical empiricism on specificationism, see Millgram, 1997, sec. 6.7.

48. Latour, 1996, attributes the failure of the large-scale engineering project whose post-mortem he is conducting to a shortage of just this virtue; compare item 4 in note 20.

49. Panelists may be quite articulate about what makes particular proposals promising, but their descriptions will normally be satisfiable by proposals that are not promising at all. Teachers will recognize the phenomenon from those sessions in which they have to explain to a student that a paper that conforms to some announced list of desiderata is nonetheless an unsuccessful paper.

50. Broadie, 1987, complains that because there is more content to the conclusion of specificationist deliberation than there was in its premises, it cannot really be *reasoning*. She is in the odd position of someone who holds that, whatever engineers were doing when they designed the Sony Walkman, or the Mosaic web browser, or the F-16, or any other innovative technology that satisfied a vague set of requirements in ingeniously new ways, it couldn't have been *thinking*. Her confusion can be traced to a more interesting problem: that in some cases of specificationist reasoning, the conditions for a successful specification are specified along with the solution itself.

Here's a famous example. Aristotle's *Nicomachean Ethics* can be read as centered around both the practical syllogism, and around specificationist reasoning – partly because, as Wiggins has argued, the practical syllogism can (anyway sometimes) bear a specificationist reading. Aristotle takes it that everyone wants to live well – to lead a happy and successful life – and his problem becomes that of specifying what such a life comes to. The *Nicomachean Ethics* is a sketch of the results of the deliberative exercise.

Or rather, the *Nicomachean Ethics* contains two different sets of results, which means, incidentally, we have a solution to one of the traditional exegetical puzzles, that of making sense of the relation between the contemplative life sketched in Book x, and the active political life of Books i–ix. It's typical of vague or indefinite goals that you can specify them in more than one way – for example, if your goal is to build a subway system, there are many very different specifications of a subway system that you could reasonably end up with – and Aristotle is simply running through the specificationist exercise twice, and ending up with two alternative blueprints.

The point I want to emphasize here is that the criteria – such as "completeness" and "self-sufficiency" – that a life must satisfy in order to count as *eudaimon* end up amounting to very different things in Books i–ix and x, respectively. And this gives the impression that there is nothing in specificationist deliberation that is not up for grabs, since the criteria for deliberative success are themselves undergoing specification simultaneously. And this is, I take it, what is really bothering Broadie. In my view, the best way to address this problem in practice is to add institutional structure, on the model of the case I've just described in the text.

You may have been wondering, for a while now, whether Aristotelian virtue doesn't require having the right premises for one's practical syllogisms, and so you may have been thinking that the account I gave of it earlier on cannot be correct. I've already mentioned a McDowellian way of speaking to that worry, and we can now supplement that with a specificationist way of doing so: The *phronimos*, who is specifying the universally shared dummy end of *eudaimonia,* will arrive at so-called middle-level ends that serve as the right premises for his further practical syllogisms.

51. The direction of explanation in this proposal is from the theory of practical reasoning to the virtues, and consequently so is the direction of persuasion: it is because you believe the theory that you are to take on the task of becoming more virtuous. There is another approach (discussed in Millgram, 2002), which begins with the persona, and is characterized by the converse direction of explanation: it is because you find the personality of Socrates compelling, or Montaigne's self-rendering frank, or Nietzsche's voice inspiring, that you have an interest in their theoretical activities, and successful theoretical engagement is in these cases not normally a matter of coming to believe their theories. That is, the other approach begins by eliciting a response that is essentially *personal.*

It is, I believe, a further merit of the conception of virtue I have been recommending that it makes possible an *im*personal answer to what seem to be those most personal of questions, What kind of a person should I be? and, *Why* should I be like *that?*

5

Murdoch, Practical Reasoning, and Particularism

Particularism is a contemporary movement in moral philosophy that it is hard to know what to do with. On the one hand, it's hard to dismiss. Its ranks include respectable – even prominent – authors such as Jonathan Dancy, Margaret Little, John McDowell, David McNaughton and Richard Norman.[1] It purports to occupy one of the two extreme positions on the spectrum of views about the generality of reasons for action, and is worth a close look just for that. And it refuses to go away: particularism is the current incarnation of what used to be called "situationism" or "situation ethics," which means that it has been around for a while. Philosophical views that stick around usually have something to them, and one is ill-advised to write them off without further ado. On the other hand, much of what is said on its behalf is either difficult to believe, or looks to be a philosophical dead end. And the view is faced with objections and difficulties – *old* objections, which for the most part one can find fielded against situationism[2] – to which it seems to have no satisfactory response.

I want to suggest here that particularism would benefit from renewing its connection to the work of Iris Murdoch.[3] I am going to recommend Murdoch's understanding of practical reasoning as a useful philosophical frame for what I will claim is the most important shared element of the particularist family of positions. In doing so, I mean to be encouraging those who work in the philosophical subspecialty of practical reasoning to add Murdoch's take on it to the contemporary menu of competing accounts.

That it is not already on the menu deserves at least brief explanation. The notion that practical reasoning and moral or ethical theory are two distinct topics for investigation, and that the former can be pursued more or less independently of the latter, is, in the philosophical community, of relatively recent currency (perhaps 1980 or so).[4] Murdoch's philosophically most productive period was probably the 1960s, a period that antedates this separation of subject matters, and so she is usually thought of as having been a powerful and insightful moral philosopher, but not as having articulated important opinions about how one ought more generally to make up one's mind about what to do. That is unfortunate: Murdoch's treatment of the subject is characteristically penetrating, and in part because she was not a member of the current generation of specialists in practical rationality, her understanding of practical reasoning can serve as a corrective to presumptions about the subject matter that are today pretty much common ground in the field.

1

If it is hard to find a crisp and uncontroversial statement of the particularist position, that is perhaps best explained by the most compelling and broadly shared moment in particularism being a *move* rather than a *claim*. Particularists will point out (call this the *defusing move*) that while a given consideration may count as a moral reason on one occasion, say for doing such and such, the very same consideration is on another occasion no reason for doing such and such, or even a reason precisely for *not* doing such and such. In an example of the phenomenon, not itself morally loaded, that Dancy borrows from Wilfred Thesiger, the hardships involved in crossing the desert on camelback are (part of) a reason to embark on the adventure – but only so long as there are no roads, "for to have done the journey on a camel when I could have done it in a car would have turned the venture into a stunt."[5] In a typical execution of the defusing move, the original consideration has not been *overridden* by another stronger reason; it is not that the charm and challenge of crossing the desert bedouin-style is trumped by some other weightier consideration, such as your ailing mother's threat to join the French Resistance while you are away. Rather, the reason behaves differently – for instance, it has a different "valence" – once the background has changed. Particularists are impressed by the apparently uniform availability of the defusing move; once you get the knack of it, you are likely to feel quite confident in your ability to produce a defusing circumstance for just about any putatively general consideration.[6] And so both proponents and opponents produce remarks like the following: "The leading thought behind particularism is ... that the behaviour of a reason ... in a new case cannot be predicted from its behaviour elsewhere." "Particularists hold that the very same properties may count morally in favour in some circumstances and against in other circumstances."[7] My sense of the territory is that characterizations of this kind are the least likely to provoke dissent, but are also less than a theoretical position. Instead, they function as expressions of confidence in the defusing move.

Particularists then do go on to provide a theoretical position, but one which is unsatisfyingly thin. To explain the success of the defusing move, they adduce the holism and context-sensitivity of reasons for action.[8] They proceed to draw lessons for our understanding of morality, and those lessons are to one or another degree antinomian: most radically, that morality has no place for rules; more modestly, that moral rules function merely as reminders, or as generalizations about the kinds of situations we tend to find ourselves in. So, for instance, one extreme version of particularism is described as holding that "it is not that general principles are insufficient to guide us in our consideration of the particular case – they simply do not exist." McNaughton has it that a particularist "believes that we have to judge each particular moral decision on its individual merits; we cannot appeal to general rules to make that decision for us." And Little tells us that "the real lesson of particularism is . . . that there is reason to doubt the existence of *any* codifiable generalities linking moral and non-moral properties."[9] These ways of talking through the success of the defusing move have looked, to some philosophers, like they require a matching metaethical view, and so, again for instance, when Frank Jackson, Philip Pettit, and Michael Smith attack particularism, they characterize it as "the view that the evaluative is shapeless with respect to the descriptive: there is no descriptive pattern unifying the class of right acts."[10]

For my own part, I find the fragments of theory that have accreted around the defusing move unsatisfying, and not nearly as convincing as the move itself. First, the gestures at holism and context do not appear as distinct components of an explanation; to say that holism is true of reasons for action is, in these discussions, just to say that how a reason works varies with context. They are not even properly an explanation, as opposed to a restatement or reification of the claim that the defusing move works. And in any case, appeals to context-dependence should set off alarm bells; they usually function philosophically as conversation-stoppers, and this subject area is no exception. They direct attention to surroundings that are arbitrarily various; variety of this kind resists accounts of how change in context effects a change in (here) the force of reasons; and so they bring one up short and leave one not knowing what to think about next.

Second, the antinomian moral conclusions fly in the face of the experience of moral argument. It is not just that they can make particularism seem like a moral theory for scoundrels (would *you* trust someone who had told you that he might treat his promise as a reason *not* to keep it?), or anyway render mysterious the social role of moral deliberation.[11] Assimilating rules of morality to the string that one ties around one's finger (one particularist attempt to make a place for them) makes it hard to see how the rule could be deployed as a premise in an argument, and we *do* use rules in this way. The heuristic value of reminders is to call to mind the premises that one will actually use ... at which point the reminders exit stage left.

Moreover, the other particularist spin on rules – treating them as summaries of rough local regularities – seems to me similarly not to match our practice. To adapt an example of Murdoch's, and one to which I will return:[12] when one learns a second language, one starts with the grammar. That grammar is used in activities as various as generating utterances, justifying one's choices of phrasing when they are challenged, and criticizing other people's prose. So the grammatical rules are not merely summaries of regularities, and they evidently do not capture merely local regularities: it is not as though we might discover a new *region* of English in which the grammar we have is entirely irrelevant. Nonetheless, mastery of a language is a very good illustration of the phenomenon of interest to particularism. As one's ear for the language improves, one finds that the defusing move can be applied to the grammar. It is not just that there is more to good style than grammar, so that stylistic sensibilities take up where the rules of grammar leave off; rather, style may require not just disregarding a grammatical rule on some occasion, but even treating the ungrammaticality as a reason for doing it that way. (Think of the occasions on which you have had to explain to a copyeditor why you are going to stet out his correction of an ungrammatical but idiomatic passage.[13]) Here we have a family of cases of particularist reasoning in which the rules do real (and not merely summarizing) work, and so we need to find a way of understanding particularism that does not preclude rules from doing work of this kind.

Third, the metaethical remarks that accompany other particularist claims prompt metaphysical objections, and while I do not think those objections ought to detain us for long, they can be understood to express a worry that needs to be taken fully seriously. The prototypical objection is that our moral concepts must surely follow discernable, usable patterns in the way things are; the particularist seems to be denying this. The objection is, again prototypically, tied to metaphysical views about supervenience that require underlying patterns. For reasons I will get to shortly, I think that this second step is a mistake. The real worry here is that the particularist does seem to be abjuring the patterns, and it is the systematic way in which we navigate these patterns that gives content and body to our claim that what we have on hand is a *reason*. When the patterns are thought of as rules, the complaint brought to bear on the particularist insistence that one has a reason, but not a general one – not one that can be recast as a rule – is that we do not know how to make reasons intelligible except through their generality.[14] Now, first, a particularist view would do best to avoid presenting a pretext for the specifically metaphysical objections. And, second, the demand that we spell out what we mean by saying that something is a reason seems to me too deep to be addressed by a specifically ethical theory, and especially by one as currently resource-poor as particularism; it would again be best to find a version of the view that would allow the question to be postponed.

2

I have been pressing toward the conclusion that the defusing move needs a better theoretical home than it has in most recent presentations of particularism. But before I claim to have gotten there, I had better have said something about the serviceability of the position that McDowell has been working up over the last few decades. That position is by now impressively well conditioned, it has strongly influenced the current cadre of particularists, and so one might think that there was no need to look any further: McDowell is developing a contemporary rendering of Aristotle, and so particularism can be thought of as a kind of Aristotelian view. It will be a reminder of what is most distinctive about the defusing move (and so of just what we are trying to find an illuminating theoretical home for) to show how this identification can be resisted.

The alternative that I want to be able to set aside is focused on the notion that moral rules have exceptions that need to be managed on a case-by-case basis, or that moral considerations compete and can override one another, also in a way that requires case-by-case treatment. Aristotle's views, and for that matter McDowell's, are of course more complex than this, so (emulating a similar hedging move by Bernard Williams) I will call the alternative the sub-Aristotelian view.[15] On the sub-Aristotelian view, ethical reasoning can be thought of as proceeding via the medium of a practical syllogism. The major premise of the syllogism expresses a general ethical consideration (or, if you like, a rule), but practical syllogisms are defeasible (that is, they can be defeated by competing considerations). For instance, my practical syllogism might proceed from the major premise that I ought to be frequenting restaurants that use organic ingredients, and the minor premise that Cafe Fanny uses organic ingredients, to the conclusion that I will frequent Cafe Fanny. But that practical inference might be derailed by the fact that I am also hunting for cafes with a lot of edge, and Fanny's edge has faded. McDowell has augmented this picture of defeasibility, in a way obviously congenial to particularists, by insisting that a defeated consideration may be not simply outweighed, but "silenced," that is, made into no reason at all. If the use of organic ingredients has become *dowdy*, then it may no longer be properly treated as a (possibly outweighed but still) positive feature; rather, organic certification may now be in and of itself a liability.

The heart of the sub-Aristotelian view is its proposal for determining when a defeasible syllogism is in fact defeated: the *phronimos*, or practically intelligent person (who is also the virtuous person), is the reference point with respect to which defeasibility (and choice more generally) is to be managed. The right thing to do is what the *phronimos* would do (or anyway what the *phronimos* would advise you to do). The choices between competing practical considerations cannot be systematized, and so the best one can do is to rely on the sensitivities of the virtuous, and their grasp of the not fully articulable ideal – *eudaemonia* or the well-lived life – that regulates their activity.[16]

But claiming the sub-Aristotelian position as a theoretical frame for the defusing move would be to give the move less than its due. For any consideration, our description of the defusing move has it, an occasion can be found on which that consideration will point in a completely different direction. And that goes for the consideration: this is what the *phronimos* would (have reason to) do. For instance, what is called for might be moral *weakness*, perhaps when your friend, in a series of akratic episodes, has made a mess of his life, and needs comfort and encouragement to put the pieces back together. The Aristotelian *phronimos* might well, in such a situation, be left helpless, his attempts at counselling being turned away with the resentful complaint that he just doesn't know what it's *like* not to be able to resist temptation, or to have done something really stupid.[17] As a morally frail person yourself, perhaps even as the graduate of a twelve-step program, you have reason to sit down for as long as it takes, and sympathetically tell your friend that you know what it's like; but you do not have reason to do as the *phronimos* would do, because the *phronimos* cannot come out with that reassurance convincingly.

A fallback position, already mentioned in passing, is to take the reference point to be what the *phronimos* would advise, rather than what the *phronimos* would do. This is only tempting as long as one has not thought about what it takes to give good advice. Allow that there is something to the Aristotelian idea that virtue is a mean between extremes. Along the spectrum whose extremes are complete obliviousness to others, and imaginative overinvolvement in others' lives, virtuous people occupy a position that is a mean; they pay some attention to others, but they do not spend too much time living vicariously, imagining themselves in others' shoes, finding out just how they are thinking of their situation, and so on. Good advisors, however, are people who are good at adopting others' points of view (if that were not the case, we would not have needed to move to the fallback position), and this is very much a skill that requires practice. So good advisors are people who spend much of their time and energy finding out about others' lives, imagining what they would do in other people's places, and so on. That is, good advisors are far too close to the gossipy, nosy, and meddlesome end of the spectrum to be anything like admirably virtuous, and so virtue should not be counted upon for good advice. Notice that the connection is not just a matter of how we go about our classifications: even if you start out with a virtuous self, over-doing your excursions into sympathetic imagination, especially when it is focused on the troubled, is likely to make you less sure-footed than when you began.[18]

Granted, the claim that the virtuous make bad advisors may seem to sit badly with the world of difference it can make to talk things out with someone whose judgment, level-headedness, integrity, and so on one admires. But talking things out is in these cases only rarely a matter of being told what to do. The helpful *phronimos* does not normally dispense instructions, and these are what the fallback sub-Aristotelian position requires.

The fallback position is unworkable, and while the pre-fallback sub-Aristotelian view may yet be workable when embedded in an Aristotelian moral theory, it is not a frame for the much more radical particularist defusing move. Apparently, Aristotelian virtue ethics and particularism occupy different locations in the space of moral theory, and the defusing move really does need a theoretical home all its own.

3

It is now time to start in on an admittedly somewhat lopsided sketch of what Murdoch had to say on the subject of practical reasoning. (Lopsided because, recall, Murdoch and her contemporaries did not distinguish her views about practical reasoning from her substantive moral views; since I am distinguishing them, I will have to take more than the usual liberties in my presentation.[19]) Most standard ways of seeing the problem space take practical reasoning to proceed from a description of a decision situation, one that is treated as simply given, to a practical conclusion: a decision, an intention to act, or anyway a realization as to what that action should be. But to Murdoch's way of thinking, the hard part of practical reasoning is getting the description of your situation right in the first place. You have to come to see your circumstances the right way, or, equivalently, to apply the right set of specialized terms, or, perhaps again equivalently, to employ the right family of metaphors; once that is taken care of, it will be obvious what to do. You might take someone to be aloof and distant, and so be rather standoffish yourself; once you come to see his manner as shy, it will be natural to be much more open towards him. It is redescribing an employer as recklessly and criminally endangering its workers, neighbors, and clients that leads the whistleblower to step forward. It is opening up the question of whether someone is really your friend – whether he *could* really be your friend, given how he had been acting – that is the most important part of figuring out how to conduct one's future relations with him.[20]

Note that particularist defusing moves can normally be recast as Murdochian moves to improved descriptions, ones in which the defusing features play a pivotal role. That a company is your employer is a reason not to leak its confidential documents to the press, but when its employees are being pressed to become complicit in its misdeeds, that you are an employee becomes precisely a reason to leak.

The idea that the real problem is getting the problem description right is pertinent not just to practical reasoning, but to theoretical reasoning as well. When they are in school, the tricky part is getting the logic or physics students to convert the story problem to the right set of formulae, and after they graduate, the even trickier part is getting them to convert the situation they are facing into the right story problem.[21] Now when one starts to think about what it takes to get the representations right in a strictly theoretical or factual domain, it is natural to start with problems in which the goal is given, and to understand the correctness of the representation in terms of its usefulness in attaining the given goal. Murdoch's recognition that getting the problem description right is just as much a difficulty in the practical case as in the theoretical case should make us more cautious here: in real-world cases, setting the goal is *part* of figuring out the description of the practical problem, and it cannot be taken as simply given.

Murdoch's insight here does not so much entail as presuppose particularism.[22] Suppose that the defusing move did not generally work. Then it would be possible to accumulate a checklist of the features of situations that operate as reasons for action. (Perhaps the list would never be completed, but we could expect that after a while it would, barring one's encountering genuinely novel circumstances, attain stability enough.) You could then construct a description of your decision situation more or less mechanically, by proceeding down the checklist and incorporating the features on the list that turn up in the decision situation into your description. And so, after some initial startup period (and after some practice with a possibly longish list), the process of arriving at the right description of one's problem would *not* be the difficult part of deliberation at all, which is to say that Murdoch's shift of focus only makes sense if the particularists are right about what I have suggested is the most important element of their view.[23]

The view against which Murdoch is moving will seem to its proponents to be metaphysically motivated: the description of the decision situation is a description of the *facts*, and so getting it right is a job for theoretical rather than practical reasoning. But that motivation begs the question, and Cora Diamond has reconstructed Murdoch's response: that insisting on the distinction between fact and value has to be understood as itself the expression of a substantive (and mistaken) evaluative position.[24] Once one is looking for it, the response is hard to miss: Murdoch throws down the gauntlet very early on in *The Sovereignty of Good*, by listing among the facts to which her account will be responsible, "the fact that an unexamined life can be virtuous and the fact that love is a central concept in morals" (1–2/299).

The problem of getting the right description is to see things as they really are, but "truth," "reality," and their paronyms, are, in Murdoch's way of using them, not to be captured by the idea of *accuracy*, of people in lab coats checking that their measurements correspond to the dimensions of the objects on the workbench. Murdoch, best known as a novelist, thinks of truth by way of novelistic truthfulness: "Truth is not a simple or easy concept. Critical terminology imputes falsehood to an artist by using terms such as fantastic, sentimental, self-indulgent, banal, grotesque, tendentious, unclarified, wilfully obscure and so on."[25] Elsewhere she warns her readers of the "philosophical difficulties [that] may arise if we try to give any single organized background sense to the normative word 'reality.'"[26] When the point is to see your way through a *practical* problem – to take a very simple example, the problem subjects were given in Maier's memorable study – it may be accurate, but irrelevant, to view a pair of pliers as a gripping tool: to bring one of the hanging cords within reach of the other, you will have to make a pendulum out of it, and to do that you will have to see the pliers as a weight.[27]

Put this way, it is obvious that getting a description right is not normally a matter of getting the *metaphysically* right description. The metaphysical objections I gestured at earlier took it for granted that one description of a problem situation (the "factual") was privileged in a way that made further descriptions (the "evaluative") acceptable only if they stood in some specified relation (for example, reduction or supervenience) to the privileged ones. But as far as Murdoch is concerned, the privilege of the "factual" description would have to be the conclusion of a *practical* or *moral* – not metaphysical – train of thought.[28] While there might be special circumstances in which the morally or practically right thing to do would be to distinguish questions of fact from further practical questions, it is not at all obvious what the argument for always so doing would be.[29] The truism that you need to keep an open mind while looking for the description that will let you make headway on a practical problem has nothing to do with – and does not entail – theses regarding the "shapelessness" of the evaluative with respect to the descriptive.

The cases that are the most natural examples of Murdoch's treatment are typically a bit to one side of the contemporary particularist's favorite examples. Perhaps that it is plagiarism is a reason to send it on to the Honor Council. The particularist applying the defusing move looks for circumstances where its being plagiarism is precisely a reason not to pursue the matter, whereas the Murdochian looks for a way to dislodge the description. (When Borges imagines someone intentionally writing a novel that is word-for-word identical with *Don Quixote*, that is no longer plagiarism, the official definition notwithstanding; it is an instructive exercise to explain why.[30]) I think we should not be put off by the way the illustrations diverge; it suffices that applications of the defusing move can be redescribed as Murdochian redescription.

4

Murdoch has a number of claims to make about the process of improving one's description of one's circumstances, and I want to sketch some of these in a manner that shows their hospitality to particularism. I do not exactly want to argue for them, but, rather, to indicate how the different pieces of the view fall into place when one is looking at the other pieces.[31] (I do think that, even when motivated, a number of her claims are quite implausible, and I will register my dissent from time to time.) The next piece of the puzzle that I want to take up is her frequent suggestion that, with the right description in place, your practical reasoning is *done*: "true vision occasions right conduct" (66/353). You are to arm yourself with descriptions that in an actual choice situation will have direct practical import; in her characterization, "the agent...will be saying 'This is A B C D' (normative-descriptive words), and action will follow naturally."[32] While I am inclined to think that here she is overstating her point, we can say something about what would make such a claim seem attractive.

Of those situations in which one seems to have on hand a description that makes practical demands, but where one still does not know what to do, many are cases in which the relevant considerations conflict or compete. "Generalists" (a particularist label for their opponents) might approach such a problem by asking which consideration was most weighty (which had greater antecedent force), but a particularist should not expect that there is a procedure that will take as inputs the weights of the considerations and produce an answer as output. After all, the defusing move works on just about anything; so, sometimes, that a consideration is weighty speaks for it, but there will be other times – for example times that call for frivolity or superciliousness – when it speaks against.[33] So the evaluatively loaded descriptions of the situations will have to *themselves* fit together in a way that resolves the practical problem, without the intervention of a weighing mechanism. (Murdoch's example of this is the unity of the virtues: while it might *seem* that one needs to choose between doing the brave thing and doing the honest thing, perceptive redescription will conveniently show that only the honest thing *is* the brave thing, and so that the conflict is merely apparent.[34]) But if conflicts must be resolved by unifying redescription, then successful description will itself have to carry one on to the ensuing action. For when there is deliberative distance between a description and an ensuing action, there are always further and conflicting considerations to intervene.

The upshot for our purposes is that Murdoch's way of framing the defusing move avoids some of the formal excesses of antinomianism. First, if accepting a description D shows the action a to be appropriate, without further intervening deliberative steps, then we have a rule that takes one from D to a. And this will allow a particularist to sidestep the objection that we cannot make sense of reasons without allowing for their generality. For on the Murdochian picture, *whenever* D is the appropriate description, a properly follows. But (and this is why particularists can allow themselves that last claim) none of the work is being done by such rules, because one cannot determine whether D *is* the appropriate description of a given situation simply by ticking off the features mentioned in D.

Second, the Murdochian picture can allow substantive rules – for example, rules of grammar – to play a guiding rather than merely heuristic role, while nonetheless making room for the defusing move. When the appropriate description has it that this is an occasion to apply the rule (as when writing English prose is an occasion to apply the rules of English grammar), then the rule functions as my reason for writing it *this* way. But when the appropriate redescription highlights the idiomatic register in which I must write on this occasion, the rule now functions as a reason *not* to write it this way.

5

Murdoch commits herself to two further, related claims. One is that the process of substituting better descriptions never ends; there is always more work to be done on, as she says, coming closer to seeing things as they really are. Second, doing so is seeing them more and more idiosyncratically; progress in moral reasoning is progress away from the shared public world and into private vision and, eventually, mutual unintelligibility: "since we are human historical individuals the movement of understanding is onward into increasing privacy."[35] When one's descriptive apparatus moves further and further away from the shared common conceptual world, a successful deliberator will sooner or later reach the point where others simply cannot understand his reasons (or, what is the same thing, his characterizations of choice situations). That point can perhaps be postponed by making one's unprecedented descriptions available to others as best one can, by for instance embedding them in fiction that conveys their content and potential relevance, and perhaps this is one explanation for Murdoch's taking the art of the novel so seriously.[36] But it will sooner or later be reached and moved beyond, if the deliberative enterprise is on track. Now there are stronger and weaker ways of reading such a claim, but the fact that Murdoch spends much of her essay on "The Idea of Perfection" arguing against Wittgenstein's Private Language Argument is convincing evidence that (what I will call) the idiosyncracy claim is meant to bear a robust construction.[37]

Once again, we can motivate this part of her view by appealing to others. Allow that conflicting considerations are negotiated by redescription. There are always further potential conflicts on the horizon, and so there is always room for further redescription. We can think of the limit in which all the demands introduced by our conflicting "normative-descriptive" terms have been resolved, and all our evaluations unified, as our apprehending an infinitely thick or fractal concept, the Good, and so we might think of Murdoch's picture of the Good as a kind of Kantian regulative ideal.[38] Convincing unifying redescriptions of this kind tend to be ingenious, clever, and surprising; they turn on highlighting some feature of a situation that one had been overlooking, and showing how it tells when it is placed next to some other overlooked feature on the other side of the situation. (Murdoch insists that the Good is enormously hard to see, and the best reason in the vicinity for that claim is that the evaluative unifications are unobvious.) They are also path-dependent: what next description will be appropriate is partly a matter of the currently available descriptions that give rise to the conflict, and these in turn have resulted from descriptions one had been working with previously. The unobviousness of each move, together with path-dependence of this kind, will promote idiosyncrasy.

I am not entirely sure how Murdochian the connection I am drawing here is. Murdoch does sketch (but only sketch) an argument for the idiosyncrasy claim. When ideal or limit concepts are in play (as they typically are in the moral domain), application of the concept cannot be anchored to a public standard. This is partly because the uninstantiated ideal limit cannot be exhibited as a reference point, and this in turn is partly because of the ways in which application of these concepts is a function of one's personal history.[39] One's history is in part a history of one's redescriptive resolutions of conflicting considerations, and since the conceptual and more generally descriptive repertoire in terms of which one sees a new conflict is a function of that history, our gesture at an argument is at any rate compatible with what Murdoch says about her reasons for idiosyncrasy.

The claim that different persons will properly work with idiosyncratic descriptive tools that they do not share with others must be distinguished from the claim that occasions for practical deliberation will require one-use, throwaway concepts, that is, ways of seeing appropriate to a single occasion. To return to an example of which I have already made some use, at the early stages of mastering a language, the action-guiding descriptions can be shared as widely as you like, and they figure into rules to which the speaker or writer must conform (for example, the grammatical concept "split infinitive," which launches the rule "Don't split infinitives"). As one's command of the language grows, however, and one becomes a better and more autonomous prose stylist, the crisply formulable rules are no longer binding (a good stylist can decide when to split infinitives), the practical guidelines to which one responds are better thought of as embodied in descriptions rather than rules, and as a strong writer develops an ear for the language and his own writing voice, the descriptions that serve him in this capacity will be – while fully responsible to the demands of the language – peculiar to him alone. They will also be quite possibly intelligible to him alone: there are many Kantians, and many admirers of James Joyce, but no one who is able to write something that would pass as another book from the hand of either Kant or Joyce; this shows that would-be imitators do not have available the conceptual repertoires that guided the respective authors. Nonetheless, because a writer may choose to maintain a consistent voice, the descriptions he deploys for this purpose will for the most part lend themselves to repeated use.

Having made the distinction, a particularist may well wonder, first, why he should take Murdoch's idiosyncrasy claim on board, or even whether it is of a piece with the defusing move (rather than just an extraneous helping of relativism). Now I am not myself insisting on the idiosyncrasy claim; I have tried to motivate it, but I haven't produced anything like an argument that would make its conclusion impossible to evade, even if one already accepted much of the rest of Murdoch's views. Still, I think the idiosyncrasy claim is worth particularist attention, and let me try to say why.

The idiosyncrasy claim amounts to a view about what patterns are to be discerned in successful applications of the defusing move. (It probably presupposes the defusing move as well; if the defusing move did not work, then your reasons would be the reasons that are relevant elsewhere to others.) Idiosyncrasy has it that for different individuals with different deliberative histories, reasons will differ. Recall the complaint that particularist gestures at context function as conversation-stoppers. If that complaint is to be addressed, particularists need to be looking for patterns with roughly the level of traction that the idiosyncrasy claim purports to have. So what I am pressing is not the demand that particularists take the idiosyncrasy claim on board, but that they use it as a model for working up other, similarly shaped claims that they *are* willing to take on board.

6

When theoretical reasoning is faced with one or another conundrum, it may refrain from drawing a conclusion on the grounds that the evidence at hand is insufficient.[40] But when practical reasoning is faced with a decision, a decision must be made, because doing nothing, it is often remarked, is a decision too.[41] (At any rate, doing nothing is a choice in a far more robust sense than skeptical *epoche* is a belief.) This asymmetry between the practical and theoretical realms gets expressed in standard pictures of practical reasoning as the notion that, in any decision situation, practical reasoning correctly performed *must* be able to produce an answer to the question: what shall I do?

Murdoch disagrees. As in the theoretical domain, you may not have available premises sufficient for deriving an answer to your question. To be sure, you may (have to) decide to do one thing or another; but in such a case, you will not be doing it because you have decisive reasons. To conclude, from the fact that you must make a choice, that you have grounds adequate for making one choice in particular (or that it doesn't much matter which choice you make), is like concluding, from the fact that your plan absolutely *must* work, that it *will* work. That is, it is allowing emotional convenience to obscure the obvious, or, as Murdoch would put it, it is letting the self – the "fat relentless ego" (52/342) – get in the way of seeing what is really there. The state of being inadequately prepared for the decision one is facing has a phenomenological character, a sense of the choice being up to one's arbitrary will. Or rather, to put it the other way around, the freedom celebrated by moral philosophers of such diverse stripes as Hare and Sartre is merely what it is like to be put on the spot without the deliberative resources needed to make an intelligent choice.

Because Murdoch thinks that the most important part of the equipment one needs is a suitable description of – or way of seeing – one's situation, those resources include a descriptive apparatus that highlights its practically relevant aspects, and it includes the ability in practice to deploy that apparatus. (I mean that if you do not take, say, grasping the concept of a bicycle to include the ability to recognize passing bicycles, then you need not just the concept, but that ability too.) It should not be assumed that either the acquisition or the application of such a descriptive epithet is immediate.[42] For example, as philosophy teachers, we try to teach our students to have on hand – and to be able correctly to recognize occasions for – labels like: an evasive moment in an argument, or a vicious circularity, or an insufficiently motivated position. It may take years for a student to develop this kind of competence . . . and even once this happens, he may exhibit a peculiar blindness when it comes to recognizing occasions for their application in his own work.

Part of the reason that augmenting one's stock of, say, concepts is so time-consuming is the one that Murdoch emphasizes: it is often a process that requires getting past an emotional stake one has in seeing things some other way. Murdoch in fact holds that the main and perhaps the only real obstacle to deliberative progress is the pull of fantasy, that is, the self's desire to avert its gaze from what is "really there" in front of one. ("Consciousness is . . . normally . . . a cloud of more or less fantastic reverie designed to protect the psyche from pain" (79/364); the production of great art is a model for practical deliberation, because beauty distracts us from fantasy and allows us to see what is "really there.") I will later try to say what I think is right about this claim; but for now, Murdoch's manner of speaking notwithstanding, it is obvious enough that resistance is by no means the only reason augmenting and deploying one's descriptive repertoire takes time. Consider Douglas Coupland, a recent example of someone who made a career of finding names for very familiar, but until then unlabeled, bits of nineties experience.[43] His success would be inexplicable if anyone could just come up with apt descriptions at the drop of a hat. Coming by the terms needed for adequately describing our world is hard enough for finding *le mot juste* a handful of times to make a bestseller (or a single telling concept, an academic's career), and for inventing a word to occasionally be an important political achievement. It wouldn't be such a big deal if it were easy.

So if you are to face decisions in which you are equipped to act for your reasons, you must do your homework ahead of time; if you wait until it is time to choose before you start thinking about what to do, too much of the time it will be too late. But if Murdoch is right about the immense difficulty of progressing to a more adequate set of practically orienting descriptions, simply starting early is not going to be enough. We have just supplemented her reason for that claim, the inertia of a frame of mind that is emotionally easy on one, with the point that it's hard to think of specially apt concepts, and the more straightforward consideration of the two shows that, even with a good deal of lead time, you will have a scanty collection of practical guides if you have to fabricate all of them by yourself. You will do much, much better if you can help yourself to the products of others' labor – as in pretty much every other part of life. But for the concepts developed by others to be usable by you, they will have to be common rather than idiosyncratic concepts.

I think there is a real difficulty for the view here. It is first of all a practical rather than a theoretical difficulty, and it is a difficulty for particularism whether or not Murdoch's full theoretical frame is being taken on. On the one hand, the lead time required to develop the means of seeing one's situation properly means that one has to prepare for deliberation ahead of time. The optimal way to do that is to acquire generic, all-purpose deliberative resources from others (because the results of one's own endeavors will simply be too sparse to suffice). A particularist reading of the moral realm, however, is constructed around an awareness of the limitations of generic deliberative resources. If the particularist reading is right, then, much of the time we are bound to deliberate poorly.

The idiosyncrasy claim provides a further reason for thinking that the way one sees things must be enough to determine, all by itself, what one is to do. If further inference is required to arrive at decision, then one's description will only be useful if it deploys terms and concepts that engage one's other inferential resources; like apt descriptions, these are also hard to come by in a timely way on one's own, and so most of them are inevitably community property. For instance, the description of a potential business partner as dishonest and unreliable is useful because one has handy a tried and tested rule of thumb to the effect that one had better not enter into close working relationships with dishonest and unreliable people. But highly idiosyncratic descriptions will not interlock in this way with other inferential resources. In Murdoch's novel *The Italian Girl*, Edmund, its narrator and protagonist, describes a stage in arriving at a decision to offer Maggie, the Italian servant of the title, a ride to Italy, and himself in the bargain:

> I could not remember that I had looked at anyone in quite that way before: when one is all vision and the other face enters into one's own. I was aware too of a bodily feeling which was not exactly desire but was rather something to do with time, a sense of the present being infinitely large. (1967, p. 168)

It is a plausible illustration of what idiosyncrasy in perception is supposed to come to, and it is plausible that only such a form of words might capture the content of one's perception on some occasion. The problem is that one is unlikely to have available rules, or even rules of thumb, like: when one is aware of a bodily feeling that is not desire but rather to do with time, etc., offer her a ride to Italy. So applications of highly idiosyncratic concepts will only be useful if they can do their work on their own, without the contribution of other interlocking pieces of intellectual machinery.

But this is not a plausible position at which to have ended up. To point out that one has to have done one's homework if one is going to be sufficiently well prepared to think about one's situation is not to have shown that one must be so well prepared that one does not even have to think. Even if our aim is to reach a state in which the gap between seeing and acting has been eliminated, it ought to be acknowledged that the aim is rarely attained; most of the time, we are still going to have to think about what to do, and so the resources we lay by for a rainy day should prepare us to do our thinking, which is to say they should be sufficiently standardized to interlock with other concepts that we have.

7

Practical reasoning is reasoning directed toward deciding what to do, and accordingly there is a long line of schematizations of practical reasoning that designate as the final step a decision, or the forming of an intention, or even an action. That connection has recently been brought into the foreground by a perceptive group of moral philosophers who hope to read off the shape of practical deliberation from the shape of the actions that are its product.[44] Now when one sees practical reasoning in this way, it is natural to see episodes of practical reasoning as themselves actions: instances of the action-type "deciding what to do" that consequently conclude successfully in actual decision.[45] Murdoch's understanding of practical reasoning does not, however, share this area of common ground in the contemporary debate, and it is interesting to see how Murdoch provides us with resources we can use to criticize some of the most interesting recent work in moral philosophy.

Let us continue to identify practical reasoning as ultimately done with a view to action.[46] As Murdoch has noticed, however, most of it must be done far ahead of time, while it is too early to have any very definite circumstances for action in mind. It follows that episodes of practical reasoning often do not, even when they are properly executed, terminate in decisions or actions. Rather, when successful they eventuate in the production of cognitive resources: metaphors or concepts or ways of seeing situations that have practical force once they are brought to bear on appropriate situations.[47]

But it is also overstating matters to say that on Murdoch's view exercises in practical deliberation *terminate*; recall that she holds that there is always further room for improvement in one's practical vision. One may leave off working on some set of "normative-descriptive" epithets for a while, in the way that one might take a break from washing the dishes; but one is never *done* with them (or should never be done with them), just as in some households one is never done with the dishes. Even when an occasion for action that deploys the concepts comes and goes, that need not mean that one is done with the job; because the kind of practical resources one is developing may be useful later, there will often be a point to trying to see a past choice better than one had managed to at the time. (And of course there may be a moral or ethical point, even if there is no future-directed reason to keep improving the descriptive tool.)

This means that, while the point of this kind of deliberative activity may still be to advance the cause of well-chosen action, because there is no visible point of closure toward which it can be oriented, the kinds of control structures that govern actions will not be appropriate for regulating it. Vogler has emphasized that because actions come with a built-in end or termination point, to which the action's previous stages are means or steps, one can check the practical rationality of a step by checking to see whether it is a step toward the termination point. (So, for instance, if the termination point has already been reached when the step is taken, as when you have already found your keys, but keep on looking for them, then your further looking is not rational but compulsive.) Since there is no end of this kind in view in much Murdochian deliberation, the stages of deliberation cannot be referred to an end in this way to see if they are practically rational.[48]

Even if action does not terminate Murdochian deliberative activity, the question remains: when is your description good enough to act on? A particularist can and ought to resist giving a general and rule-like answer. (Compare: when is a painting good enough? A walk through your local museum will convince you that curatorial decisions are particularist; that it is by a minor artist of such and such a school is a reason not to hang it in one exhibit, and just as much of a reason to hang it in another.) Still, we might be worried about a looming regress. Whatever a particularist has to say about whether a given description is good enough to act on will presumably be itself a (second-order) description. But when will the second-order description be good enough to act on?

I earlier worried that the particularist gesture at the dependence of reasons on context had the effect of bringing discussion up short, and I have been trying to suggest that we will do better by reimporting Murdoch into that discussion. The hard part, once again, of figuring out what to do is supposed to be getting the description of your situation right; so what we need to think about next is how you ought to go about getting the right description. This might sound like a proposal for a manual that would instruct us in producing practically relevant portrayals of one's circumstances (think of something along the lines of the journalist's "Five W's," only more so). A particularist will not find such a project promising at first glance, and now that we have reopened the question of the kind of control structure the descriptive phase of practical deliberation has to have, it will seem even less promising at second glance. Manuals work best when they are explaining how to achieve some fairly definite end.

Murdoch has it, we saw, that the primary obstacle to seeing matters as they really are is being distracted by oneself: by the desire to be vindicated, by comforting fantasies, and the like. Her prescription is to redirect one's attention away from the self, and she holds that this can be done only incrementally, and that it will normally require external aids. (She recommends great art, nature, and, possibly, prayer.) This diagnosis, I argued, is difficult to accept as stated; the distractions of the self are some among many other obstacles, though I am willing to believe that in the moral domain they are especially important. But there is something that Murdoch is getting right about practical reasoning, and I would like to conclude by trying to say what that is.

Getting one's descriptions right – seeing things in the right way – is most importantly a matter of what one notices.[49] And so the task here really is that of directing or redirecting one's attention. Now while there is some degree to which one can force one's attention this way or that, and so to which attending or noticing can figure as stages in a plan, to a great extent attention resists voluntary direction. You can't keep your eyes from sliding off the pages of some books; you suddenly realize that, despite your firmest intentions, you cannot remember the last ten or so minutes of a talk that you are now willing to describe as tedious; you are unable not to notice an interlocutor's verbal tics. Attention follows responses like interest or curiosity, in something like the way that the growth of plants follows their responses to light.[50]

Let me press the analogy just a bit further. Plants solve practical problems, but they do not typically (there are occasional exceptions, as in the carnivorous plants) *act.* Agency involves a kind of coordination that requires centralized command, but plants produce outcomes (such as efficient configurations of leaves) without coordination of this kind.[51] (When one root encounters a concentration of nutrients, and so branches, there is no central nervous system deciding whether this root should branch, or some other.) And since actions require a high degree of coordination of this kind, plants do not produce actions. When a plant grows toward the light, there is very often no determinate end point against which the previous stages of growth can be positioned as steps in a plan. (Rather, the plant will continue growing as long as the light attracts it – sometimes to its detriment, as when a tree breaks under its own weight.[52]) Our practical vocabulary is specialized around agency, but we need to come to recognize this as a practical hinderance: not all practical problems are solved by *doing* something.

The thought that human beings engage in, or are the locus of, activity that is less than action is not unfamiliar. Our bodies grow, digest, and all the rest of it, and the notion of "subpersonal cognitive processes" has been fairly well assimilated into the current picture of human psychology. But we have not yet managed to reject a view, perhaps inherited from as far back as Aristotle, of where these processes fit into the organization of the person – a view that is more an expression of pre-Copernican evaluative bias than it is an honest description of what we are really like. On this view, some creatures have merely vegetative souls; these solve their practical problems through devices like phototropism. Creatures with animal souls – that is, creatures that solve their practical problems by acting on the basis of what they perceive – have, as it were, a vegetative substratum, but this is subservient to the governing animal organization of such a creature. Creatures with rational souls – human beings – have vegetative and animal substrata in turn, but these lower layers serve the higher rational organization, and in particular the animal (viz., perceptual and active) aspects of human activity are directed by the highest and autonomous layer, the person's rational agency.

What Murdoch has right is that, in human beings, agency and the actions it produces are themselves directed by processes that resemble, in the terms of the Aristotelian picture, activity of the vegetative part of the soul. The agential structure of persons is better thought of not as the governing top layer, but as one of the middle layers in a sandwich. This is why the stages of practical deliberation that Murdoch is focusing on do not look like actions oriented toward definite termination points.[53]

The aspects of rationality that we most value turn out to belong to what we have the unjustifiable habit of regarding as a "lower" part of the soul. That idea is likely to generate a certain amount of resistance. First, it will be objected, plants grow toward the light *blindly*; how can a process of that sort count as rational – and, particularists will add, how can we expect it to be more flexible than the rules they are rejecting? Second, the compelling force of rational inference is lacking: if it is all noticing and attention, the practical reasoning cannot lie in arriving at the description of one's problem, because there is – as Jonathan Dancy vividly put it to me – no *therefore* in mental movements of this kind.

But, on the first count, humans do differ from plants in that we can to some extent train the responses that guide our attention (and so our ability to notice what we need to). Taking the response of interest as representative, along with a nearby example, recall that what it is to become a philosopher is in part to acquire a sense of what is philosophically interesting; if things are going well, what one finds interesting will change not only as one comes to understand the field better, but as the field itself changes. It is their mutability, their ability to track or underwrite content-rich assessments such as "interesting," and the traction they allow for criticism that makes the responses that direct our attention less hidebound than the unvarying reasons that so frustrated particularists. So if the hardest part of thinking through our practical problems is arriving at the right way of seeing them, the next thing to think about is how to modify and adjust the responses that determine our attention, so that we will be able to notice what needs to be noticed. That is itself a practical problem, and if Murdoch is right, we will have to address it situation by situation, starting off by trying to describe what the impulses that direct our attention are responses to, and how well they are doing their job.

On the second count: Perhaps there are no rules that attention must follow, in the way that inferences can follow logical rules; but since a particularist should not allow that inferences are carried along by rules, that is no reason for agreeing that the "therefore" is missing. I don't have a satisfactory account of the force of a "therefore," and while sometimes that does not preclude arguing for its presence, I'm not going to attempt that here. Instead, by way of suggesting that we should be less certain about the alleged contrast than the objection has it, I want to point out that what looks like a symptom of this kind of compellingness is present. That one cannot believe at will is best explained by the fact that beliefs stand in inferential relations to other beliefs, and that we also cannot notice at will, and have a great deal of difficulty paying attention at will, may likewise be best accounted for by something of a piece with the force of (uncontroversially rational) inference.

8

I have been advancing a series of suggestions about how to proceed in the development of an area of moral theory. I pointed out that the sub-Aristotelian position is a poor fit for particularism, and that particularism needs a better theoretical home if it is not to function as a philosophical conversation-stopper. I introduced Murdoch's idea that the early-on descriptive phase of practical reasoning should be the focus of our attention, because that is where all the hard deliberative work has to get done. This does seem to me to be a promising way to think about the defusing move, which I suggested was the heart of particularism. However, I tried to show how pressure develops in Murdoch's view (and possibly more generally, in views of this kind) to connect description directly with action, at the expense of subsequent deliberation. I inspected Murdoch's notion that successfully executed redescription will tend to be idiosyncratic; while I am not entirely convinced, I think that particularists ought to be entertaining claims with roughly this look and feel. I have just been asking you to notice how Murdoch's understanding of practical reasoning is tied to a nonstandard picture of the place of agency in the person. And I hope that the way I have laid matters out makes the idea of pairing particularism with Murdoch's take on practical reasoning attractive. But argumentatively inclined readers may be thinking that we have had far too much in the way of suggestion, and not nearly enough in the way of argument. So this would be an appropriate place to remind them that, on the account of practical deliberation that we find in Murdoch, this is just what deliberation with a practical point is supposed to be like.

Notes

An earlier version of this paper was presented at the Virgil Aldrich Colloquium at the University of Utah; I'm grateful to panelist David Sussman for his reply, and to members of the audience for the discussion. The paper benefited as well from discussion with Lori Alward, Alice Crary, Gerald Dworkin, Amy Johnson, Tamar Laddy, Ram Neta, Michael Ranney, Connie Rosati, Matt Shockey, Ken Taylor, Lauren Tillinghast, and Candace Vogler, and from very helpful comments on its predecessors by Lanier Anderson, Chrisoula Andreou, Carla Bagnoli, Michael Bratman, Sarah Buss, Roger Crisp, Jonathan Dancy, Edwin Frank, Ulrike Heuer, Eric Hutton, Maria Merritt, Tamar Schapiro, Yonatan Shemmer, Gopal Sreenivasan, and Valerie Tiberius. Work on this essay was supported by fellowships from the National Endowment for the Humanities and the Center for Advanced Study in the Behavioral Sciences; I am grateful for financial support provided through the Center by the Andrew W. Mellon Foundation.

1. Dancy, 1993, pp. 55–119; Dancy, 1985; Little, 2000; Little, 2001b; McDowell, 1998, esp. ch. 3; McNaughton, 1989, esp. p. 62 and ch. 13; Norman, 1997, esp. pp. 122 ff. It's not clear that McDowell self-identifies with the movement, but the movement does seem to identify with him; I will return to the question of the fit between them.

2. See, for instance, Kolnai, 1970.

3. As it happens, there is a history of influence to be recovered: McDowell is (modulo the qualification mentioned in note 1) probably the most influential of the contemporary particularists; other particularists have been strongly influenced by him, and McDowell was himself influenced by Murdoch. Most particularists are either not aware of or do not devote much attention to the connection; it is indicative of how little that a recent anthology titled *Moral Particularism* contains only one reference to Murdoch, and that reference gets the title of her best-known philosophical publication wrong: Hooker and Little, 2000, p. 292n. For traces of the pattern of influence, see Dancy, 1993, pp. ix, xii; McDowell, 1998, ch. 3, notes 35–7; McNaughton, 1989, p. ix.

4. Of course, the idea itself has been around for a long time; decision theorists have taken it for granted since, anyway, the 1940s, and (as Michael Thompson has reminded me) G. E. M. Anscombe famously made a point of choosing examples of reasons for action that went against the moral grain. Note that the distinction I am invoking here is not to be confused with that between ethics and metaethics, which was quite popular for much of the twentieth century; if this latter distinction can be sustained, both substantive theories of practical reasoning (in particular, those that specify the forms that practical inference takes) and substantive moral theory will come down on the same side of it.

5. Dancy, 2000, p. 144, quoting from Thesiger, 1959; he produces the example in the course of a discussion of the Sure-Thing Principle, and does not seem to think of it as an illustration of the defusing move. Dancy, 1999, p. 144, acknowledges that particularism has had to get by without having a "canonical expression."

6. To be sure, not everyone agrees that the defusing move always works. For instance, Brad Hooker is willing to insist that pleasure, at any rate when it's not a sadist's pleasure, is always a "moral plus" (2000, p. 8), and David Bakhurst, even while agreeing that it is not always in the same way a reason for action, likewise holds that "suffering is enduringly significant... [and] not something that... [a morally sensitive] agent could leave out of a moral description" (2000, p. 173). A similarly hedged resistance can be found in Brännmark, 1999. But disagreement of this kind is, on the occasions I have run into it, premature. To continue with pleasure and suffering, variations on the camelback adventure will serve as defusing surrounds; or again, climbing a mountain might be motivated by the extreme limits to which one will be pushed, that is, by the pain and suffering it will involve. When people choose to undergo real suffering on their way to the next peak or oasis, the suffering may well *not* belong in a morally oriented description of the situation.

One line of resistance to particularism is to insist that the defusing move works for derivative or secondary considerations, but not for basic ones.

However, pleasure and pain are the standard and typical candidates for being context-resistant "basic" reasons; they don't fare well when examined, and there is this to be said for particularism: I've yet to see an alleged basic reason that does any better. There is an interesting and plausible objection in this vicinity to other standard ethical views: perhaps utility, or universalizability, will be the significant consideration in a given choice, but it would be hubris to be sure that utility, or universalizability, will always be the only relevant consideration. (See the opening paragraph of Gass, 1957, for a case in which the basic or primary considerations deployed by the standard moral theories seem weirdly inappropriate; I'm grateful to Hilary Putnam for bringing the piece to my attention.)

7. Dancy, 1993, p. 60; Hooker, 2000, p. 6.

8. Dancy, 1993, pp. 60–2; Dancy, 2000.

9. McNaughton and Rawling, 2000, p. 257 (the view they are describing here is not their own); McNaughton, 1989, p. 190; Little, 2000, p. 288; Little also adopts the generalization explanation of rules. The reminder view of rules can be found in Dancy, 1993, p. 67; he gives a related account of the moral uses of imagined situations at Dancy, 1985, 150–1. See also McDowell, 1998, pp. 57–8, on what he subsequently calls the "thesis of uncodifiability," and the quoted characterization of particularism at Dancy, 1985, p. 149.

10. Jackson, Pettit, and Smith, 2000, p. 99; compare Dancy, 1993, pp. 73–9.

11. For the objection, see Hooker, 2000, pp. 16ff.

12. Murdoch's *Sovereignty of Good* (1970) is perhaps the most widely available of her philosophical works, but *Existentialists and Mystics* (1998) stands a good chance of becoming the canonical collection of her nonfiction. (It is not to be treated as a critical edition; for instance, her important paper, "On Vision and Choice in Morality," has been abridged so as to remove its original concessions to Aristotelian Society format.) The essays in *Sovereignty* appear in *Existentialists* as well. Accordingly, for the remainder of this chapter, slashed cites in the text will give first the page in *Sovereignty*, followed by the page in *Existentialists*; unslashed cites give the page in *Existentialists*. This example is to be found at 89–90/373.

13. Compare McNaughton, 1989, p. 203, on rules of style.

14. For this last claim, see Raz, 2000, pp. 66–7.

15. Williams, 2001, p. 78.

16. For a particularist gesture at the sub-Aristotelian position, see Dancy's "account of the person on whom we can rely to make sound moral judgements" (1993, at p. 64). Perhaps compatibly, McNaughton, 1989, pp. 203–5, expresses his qualms about using the professional ethicist (who is to be distinguished from the *phronimos*) as a moral reference point.

17. The point is related to one made by Williams against Aristotelian alternatives to his "internalism" (1995). Because your differences from the *phronimos* can give you reasons for action, what the *phronimos* has reason to do may not be what you have reason to do: the virtuous person is temperate and so has no need to lock his liquor cabinet, but if you are an alcoholic, you may have all the reason in the world to lock it up and throw away the key. (Perhaps if we mute Aristotle's insistence that the *phronimos* have been well brought

up we can allow for one who remembers, for instance, an akratic past. But we obviously cannot have a *phronimos* who has lived through all the possible fallings-away from virtue.) The counterexamples exploit what Shope (1978) has labeled the "conditional fallacy."

We do have to allow that an Aristotelian virtuous man can make the best of some situations for which a virtuous man could not be responsible. (For example, a soldier ordered onto a battlefield by incompetent and vicious generals – a circumstance dramatized on film in *Gallipoli* [Weir, 1981].) That is still not the same as drawing on resources that require him to be less than virtuous himself.

18. Three remarks. First, the effect should be familiar from the identity crises suffered by senior-year applicants for fellowships abroad – the upshot of having worked up four or five rather different projects and accompanying interview personalities. Second, perhaps there are people one could legitimately call virtuous advisors, but these would be people who possessed the advising virtues, not people who were both virtuous and advisors. (See Geach, 1956.) And third, there is not much point in taking refuge in the insistence that the *phronimos* does everything right *by definition*, and so of course dispenses good advice. If we cannot make the *phronimos* intelligible to ourselves as a human personality, then the concept cannot play the role of ideal or model that Aristotelian theory assigns it.

19. Murdoch herself tended to think of the background to her ethical views as philosophy of mind or moral psychology; see 4/301–2.

20. These examples are due to Lori Alward and Amy Johnson.

21. Psychologists and cognitive scientists have found these issues of interest for much of the last century; see, e.g., Duncker, 1945, or, more recently, Chi, Feltovich, and Glaser, 1981.

22. She does explicitly endorse views of a piece with contemporary particularism at 85ff.

23. The checklist metaphor, differently deployed, crops up in discussions of particularism, including Dancy, 1985, p. 150, McNaughton, 1989, p. 62, and Little, 2000, p. 287.

24. Diamond, 1996.

25. Murdoch, 1992, p. 86.

26. 40/332; compare 37/329, 64/352.

27. Maier, 1931.

28. It is here that keeping track of particularism's historical debt to Murdoch could especially have prevented wasted motion. Jackson, Pettit, and Smith, for instance, begin their discussion of particularism by introducing "the distinction between, on the one hand, the descriptive, non-evaluative, factual, natural, etc. and, on the other, the evaluative, ethical, normative, moral etc." as a distinction without which the view they oppose cannot be so much as stated (2000, p. 81). But perhaps they would have been less confident on this point had they identified Murdoch as a member of the particularist tradition. Murdoch was, after all, thought of until recently by philosophers in the analytic tradition primarily as the source of the view that what are now called "thick ethical concepts" can be used as an objection to the

fact-value distinction. (The term was made familiar by Geertz, 1973, ch. 1, who in turn attributes it to Ryle; I'm grateful to Gopal Sreenivasan for helping me follow the citation trail. See Millgram, 1995, for the way in which Murdoch's ideas were adapted by writers such as McDowell, Putnam, and Williams.)

I don't, however, want to suggest that the analytic appropriation of Murdoch was faithful to her views. As she was appropriated, the objection was supposed to be that concepts such as "devious," "sleazy," "cute," and so on have both evaluative or prescriptive and factual or descriptive aspects, but that they cannot be factored into separate evaluative and descriptive components; the conclusion that was supposed to follow was that the fact-value distinction is impossible to sustain. But there is, as we might expect, no argument to that effect in Murdoch's own discussion; her claim is rather that it is *inadvisable* to sustain the distinction.

29. I'm grateful to Carla Bagnoli for discussion on this point. Murdoch herself seems to think that there might be arguments for sometimes but not always doing so; she describes the demand as part of "a Liberal ideal" (1992, p. 84).

There is a further way to see how the allegedly metaphysical distinction is beside the point. Return to the grammar example, and call *grammatical particularism* the thesis that the defusing move works *within* the grammar of a language. In a language of which grammatical particularism was true, that a noun was masculine, say, would be a reason for using the masculine article . . . except that there would be a not fully systematizable array of contexts in which it was a reason for using the feminine or neuter article. (If the defusing contexts are really unsystematizable, they cannot be judged grammatical or ungrammatical by appeal to a nontrivial rule, but we can suppose that native speakers classify them as acceptable and unacceptable.) We can imagine languages of which grammatical particularism is true; I sometimes suspect that it is almost true of French and English. It is evidently possible to modify arguments against particularism of the type advanced by Jackson, Pettit, and Smith, 2000, to conclude that grammatical particularism cannot be correct: that there must be codifiable rules that determine some patterns of the linguistic elements (such as words, phonemes, or letters) to be the grammatically correct constructions.

Now notice that when the metaphysical or metaethical contrast between "evaluative" and "descriptive" is drawn, the elements that the grammar governs – words, sentences, and even letters – are not so much as identifiable using only those features that those who draw the distinction could defend placing on its descriptive side. This strongly suggests that the concerns regarding particularism do not at bottom have anything to do with the contrast between evaluative and descriptive, and that arguments that so present them are their less than faithful expressions.

30. Borges, 1998.

31. Murdoch does not present anything like a standardly shaped argument for them herself. In Millgram, 1998, I outlined and assessed what I took to be Murdoch's strategy for supporting her theses, that of using her own novels as arguments for her view. I am now less certain that I correctly understood

her intentions. As we will see, on Murdoch's account, moral progress is a matter of gradually redirecting one's attention; this happens incrementally, and can be assisted, but not compelled, by providing better objects on which to fix one's attention. So we should not expect an *argument*, even a novelistic argument, that is intended to force an abrupt turn in one's moral life; at most we will be provided with, or reminded of, other things to think about, and terms to think about them in, and it is likely that this is the way she intends *Sovereignty* to operate.

32. 42/333; actually, she seems to be suggesting not just that one need not do further practical reasoning, but that one *cannot*. She writes: "One is often compelled almost automatically by what one *can* see" (37/329). She speaks repeatedly of "a world which is *compulsively* present to the will"; "we cannot suddenly alter what we can see and ergo what we desire and are compelled by" (39/330f); "man ... is a unified being who sees, and who desires in accordance with what he sees ..." (40/332) (her emphasis throughout).

33. Alternatively, one will not be in a position to say, before arriving at one's answer, what the weights are. Compare McNaughton, 1989, pp. 199–200.

34. 57–8/346–7; 95/378.

35. 29/322, and compare 33/326: "Reasons are not necessarily, and *qua* reasons, public." This may be Murdoch's view of specifically moral thought, rather than a rendering of practical deliberation more generally; certainly she allows that many concepts whose structure is simple and public – "red light" and "green light," for example – are fine as they are.

36. Compare: "in Shakespeare or in Dostoievsky charity wears a strange and unique face. We are not classifying, but experiencing something new, if we give it that name" (Murdoch, 1989, p. 145).

37. 11ff/307ff; I am not claiming that Murdoch has the (very controversial) Private Language Argument right, and so I don't need to take a stand myself on what the Argument is or how it works. What matters for the point at hand is its reception in the 1960s: Murdoch is arguing against the claim that the private is logically parasitic on the public, and so that thoughts whose contents are in principle incommunicable cannot be made sense of. This was understood at the time as a claim about the metaphysics of mind.

For obvious reasons, one should not expect convincing and worked-out examples of robustly idiosyncratic reasons (though I will present a surrogate for one below). Difficulties of this general flavor are typical of particularism; compare Lippert-Rasmussen's complaint that Dancy is not in a position to treat his imagined cases as arguments for his view (1999, p. 106n).

38. See 42/333. I don't see how a particularist could have a guarantee that such evaluatively unifying redescriptions will always be available; an argument to that effect would have to turn on some feature of situations that was guaranteed always to be present and always to be practically relevant, but the central motivating thought of particularism is that there can be no such feature. Murdoch seems to acknowledge this when she says that while "the search for unity is deeply natural ... [it] may be capable of producing nothing but a variety of illusions" (76/362).

39. 28 ff/321 ff, and especially the following remark: "...if M [a mother-in-law in a famous example] says D [her daughter-in-law] is 'common'...this use of it can only be fully understood if we know not only D but M" (33/325).

40. Of course, in-principle sufficiency is not all there is to it: the theoretical reasoner may fail to see *how* the evidence is sufficient. The science student may know full well that the questions in the problem set have solutions, but nonetheless refrain from turning answers in because he cannot tell what the supplied information is sufficient *for*.

41. A typical remark of this sort: "Even to omit to do anything positive, and to remain passive, is to adopt a policy; Oblomov had his own solution to the practical problems confronting him; his was one possible solution among others" (Hampshire, 1954, pp. 162–3).

42. Particularists sometimes use metaphors which suggest that perception, or a faculty resembling it, might bypass these difficulties. For instance, Dancy frequently talks about "shape," and it's easy to think that shape is something you can just see.

43. See especially his breakout novel, *Generation X* (1991), which has the dubious distinction of having become a culture icon almost entirely on the basis of its title and marginalia.

44. Vogler, 2002, argues for the primacy of instrumental reasoning on the grounds that actions are instrumentally structured. The product of successful practical reasoning is action, and consequently practical reasoning must trace the means-end outline of the action it is generating; other forms of practical rationality are optional, but this one is not. Vogler regards her view as descended from Anscombe and, indirectly, Aquinas. Schapiro, 2001, suggestively argues that actions are moves in a practice, and I take it that the suggestion is that practical reasoning will have to be something like reasoning about what move to make in a game (and so will accordingly conform to something like Kant's Categorical Imperative). Korsgaard, 1999, develops an argument for similarly Kantian conclusions turning on what it takes to attribute actions to agents.

45. Vogler, 2001a, p. 461.

46. The reader might reasonably wonder if Murdoch herself would concede that much; she makes much of the idea that moral progress is valuable even when it has no consequences for action at all. (Compare 3/301, 17/312, and her essay on "Vision and Choice in Morality," 76–98.) But since, as I have remarked, she does not distinguish her substantive moral theory from her account of practical reasoning, it is hard to know what aspect of her view to pin this idea to.

47. Vogler, 2000, points out that the development of such cognitive resources (her own example is writing a cookbook) cannot simply be assumed without further ado to be a stage in what I am inclined to think of as the normal and central case, practical reasoning interrupted or divvied up between persons. "Once the [cook]book is done," she reminds us, "it can be read for pure entertainment and the author need never again cook another French meal (this could be why he writes the book – in order to be done with French food forever)." But it is important that (to switch to an adjacent example)

when a manufacturer cans garbanzos, it is taking over a phase of my own food preparation, viz., saving me the trouble of boiling them myself; that is the point of providing the ready-made ingredient, even if the manufacturer does not know of me personally, or of my cooking plans, or even whether that particular can is slated to be used as food or an impromptu doorstop.

48. For a response, see Vogler, 2002, pp. 28–9, esp. n5.

49. For examples in a nonmoral subject area, see Duncker, 1945, esp. chs. 7–8.

50. That said, it's important not to overstate the point. Most of the jobs in our economy are tedious, but the people who hold those jobs have no alternative but to stay focused on them anyway, and they manage to do this to a greater or lesser degree. (I'm grateful to Tamar Laddy for pressing me on this point.) However, we may be on our way to a new reason for endorsing the view, often identified with the early Marx, that this is not the way we should want our economy to work.

51. An important account of agency as a response to the need for coordination is worked out in Korsgaard, 1996a, ch. 13.

52. Having said that, let me qualify it. A good deal of plant activity *is* characterized by the stepwise progress toward a termination point that is central to Vogler's account of action. Even when it is not governed by a central command center, we find a plant, say, first blooming, then bearing fruit, then shedding its leaves, and then hunkering down for the winter.

53. This idea is not unique to Murdoch – for instance, Bratman takes the disposition to reconsider one's plans on some occasions but not on others to be more or less of this type (1987). But the amount of emphasis Murdoch places on it is distinctive. For further discussion, see Millgram, 2004.

6

Was Hume a Humean?

When it comes to talking about practical reasoning, "Humean" is a synonym for "instrumentalist." That is, a "Humean" view of practical reasoning is one on which only means-end reasoning directed towards satisfying antecedently given desires counts as practical reasoning at all. Witness, for instance, Michael Smith's fairly recent paper, "The Humean Theory of Motivation," which advances just this view; Smith, who does not discuss Hume himself, simply takes it for granted that the label "Humean" fits.[1] It wasn't always this way: when Aurel Kolnai, some years back, wished to criticize instrumentalism, he described the view as Aristotle's, an attribution that would be unlikely now.[2]

Why care about a name? There are two reasons. First, if any theory of practical reasoning today deserves to be considered the received view, it is instrumentalism. Calling it Hume's not only gives it the cachet that comes of association with a distinguished member of the philosophical pantheon, but invokes in its favor the arguments – and the rhetoric – Hume produces in the *Treatise*. Arguments for instrumentalism are hard to come by, but the lack is perhaps less urgently felt than it might be because it is assumed that Hume's arguments are already on hand. Second, the label gets in the way of reading Hume, and so obscures our vision of a characteristically ingenious and subtle philosophical mind: if we know what Humeanism is, and we consequently think we know what Hume thought, we are much less likely to see, and learn from, what he actually did think.

I'm going to argue that linking Hume's name with instrumentalism is as inappropriate as linking Aristotle's: that, as a matter of textual point, the Hume of the *Treatise* is not an instrumentalist at all, and that the view of practical reasoning that he does have is incompatible with, and far more minimal than, instrumentalism. Then I will consider Hume's reasons for his view, and argue that they make sense when they are seen against the background of his semantic theory. And finally, I will try to say why it is that Hume has nonetheless been read as he has.

Nailing down Hume's views on practical reasoning is a fairly ambitious project, and if this chapter is to be kept within manageable bounds, we will need to restrict its scope. While I will discuss the body of argument preceding the famous "is-ought" paragraph in Chapter 7, I will not discuss the first Appendix to the second *Enquiry*; it deserves stand-alone treatment, since there is reason to believe that Hume changed his mind on some of these issues as he was finishing up the *Treatise*. That means that I will be focusing on the discussion surrounding Hume's well-known pronouncement that "reason is, and ought only to be the slave of the passions, and can never pretend to any other office than to serve and obey them."[3]

1

The instrumentalist appropriation of the battle cry, "Reason is the slave of the passions," identifies Humean passions with desires, as they are conceived by the contemporary philosophical community, and understands reason's slavery to consist in its being allocated the task of finding the means to satisfy them. But a second glance at the trope should make it less than obvious that this is what the passage means. The point of practical reasoning, on the instrumentalist model, is to generate subsidiary motivations – desires or intentions – for the means to satisfy one's initial desires. Practical reasoning of this kind has a critical and coercive function: as Kant was to later point out, he who wills the end *must* will the means. (While an instrumentalist believes that *only* means-end reasoning is practical reasoning, he *does* believe that means-end reasoning is practical reasoning, and so that one is committed to the conclusions of one's means-end reasonings.) In terms of the kind of image the passage is likely to evoke, the instrumentalist's passion is not a reclining pasha who sends reason scurrying off to bring back this or that object of desire; rather, reason returns with further passions, which the initial passions *must*, on pain of irrationality, adopt. (Actually bringing back the objects of desire is a job for the agent, not one of the agent's mental parts.) This is not at all the role of a slave, and what it has reason doing does not match what Hume says in the second half of his battle cry: that reason "can never pretend to any other office than to serve and obey them." The rhetorical device and the instrumentalist construal of the passage do not fit very well together, and this should be enough to keep us open-minded about the force of these lines.

If it is not obvious what the claim that reason is the slave of the passions means, how can we determine what it does mean? The claim is presented as the conclusion of two adjacent arguments. This means that the content of the claim that reason is the slave of the passions must be whatever the conclusion of those arguments turns out to be. (This application of the principle of charity is licensed by the fact that Hume, like most philosophers, takes valid argumentation very seriously.[4]) To find out what the claim comes to, then, we must reconstruct the arguments for it.

Fortunately, both arguments are quite straightforward. The first has the following skeleton:

1. "The understanding exerts itself after two different ways, as it judges from demonstration or probability..." (T 413:21–2). With only minimal anachronism, we can rephrase this as the claim that all reasoning is either mathematical reasoning, or empirical reasoning about matters of fact.[5]

2. "Abstract or demonstrative reasoning...never influences any of our actions..." (T 414:9–10). That is, mathematical reasoning on its own does not produce practical conclusions.

3. Empirical reasoning on its own (or supplemented with mathematical reasoning) does not produce practical conclusions (T 414:13–34).

4. Therefore, "reason alone can never produce any action, or give rise to volition" (T 414:35–6). That is, reasoning (or the understanding) does not produce practical conclusions.

The conclusion of the argument running from 413:21 to 414:36 is evidently not that all practical reasoning is instrumental, but that there is no such thing as practical reasoning at all.[6] The conclusion is explicitly stated, and, more importantly, if Hume's argument is to be valid, this is what the conclusion must be. So if "reason is the slave of the passions" is the conclusion of this argument, then this is what it must mean.

This conclusion is reinforced by Hume's second argument, which appears at T 415:20–33 (and is repeated at T 458:7–18). The argument runs:

1. "A passion is an original existence"(T 415:23); "original" is being contrasted with "representative," so what this means is that passions don't represent anything.

2. Since truth and falsity require representation (the agreement or "disagreement of ideas, consider'd as copies, with those objects, which they represent"; T 415:31–3), passions can't be true or false.
3. Reason concerns itself only with truth or falsity.
4. Therefore, a passion cannot be opposed (or, for that matter, endorsed[7]) by reason; practical states of mind cannot be produced by reasoning.

While the argument's structure is not as clearly highlighted as its predecessor's, it is evident that the argument has something very like the form just outlined; and if this is right, then its conclusion is tantamount to the claim that there is no such thing as practical reasoning, since if there were, reason would be able to endorse or oppose some motivational states. As before, if the argument is to be valid, its conclusion must amount to a denial of practical reasoning. And since both of the arguments for reason's slavery to the passions converge on this conclusion, this must be what "reason is the slave of the passions" means.

What this shows is that Hume is not an instrumentalist. An instrumentalist holds that there is one (but only one) kind of practical reasoning, viz., means-end reasoning. Hume holds the rather more minimalist view that there are *no* legitimate forms of practical reasoning: he is, to adapt a phrase of Christine Korsgaard's, a skeptic about practical reasoning. There are different ways to call someone a skeptic; this way has the skeptic about practical reasoning not merely doubting but denying that there is such a thing as practical reasoning, and, a fortiori, such a thing as instrumental practical reasoning. Korsgaard describes "a sort of being who could engage in causal reasoning and who could, therefore, engage in reasoning that would point out the means to her ends, but who was not motivated by it." On the view of the skeptic about practical reasoning, as I am proposing to use the term, this creature has got practical rationality *right*.[8] Hume differs from the instrumentalist in thinking that not even means-end reasoning is legitimate.

We can confirm this conclusion – and see a little more of what it comes to – by turning to the subsequent discussion in the *Treatise*. Hume acknowledges that we do sometimes describe passions as unreasonable; and he also acknowledges that passions often seem to be responsive to certain kinds of reasoning – in particular, reasoning about what is a means to what, which is perhaps why he has been so widely mistaken for an instrumentalist.[9] His explanation for these facts invokes the judgments that often accompany, or provoke, passions. These judgments can be true or false, they can be the conclusions of reasoning, and they can be criticized as irrational. And these judgments are causally effective in producing and removing passions:

> I may desire any fruit as of an excellent relish; but whenever you convince me of my mistake, my longing ceases. I may will the performance of certain actions as means of obtaining any desir'd good; but as my willing of these actions is only secondary, and founded on the supposition, that they are causes of the propos'd effect; as soon as I discover the falshood of that supposition, they must become indifferent to me. (T 416:36–417:8)

But these connections between reasoning and the passions are not enough to make the reasoning genuinely practical: Hume is careful to insist that not only must "a passion ... be accompany'd with some false judgment, in order to its being unreasonable": "even then 'tis not the passion, properly speaking, which is unreasonable, but the judgment" (T 416:25–8); or, as he puts it after his second pass over one of the arguments we have just reviewed, "these false judgments ... may be said to render [the associated passions] unreasonable, *in a figurative and improper way of speaking.*"[10]

Suppose, to adapt the example we just quoted, I desire a persimmon because I expect it to taste delicious. I, like most people, am built so that, when I realize that the persimmon will not taste as good as I had thought – perhaps it is still unripe, and will have the chalky taste characteristic of unripe persimmons – I stop wanting the fruit. Similarly, if, desiring a persimmon, I conclude that I can get one by making a trip to the corner produce market, I am likely to acquire a desire to drop by the produce market. And I am constructed so that when I discover that the produce market will be out of ripe persimmons after all, the desire to go there fades. Because my judgments as to the flavor of persimmons and ways of getting them can be rationally arrived at, and rationally criticized, my desires are sensitive to my reasoning. And, miraculous as it may seem that I am built this way, it is, from an evolutionary standpoint not available to Hume, not all that surprising: organisms that exhibit this kind of sensitivity are likely to do better than organisms that do not.

But this sensitivity is not itself an aspect of rationality, and failure of such sensitivity does not expose one to the criticism that one is being irrational. If I realize that the persimmon is unripe, and continue to desire to eat it, there is no mistake I am making. If, after I recall that the corner produce market has no ripe persimmons, I still want or intend to make a trip there, I am not being in any way irrational.[11] And, conversely, if I desire the persimmon, arrive at the conclusion that I can have one by retrieving it from the top of the refrigerator, but, even when there are no competing desires, do not come to desire or intend to fetch it, I am not being irrational in that case either. In the face of these considerations, I can shrug my shoulders, and point out that none of them amounts to a reason to do, or want to do, or not do, or not want to do, *anything* – since nothing could count as such a reason.

The attribution of instrumentalism to Hume is sometimes defended by appeal to Hume's statement that "reason alone" does not produce practical conclusions; the point of Hume's phrasing, on this account, is that instrumental reasoning requires desires. But this way of reading Hume is confused. On the instrumental model, desires are among the *premises* of practical reasoning, together with beliefs about what is a means to what. But if needing premises is enough to make it the case that "reason alone" is not doing the work, then nothing particular to practical reasoning can have been shown, since – with the possible exception of mathematical reasoning, which Hume may have thought did not need to be supplied with premises – *all* reasoning requires premises. What Hume is saying here is, rather, that once reasoning has arrived at the judgments that are its conclusions, those judgments must be supplemented with passions in order to "produce any action, or give rise to volition." And this interaction of judgment and passion does not count as reasoning.

So much for setting the record straight regarding Hume's alleged instrumentalism. Hume is a skeptic, not an instrumentalist: if nothing could count as a reason for action, then the considerations adduced as instrumental reasons cannot count as reasons for action either. Let us return for a moment to the figure of the slave: at their whim, the passions send reason searching for information about their objects and the ways of obtaining them. But that information, once obtained, exercises no coercive force whatsoever over the passions: the slave does not issue commands to its masters, or tell them what to do with the information it has gleaned. The passions will do whatever they like, and when they do, their slaves will not be the ones to call them to account.

2

Skepticism about practical reasoning is a counterintuitive position, and because one does not adopt counterintuitive views without reason, we can take it that Hume had what he took to be compelling reason to hold it. Since we know Hume to have been an intelligent and thoughtful philosopher, it is worth trying to figure out what his reasons might have been, if only in order to ask whether they are good enough for us to join him in his skepticism. Now since we have just seen his arguments for the view, we might think that his reasons must already be out on the table; another look at the arguments, however, will persuade us that they are not.

The arguments are valid: this was, after all, what made it so easy to determine what their shared conclusion was. But why did Hume believe their premises? I will not try to say whether or not the premises are true; what matters just now is that they are certainly question-begging. Consider the major premise of the first argument, that all reasoning is either mathematical or empirical. This is a terrible premise to use in an argument whose conclusion is that there is no such thing as practical reasoning: anyone who needed to be persuaded of the conclusion would be extremely unlikely to concede it. (After all, why isn't practical reasoning a third kind of reasoning?) The other argument seems little better, although the problem with it could be located in any of several places. Why should someone who is seriously entertaining the possibility of practical reasoning agree that "reason is the discovery of truth or falshood" (T 458:6), thereby excluding the process of correctly arriving at new desires and intentions? Or why should he agree that "a passion is an original existence" (T 415:23) – that is, not representing, and so not responsible to, further facts or states of affairs? Why can't mental states be both world-guided and action-guiding – as, indeed, actual emotions seem to be? Some explanation is required of Hume's willingness to accept these premises, despite their being close enough to his conclusion to deprive the arguments of most of the work they ought to be doing.

We can explain Hume's views on practical reasoning – and, along the way, some of his psychological views – using his semantic theories. Of immediate interest is the well-known fact that Hume took content-bearing mental entities to be very much like mental pictures.[12] Importantly, this isn't just naive or antiquated empirical psychology; it is, rather, an expression of the semantic view that content is carried by resemblance. A familiar way of explaining Hume's views is to invoke his psychology (the so-called theory of ideas). But a counterintuitive and apparently unmotivated philosophical view isn't explained by deriving it from a counterintuitive and apparently unmotivated psychological view. Hume's philosophical psychology and his views on practical reasoning should not be considered two distinct bodies of doctrine, one of which can be invoked to explain the other. (If anything, Hume can only find the psychology plausible if he finds the theory of practical reasoning embedded in it plausible.) They are two sides of the same coin, and must be explained – or go unexplained – together.

Semantic theories, which I am suggesting will do the explanatory job, have to account for, first, the contents of mental items, their being *about* things, and, second, the different roles mental items play in thought: what makes the content of an attitude (propositional or otherwise) the content it is, and what makes an attitude the particular attitude *it* is. So, contemporary philosophers might explain how items with semantic properties – for example, words or sentences – have contents using theories of reference together with recursive definitions of the contents of a complex item from the contents of its components. And they might distinguish between the attitudes held towards these contents – such as believing, wanting, or merely imagining – by appealing to, say, functional-role theories. Hume's semantic theories have to cover the same territory, just because this is the territory that *any* body of semantic theory has to cover. But Hume does not have the focus on language so characteristic of the philosophy of this century. (This means that in using the term "semantic," I am not assimilating Hume's views to theories of language. Hume differs from us most interestingly in that the objects of the attitudes are not propositions – that is, idealized sentences – but something very much like pictures, that is, not linguistic items at all.) And so his theories do the job rather differently than ours.

Hume takes the contents of mental items to be carried by resemblance, but not just resemblance to anything; like contemporary causal theories of reference, contents derive from preceding links in a causal chain leading back to an initial object. "Ideas," says Hume, "always represent the objects or impressions from which they are deriv'd."[13] Resemblance is the mechanism that transmits content from one link in the chain to the next. Let's call this the *causal resemblance theory* of mental content.

If the causal resemblance theory covers – to a first approximation – the territory covered by modern theories of mental content, what does Hume have to cover the area we leave to functional-role theories? It is clear that mental entities play different roles in thought (for example, imagining, believing, and wanting), and that Hume must somehow distinguish these roles from one another. A thought of a golden mountain may be merely a fancy I am toying with; it may be a belief that there is a golden mountain somewhere; or it may be a desire to come by a golden mountain.

As I remarked a moment ago, one upshot of the causal resemblance theory is that content-bearing mental entities are conceived of as something very like mental pictures. Now when pictorial resemblance constitutes representational content, the pictorial features of mental entities are fully determined by their contents. Consequently, those features cannot be varied to distinguish one role from another. If you were to take an idea representing, say, a landscape, and write "belief" on the upper part of it, you would get, not a representation of the landscape serving the function of a belief, but a representation of a different landscape (one with skywriting that says "belief"), whose mental role would have been no further determined.[14]

What further features of a mental picture can serve to distinguish mental roles? Hume's first proposed answer is *vivacity*: roughly, the brightness of the picture.[15] (A vivacious idea [bright picture] of a golden mountain is the belief in a golden mountain, whereas a less vivacious idea of the same thing is a fancy that does not amount to belief.[16]) Vivacity varies along a single dimension: the only way to vary the vivacity of a perception is by making it *more* or *less* vivacious, just as there is only one way pictures can become dimmer or brighter.

When you wou'd any way vary the idea of a particular object, you can only encrease or diminish its force and vivacity. If you make any other change on it, it represents a different object or impression. (T 96:13–16)

Now if vivacity is the *only* way to distinguish representational states, Hume will have to be careful not to squander his sole available resource. Hume needs to distinguish not only imagination from belief, but belief from hallucination or sensation, and these from memory, probabilistic belief, and so on. The way he does it is to assign bands on the vivacity spectrum to the different content-bearing mental states. In descending order of vivacity, these are: impressions, memories,[17] beliefs, judgments of probability,[18] poetical near-beliefs,[19] and imaginings.

However, simply because it varies along a single dimension, vivacity *alone* will not suffice to tell beliefs, desires, and imaginings apart. Believing must be more vivid than imagining; given this, where on the scale of vivacity can we locate desire? Desire is also, one would think, more vivid than mere imagining, which leaves us two choices: either desire is more vivid than belief, or it falls somewhere between imagining and belief. But it's implausible that desire is more vivid than belief, since you can't transform a belief into a desire by making it more vivid (say, by increasing the evidence for it).[20] Similarly, you can't transform a desire into a belief

```
        impressions
         memories
          beliefs
   probability judgments
   poetical near-beliefs
         imaginings
```

FIGURE 1. Vivacity or forcefulness distinguishes different types of representational mental states.

by making it less vivid. And the alternative, that desire is more vivid than imagining but less vivid than belief, is hardly better: making imagination vivid need not transform it into desire, making a desire more vivid does not transform it into a belief, and, finally, making a belief less vivid does not transform it into a desire – even if occasional cases of daydreaming or wishful thinking appear to fit some of these descriptions.[21]

Types of representational mental states are distinguishable only by vivacity, but vivacity can't be used to distinguish beliefs and imaginings from desires. There is only one way out: desires cannot be representational. There is another way to make this point. Think of whether a mental state is representational or not as a stable property: its *representationality*.[22] The problem, recall, was to distinguish types of mental states from each other; and it turned out that vivacity was not enough to do the job. Representationality is a further feature that can be used to distinguish types of mental states from each other; in Hume's scheme of things, passions are *identified as such* in part by being nonrepresentational.

Humean passions differ from the contemporary philosopher's notion of desire in being multitudinous and qualitatively varied. So Hume needs not only to be able to tell passions from beliefs; he must be able to tell passions from each other. But once passions are nonrepresentational, this is no longer a difficulty. The problem that vivacity was needed to solve was that of distinguishing *representational* mental states; Hume was forced into using vivacity because the pictorial features of a representational perception are all controlled by the content, leaving nothing left over to mark what *kind* of mental state it is. But once we turn to impressions of reflection, we are leaving representation behind. So Hume can distinguish one kind of nonrepresentational impression from another by its "peculiar" feeling, rather than by its vivacity.[23]

We are now in a position to explain why the premises of Hume's arguments seemed so natural to him. These premises have to be seen against the background of Hume's semantic theory – a theory in which, while writing the *Treatise*, Hume must have been entirely immersed.[24] The semantic theory makes more or less inevitable, in the manner just outlined, a philosophical psychology in which mental states either have contents or motivational force, but not both. (The view is a precursor of contemporary belief-desire psychology, but is more radical in that Humean passions cannot have the analog of the propositional objects allowed desires; the intentionality of the passions must be simulated by causally linking a passion with a content-bearing judgment.[25]) Once motivating mental states, or passions, are understood not to bear contents, that passions are not the objects of reason should cease to be surprising: reasoning manipulates only mental states with contents.

Let's return briefly to the premises of Hume's two arguments. Recall that the causal resemblance theory of mental content gives rise to a way of thinking on which mental contents are rather like mental pictures. What mental operations on such contents might count as forms of reasoning? Evidently, one can highlight structural features of one's mental pictures (that is, trace out what Hume calls "relations of ideas"), or one can investigate the ways in which one idea gives rise to another (here, only the patterns that track causal connections are candidates for the honorific term "reasoning"). So, against this background, the first premise of Hume's first argument is quite natural: reasoning will either regard "the abstract relations of ideas" (that is, be mathematical), or the relations of the objects that the ideas represent, and which are responsible for the ways in which the ideas succeed one another – that is, "those relations of objects, of which experience only gives us information" (T 413:23–4).

Hume's second argument falls into place against this background picture as well; in fact, it is almost a direct expression of it. We have explained why passions are "original existences," and it is now also clear why reasoning is responsible only to the agreement or "disagreement of ideas, consider'd as copies, with those objects, which they represent" (T 415:31–3): given what the contents of mental entities are like, on the background semantic theory, there is nothing else for reasoning to be responsible to.[26]

Let us quickly take stock of our location in the argument. Hume is not an instrumentalist but a skeptic about practical reasoning. And now that we are in a position to see what drives Hume's skepticism, it is clear that the very considerations that would require him to abandon all but instrumentalist reasons for action require him to abandon those reasons as well. Hume does not arrive at his skepticism on a case-by-case basis, rejecting one type of putative practical reasoning after another until none are left. The semantic theory that is the engine of his views is unable to distinguish between types of reason for action, and so when it is put into gear, it makes a clean sweep of all of them. The motivating states that are the only candidates for reasons for action turn out to have no contents. And content-free mental states cannot be reasons, instrumental or otherwise. Hume's skepticism about practical reasoning is by no means an independent dogma, but is generated by the semantic views that shape so many of the arguments in the *Treatise*.

That said, it needs to be qualified; I will do that by considering a pair of problems with the story I have just sketched. Practical reasoning is not possible, on Hume's view, because passions cannot be representative states. And we saw that this was inevitable because they could not be accommodated in the ladder of vivacity used to distinguish representational mental states from one another. But this might have been avoided by allowing different kinds of vivacity: one for motivation, one for belief, and so on. The first problem, then, is the objection that Hume in fact did allow for different kinds of vivacity.[27] Assuming this objection can be met, the second problem is that of explaining why Hume didn't help himself to different kinds of vivacity.

The objection that Hume actually did allow for different kinds of vivacity is supported by lists like "more vivid, lively, forcible, firm, steady conception of an object" (EHU 49); the objection has it that the point of such lists is not to compensate for linguistic imprecision but to express the disjunctive context-dependent character of the denoted quality. But there are, I think, passages that make it clear that the vocabulary is meant to express a single notion for which there is no good single term, rather than to list many notions: for example, "the same quality, call it *firmness, or solidity, or force, or vivacity.*"[28]

What is interesting is that Hume later recanted this position, acknowledging it to be an "error," albeit one "of less importance" than the incompatibility of his views on causation and personal identity. The relevant passage is to be found in the Appendix to the *Treatise*, where Hume is in the process of changing his mind about various things (T 636:25–31);[29] the passage it refers to shows that in the *Treatise* proper, "vivacity" is univocal (T 96:13–16; previously quoted). This is why Hume's arguments in the second *Enquiry* do not include successors to the arguments I have construed as depending on this view about vivacity.[30] Hume's change of mind on this topic goes some distance toward explaining the fifth argument in the first Appendix to the *Enquiry*, which has a distinctly instrumentalist cast:[31] perhaps, as the background semantic view became more flexible, Hume found himself able to admit instrumentalist patterns of practical reasoning into the fold.[32] That Hume abandoned the arguments surrounding the "slavery" passage upon abandoning this view about vivacity is strong circumstantial evidence in favor of an interpretation that takes this view of vivacity to be essential to those arguments.

Why did Hume take vivacity to be univocal and unidimensional when he was writing the *Treatise*? It is, of course, possible that the alternative simply hadn't occured to him, perhaps due to the controlling power of a metaphor or analogy: real pictures have only one kind of brightness. Still, why doesn't Hume appeal to the fact that different physical representations of the same object can have different looks and feels, in the way that oil paintings, drawings, and photographs *look* different, even when they have the same subject?

If Hume found the option unappealing, perhaps the reason is that the difference in look would have to *explain* why one perception was motivating and another was not. If the different looks were, say, the watercolor look and the oil-painting look, an image of a soufflé with the watercolor look would have to be mere imagining of or belief about a soufflé, while the oil-painting-like mental image would – just *in virtue* of its being an oil-like image – have to *motivate* me to go for the soufflé (regardless of what the soufflé was depicted as being like). And it is implausible that this kind of difference in look could explain motivation.[33]

3

I began by noting that "Humean" is often used as a synonym for "instrumentalist." But if Hume is a skeptic rather than an instrumentalist about practical reasoning, this usage calls for explanation. It is not as though the passages I have adduced have been other than in plain view, and it is too much to suppose that they have gone entirely unnoticed by Hume's readers. If they suffice to show Hume to have been a skeptic about practical reasoning, why has anyone ever thought otherwise? If Hume's skepticism is as obvious as I have made it out to be, why don't other readers read Hume the way I do? Some, of course, have and do. But an explanation is still needed for the majority who do not. By way of concluding, I will sketch two possible explanations, and draw a moral from each.

The first is that Hume's readers have not seen why Hume *had* to be a skeptic about practical reasoning. The considerations laid out in Section 2, which make Hume's skepticism inevitable, have been overlooked for two contrasting sets of reasons: they were, in Hume's day, too obvious, and, in our own, too obscure. They turn on a semantic theory that once receded into the background because it was taken for granted, and that now is so alien, and so thoroughly discredited, that when connections that rely on it are not explicitly drawn, they simply fail to be noticed. I have argued that Hume was committed to his view about practical reasoning by his semantic theories, which we no longer share; this means that Hume had grounds for taking his skepticism about practical reasoning seriously even if he found it to be counterintuitive. It also means that, while there is much to be learned from examining Hume's arguments, we should not, so long as we reject the semantic theory that is their starting point, expect to be able to appropriate those arguments ourselves. If I am right, instrumentalists err in invoking Hume's authority not just because they are mistaken in thinking that Hume shares their view, but in that they suppose that Hume's arguments, perhaps slightly modified, can be adapted to the uses of a contemporary philosopher. They cannot.

A second, and, I am inclined to think, more important explanation for the invisibility of Hume's skepticism is that Hume has not been read as a skeptic about practical reasoning because, even when the passages that support such a reading have been noticed, it has been thought uncharitable to construe Hume in this way.

There are two points to be made here, regarding method and content, respectively. First, the so-called principle of charity, when taken as the principle that interpretation should make its text out to be, as far as possible, correct, has its dangers. In particular, it prevents one from learning from those whose views are very different from one's own. The greater the difference between views, the more wrong-headed the contrasting view is likely to seem; and the more wrong-headed it seems, the less likely charitable interpreters will be to hear the "wrong-headed" view at all, as opposed to a reconstruction conforming to their own sense of what is plausible. But the greater the difference in views, the more interesting the contrasting view: we will learn more from listening to those who disagree with us than from those who repeat to us that of which we are already convinced. The principle of charity, understood as an injunction to maximize truth in interpretation (rather than, for instance, tightness of argument), tends to become a way of filtering out precisely those philosophical views that are most interesting and most important. The reception of Hume's skepticism regarding practical reasoning is a case in point,[34] and the problem does not just arise in reading Hume. It often seems that the more interesting the philosopher, the less commentators are willing to take him at his word. When this happens, nobody is doing anybody any favors, charitable intentions notwithstanding.

And – proceeding now to content – skepticism about practical reasoning *is* philosophically interesting and important. Skepticism should be a reference point in the discussion of practical reasoning: the always-present null hypothesis against which other accounts must vindicate themselves. It is not an artificial or uncompelling hypothesis. One is either extremely fortunate or unfortunately complacent if one has not had bleak mornings during which it seems suddenly clear that purported reasoning about action is nothing more than empty posturing, the attempt to proceed under the comforting but unsupportable notion that actions or decisions, or the mental activities leading up to them, might be right or wrong, because rational or irrational.

Notes

For comments on an earlier draft of this paper, I'm grateful to Don Garrett, Elizabeth Radcliffe, and Wayne Waxman. A version of this paper was read to the Hume Society in March 1994; my thanks to Justin Broackes for his response and to members of the audience for objections and discussion. An ancestor of parts of this paper benefited from comments from Alyssa Bernstein, Hilary Bok, Lindy Cassidy, Steve Engstrom, Don Garrett, Robert Nozick, Hilary Putnam, Tim Scanlon, and Candace Vogler.

1. Smith, 1987. This is not at all an isolated case. By way of further example, Lewis, 1988, begins by describing instrumentalism as a "Humean thesis about motivation."

2. Kolnai, 2001.

3. Hume, 1888/1978, 415:18–19. Subsequent references to Hume's *Treatise* will be to T, page number, and, where this is useful, line numbers; T 5:6–8 would refer to Hume, 1888/1978, page 5, lines 6–8. The *Enquiries* are cited respectively as EPM and EHU, with page and line numbers likewise from Hume, 1777/1978.

4. Hume's enthusiasm for tight argument may be even greater than the philosophical run of the mill: there's an almost erotic tone to his description, at T 30:10, of an argument as "very strong and beautiful"; and his subsequent tirade against philosophers who won't accept the force of a conclusive argument (T 31:27–36) is an indication of the weight Hume himself put on such arguments. I will return to the principle of charity in Section 3.

5. The element of anachronism has to do with the ways in which Hume's conception of mathematical reasoning differs from our own. As far as the argument at hand goes, it's worth noting that recasting the dichotomy as between deductive and inductive reasoning would not do; it should not be at all obvious that deductive reasoning cannot produce practical conclusions. It is also worth remarking that Hume's well-known arguments elsewhere about

the workings of reasoning about causation – the empirical reasoning he has foremost in mind here – complicate the contrast being drawn here: given Hume's views there, do we want to allow that causal inferences deserve the (for us) honorific title "reasoning"? I'll leave these qualms to one side for the present.

6. This is to understand practical reasoning as reasoning that terminates in a practical conclusion such as an intention. If one were to call "practical" reasoning lying in the causal history of an intention (or, alternatively, reasoning that makes a difference to what intentions are formed), then one would need to redescribe Hume's conclusion as the claim that reasoning, while perhaps practical, cannot terminate in a practical conclusion. (I'm grateful to Wayne Waxman and Justin Broackes for pressing me on this point.)

However, there are reasons not to use "practical" this way. First, it will not help defend the attribution of instrumentalism to Hume. An instrumentalist is someone who believes that all practical reasoning is means-end reasoning. On the alternative use of "practical" that we are now examining, the claim that Hume was an instrumentalist would amount to the claim that *only* reasoning about what is a means to what makes a difference to what intentions get formed, and what actions get performed: that only instrumental reasoning could have effects on our actions. But what has an effect on what Hume famously held to be a contingent matter; and he in fact argued that forms of reasoning other than instrumental reasoning create passions and cause actions. (See note 9.) So, on this use of the word "practical," Hume was not an instrumentalist either, since many kinds of reasoning other than means-end reasoning make a difference to action.

Second, we can now see that using "practical" this way is a waste of a good word: there is no point in drawing a distinction when nothing lies beyond the line being drawn. *Any* reasoning can causally influence subsequent action; so if reasoning is practical when it could lie in the causal history of a practical attitude such as an intention, then all reasoning is practical. Better to use the term to invoke the responsiveness to logical canons that distinguishes intelligent thought from free association: to show that reasoning is practical would then be to show that actions and motivating attitudes are governed by the same logical canons that control the sequences of thoughts that make up intelligent thinking; and *this*, I hold, is what Hume is concerned to contest.

7. Hume provides a quick argument, at T 414:35–415:13, to the effect that reason's inability to produce what we might call "positive" practical conclusions – for example, decisions to do something that one had not already been inclined to do – entails its inability to produce "negative" conclusions, that is, decisions *not* to do something one was already on one's way to doing. Although Hume does not say this, if the argument works, it works in the other direction as well – as, on my reading of Hume, it ought to. So I am going to shorten the exposition by describing Hume's conclusion as covering both "positive" and "negative" practical reasoning.

8. Korsgaard, 1996a, ch. 11. My use of the word "skeptic" is of course not continuous with Hume's, and it also diverges from that of Korsgaard, who presents an instrumentalist reading of Hume as the "classical formulation" of skepticism

about practical reasoning. My excuses for assuming the risks of confusion involved in shifting the use of the term are that this is the best term for the job, and that this is the cleanest way to cut up the territory. Note that, on my use of the term, and on the reading of Hume for which I am arguing, Korsgaard comes out right: the passages in question *are* the classical formulation of skepticism about practical reasoning after all.

9. There are, in fact, other types of reasoning to which Hume takes the passions to be responsive. Some are obliquely related to instrumental reasoning. For instance, "we are no sooner acquainted with the impossibility of satisfying any desire, than the desire itself vanishes" (T xviii:5–6). Or again, instrumental reasoning can seem to work in reverse, as when our hunger is diminished by "whatever inclines us to set our victuals at a distance" (T 394:29–395:6; cf. T 536:3–4). But not all responsiveness of passion to reasoning is a response to reasoning about what would bring about what; the most prominent case of this is sympathy, in which the inferred belief as to another's feelings gives rise to qualitatively similar feelings.

10. T 459:26–9, my emphasis; nearby, he describes this attribution of the properties of a judgment to the action with which it is associated as "an abusive way of speaking, which philosophy will scarce allow of" (T 459:6–7).

11. Which Hume actually thinks is not unlikely to happen, if I am already on my way (T 451:16–19; cf. also 452:5–11). This should count as a qualification to the just-quoted "as soon as I discover the falshood of that supposition, they must become indifferent to me"; they – the actions I had supposed would attain my goal – may well not.

12. Of course, this description needs to be complicated, for instance, to accommodate the variety of sensory modalities; for our purposes, these complications will not matter. The picture in the head metaphor, however, is not just an expository convenience; while Hume doesn't rely on it explicitly, it does seem to shape his thinking. Cf., e.g., T 20:11, where he describes an (abstract) idea as an "image in the mind."

13. T 37:29–31; also see, e.g., T 157:30–1, 161:9–10, 233:1–3; at T 163:14 he describes the claim as "our fundamental principle."

14. Cf. T 94:32–95:3.

15. See, for example, T 96, EHU 47ff; 58:31–4.

16. See, again for example, T 116:25–7; 119:34–120:1; 120:16–20.

17. T 85:15–18; 86:1–9; 8:26–9:11; 371n.

18. T 129–31. Cf. T 143:9–12, where Hume describes "the shading of those colors, under which [an impression] appears to the memory or senses"; the problem is that remoteness imitates the effect of probabilistic judgment. For our purposes, the passage is useful in that it shows that probabilistic judgment is a matter of "the shading of those colors." (It is also a nice illustration of the way in which Hume thought in terms of mental pictures.)

19. T 123:30–2; 630:24–7.

20. There is, according to Hume, an interesting class of exceptions: beliefs about desires or passions, which figure most prominently in Hume's discussion of sympathy. Hume's account of sympathy deserves more extended treatment than I can give it here; for now, it suffices that, if only because not all beliefs

are beliefs about passions or desires, the special case does not solve the general problem of distinguishing belief from desire.

21. For simplicity of presentation, I am ignoring the further just-mentioned uses to which vivacity is put. The reader may experiment with fitting desire between adjacent bands of the full spectrum to verify that these further uses do not affect the present point.

22. This stability might be contested: surely modifying the functional role can make a representational state nonrepresentational. (Candace Vogler has instanced a seventies artist who blew photographs up into nonrepresentational abstracts.) But that is to allow representation to be determined by functional role, rather than by causation and resemblance alone. The appeal to functional role may be the right appeal to make, but it is not in Hume's bag of tricks; if it were, and were thought through with Hume's accustomed rigor, the qualitative resemblance of ideas to impressions would have quickly proved to be a superfluous part of the account.

23. T 472; compare also T 617:28–30, where Hume concedes that this way of doing things is not all that illuminating: "there is something very inexplicable in this variation in our feelings."

24. This isn't the place to amass evidence for this claim; suffice it for now that the *Treatise* begins with an exposition of the basis of the theory, and the semantic theory is appealed to in the course of argument after argument.

25. By contrast with belief, "*will* and *desire* are annex'd to particular conceptions of good and pleasure" (T 625:3–9). For an example of how propositional objects are simulated, see T 278, where Hume describes the "object of [the] passions of [pride and humility]" as "that to which they direct their view, when excited"; "that passion, when excited, *turns our view* to another idea" (my emphasis). The objects of the passions are a contingent matter, "determin'd by an original and natural instinct, and . . . from the primary constitution of the mind" (T 286:5–7; compare EPM 213n). Cf. also T 287:9–11, 15–17 (note the use of the word "produce"); T 367–8 (contingency of the objects of love and hatred), and T 399 (definition of the will as an internal impression, picked out not by its logically necessary object but by the circumstances in which it normally arises).

26. Annette Baier has dismissed this argument as a "very silly paragraph," "deplorably" inserted into the *Treatise* (1991, p. 160). Baier's grounds are, first, that Hume elsewhere extensively discusses the passions, in a way that seems to allow them intentional objects; second, that the *Enquiry* does not repeat this argument; and third, Hume's insistence that the passions are causally influenced by beliefs arrived at by reasoning. On the first point, Baier is right that Hume is quite sensitive to the way emotions work, but mistaken to think that Hume regards what we would think of as their intentional objects as a logical component of the passions, or as individuating them. (See note 25 for examples of causal locutions used where the modern reader would expect logical or constitutive ones.) I will in a moment present a better explanation for the argument's absence in the second *Enquiry*, and for now note that the suggestion that the argument is a momentary oversight conflicts both with Hume's willingness to repeat it, more or less verbatim, some 43 pages

later, and with the convergence of its conclusion with that of the argument on the immediately preceding pages. Finally, the appearance of reasoning in the causal history of a passion is irrelevant to whether the passions fall under the aegis of reason; on this point, see note 6, above. Baier seems to take Hume's insistence on the nearly ubiquitous causal role of beliefs in the formation of impressions of reflection as the view that passions "incorporate the influence of reason . . . [and] presuppose beliefs" (159); but the argument we are considering gives us every reason to think that Hume did not make the mistake of confusing causal with logical influence. For discussion of Baier's views, see Cohon, 1994.

27. The objections considered in the remainder of this section are due to Steve Engstrom; I'm grateful to him for his thoughtful comments.

28. T 106:9–10; cf. also T 628:28–629:14; EHU 48–9.

29. Actually, what Hume says is not that vivacity can be multidimensional, but that there are differences in feeling over and above differences in vivacity that can be varied without changing the content of an idea. For our purposes, the distinction between these is terminological only: the question of interest is, is there more than one parameter that can be varied to distinguish ideas with the same content?

30. They do include recast descendants of some of the arguments preceding the famous "is-ought" passage.

It might be suggested that there is a simpler explanation for the omission of these arguments from the *Enquiry*: in hopes of popularizing his views, Hume left out the counterintuitive and hard to assimilate material. But even if this is a correct account of what went into the second *Enquiry* proper, it quite evidently does not apply to its first appendix, which contains arguments as difficult to swallow, and whose conclusions are entirely as radical, as anything in the *Treatise*.

31. As does EPM 277:2–6.

32. This is not, of course, anything like a sufficient account. For one thing, it fails to explain how the fifth argument can be compatible with the first four. In any case, reconstructing the arguments of the second *Enquiry* is a project that would require a paper to itself.

33. But how can vivacity do any more explanatory work than looking like an oil painting? Vivacity is not meant to be quite the brightness of a picture (which would, after all, amount to a picture of a bright object), but the forcefulness with which the picture strikes you. And there, Hume thinks, explanation may be allowed to stop: "it will not be very necessary to employ many words in explaining this distinction. Every one of himself will readily perceive the difference between feeling and thinking" (T 1:14–2:2). It is interesting, however, that this forcefulness is inseparable from the picture with its particular contents – plausible for the brightness of a picture, but also for the forcefulness of belief: you can't have the forcefulness without an object. By contrast, we are all familiar with desire without an object: that yearning without a name ("I want *something*, I just can't figure out what") that often expresses itself as unfocused restlessness, or repeated searching through the kitchen cupboards. So construing belief as inseparable vivacity

and desire as separable passion is faithful to experience, as Hume claims it is (T 625:26–626:17).

34. So too, I think, is the insufficient attention accorded Hume's sentimentalist account of morality. Hume's remarkable achievement, the reconstruction of our moral lives using the apparatus of feeling rather than practical reasoning, can only be fully appreciated when it is seen against the background of the skepticism that made practical reasoning unavailable, and the restriction to sentiment necessary.

7

Hume on "Is" and "Ought"

The claim that "'is' does not entail 'ought'" is so closely associated with Hume that it has been called "Hume's Law."[1] The interpretation of the passage in Hume's *Treatise of Human Nature* that is the *locus classicus* of the claim is controversial. But the passage is preceded by three main bodies of argument, and, on the working assumption that the passage in question is closely connected to the argumentation that leads up to it, I will here examine the third of these, running from T 463:7 to 469:18.[2]

While interpretations have differed from one another, they have agreed in attributing to Hume uncharacteristically weak arguments.[3] I propose to show that Hume's arguments are both stronger and more interesting than has been allowed. But – I will argue – they exploit and consequently depend upon a semantic theory that contemporary philosophers are no longer able to accept.

Hume must be assigned a good deal of the responsibility for making "'is' does not entail 'ought'" part of philosophers' (and not just philosophers') commonsense. If I am right both about Hume's influence and about the presuppositions of his arguments, then the interest of these conclusions is not merely historical. Today Hume's Law is a philosophical near-truism, and the burden of proof is taken to rest squarely on the shoulders of its opponents. But if Hume's Law is inherited from Hume, and was originally accepted on the basis of arguments that we can no longer find acceptable, this may require a reassessment of just where the burden of proof may be presumed to lie.

1

It will be helpful to have a rough outline of Hume's semantic theory in front of us, and I will accordingly begin by summarizing it and indicating some of its consequences. If mental items (perceptions, in Hume's terminology) have contents, these must come from somewhere. Hume looks for their source and finds it in a surprisingly familiar place: to determine the content of a mental item, follow the causal chain it terminates back to its origin.[4] An idea derives its content from the idea(s) or impression(s) that caused it, and impressions derive their contents (when they have any) from whatever caused them. Thus my idea of golden mountains is about golden mountains in virtue of being derived from ideas of gold and of mountains; and these are about gold and mountains because (let us suppose) at some time or other I have had impressions of gold and of mountains from which these ideas are derived. To be sure, causation itself is not enough: my mental entities are not about *all* the things that caused them. In modern theories, this difficulty is usually met by incantations of the phrase, "causal chain *of the appropriate type*"; Hume's way of addressing this problem – determining that resemblance must be added to causation to transfer content – has, at any rate, the merit of being more substantial than contemporary alternatives.[5] We can label this part of his view the *causal resemblance theory* of mental content.[6]

At least part of the account I have just given should be familiar under the name "the theory of ideas." My description is intended to bring into focus the following point. The "theory of ideas" is usually thought of as a doctrine in what we would today call philosophy of mind; and so the temptation is to blame aspects of Hume's views that are derived from it on an outmoded empirical psychology. But Hume's philosophical psychology is, like our own, hardly empirical at all. He does not discover what the contents of the mind are by, say, cutting open heads and looking. Rather, like contemporary philosophers of mind, he derives his theory of the mind from his theory of representation; just as contemporary philosophers, who take content to be borne by propositions, find the mind to be stocked with propositional attitudes, so Hume, who takes content to be borne by resemblance, finds the mind stocked with impressions and ideas. The *explanatory* account is semantic, not psychological: it is a view about how, and under what conditions, representation is possible.

The causal resemblance theory of content has two important consequences, corresponding, more or less, to the two conditions it imposes on representation. First, because we may not have examined the resemblance-preserving chain that is responsible for an idea having the content it does, we may be in error as to what the contents of our ideas are. (Hume accordingly devotes much of the *Treatise* to establishing what the contents of our ideas are in philosophically important cases.) An idea can be simple or complex. If complex, its content is determined by the way its structure relates simple ideas. If an idea is simple, its content is determined by the impressions and objects it derives from and resembles. It follows that one can establish the content of an idea by analyzing its structure, if it is complex, and by tracing the relevant chains of resemblance-preserving causation back to their origins. In doing so, one can discover what it really was that one was thinking about when one entertained and used an idea – a surprising claim, since it might turn out that what one was *actually* thinking about was not at all what one *took oneself* to be thinking about.[7] In the next section I will examine two instances of this use of the causal resemblance theory.

A second consequence of the theory is to be found in Hume's understanding of mathematical reasoning, that is, deduction or demonstration.[8] Hume's theory of content is, indirectly, a theory of what contents of thought are possible: if content is borne by resemblance, thoughts can have only those contents for which resemblance can be responsible. Contents must be, roughly, *pictures* of what they represent. ("Roughly," because we have other modalities of perception than the visual; we hear, taste, smell, and feel. So not all ideas are literally pictorial.) Because thought is the mental manipulation of contents, Hume's understanding of thinking in general, and deductive thinking in particular, is shaped and constrained by his pictorial theory of content, just as ours is presumably shaped and constrained by our propositional theory of content. That is, since in Hume's view all reasoning consists in the manipulation of ideas, which Hume tends to think of as something like mental pictures, deductive reasoning must be reconstructed as the manipulation of (roughly) mental pictures.[9] The general shape of Hume's pictorial view of deductive arguments is nicely rendered by Harrison:[10]

two and two are four – an *a priori* necessary truth, discoverable by reason – can be known to be true by comparing our idea of, say, two spots and another idea of two spots, and seeing that they must be equal in number to our idea of four spots.[11]

We should bear in mind that in Hume's day the foremost deductive science was geometry, in which the reasoning was explicitly pictorial.[12] And, of course, the deductive techniques codified by Frege were not available to show how propositionally oriented forms of deduction could be powerful tools of inference – something the syllogistic was most definitely not. So Hume's thinking of deduction as something done with pictures was not nearly as far-fetched as it would be today. In Sections 3 and 4 we will see how Hume's discussion of the view that morality might be a demonstrative science is controlled by his pictorial understanding of deductive argument.

2

The stated aim of the stretch of argument we are examining is to show that beliefs about what ought and ought not to be done – about "the boundaries of right and wrong" – cannot be arrived at by reasoning. Later I will say a little about the role of this claim in Hume's larger argument. For now, we need only note that the considerations Hume allows himself in these arguments are not morality-specific, and so do not apply only to beliefs containing a "moral ought." (I will call the beliefs with which Hume is concerned "deontic beliefs"; I mean the term to cover beliefs naturally expressed using a "should" or an "ought" whether or not they contain a "moral ought.")

The argumentation is organized by a familiar dilemma:[13]

> If the thought and understanding were alone capable of fixing the boundaries of right and wrong, the character of virtuous and vicious either must lie in some relations of objects, or must be a matter of fact, which is discovered by our reasoning. (T 463)

The two tines of Hume's standard fork are subsidiary arguments to the effect that moral beliefs (or, more generally, deontic beliefs, that is, judgments of what ought to be done) cannot be the conclusions of deductive reasoning (reasoning about relations of objects), and that they cannot be the conclusions of what we can call empirical or experimental reasoning (reasoning about matters of fact). I will treat the second tine first; it runs as follows:

> Take any action allow'd to be vicious: Wilful murder, for instance. Examine it in all lights, and see if you can find that matter of fact, or real existence, which you call *vice*. In which-ever way you take it, you find only certain passions, motives, volitions and thoughts. There is no other matter of fact in the case. The vice entirely escapes you, as long as you consider the object. You can never find it, till you turn your reflexion into your own breast. (T 468–9)

Now on a first reading, this argument should seem to beg the question. Why not say that you *do* perceive the vice?[14] It seems unlikely that opponents will agree that they do *not* perceive it in the imagined situation. To see why Hume thinks that this claim is legitimate we must bring to bear his semantic theory. If I judge some state of affairs to be virtuous or vicious, I must have an idea of vice or virtue. What is the content of this idea? Hume's way of addressing this question is to invoke what I am calling the causal resemblance theory of mental content.

There are similar applications of this technique elsewhere in the *Treatise*, and it will be useful to first consider one of these: Hume's treatment of necessity is suitably explicit. He asks:

> *What is our idea of necessity, when we say that two objects are necessarily connected together.* (T 155, Hume's emphasis)

We make judgments to the effect that two objects are, or are not, necessarily connected. What is the content of the idea of necessary connection? Hume turns to the causal chain of ideas and impressions from which the idea in question is derived:

> Upon this head I repeat what I have often had occasion to observe, that as we have no idea, that is not deriv'd from an impression, we must find some impression, that gives rise to this idea of necessity, if we assert we have really such an idea. (T 155)

Hume considers the two objects that we might have thought were the other end of the causal chain, and concludes that the impression of necessary connection is not derived from them. One reason for this may be a picture of the physical mechanisms that mediate sensation and the information they are able to convey; light carries information about the colors and (perhaps) the spatial dispositions of objects, but not about necessitation.[15] Hume also has a further argument. The derivation must not be merely causal: the derived idea or impression must *resemble* its cause. So we need to examine the putative cause to see whether we can find an aspect of it that resembles the idea under consideration. Hume says:

> I turn my eye to two objects suppos'd to be plac'd in that relation; and examine them in all the situations, of which they are susceptible.

He immediately discovers the spatial relation of contiguity and the temporal relation of succession, both of which have their correlates in his ideas; but no feature resembling the full force of necessary connection is apparent in the objects, since a similar-*looking* pair of objects could prove to be only coincidentally connected.[16] So the objects cannot be the source of the *entire* content of the idea.

The content of the idea of necessary connection must derive from something in the circumstances in which the judgment of necessary connection is made: if not from an external impression, then from an internal one.[17] Examining the surrounding circumstances reveals that the repeated observation found to give rise to such judgments

produces a new impression, and by that means the idea, which I at present examine. For after a frequent repetition, I find, that upon the appearance of one of the objects, the mind is *determin'd* by custom to consider its usual attendant, and to consider it in a stronger light upon account of its relation to the first object. 'Tis this impression, then, or *determination*, which affords me the idea of necessity. (T 155f)

Tho' the several resembling instances, which give rise to the idea of power, have no influence on each other, and can never produce any new quality *in the object*, which can be the model of that idea, yet the *observation* of this resemblance produces a new impression *in the mind*, which is its real model.[18]

Notice the role played by resemblance in this account – over and above that of the resemblance between instances of causally interacting objects. While the mental impression from which our ideas of causation are derived is itself caused by the objects we naively take the idea to be about, semantic content is only transferred between resembling links of the causal chain. The impression of determination does not resemble the external objects, so, even though it is caused by them, it does not derive its content from them; consequently, the impression of determination terminates the semantic chain. In short, applying Hume's semantic views shows the content of our idea of necessity to be (in part) derived from an impression of reflection rather than the "necessarily connected" objects themselves. It follows from this that necessary connection is not any matter of fact *about the objects*, and so that empirical reasoning about the objects will not establish their necessary connection.

The reasoning is similar, albeit more terse, in Hume's discussion of the case of willful murder. We make moral judgments, such as those regarding virtue and vice.[19] What are the contents of the ideas involved in those judgments? The content of an idea (of, say, vice) must be derived, directly or indirectly, from some impression. Can this content be derived from impressions of vicious events? On considering a vicious event (willful murder), Hume decides that it cannot. As in the argument about necessary connection, Hume's view is probably shaped in part by a conception of the mechanisms involved in sensation: sound and light convey information about, for example, color, but not, at any rate in the same way, about vice.[20] More importantly, a derived idea must resemble its cause. What, in the murder, resembles the *idea* of vice, with its felt repugnance, motivating power, and disapproval? Quite evidently, nothing. But when "you turn your reflexion into your own breast, [you] find a sentiment of disapprobation, which arises in you, towards this action" (T 468–9). This sentiment does possess the requisite felt qualities, and must therefore be the source of the idea's content. Notice again the role played by resemblance in terminating the causal chain with the "sentiment of disapprobation" rather than with the nonresembling event acknowledged to have caused the sentiment. The murder causes the sentiment, but since the sentiment doesn't resemble the murder, the sentiment doesn't derive its content from the murder; and consequently ideas that derive their content from the sentiment cannot be thereby deriving their content from the murder itself.

The conclusion is

that when you pronounce any action or character to be vicious, *you mean nothing, but* that from the constitution of your nature you have a feeling or sentiment of blame from the contemplation of it.[21]

Since vice is not a matter of fact about the "vicious" object, you cannot establish that an object is vicious by experimental reasoning about the object. But viciousness, recall, was just an example of a moral (or deontic) fact. Generalizing, the conclusion of the argument is that moral (or deontic) facts cannot be established by experimental reasoning that is solely about the objects that are the putative subject matter of those facts.

Now we might wish to resist Hume's analysis on the grounds that the "sentiment of disapprobation" cannot possibly capture the full force of the idea of vice. (In what way, we might ask, does disapprobation *resemble* vice?) It is clear enough what Hume thinks the feeling supplies: if part of the idea of vice is that it is (something like) repulsive, that can be accounted for by appealing to an actual feeling of revulsion.[22] The problem here is that if "disapprobation" is something on the order of a feeling of revulsion in the pit of one's stomach, it will not have the richness needed to reconstruct the cognitive role of the idea of vice; but if, on the other hand, it is sufficiently complex – if it is *disapprobation* – then it will have too much cognitive content to be construed as derived from an impression of reflection, that is, from something on the order of a feeling of revulsion in the pit of one's stomach. These problems are a good place to dig in one's heels; however, for our present exegetical purposes, we need only consider whether they should give rise to second thoughts about our reconstruction of Hume's argument. And here parity considerations settle the issue. It is just as implausible that a *feeling of determination* could account for whatever content the idea of necessity has over and above constant conjunction. (How does a feeling of determination – perhaps something, as James might have thought, like a tension in the upper chest – *resemble* necessity?) But Hume's treatment of necessity is given at much greater length, and it is clear that he accepts just this analysis. So we should not be surprised that he accepts a similar analysis in the case of vice as well.

3

We've just finished reconstructing one horn of a dilemma. If moral or deontic beliefs can be arrived at by reasoning, they must be arrived at either by experimental reasoning or by deductive reasoning. We have seen Hume's argument that they cannot be arrived at by experimental reasoning. Hume presents two further arguments to the effect that they cannot be arrived at deductively, or, in his language, cannot consist in "relations of objects." These arguments are intertwined in the text, and commentators often fail to distinguish between them.

The first argument in the antideductivist horn of Hume's dilemma aims at showing that the relations of objects that a moral or deontic fact would consist in cannot even be specified. (If they cannot be specified, "thought and understanding" cannot be "alone capable of fixing [their] boundaries" [T 463].) Since much of this argument has been adequately discussed, I will, in surveying those parts of it that have, provide just enough detail to frame the part that has not. Hume first points out that these relations have never actually *been* specified (T 463:25ff); this fact puts the burden of proof squarely on the shoulders of his opponent. (Hume remarks, " 'tis impossible to refute a system, which has never yet been explain'd" [T 464:15–16].) Moreover, he insists that the relations in which deontic facts allegedly consist must be specified in terms of the four relations of "resemblance, contrariety, degrees in quality, and proportions in quantity and number" (T 464:4–5, emphasis removed); and it is (he will argue in a moment) very unlikely that deontic facts could be specified using only these relations. This restriction is not as question-begging as it might sound.[23] First, Hume claims, no one has ever proposed any *other* relation to play this role (T 464:10–15). And second, recall that these relations are supposed to play a role in deductions or demonstrations, and that Hume's understanding of deduction is pictorial. Since deductive reasoning is to be reconstructed as the manipulation of mental pictures, the relations in question must be the kind of relations that can be used in a deduction, pictorially conducted: that is, in a deduction that proceeds in roughly the manner of the proofs of Euclidean geometry. This explains why it is reasonable to restrict the allowable relations to the four Hume mentions; and even if he has overlooked one or two, it is implausible that relations relevantly similar to *these* could suffice to specify the moral or deontic facts.

Hume supports the implausibility claim with an argument.

As moral good and evil belong only to the actions of the mind, and are deriv'd from our situation with regard to external objects, the relations, from which these moral distinctions arise, must lie only betwixt internal actions, and external objects (T 464:21–465:1).[24]

But it is very unlikely that the allowable relations will suffice to rule in all the situations of moral import while ruling out those to which morality is irrelevant. Hume supports the point with a well-known illustration:

To put the affair, therefore, to this trial, let us chuse any inanimate object, such as an oak or elm; and let us suppose, that by the dropping of its seed, it produces a sapling below it, which springing up by degrees, at last overtops and destroys the parent tree: I ask, if in this instance there be wanting any relation, which is discoverable in parricide or ingratitude? (T 467:2–8)

There are obvious differences between oaks and persons, and between their respective relations; but the problem is to capture these differences in terms of the allowable relations, those that could plausibly play a role in pictorially executed deductions. Hume is quite right to think that it is unlikely that they can be captured in this way; once again, if Hume's opponent claims that moral (or more generally, deontic) facts can be specified in terms of relations of ideas, the burden of proof is squarely on him.

But burden of proof arguments, no matter how plausible, are not decisive. After all, perhaps some very complicated, not at all obvious way of combining relations of the allowable kinds will allow one to distinguish situations in which morality has a purchase from those in which it does not. Hume accordingly concludes his argument against the specifiability of the moral relations with a circularity argument that "deserves to be weigh'd, as being, in [his] opinion, entirely decisive" (T 468:19–20).

The circularity argument, running from T 467:24 to 468:20, purports to show that it is not merely unlikely that the requisite specifications be produced: it is in fact impossible. The circularity argument invokes a further fact (presented as an opponent's objection) about what such a specification would have to express. We *know* what the relevant difference is between inanimate objects, plants, and animals, on the one hand, and persons, on the other: *people (should) know better*:

> I would fain ask any one, why incest in the human species is criminal, and why the very same action, and the same relations in animals have not the smallest moral turpitude and deformity? . . . this action is innocent in animals, because they have not reason sufficient to discover its turpitude; but . . . man, being endow'd with that faculty, which *ought* to restrain him to his duty, the same action instantly becomes criminal to him (T 467:24–32).

Hume's reply is that

> this is evidently arguing in a circle. For before reason can perceive this turpitude, the turpitude must exist; and consequently is independent of the decisions of our reason, and is their object more properly than their effect. (467:33–6)

Hume's appeal to circularity here should be puzzling. The problem, it will be recalled, is to *specify* the relevant moral features of situations in a way that allows of moral demonstrations or deductions; Hume, then, is claiming that such a specification cannot be given because it would be circular. But not all circularity is vicious. It is true enough that circularity of a kind may be found here: on the proposed view, a moral fact holds of a situation if and only if certain "relations of objects" can be found in the situation; one (not the *only* one) of these must be an awareness (or the capability of having an awareness) of those relations obtaining.

But why is this any worse than circularities like these? You can be a member of the Rule Club only if you know the rules of the club, and these rules contain clauses stating that they apply only to members. One might feel proud of, among other things, one's appropriate pride in oneself; and one might even believe that one is not worthy of pride if one does not esteem oneself properly. Again, perhaps part of being intelligent is recognizing that, and how, one is. There is nothing wrong with these circularities; what then is wrong with the similarly circular specification of vice?[25] To the best of my knowledge, this difficulty has been entirely overlooked by Hume's commentators.

Now in more recent times, philosophical resistance to seemingly innocuous circularity has been motivated by features of the technical apparatus used to reconstruct representation and reasoning. (I have in mind uses of the theory of types.) This suggests that to explain Hume's circularity argument, it may be once again helpful to turn to his semantic views. What requirements, we should ask, do these views impose on the reconstruction of the distinction between persons (who are aware of the morality-relevant relations in their situations) and animals (who are not)?

Content is, on Hume's view, a matter of (causally controlled) pictorial resemblance. For a person to be aware of the relations of objects that make, say, a certain moral response appropriate is for that person's mind to contain an idea of those relations: that is, for there to be in his mind an idea that pictorially resembles those relations (and is causally connected to them in the appropriate way). Very crudely expressed, being aware of the relevant relations of objects involves, among other things, having a picture of those relations in your head.[26]

But what must this picture look like? One of the facts it must picture is that you are (or could be[27]) aware of the relevant relations: this is, Hume points out, what is acknowledged to be the relevant difference between persons and animals or trees. So the picture must picture the fact that you (could) have a picture in your head; and not just any picture, but that very picture itself. Now content is, to reiterate, a matter of pictorial resemblance; to picture the fact that you have this very picture in your head, the picture must *contain itself*. And of course the smaller, contained picture (since it is identical to the larger, containing picture) must contain within itself a still smaller copy of itself, and so on, *ad infinitum* – much like those pictures on the labels of cans that show the can itself, with a picture of the can on the label, that shows a still smaller picture of the can ... In short, on Hume's semantic views, the circularity turns out to involve an infinite regress within the representation of the putative moral fact.[28] (Of course, one need not crudely think of ideas as literally in the head; and, recall, not all ideas are visual. But the regress remains when these expository conveniences are left behind.)

Still, just as not all circularity is vicious, not all regresses are vicious either. Why is Hume unable to find this one acceptable? We are going to have to speculate, since Hume does not explicitly discuss the matter; but there are two considerations that come to mind. The first is simply that such a representation is not well suited to be an element of a pictorially understood deduction. The second, which would be in Hume's view decisive, has to do with what we could call the possible granularity of a mental representation. Hume devotes Part II of Book I of the *Treatise* to arguing that our ideas of space and time are not infinitely divisible. Without reviewing Hume's arguments on this point, we can say that Hume's view was that infinitely nested representations of the kind we are considering are just not possible, since nesting of this kind would require a kind of infinitely fine detail that our ideas cannot have. Hume took this position very seriously; this is indicated by both the length and location of his treatment, which suggest that Hume saw it as central to his account, and by the fact that, on the basis of this claim, Hume was willing to adopt the extremely counterintuitive position that Euclidean geometry is only approximately true.[29]

Recall our current location in Hume's move tree. The task of the second horn of the dilemma is to show that deontic facts are not demonstrable – that morality cannot be thought of as a mathematical science. (It is interesting to see how much more time Hume commits to this horn of the dilemma than to the other, empirical, horn; we can get some comparative sense from this of how *live* the two options were felt to be in Hume's day.) We have just seen his first argument (or rather, a short series of connected arguments) for that conclusion; its (or their) point was that the premises from which a moral demonstration would proceed cannot be specified, and that the proofs that the mathematical moralist hopes for cannot be so much as begun. This argument has been seen to turn on Hume's pictorial understanding of representational content. On the one hand, the argument is much tighter than commentators have taken it to be; on the other, once we see how it works, it becomes clear that this is not an argument that can be appropriated by a contemporary moral philosopher.

4

The horn of the dilemma that argues against the deducibility of deontic beliefs contains a second argument (T 465:17–466:11, 15–18), which commentators have given particularly bad treatment. Some have simply ignored it, some have mistaken it for a part of the previous argument (easy to do because they share an illustration), and most have taken it to be a hopeless argument for a plausible conclusion.[30]

The argument runs as follows:

According to the principles of those who maintain an abstract rational difference betwixt moral good and evil, and a natural fitness and unfitness of things, 'tis not only suppos'd, that these relations, being eternal and immutable, are the same, when considered by every rational creature, but their *effects* are also suppos'd to be necessarily the same. (T 465:18–24)

But

'Tis one thing to know virtue, and another to conform the will to it... even in human nature no relation can ever alone produce any action; besides this... it has been shewn... that there is no connexion of cause and effect... of which we can pretend to have any security by the simple consideration of the objects... we cannot prove *a priori*, that these relations, if they really existed and were perceiv'd, wou'd be universally forcible and obligatory. (T 465:27–9; 466:1–7, 15–18)

The large structure of the argument is clear: it is a Modus Tollens with two premises:

1. If moral conclusions can be derived through reasoning about relations of ideas or objects, then "their *effects* are... necessarily the same."
2. The effects are not necessarily the same.

Leaving open for the moment just what these moral conclusions are, just what these effects are, and what they are effects *of*, note that from these premises it will follow that moral conclusions cannot be derived through reasoning about relations of ideas, or, as we might put it today, that morality is not a priori, or analytic, or conceptually true. The difficulty is that it is hard to see what Hume might mean by the premises so as to make them plausible, and the argument sound.

Now the first premise, that the effects (whatever they are) are necessarily the same, need not be Hume's, since the premise is introduced as how things stand "according to the principles of those who maintain an abstract rational difference betwixt moral good and evil" (T 465:18–21). Interpreters have accordingly assumed that the argument is merely directed against *actual* opponents who did in fact accept (1). But this view has two difficulties. First, as we shall see, the argument would then be directed against straw men[31] – even if these particular straw men actually happened to exist. (We will see in a moment that it is not plausible to suppose that they did.) Second, it would fail to do the work required by Hume's larger argument. In order to show that morality is not established by a priori reasoning, it does not suffice to show that people who think it is, and who *also* happen to believe (1), are mistaken. We must, rather, construe Hume as arguing that anyone who believes that morality is established by a priori reasoning is committed to (1), and therefore is mistaken. Hume's own language supports this point: "according to *the principles of* those [philosophers]," he says; *not* "according to those [philosophers]."

Why anyone would believe (1) should seem obscure when one considers just what the necessarily following effects must be if the argument is to go through. Commentators who try to take (1) as explicitly acknowleged by Hume's opponents appeal to the following passage:

> 'Tis one thing to know virtue, and another to conform the will to it. In order, therefore, to prove that the measures of right and wrong are eternal laws, *obligatory* on every rational mind, 'tis not sufficient to show the relations upon which they are founded: We must also point out the connexion betwixt the relation and the will; and must prove that this connection is so necessary, that in every well-disposed mind, it must take place and have its influence. (T 465:27–35)

On the basis of this passage, the effects in question are taken to be *motivational*, that is, to be an acknowledgement of the action's obligatoriness or an urge to perform the action.[32] These effects are taken to be effects of doing the demonstrative reasoning. They are supposed to be effects of relations of ideas, in a very concrete sense: the ideas are the ideas of the agent, and their effects are the choices or intentions or motivations of the agent. But this construal is mistaken.

In order for the Modus Tollens to be valid, the effects in question must be not merely motivations, but *actions*, for (2) claims that *actions* are what do not necessarily follow: "no relation can ever alone produce any action."[33] And this claim is supported not by any fact specific to human reason or motivation, but by appeal to general facts about causation. Now *no one* should find it plausible that actions necessarily follow upon appreciation of an a priori demonstration that some action is right – not even Hume's rational intuitionist opponents. Bluntly put, you may be hit over the head before you get a chance to carry out the action. (Recall also that Hume's Christian opponents believed in the possibility of sin, which, on their view, involves knowing the right, but not acting on it.) In short, for the argument to be valid, the effects must be actions rather than just motivations; the principle of charity consequently requires that we refrain from identifying the effects of the "relations" as motivations alone, *even though* it is implausible to attribute this view to Hume's opponents.

There is another reason for thinking that the effects in question should not be thought of as motivational, having to do with what I take to be the function of the arguments we have been examining. Hume is arguing against practical reasoning, against the notion that action can be correct or incorrect in the light of reason for or against it. He has already argued that neither the action, nor the passion that mediates the transition from theoretical conclusion to action, can be *mistaken*; consequently there is no room for describing such transitions as reasoning. This is (part of) the force of his earlier claim that reason is and ought only to be the slave of the passions.[34] Now suppose that an opponent does not accept this claim, but insists that agents' actions can be rationally required by certain beliefs they hold. Hume can concede this without conceding that practical reasoning is possible. For even if holding a belief can rationally require action, there is still no room for practical reasoning unless the belief that compels action can itself be arrived at by reasoning. And the purpose of the body of argument that this chapter is examining is to show that deontic beliefs cannot be arrived at by reasoning.

So the argument we're looking at has work to do in Hume's larger argument; and if I am right about its role, then this is the wrong place for taking the effects in question to be simply motivational. For Hume has *already* argued that reason does not motivate, and has also argued that because reason does not motivate, deontic beliefs cannot be arrived at by reasoning (T 457:6–458:18). It is now time for him to concede the possibility of motivating beliefs, if only for the sake of argument, and to show that even if some beliefs did motivate, this would not show that there was such a thing as practical reasoning. These role-directed considerations favor construing Hume's argument as not depending on the claim that reason does not motivate. On the conventional interpretation, however, this is the force of (2).[35]

The effects, then, are not simply motivations, but actions. But if the effects are actions, we have to explain why the proponent of the view that relations of ideas ground morality is committed to the claim that the actions that follow upon particular relations of ideas must always be the same. To do this, we must return to Hume's semantic theories.

Recall that what the *contents* of deductively manipulated ideas are must be compatible with the causal resemblance theory. And restrictions on what these contents can be may constrain which deductive inferences are possible. Thus, for example, because Hume takes there to be a limit to the precision of one's mental pictures, he is willing to conclude that Euclidian geometry is only approximately true. His semantic analysis of the contents of geometrical ideas constrains the consequences of admittedly deductive argument.[36]

Now consider an alleged inference from relations of objects to (something like) the appropriateness of an action. We must picture, first, the relevant relations of objects, and, second, the appropriateness of a particular action. (Call these picture$_1$ and picture$_2$; we have already seen Hume's argument that you are not going to be able to render picture$_1$.) Now how is picture$_2$ to depict the *appropriateness* of an action? How would a picture of an action *differ* from a picture of an action's appropriateness? All the picture can do is depict the action's being *done*. Therefore, the content of the ensuing judgment must be, that the action is *done*. (This, of course, is Hume's opponents' problem, not Hume's. Hume can analyze appropriateness by adjoining to picture$_2$ a nonrepresentational feeling of (say) approval. This is because Hume is not committed to the feeling being *deduced* from picture$_1$. But his opponents do not have this option; only pictures can be deduced from pictures by comparison of ideas.)[37]

On Hume's general views about conceptual possibility and necessity, if picture$_2$ is demonstrable or deducible from picture$_1$, then what picture$_2$ depicts is necessitated by what picture$_1$ depicts.[38] Since what picture$_2$ will depict is an *action*, Hume's opponents, by virtue of their claim that morality is established deductively, are committed to the claim that action ensues necessarily on the occurrence of those relations of objects that make it appropriate. This makes Hume's response – that there are no such necessary connections – reasonable.

Recall Hume's unusual way of putting his standard fork, using the locution "relations of objects" instead of "relations of ideas."[39] The relations of objects are mirrored by the relations of ideas that represent those objects. Deductions proceed from initial relations of ideas to further relations of ideas; these latter relations of ideas, however, mirror relations of objects: if the initial relations of ideas correctly mirrored the objects they represent, then so do the latter. Therefore, if from a representation of a situation it were possible to deduce a representation of a certain action occurring in that situation, this would show that in such a situation that action would, necessarily, occur. This feature of deduction is not specific to Hume's pictorial conception of it; the same holds for our propositional conception: If from a statement representing a given state of affairs it is possible to deduce a further statement that in that state of affairs some action will occur, this shows that in the actual state of affairs the action will, necessarily, occur.

Here's an illustration of the difficulty Hume takes his opponents' views to have. (I'm going to modify the one Hume gives; his illustrates both this argument and the one immediately preceding it, which makes it messy to untangle.) Consider what a deductive demonstration of the evil of parricide would have to look like. The premise of this deduction would be a representation of the relevant relations of objects. (For expository purposes, we can imagine this as, say, a picture of a father and his child. Of course, an idea capable of capturing the notion of parenthood would have to be complex in the extreme, and to the extent that it involved specifically causal notions would be partially nonrepresentational for reasons that Hume discusses elsewhere. I propose to ignore these complications for the present.) The conclusion of the deduction would be a picture, the force of which would be that parricide is evil, or ought not to be done. How could a picture have this force? The closest we can come is a picture of someone doing what he ought, that is, not murdering his father. So the conclusion of the demonstration would be, not that people *ought* not to murder their fathers, but that they *do* not murder their fathers. But whether people murder their fathers or not is a contingent matter, not amenable to being settled a priori.

Now that we have accounted for Hume's emphasis on effects that are actions, we can fine-tune the view to accommodate effects and necessary conditions that are motivational as well. It might be suggested that for action to follow, the agent has to recognize that it is required: the agent must "know virtue" (T 465:28). Furthermore, the agent must have the right moral character: he must be "well-disposed" (34). And finally, what is required in some cases may be not actually *action*, but rather the attempt or the motivation: what can be morally required is only that the agent "conform the will," that "in every well-disposed mind, [the connexion betwixt the relation and the will] must take place and have its influence" (23, 34–5). We can now see that these qualifications, which Hume gracefully concedes, are irrelevant to the argument. If these are what morality requires, his deductivist opponents are committed to their necessarily occurring in the appropriate situation; but motivation and attempts, even on the part of well-disposed agents, are as contingent as action. We have now accounted for the passages that seemed to support the conventional reading of the argument.[40]

To recapitulate: Because deductive relations, pictorially understood, can hold only between contents that can be pictured, someone who claims that morality is deductive can at best mean that pictures of actions can be deduced from pictures of situations that (morally) require them. This would entail that (morally) appropriate actions necessarily occur in the situations that (morally) require them. The fact is they do not, at any rate, not necessarily. Therefore, morality cannot be deductive. Moreover, since the argument was not morality-specific, it establishes more generally that deontic facts cannot be arrived at by deductive reasoning.[41]

It is well known that pictorial theories of thought have difficulty accounting for what we think of as logical connectives, such as negation:[42] how is one to distinguish a picture of some state of affairs from a picture of its negation? What is important as regards the present point is that this difficulty extends to what we regard as modal and deontic operators. How is one to distinguish a picture of a state of affairs' holding from a picture of its necessarily holding? How is one to distinguish a picture of a state of affairs' holding from a picture of its being obligatory?[43] It cannot be done using the representational elements of the picture. The easiest way to see this is to imagine trying to use a picture of a state of affairs to represent the necessity or obligatoriness of that state of affairs by modifying the representational elements of the picture – perhaps by scrawling "Necessary" or "Obligatory" across the top. The attempt is bound to fail: what one will get is not a picture of necessity, but a picture of, say, a landscape marred by peculiar skywriting. But if the representational elements of the picture cannot be used to distinguish obligation from fact, the remaining option is to *adjoin* to the picture a nonrepresentational impression; and this is what Hume does.[44]

5

The passage generally read as claiming that "is does not entail ought" (T 469:19–470:4) is often considered to be a mere afterthought to the previous argument,[45] a further independent but very brief argument presented as a rhetorical question: Hume professes not to understand transitions from "is" to "ought," and demands an explanation. We are now prepared to take a position on the force of that rhetorical demand.

If the passage is read on its own, it is extremely weak, just because no argument *is* presented. Hume's opponents are likely to think they *have* an account (for example, one that appeals to divine will, or fitness in relations of objects or ideas), and the *mere* rhetorical question will not (and should not) carry conviction.[46] I suggest that a better reading of the "is-ought" passage would take it as a corollary to the previous argument; this is dictated by, at least, the principle of charity. By seeing just how the previous argument supports the claim we will be able to explain just what its force is supposed to be – on the assumption that the most reasonable interpretation is the one supported by the arguments Hume actually gives.

The arguments we have already seen are supposed to have established that judgments of obligation involve ideas whose contents derive, not from the situation that supposedly generates the obligation, but from the sentiments of the observer. Consequently, reasoning from a description of such a situation to such a judgment will involve the introduction of such a sentiment-derived idea. But reason is conservative, in that the conclusion of an inference can only contain elements contained in its premises; as Hume puts it elsewhere (describing it as one of two "very obvious principles"), "reason alone can never give rise to any original idea" (T 157:18–20). So one cannot arrive at "ought-judgments" by reasoning about circumstances.

The point is this. Since the idea derived from the sentiment is *ipso facto* not derived from the situation being examined, it will not appear in a description of the situation. If the premises of an argument are the description of that situation, the idea needed in the argument's conclusion will not appear in the premises, and, since reason is conservative, cannot figure in the argument's conclusion.

The "is-ought" passage can now be seen to be, not an afterthought, but an argument that relies on the conclusions of the immediately preceding arguments. And the force of its conclusion is just what it sounds like: "is" does not entail "ought." Specifically, you can't start with a description of some situation and reason your way to claims about what, in that situation, ought to be the case.

The "is-ought" passage does not itself invoke the considerations, deriving from the causal resemblance theory of mental content, whose importance for the previous arguments I have been emphasizing. But it does invoke the conclusions of arguments that do turn on those considerations, and so we should see the causal resemblance theory of mental content as underwriting Hume's acceptance of the eponymous law, that "'is' does not entail 'ought.'" We are not yet fully equipped to assess the degree of this dependence, since we have surveyed only one of the three bodies of argument that lead up to the "is-ought" passage; were the others to prove not to turn on causal resemblance considerations, it would be possible to surrender the causal resemblance theory and still have Hume-supplied reasons to accept Hume's Law. I will not here anticipate the outcome of examining these other arguments.

6

We've reconstructed a few of Hume's arguments on the subject of practical reasoning, and found them to be a good deal better than commentators usually acknowledge them to be. We've also found them to rest, at least in part, on a body of semantic theory that is no longer acceptable to-day. What does this buy us? Well, first, it's nice to know that Hume repays close reading; that, on examination, his arguments turn out to be tight and ingenious attempts to arrive at dramatic (if unlikely) conclusions, rather than boring, bad arguments for obviously true conclusions. Second, it may be worth rereading other arguments in the *Treatise* in light of these reconstructions; perhaps they too will turn out to be dependent on Hume's semantic views in interesting ways. Third, as I suggested at the outset, this interpretation may have consequences for contemporary moral philosophy: I take it that the presumption that the burden of proof rests on opponents of Humean views about practical reasoning is in part due to the historical influence of the arguments we have been considering. But if this is right, finding these arguments to depend on a body of semantic theory that we no longer believe puts modern philosophers who believe Hume's Law on the spot: they must be prepared to show that they have not merely *inherited* Hume's Law, but that they can adduce good reasons for it. That "'is' does not entail 'ought'" may, today, seem obvious; but if this obviousness is an effect of the arguments we have been examining, a defense of Hume's Law should not appeal to its obviousness.

There is a fourth moral to draw from our discussion of Hume's arguments. Consider the question of the penumbra of commitments surrounding the causal resemblance theory. The puzzle here is that several aspects of the causal resemblance theory do not seem to get anything like the amount of explicit consideration that they deserve, given their central role in Hume's arguments. For example, while the pictorial view of deduction seems essential for reconstructing several of the arguments, the *Treatise* lacks the kind of discussion of pictorial deduction that we might hope for and think warranted by the uses to which the view is put. (While there is an extended discussion of geometry early on in the *Treatise*, this reads like an application of the view to a branch of mathematics, rather than a treatment of the view itself.) Or again, consider the argument discussed in Section 4, against the deductivist view of morality. The argument turns on a very straightforward consideration: that the would-be conclusion of such an argument cannot be fully represented, and so cannot be the conclusion of a demonstration. So why doesn't Hume simply *say* this?[47] Now as a matter of fact, he *does* say something very much like this elsewhere; I take it that this is more or less the force of T 415:23–33 and 458:12–22. But even granting this, why does the later argument express such an uncomplicated consideration in such a convoluted manner?

What I think is happening is this. Much of the causal resemblance theory was, in Hume's time, a widely held view (remember "the theory of ideas"); and Hume accordingly takes many of its commitments for granted. He does not feel that they need discussion, in roughly the way that a contemporary philosopher writing a treatise on mind or morality would be unlikely to feel that the propositional understanding of deduction needs discussion. And because of this, he does not see how much work these commitments are doing in his arguments. They are the platitudinous and frequently suppressed premises without which the argument does not make sense, but which are not worth spelling out for a contemporary and sophisticated audience. One doesn't tend to think that the dialectical work is being done by one's platitudinous premises, and so one frames one's arguments so as to highlight the premises one takes to be substantive. However, from a distance of two hundred and fifty years or so, it is precisely the platitudinous and often suppressed premises that seem to be the hinges on which the arguments turn.

The moral, then, is that we should take very seriously the thought that we are in Hume's position ourselves. Like Hume, we take for granted and rely on semantic theories; and the arguments we construct – whether for updated versions of Hume's Law or for other claims – will tend to depend on those theories in ways that are not obvious to us. It is worth remembering how likely it is that, in two hundred and fifty years, our current semantic theories will appear merely quaint. For this reason it is worth taking special pains to avoid, where possible, having one's arguments in moral philosophy depend on the apparatus supplied by contemporary philosophy of language.

Notes

Thanks to Annette Baier, Alyssa Bernstein, Hilary Bok, Lindy Cassidy, Cora Diamond, Steve Engstrom, Don Garrett, Hillel Millgram, Robert Nozick, Hilary Putnam, Geoff Sayre-McCord, Tim Scanlon, Candace Vogler, and Margaret Wilson, who read and commented on earlier drafts of this chapter. I'm also grateful to Sanford Shieh for helpful discussion, and to an audience at Brown University for questions and objections.

1. Hare, 1963, p. 108.
2. For citation conventions, see note 3 in Chapter 6; The "is-ought" passage is at T 469. The first stretch of preceding argument (T 457:6–459:10) recapitulates points made at T 413–17, and cannot be adequately discussed without considering those passages as well; limitations of space prevent me from doing that here. The second (T 459:11–463:2) deploys considerations that are morality specific, and are for this reason also best treated separately.

3. I will discuss some of these interpretations in what follows. For now, we may note that my assessment of the reconstructed arguments as weak is typically shared by the commentators who have advanced those reconstructions. Stroud, for example, wraps up his account of the arguments I will consider in Sections 3 and 4, below, by remarking that "it need hardly be said that this argument is not completely decisive," attributing the arguments' not fully spelled-out shortcomings to "the vagueness and imprecision of the views Hume is arguing against" – and to "unjustifiable restrictions on what is demonstrable" (1977, 175–6). Fogelin ends up describing the arguments in question as "embarrassingly weak" (1985, p. 127). Harrison states that "not only does Hume's proof of the conclusion that morality is not susceptible of demonstration fail...; his conclusion is also false, and rather obviously false at that" (1976, p. 49).

4. T 37:29–31. "'Tis impossible perfectly to understand any idea, without tracing it up to its origin, and examining that primary impression, from which it arises" (T 74:36–75:1; 83:11–29 could be construed as involving an extremely long chain of this kind). Abstract ideas are trickier but are treated by Hume as derivative from the straightforward case: T 17ff, esp. 17:17–20; 20:9–13; 22:11–24; 24:24–6; 34:30–5.

   The causal analysis of reference may seem to sit uncomfortably with Hume's subsequent discussions of causation and of external objects. I do not think this difficulty can be explained away, say, by somehow combining the accounts – I think that they really *are* incompatible. And I do not think that Hume was unaware of this: in fact, I suspect that eliciting such incompatibilities was part of Hume's philosophical project (the part that justifies calling Hume a skeptic). (For discussion of one such incompatibility, see Garrett, 1981.) An adequate discussion of these issues is beyond the scope of this chapter; for the present, I will adopt the expository policy of treating items given nonstandard or skeptical analyses in one argument as, nonetheless, meant to be thought of in an ordinary, unanalyzed way in others, unless appeal to those analyses is made specifically. (See note 6.)

5. To see that these are distinct conditions, notice that Hume states that "secondary, or reflective impressions are such as *proceed from* [i.e., are caused by]...original ones" (T 275:16–17, my emphasis). Here we have impressions caused by others they do not resemble, and whose content they do not assume.

6. Notice that if, contrary to the policy adopted in note 4, one were to attempt to combine the causal resemblance theory with Hume's account of external objects (roughly, there are no external objects, and if there were, impressions could not resemble them), one would have to adopt a view on which impressions of sensation had no representational content; on such a view, representational content could be had only by ideas. (One would then have to choose between saying that impressions have no contents at all, or saying that there is a thinner, nonrepresentational notion of content exhausted by the merely intrinsic qualities of impressions. One would also have to assume the exegetical task of reading away references to objects in passages like the one just quoted [T 37:29–31].) Since I wish for the purposes of this chapter

to remain agnostic on this point, I will for simplicity of exposition continue to speak of external objects as the possible sources of contents of ideas and impressions; but I intend my discussion to be compatible, *mutatis mutandis*, with a reading of Hume of this more exotic variety. (I'm grateful to Cora Diamond for pressing me on this point.)

7. Mackie, 1980, p. 58, is unable to believe that Hume was willing to endorse this conclusion, and chooses to reconstrue Hume "as intending to say that this is what you ought to mean, because that is all that, on reflection, you could maintain." Stroud also finds this unlikely (1977, pp. 180–1), as does Hudson (1968, p. 297); and Fogelin has his qualms as well (1985, p. 137). But see EHU 62:8–63:5, esp. 62:21–5, and, on a slightly different but related point, T 23:14–18; 33:9–18 (esp. 15–18). Hume also thinks that we can use names with no idea of what we are naming; this is a risky practice, and following the procedure for determining what the content of an idea is may actually establish that some of our words are meaningless: EHU 74:14–20; 78:2–4; T 61:36–62:1; compare T 162:20–5; 168:7–29; 224:6–14.

    Even if textual evidence seems to show that Hume held this view, isn't it too outlandish to be attributed to him charitably? Is it Hume's view that, for example, I could really be thinking about a can of cat food when I *think* I'm thinking about my Form 1040? (I'm grateful to Felicia Ackerman for the example, and for pressing the objection.) To see that Hume has ways of handling this kind of case, recall the role of resemblance in controlling reference. How are we to imagine such a case? Suppose we have a mental picture that (we would say) qualitatively resembles a Form 1040, but is causally connected to a can of cat food. In this case, the content of the picture cannot be the can of cat food because it fails to *resemble* the can of cat food. Suppose we substitute for this picture one that qualitatively resembles a can of cat food; now there is no trouble in seeing that it is a picture of the cat food, but it is implausible that I should mistake *this* picture for a picture of my Form 1040. (Dan Brock has suggested that the problem might be kept in play by considering a chain of partial resemblances. I'm not sure what the Humean response would be here, but I doubt that Hume considered this problem himself.)

8. The closest contemporary rendering of "demonstration" is "deduction," and treating these as synonyms is a helpful reminder that they play analogous roles in their respective philosophical environments. However, it is important to remember that the fit is not precise.

9. In this context, ignoring mental contents that are not visual images is not unreasonable. It can be at least at first glance sensible to imagine deductive thought as done with pictures; but it would be another matter entirely to conceive of deduction as performed with, say, olfactory sensations.

10. Harrison, 1976, p. viii. Harrison's view of the upshot (p. 34) is that "since [Hume] confuses propositions with ideas or mental images, he confuses entailment, which is a relation between propositions, with relations such as resemblance between mental images." This parochial and tendentious statement of an important point is worth rephrasing: Since Hume has a different understanding of thought than we do (one not necessarily more

confused than our own), he has an appropriately different understanding of deductive inference. I have not yet come across an adequate treatment of this subject, which I can only touch on in this chapter.

11. I don't mean to suggest that one would choose this example if one wanted to explore Hume's views of demonstration in greater depth; while it illustrates the way in which demonstration must be pictorial, it may not be helpful when considering other features of demonstration. For instance, its very simplicity makes it at best a borderline case; since the relation of equality is "discoverable at first sight, [it] fall[s] more properly under the province of intuition than demonstration" (T 70:9–10).

12. It might be objected that Hume finds arithmetic and algebra more precise than geometry, and that we should consider them, rather than geometry, "foremost" for Hume. Moreover, since Hume imputed the "defects" of geometry to the fact that its "original and fundamental principles are deriv'd merely from appearances" (T 71:30–2), we might conclude that algebra and arithmetic owe their "perfect exactness and certainty" to their nonpictorial nature. I won't try for a judgment call on which of the mathematical sciences was Hume's favorite; note, however, the amount of discussion that geometry receives in the *Treatise*, as opposed to arithmetic or algebra (cf. also T 181–2). And as to whether Hume considered algebra to be at bottom nonpictorial: he reiterates, on the following page, "that principle so oft insisted on, *that all our ideas are copy'd from our impressions*"(72:32–3); it follows that arithmetic and algebra are unlikely to be exceptions.

13. Actually, the dilemma here is not *entirely* familiar, since Hume has substituted "relations of objects" for "relations of ideas." I take it that he chose this way of putting the point partly in light of opponents' views that moral facts can be discerned in relations of objects (the locution being the opponents' rather than Hume's: cf. Mackie, 1980, ch. 2). Since perceptions of objects will represent whatever relations are to be found among the represented objects, it does not much matter for Hume whether he is considering relations of objects or relations of ideas. (Cf. T 456–7: "All these systems concur in the opinion, that morality, like truth, is discern'd merely by ideas, and by their juxta-position and comparison." See also T 20:1–2 and T 29:3–6.) Nonetheless, as we'll see, the emphasis on relations of objects turns out to be a pointer to the way the argument actually works.

14. See Mackie, 1980, pp. 53–4, or Harrison, 1976, p. 63, for something like this objection. Harrison says elsewhere that "this is mere assertion, and Hume is guilty of appealing more to rhetoric than to argument" (p. 61). Stroud makes a related point as well (1977, pp. 179–80).

15. T 34:6–9: "my senses convey to me only the impressions of colour'd points, dispos'd in a certain manner." Cf. also EHU 63:13–5 and T 56:23–7. In any case, as Steve Engstrom has reminded me, the realization that modal facts are not directly perceptible predates Hume.

16. The claim should be distinguished from the separate point, that no proof can be given that two distinct objects are necessarily connected. That very different argument would be the structural analog of arguments we will presently consider. Cf. EHU 63:33–64:7.

17. Cf. EHU 64:8–12.
18. T 164f, Hume's emphasis. Cf. also EHU 75:19–24; 78:10–18.
19. Or, more generally, judgments that play the role in action that moral judgments play in moral action; the argument is more general than morality.
20. This of course is not to say that vice is, on Hume's view, in the object but causally ineffective with respect to our sense organs. At this point in the argument, however, this possibility has not yet been ruled out. The claim that vice is not in the object is the *conclusion* of the argument.
21. T 469:4–8, my emphasis. Notice that this is not a skeptical conclusion – that there is no such thing as, say, vice – but the hard-won result of semantic analysis, which does not dispose of the concept of vice, but rather tells us just what it is a concept *of*. Hume's skepticism lies elsewhere.
22. Thinking of the surplus content as repulsiveness may be too strong. Hume tends to describe the feeling as "uneasiness" (e.g., T 499:25–8; 471:5–9); at one point he suggests that it can be distinguished from other kinds of uneasiness, but does not say much about its "peculiar" qualities (T 472).
23. For variations on this complaint, see Harrison, 1976, p. 48, Fogelin, 1985, p. 135, and Stroud, 1977, pp. 175–6.
24. It might be thought that this argument is morality-specific, and does not settle the question with respect to deontic facts more generally. But this would be to misconstrue the intent of the argument. Moral facts are a subset of deontic facts; from a moral argument one concludes that one *ought* to do such and such, just as one might conclude, from a prudential argument, that one *ought* to do something else. If moral facts cannot be specified in terms of available relations, this will suffice to show that not all deontic facts can be so specified.
25. Notice that the circularity in these cases is only partial; there is more to being intelligent than thinking that one is, more to the object of justified pride than the pride itself, and, presumably, more to being a member of the club than knowing the rules. But vice has the same structure; there is more to being vicious than thinking that one is.
26. It must of course involve other things, if only because the representation of the objects may present you with many more relations between them than the small number that now have your attention. But I cannot here discuss Hume's answer to the question: what picks out one represented relation as the object of my thought?
27. The modal aspect of this fact raises difficulties which we shall touch upon later, but ignore for now.
28. Annette Baier has pointed out to me that intention is liable to involve a similar circularity, and that this will be a problem for Hume. However, the feature of intention that makes it problematic is specifically its reflexivity: intending to do ϕ is, in part, intending that that very intention be causally effective in bringing it about that one ϕs. But as this feature of intention has come in for attention only recently, we may wonder whether Hume saw that there is a problem here. He defines the will as "the internal impression we feel and are conscious of, when we knowingly give rise to any new motion of our body, or new perception of our mind" (T 399, emphasis removed).

The knowingness is not part of the impression that is the will, but is only a surrounding circumstance; and whether it is a problem depends on what Hume takes it to be a knowingness *of.* The circularity problem only arises here if knowingness consists in having an idea of, among other things, having that very idea; an idea of, for instance, a passion causing an action would be innocuous.

29. This brings out an interesting tension in the view I am attributing to Hume. On the one hand, I am suggesting, the availability of Euclidean geometry, then the paradigm of deductive reasoning, made plausible to Hume the thought that demonstrative inference could be reconstructed within the pictorialist constraints of his semantic theory. On the other hand, however, his semantic theory required him to insist that Euclidean geometry could not be understood in the standard way.

30. Broad, for instance, ignores it, perhaps, one senses, out of embarrassment (1930/1951, pp. 104–15). Raphael, normally a sympathetic and careful reader, quotes the argument in its entirety and then, in a short paragraph, dismisses it as "depend[ing] on an absurd identification" and "rest[ing] on a confusion" (1947, pp. 60–2). Some commentators manage to do more than one of these. Harrison conflates this argument with the previous one. He also manages to accuse Hume of begging the question, of tautological vacuity, and of vulnerability to the objection that men have a "passion for morality" – even though Hume went to great lengths to defend this very view, making it hard to believe that this was an objection he had overlooked (1976, pp. 53ff).

31. Mackie, 1980, cites Harrison as raising this objection (1976, pp. 53–4), and defends Hume by "not[ing] how big a concession this [i.e., surrendering (1)] would be, and how reluctant Clarke, for instance, or Butler would be to make it" (p. 54; see also p. 57). Compare Fogelin, 1985, p. 127.

32. Harrison, for example, attributes to Hume the "premiss that if morality consists in relations apprehended by reason, morality must *necessarily* move us," and asks whether "there [is] ... any reason why this ... premiss should be true" (1976, p. 35). Mackie takes Hume to be concerned with "the connection between the supposed moral relation and *choice* by any rational agent" (1980, p. 57, my emphasis).

33. There is a potential ambiguity in this passage: "action" might mean a product of human agency, or merely an event. (If the latter – and this reading could be supported by the introductory phrase, "even in human nature" – then an "action" might be an instance of coming to have a motivation, after all.) Hume uses the word both ways, and the sense seems to be controlled by context: when he is discussing morals, he generally means human action; when he is discussing inert objects, he means (roughly) events. Because Hume is here discussing morals, I take it that here he means by "action," human action. If this is right, it removes the ambiguity of the earlier phrase, "conform the will." "Conforming the will" might be a matter of good intentions, or it might require actually *doing* something. But on the former construal, pointing out that actions do not necessarily follow would be irrelevant, since one can have the best of intentions, yet not act.

Now suppose I am wrong on this point. As we will see, when we consider Hume's way of handling moral theories that require not actions but merely good intentions, it turns out not to matter. Once we see *why* "effects" must be "necessarily the same," we will see that even when Hume's opponent has a moral theory that does identify some (or even all) "effects" with motivations, Hume's argument will work anyway. But we will also see another reason that it is unlikely that Hume has in mind only motivations and not actions. Hume's argument makes the "effects" out to be what his opponent's moral theory requires of agents. Now moral theories that require *only* meaning well are rather rare: most moral theories require agents to actually act, at least in some circumstances. And in these cases, the "effects" will be full-fledged actions, not mere events.

34. For these passages, and discussion, see Chapter 6.

35. There is yet another reason for resisting the identification of effects with motivations. The argument construed as turning on motivations would be unsatisfactory, because it would prove too much. The point of the argument is to establish a *contrast* between genuine deductive reasoning and moral or practical reasoning. On the conventional interpretation, this is done by showing that while the conclusions of deductive reasoning are necessarily adopted, the conclusions of moral or practical reasoning are not. But recall that the argument appeals to a very general fact about causation – roughly, the fact that effects cannot be deductively inferred from their causes. If this fact establishes that the conclusions of practical reasoning – understood as ideas of the reasoning's conclusion, or motivations – do not necessarily ensue on the mental processes that would in normal circumstances produce them, it seems equally to establish that the conclusions of deductive reasoning – similarly understood as mental entities – do not necessarily follow either: if you believe p, and you believe $p \supset q$, you may be hit over the head before you get around to concluding q. So the argument, construed in this way, would, if it worked in the case of practical reasoning, work in the case of deductive reasoning as well: it would have to establish that there really is no deductive reasoning either. Leaving to one side the intrinsic merits of such an argument (it looks pretty bad), we may note that since its purpose was to establish a contrast between deductive and moral or practical reasoning, the argument, so construed, would fail by virtue of overkill.

36. T 26–65; esp. 45:4–7. It might be suggested that the arguments are not admittedly deductive, since Hume says that "with regard to such minute objects, they are not properly demonstrations" (45:1–3). This, however, is precisely the point: without ideas of such objects, you cannot have deductions that take them as their subject; this is the way in which the scope of deductive argument is constrained by Hume's semantic theories.

37. Two points need mentioning here: First, lacking an adequate treatment of Hume's understanding of deduction, I wish to leave open the question of whether picture$_1$ and picture$_2$ need in fact be *different* pictures. (A geometrical demonstration may start and finish with the same picture.) Second, recall that the "pictures" need not be entirely visual; my idea of a heavy object may

involve simple ideas derived from tactile rather than visual impressions. But this complication does not affect the present point.

38. For Hume's views on these matters, cf., e.g., T 18:22–8; 19:36–20:1; 29:11–14; 32:17–23; 36:17–22; 40:26–8; 43:5–13; and esp. 29:3–6.

39. See note 13.

40. Now that we have seen the argument, it might be thought that there is a further reason that the effects cannot be motivations: motivations cannot be represented either. (This would make it difficult to understand Hume's subsequent insistence that motivations rather than actions are the appropriate object of moral judgment; cf., e.g., T 477:13–17.) But motivations can be represented. I can have impressions of reflection; and have ideas that are derived from them, resemble them, and consequently represent them.

41. Understood in this way, Hume's argument evades the overkill objection discussed earlier (note 35). When one idea is demonstrable from another, the holding of the state of affairs depicted by the latter *does* entail the holding of the state of affairs depicted by the former. Whenever you have an *idea* of two spots together with another two spots, you have an *idea* of four spots; and whenever you *have* two spots together with another two spots, you *have* four spots. Showing that moral (or, more generally, action-guiding) reasoning is not like this establishes a contrast with genuine deductive reasoning that is sufficient to show action-guiding reasoning to be nondeductive.

42. Cf. Harrison, 1976, pp. 30, 32–3, Stroud, 1977, p. 75. Stroud's point is quite general, and is closely related to the central themes of this chapter. But he fails to exploit it to elucidate the large body of Humean doctrine it bears upon.

43. This may be a difficulty for philosophers other than Hume who are committed to pictorial construals of content; perhaps the early Wittgenstein is an example of this. Cf. Hudson, 1983, pp. 107ff.

44. It is worth remarking that the territories covered by modern theories of content and by Hume's are only identical to a first approximation. Modern accounts of necessity tend to be extensions of non-modal semantics, such as possible-world semantics. But Hume must rely on radically different tools (impressions of reflection) to reconstruct modal notions. So while we can think of a proposition with a modal operator in it as fully representational if we want to, Hume cannot.

If only representational items come under the aegis of deductive inference, it will follow from this that necessity cannot be established by a priori deductive inference. It is, I think, useful to read certain of Hume's arguments regarding induction and necessity with this in mind.

One worry that might be raised here is that Hume seems to be committed by this account to a view on which mathematical necessity will not be representable or expressible; but since he has been arguing that mathematical necessity will not account for obligation, it must be possible, somehow or other, to express the notion. Here it suffices to note that Hume's treatment of mathematical necessity can be expected to be continuous with his treatment of causal necessity and obligation: he writes that "the necessity, which makes two times two equal to four, or three angles of a triangle equal to two right ones, lies only in the act of the understanding, by which we consider and compare these ideas" (166:5–10); and he does so in the course of drawing a comparison between mathematical necessity and causal necessity, the account of which we sketched in Section 2.

45. As, for example, Mackie, 1980, p. 61, is inclined to: "the passage about 'is' and 'ought'. . . is plainly an afterthought for Hume himself." Stroud, 1977, p. 187, similarly states that "Hume apparently added it as something of an afterthought he hoped would be helpful." And the view echoes at Harrison, 1976, p. 69, who refers to the passage as an "argument, inserted almost as an afterthought." On the other hand, Atkinson, 1968, p. 274, regards it as a continuation of the previous argument, and Fogelin, 1985, pp. 138–9, takes it to be a recapitulation of the argument at 463:17–468:20.

46. Harrison, 1976, pp. 69–82, summarizes a number of (generally modern) responses of this kind. Moreover, even if Hume's opponent does not take himself to have such an account, he may not concede that he has to shoulder the burden of proof: it is, he may suggest, no more reasonable to demand such an account of him than it is to demand an independent justification of the transition from a proposition universally quantified throughout to one containing proper names. The building blocks of practical reasoning, he may claim, are not to be expected to be amenable to any more justification than are other building blocks of reason.

47. I'm grateful to Jaegwon Kim and Martha Nussbaum for pressing me on this point.

8

Hume, Political Noncognitivism, and the *History of England*

Hume was a nihilist about practical reasoning, that is, he held that there is no such thing as reasoning about what to do, because nothing could count as an inference to a practical conclusion. This was not just a counterintuitive position to hold – don't we have, after all, a well-entrenched practice of moral and especially political argumentation? – but a challenge to Hume's sense of intellectual responsibility: "nothing," he thought, "is a clearer proof, that a theory [having to do with morals] is erroneous, than to find, that it leads to paradoxes, repugnant to the common sentiments of mankind, and to the practice and opinion of all nations and ages."[1] In what follows, I want to sketch Hume's attempt to persuade himself that his views on practical reasoning could accommodate not just the existence of the practice, but a nondismissive attitude towards it. I will explain how Hume's *History of England* was meant as an extended political and moral argument, and so as a very lengthy demonstration of how such argument (in a suitable sense of the word) could be managed even by someone who believed that practical reasoning was strictly speaking an impossibility.

Humean nihilism has attracted remarkably little attention, and showing how his *History* addressed an objection to it may accordingly seem to be of less than general interest. So I am going to superimpose on a relatively terse historical treatment some discussion of a problem in contemporary public life on which, I will suggest, Hume's efforts are an instructive preliminary attempt. I will call the problem *Political Noncognitivism*, and let me start with that.

1

Back in the late 1960s, one could determine an American male's views about East Asian foreign policy by looking at his haircut. This was an especially memorable instance of a widespread and familiar phenomenon, namely, the yoking together, by party affiliation, of a number of logically unrelated positions. As I write this, knowing what an American thinks about any one of such topics as taxation, foreign affairs, penal policy (especially executions), or various sorts of intervention in human reproduction will allow you to predict, with varying but often high reliability, what he thinks about the others. The arguments fielded on these topics do not share premises to any significant degree. Therefore, if the positions travel together, they are not the conclusions of arguments. Arguments exhibit the way reasons bear on a position, and so – this is what I mean by "Political Noncognitivism" – the constellations of positions making up a party doctrine are not held for reasons.[2]

"Noncognitivism" is a label standardly used to describe a series of progressively more sophisticated positions in twentieth-century metaethics, on which what look like moral judgments, responsible to matters of moral or evaluative fact, are, in one way or another, not actually that at all: emotivism, which held evaluations to be merely expressions of emotion, on a par with cringes or yelps of joy; prescriptivism, according to which what seem to be ethical assertions are really disguised commands; projectivism, according to which they are projections of one's emotional states onto the world; and so on.[3] Now, Political Noncognitivism, early twentieth-century metaethical noncognitivism and Humean nihilism are distinct positions, which nonetheless have strong affinities with one another. On the one hand, political debate, or what passes for it, is substantially practical; it is, in the end, about what to do. So Hume's nihilism entails that what looks like political argument is not, in the philosopher's or logician's sense, really argument at all. And Hume's arguments for nihilism turn on an idea shared with the earlier metaethical noncognitivists, namely, the nonrepresentational status of the practical elements of a thought: a *should* or an *ought* derives its content, not from the way things stand in the world, but from a *feeling*. On the other hand, you can think that political positions are not held for reasons even if you do think that evaluative claims really *are* claims, and even if you think that the notion of reasons for action makes perfectly good sense. And Political Noncognitivism does not have to put feelings or emotions center stage; we will shortly see versions of it that don't.

Early noncognitivist views such as emotivism and prescriptivism foundered on their inability to reconstruct moral argument – or rather, since it would beg the question to insist that would-be moral argument really *was* argument, on their inability to allow for anything with the look and feel of moral argument. And so you would expect that the objections that broke the back of emotivism and its ilk would be decisive against Hume's position also.[4] Moreover, Hume's *Treatise of Human Nature* and his second *Enquiry,* in which philosophers generally take his moral philosophy to be found, might seem to bear out the concern that Hume's theory of practical reasoning leaves no place for political or moral argumentation. The *Treatise* proposes a taxonomy of traits into virtues and vices (the moral categories that appear to be of most interest to him), but provides insufficient resources for arguing about them. The principle of classification appeals to reactions of approval and disapproval, and so there is room for arguing over whether we do in fact collectively approve or disapprove of some trait; but not, apparently, for constructing an argument that would override those reactions. Disputes about grammar are thin in just this way, and Hume remarks that "it belongs to *Grammarians* to examine what qualities are entitled to the denomination of *virtue*" (T 610:4–6).

Hume could not have anticipated objections to his view cast in the signature style of mid-century analytic philosophy, but he took the generic problem of accounting for the look and feel of political (and moral) argument much more seriously than the emotivists and their successors. It is important not to think of his subsequent *History of England* as something that he also *happened* to write. The *History,* comprising six massive volumes, was an ambitious enterprise; it became a bestseller, and the work Hume was best known for during his lifetime. Moreover, it has withstood the test of time: historians still seem to read it, and occasionally produce quotes one could mine for jacket copy (as when Hume gets described as "the only major philosopher to have produced a major work of historiography").[5] The usual explanation for Hume's turn to history is that when his philosophical writing failed to gain a broad readership, he moved on to other ways of making a name for himself in the "republic of letters." But whether or not that is the truth, or part of it, were we to assume that Hume did not use subsequent work to address the unresolved intellectual problems of the *Treatise,* we would underestimate him. The *History* constitutes a political and moral argument – in fact, just what we had been led by the *Treatise* (and the first appendix to the *Enquiry Concerning the Principles of Morals*) to suspect was impossible.

Here are two theses of the many for which Hume's *History of England* argues. The dramatic episodes of statecraft – battles and wars, diplomatic coups and catastrophes, alliances and crises – do not matter nearly as much as one is naively inclined to think, and in particular, they matter far less than the gradual changes in manners, arts, and what the Enlightenment called "police," the social regulation and control of civil and material culture. Manners and "police" really do change, and, when a sufficiently long-term view is taken, for the better: the seemingly endless catalog of indiscriminate slaughters committed by heptarchs and their successors, and the generally casual attitude toward one person's killing another, give way to more restrained and more refined behavior.[6] Acknowledging that the change is an improvement amounts in turn to acknowledging that the "virtues" of barbarian warriors, and, later on in the narrative and for similar reasons, the "virtues" of the Catholic clergy and Protestant rebels – all of which a reader may be accustomed to celebrating *as* virtues – are not actually that at all, but the vices of short-sighted brutality, superstition, and fanaticism, respectively.

In the second *Enquiry* Hume had pointed out that "luxury, or a refinement on the pleasures and conveniences of life, had long been supposed the source of every corruption in government, and the immediate cause of faction, sedition, civil wars, and the total loss of liberty. It was, therefore, universally regarded as a vice . . . Those, who prove . . . that such refinements rather tend to the increase of industry, civility, and arts regulate anew our *moral* as well as *political* sentiments, and represent, as laudable or innocent, what had formerly been regarded as pernicious and blameable" (EPM 181:13–23). In the *History*, Hume takes up the "proof." Many reasons are marshalled for this conclusion, and here is just one representative example. Luxuries are manufactured and distributed by craftsmen and tradesmen, rather than the retainers of a noble household. When the nobility spends its money on "mechanics and merchants," it has to give up its retainers, or most of them. Dependent household retainers had made up a reserve of armed men that the barons used against their political opponents. So luxury neutralizes a source of political violence and instability, and, to make a longer story short, virtue is fostered by a rising standard of living.[7]

The understanding of Hume's enterprise as moral and political argument is confirmed by Edward Gibbon's attempt to imitate and improve on it. Gibbon was a later contemporary of Hume's who read Hume's work and corresponded with its author. Gibbon's *Decline and Fall of the Roman Empire* is very clearly an attempt at moral and political argument in the historical medium.[8] One of its primary agendas is to display the contribution made by some character traits to the early success of the Republic and Empire, and by others to its progressive disintegration, and so to convince you that the former were virtues and the latter were vices. In doing so, Gibbon is taking issue with Hume's claim that a rising standard of living makes for better people. Gibbon's argument, you will recall, is that becoming accustomed to a civilized standard of living makes one unwilling to tolerate the discomforts of military life; that a well-off citizenry ends up leaving defense and security to mercenary and, eventually, barbarian armies; and that the well-off polity eventually but inevitably becomes the prey and prize fought over by ruthless savages.[9] What Hume tried to convince his readers was virtue, Gibbon is arguing, is just the opposite; what Hume argued was conducive to virtue is in fact conducive to vice and ultimate catastrophe; and Gibbon is undercutting Hume's claim that, over time, the human condition improves, and that, just as the present is better than the past, so we can look forward to the future being better than the present: sometimes, and in a way that is very hard to forestall, it is not. Like Hume's *History,* Gibbon's *Decline and Fall* is lengthy; I will say something about why that is so in due course. For now, the point I want is that Gibbon, who was much closer to Hume than we are, took Hume to be doing what he then went on to do more of; and what he went on to do more of was history as moral and political argument.

Not a few of the *Essays* are also devoted to argument with a political or moral agenda, but the *History* marshalled Hume's full efforts to produce a very extended argument of impressive scope and depth, and accordingly is the one we should use to examine his views about how such argument ought to be conducted. But how could he have embarked on such an enterprise, given the nihilism of the *Treatise?* Do we have to imagine that the *History* was an *oversight?* That would not be unprecedented: Mackie, after famously insisting that moral judgments are merely projections of one's emotions onto the world, and that they are accordingly uniformly mistaken, proceeded, apparently oblivious to the pragmatic contradiction, to lay out his own substantive moral theory. But I do not think that we need to adopt such an uncharitable opinion of Hume. Before I get to Hume's account of what his *History* was doing, however, I want to further consider the problem posed by Political Noncognitivism.

2

An observant metaethicist might have been wondering whether there *is* a problem about Humean nihilism, or, for that matter, noncognitivism. The problem was supposed to be that nihilism and noncognitivism more generally cannot account for the practice of observed moral and political argument.[10] But why think that (in any but trivial cases) we *do* engage in such argument? (If you've been reading the notes: why think that the Frege-Geach argument scales up?) Consider a few reminders of what public political debate looks like.

First, the point of an argument, as philosophers are trained to understand the notion, is to convince someone (perhaps oneself) of its conclusion. But public political argument, whether conducted in bars, on talk radio, over the dinner table, or anywhere else, does not normally change the opinions of the participants. Induction from past cases ought to make that fact clear enough to participants, which raises the further question of why they bother. It cannot be because they reasonably expect to talk their opponents around to their own point of view.

Second, political argumentation does not normally stay on point; instead it *skids* from one topic to another. You may start out arguing about the current war, but within moments you will be talking about, say, health care policy, and moments later, about taxation. Even when conducted as a monologue, political argument exhibits skidding; think of how typically political documentaries, which generally have the floor for ninety minutes or so, slide from topic to topic, often retaining only the barest connection to their announced focal issue.

Third, in a proper argument, belief in the premises explains belief in the conclusions. In public political debate, the direction of explanation runs the other way around: the practical conclusions endorsed by the participants account for their belief in the factual premises. In particular, the participants in a political debate normally refuse to accept purported facts adduced by their opponents. During the 1980s, Democrats and Republicans could not agree, to within an order of magnitude, on the number of people living on the streets of America's cities (a straightforward matter, one would have thought, of counting heads). As I write, party affiliation is the best predictor for what someone believes the facts about global warming and climate change to be.[11]

Fourth, the conclusions of political arguments are almost uniformly familiar positions on an available political spectrum; they are hardly ever novel, or surprising. As experienced philosophers know, following the argument where it goes quite often takes you to a novel and startling position; accordingly, in nonpolitical regions of philosophy, such as philosophy of mind, or philosophy of language, there is almost no conclusion so offbeat but that you cannot find some philosopher defending it. Ergo, political argumentation isn't real reasoning or argument.[12]

Emotivism and its successors were rejected because they could not reconstruct moral and political argument; Hume's nihilism, it was suggested, faces the same problem. The metaethical rejoinder on behalf of this family of theories was that there is so little in the way of real argument about politics or morals that there is no need to reconstruct a practice of genuine moral and political argument; the inability to do so does not count as an objection to nihilism about practical reasoning (or to related forms of noncognitivism). Stanley Cavell presented Charles Stevenson, the sometime champion of emotivism, as someone who had forgotten what moral argument was like; the rejoinder we are considering is that, on the contrary, it is everyone *but* the emotivists who have forgotten.[13]

What I have been saying describes not just arguments in bars, and not just political journalism, but much of what passes for academic writing, both in political theory and political philosophy. It also describes, at least as soon as we leave the more rarefied regions of moral theory, not just political but moral discourse – partly because it is hard to distinguish them. (Is the contemporary debate over abortion *political,* or *moral?* To put the question is to see that these are not, in this case, genuine alternatives.) I will consider another explanation shortly, but notice that we do need to qualify the rejoinder. Unless one is already a metaethical noncognitivist, one will take Political Noncognitivism to be an idealized or approximate description of a messier state of affairs. The various phenomena we have gathered as supporting evidence are evidently only present to one degree or another. For instance, that a political opinion on one topic reliably predicts opinions on other topics is true only to a certain extent.[14] Sometimes verbal agreement masks disagreement among the partisans. Sometimes people do change their minds (often, when they do, pretending that they haven't). And even if Political Noncognitivism is true of public political debate, it is a delicate question, and one which the arguments on the table leave open, how far it holds of political decision making conducted behind closed doors. While politicians are not necessarily *immune* to the flow of public political debate, we should not assume that a politician's deliberative resources are confined to the argumentative displays put on by his party's spokespersons.[15]

These qualifications notwithstanding, we can now recognize Political Noncognitivism as an urgent practical problem, and one that should concern us especially if we think that nihilism (or emotivism, or whatever) is mistaken. To the extent that public political debate controls policy choice (as in a democratic polity it is supposed to), we make our political (and moral) choices *as though* we were noncognitivists, and *as though* nihilism about practical reasoning were true. Emotivism was the earliest and most straightforward of the analytic noncognitivist positions, and it was meant to be dismissive: its point was that when you produce a moral or ethical evaluation, you're not really *saying* (or *thinking*) anything at all. (More recent forms of noncognitivism have attempted to mute the dismissiveness.) In suggesting that Political Noncognitivism is the correct account of much of our political discourse, I mean to be every bit as dismissive as the logical positivists were, when they advanced emotivism as their metaethical theory.[16] To treat Political Noncognitivism as the right idealization to work with is to say that, with exceptions that are almost too unusual to matter, people who argue politics in public are only *pretending* to think. If choices which are made for good reasons are normally better than choices which are made without reasons, and if public debate really does shape policy, this is a practical disaster.

3

Hume also saw the problem of making room for political argumenta-tion as not merely theoretical. One of the threads running through the *History* is Hume's concern with party politics, a familiar part of the polit-ical landscape to us, but relatively new to Hume's time. (The Whigs and the Tories had only just evolved out of their religious predecessors.) You might think of someone who is willing to die for his political beliefs as a man of principle, and admirable for that reason, but Hume uses the *His-tory* to argue that "party zeal" is not a virtue but a vice. As in the previously mentioned arguments of the *History*, many different considerations are put into play; I'll sketch one path through the discussion, starting out with points Hume makes in his *Essays*.

It has become the case that

> no party, in the present age, can well support itself, without a philosophical or speculative system of principles, annexed to its political or practical one; we ac-cordingly find, that each of the factions, into which this nation is divided, has reared up a fabric of the former kind, in order to protect and cover that scheme of actions, which it pursues.[17]

But demarcating factions by (what we would now call) political ideology brings out the worst in people.

> It is no wonder, that faction is so productive of vices of all kinds: For, besides that it inflames all the passions, it tends much to remove those great restraints, honour and shame; when men find, that no iniquity can lose them the applause

of their own party, and no innocence secure them against the calumnies of the opposite.[18]

As unscrupulous politicians rise to the top, they take advantage of the fact that "party zeal is capable of swallowing the most incredible story" (HE vi 495n), and Hume recounts at great length such instances of the phenomenon as the "popish plot." (Briefly described: the McCarthyism of late seventeenth-century England, an episode in which "men reasoned more from their fears and their passions than from the evidence before them" [HE vi 340].) "We know not to what length enthusiasm or other extraordinary movements of the human mind, may transport men, to the neglect of all order and public good" (EMPL 528–9). In particular, "controversy may appear so momentous as to justify even an opposition by arms to the pretensions of the antagonists" (EMPL 493). Hume's narrative shows us what happens when that barrier is crossed, rehearsing what has become the all too familiar progress of revolution: the progressive shift of control to the most extreme faction, the triumph over the old regime and the execution of the monarch, the terror and the revolution devouring its children, and finally, Hume finds that "illegal violence, with whatever pretences it may be covered, and whatever object it may pursue, must inevitably end at last in the arbitrary and despotic government of a single person" – Cromwell, in this case (HE vi 54).

There are two points to pull out of this capsule description of what, when you add up the parts of Hume's treatment devoted to it, is a dauntingly long argument. First, political or religious fervor, however sincere and well-intentioned, is a recipe for disaster, and therefore vicious. And second, part of the reason it is a recipe for disaster is that, along the way, the (putative) reasons given for a party's policies come to exhibit the features I earlier claimed were characteristic of public political debate; no longer responsible to the normal standards of factual evidence, they amount merely to markers of party membership. The (or a) problem with party politics is that it produces Political Noncognitivism.

4

In "The Skeptic," Hume sets up the theoretical problem that I take it the *History of England* is meant to address. The essay is one of a group of four, which present for the lay but literate reader prominent philosophical schools of the Hellenistic world, and so one might wonder whether its views can be safely attributed to Hume himself. That hesitation is unnecessary; unlike the other essays in the group, which self-consciously adopt an archaic and exaggerated prose style, the essay on skepticism is written in Hume's characteristic voice, and includes, almost verbatim, stretches of argument (covering his views on practical reasoning) taken from the appendix to the second *Enquiry*.

As we should expect, the problem is that there really is no such thing as practical reasoning: "To diminish . . . or augment any person's value for an object, to excite or moderate his passions, there are no direct arguments or reasons, which can be employed with any force or influence" (EMPL 171). However, evaluations are the result of those passions produced by considering an object, and one does not normally, in the course of forming them, consider only the official object of the evaluation. (Hume's example is a diamond: in judging it to be precious, we respond not just to the glittering little crystal, but to its rarity.) So our evaluative judgments will be sensitive to *which* objects are considered, and "here, therefore, a philosopher may step in, and suggest particular views, and considerations, and circumstances, which otherwise would have escaped us; and, by that means, he may either moderate or excite any particular passion" (EMPL 172). What has the look and feel of reasoning about evaluative (and so, moral and political) matters will turn out on closer inspection to be, not a sequence of logically valid inferences, but a series of reminders, redirecting an interlocutor's attention so as to suitably stimulate his emotional responses.

This redirection of attention may involve reasoning properly so called, and this is how we find Hume elsewhere squaring the opposing views about the possibility of moral argument.

The final sentence . . . which pronounces characters and actions amiable or odious, praise-worthy or blameable . . . depends on some internal sense or feeling . . . But in order to pave the way for such a sentiment, and give a proper discernment of its object, it is often necessary, we find, that much reasoning should precede, that nice distinctions be made, just conclusions drawn, distant comparisons formed, complicated relations examined, and general facts fixed and ascertained.

Moral argument, in this respect, is much like art criticism:

in many orders of beauty, particularly those of the finer arts, it is requisite to employ much reasoning, in order to feel the proper sentiment; and a false relish may frequently be corrected by argument and reflection. There are just grounds to conclude, that moral beauty partakes of this latter species, and demands the assistance of our intellectual faculties, in order to give it a suitable influence on the human mind. (EPM 172:33–173:24)

But not all such reminders will end up looking like reasonable argument, reasonably conducted, to a successful conclusion, and in particular, specifically philosophical reminders will not. Much of the remainder of the essay is devoted to pointing out that philosophers' doctrines are ineffective when deployed in normal debate. First, philosophical arguments are too complex and too distant from one's tangible concerns to keep in focus; one's attention quickly slides away from them, and back to the concerns they were meant to override or counterbalance. But a "consideration...which we cannot retain without care and attention, will never produce those genuine and durable movements of passion, which are the result of nature, and the constitution of the mind" (EMPL 172). Second, they do not discriminate between one local concern and another: "In vain do we hope to direct their influence only to one side" (EMPL 173). Hume's examples of "philosophical" considerations include the fact that we all die in the end, anyway, and that the world is an insignificant speck in the vastness of the universe; pointing out that we all die in the end anyway does not select, say, this mayoral candidate over that; rather, the consideration distracts one from the choice.

Evaluative or practical argument (or the best surrogate we have for it) consists in drawing attention, often argumentatively, to hitherto overlooked considerations. Philosophical considerations are inappropriate to argument (or "argument") meant to address the sorts of practical questions that come up in ordinary moral or political contexts. However (and here we are moving beyond what we find in "The Skeptic"), history does better than philosophy on this count. Historical facts and narratives are concrete, vivid, and easy to keep in mind; they discriminate between evaluative stances in ways that the more distant "philosophical" considerations do not. And when we pick up the *History of England*, we find that Hume's arguments conform to this model. For instance, he tells us that if "the spectacle...of those times...seems horrid and deformed, we may thence learn to cherish with the greater anxiety that science and civility, which has so close a connexion with virtue and humanity...";[19] by providing historical context for present science and civility, Hume is trying to prompt an emotional response which might go missing if someone brought up in a culture that takes these things for granted were to consider them on their own. Or again, the *History of England* is organized by reigns, and, on the death of each monarch, Hume pauses for a briefer or lengthier assessment of his or her character, explicitly conducted in terms of the monarch's virtues and vices. With all the relevant facts in front of them, the readers follow along with Hume as he summons up

the appropriate passions which together constitute the appropriate ethical judgment: their "hearts beat with correspondent movements to those
which are described by the historian" (EPM 223:15–17).

Hume had high hopes for this mode of argumentation. He observed
that historical narrative, by and large, comes down on the side of virtue:
even Machiavelli, he remarked, ceased to maintain the cynical amoral-
ity of his political doctrines once he got around to retelling the history
of Italy (EMPL 567). In thinking historiography to be a mode of argument that could escape the pernicious influences of party zeal, he put
his money where his mouth was, claiming the last two volumes of the
History of England to be the first nonpartisan history of the events that put
in place the regime under which he lived. (A good deal of the *History* is
devoted to contesting the claim that England's political convulsions had
been about restoring the ancient liberties of the people; while Hume was
satisfied with the outcome, there had been, if you looked at the past hon-
estly, no ancient liberties to restore.) What were Hume's reasons for his
optimism?

5

An early essay, "Of the Study of History," provides the first of Hume's
reasons for turning to history.[20] Virtue and vice, Hume had argued in
both the *Treatise* and second *Enquiry*, have to be felt. The vocabulary of
moral assessment is selected precisely as vocabulary that expresses shared
or common sentiments; to master the "general unalterable standard, by
which we may approve or disapprove of characters or manners" is to learn
to correct for idiosyncratic deviations from "general language . . . [which]
affix[es] the epithets of praise or blame, in conformity to sentiments,
which arise from the general interests of the community."[21] Since moral
vocabulary is introduced to distinguish emotional responses that are universally shared from those that are idiosyncratic – the moral response
is by definition the nonidiosyncratic one – the problem of moral argument will be to assure that, although driven by emotion, it is conducted,
assessed, and regulated by a shared set of standards.

Now, history is a happy medium on a spectrum that has both fiction
and "life and action" lying at one extreme, and philosophy at the other.
Rehearsing a philosopher's arguments "leaves the mind so cold and un-
moved, that the sentiments of nature have no room to play"; the emotional response necessary for moral evaluations goes missing. There is no
shortage of emotion in the assessments of a "man of business," but they

are likely to be driven by self-interest: "his judgment [is] warped on every occasion by the violence of his passion." And because "poets" must above all keep their readers engaged, they will avail themselves of any means they can to provoke vivid emotional responses, and consequently "often become advocates for vice." (We can, if we like, treat this as the Humean response to the suggestion recently advanced by Martha Nussbaum, that reading fiction will improve our moral discrimination.) But "the writers of history, as well as the readers, are sufficiently interested in the characters and events, to have a lively sentiment of blame or praise; and, at the same time, have no particular interest or concern to pervert their judgment."[22] The sort of specialized training in argument that seemed too recherché to support the man in the street's assent to moral and political conclusions is not required to appreciate historical narrative; it was no accident, Hume must have decided, that his *Treatise* "fell dead-born from the press," while his *History of England* became such a bestseller that "the copy-money exceeded any thing formerly known in England."[23] In short, even in the absence of academic training, historical writing produces emotional responses, but not idiosyncratic ones; to the extent that this is true, both historians and their readers will – by definition – come down on the side of virtue.

Hume's second reason for thinking historical writing could serve as moral argumentation has to do with what we would now think of as the logical form of historical theory. The social and political sciences, history among them, do not fit the so-called Deductive-Nomological model of science, on which the exceptionless laws invoked in explanations can be disconfirmed by even a single balky instance. Hume devotes a full essay, "Of Some Remarkable Customs," to showing that there are exceptions to even the best-grounded generalizations of such sciences. The exceptions should not lead us to dismiss generalizations supported by the preponderance of evidence; general historical conclusions (such as our earlier examples: manners matter; luxury is a good thing) must be established by piling instance upon instance, until the supporting evidence outweighs the odd exception. History is a science in which argumentation proceeds *cumulatively.* I have already gestured at the sheer length of Hume's and Gibbon's histories; we now have a principled explanation for that feature of their writing.

The cumulative nature of historical argumentation promises to make political argument more tractable. Members of opposing parties may have irreconcilably different renderings of this or that historical event. But the important lessons of history are generalizations (again: a rising standard of living brings about an improvement in manners), and these general-izations depend on the preponderance of the evidence, and not on any particular bit of it: in constructing such an argument, the local and parti-san disagreements wash out. If everyone can agree on the generalization, then the generalization can be used as a shared basis for formulating present policy.

Again, Hume is aware enough that ideological commitments may pro-duce irresolvable disagreements about the course of one or another his-torical event. "There are ... three events in our history, which may be regarded as touchstones of partymen. An English Whig, who asserts the reality of the popish plot, an Irish Catholic, who denies the massacre of 1641, and a Scotch Jacobite, who maintains the innocence of queen Mary." He describes such polemicists "as men beyond the reach of argu-ment or reason, [who] must be left to their prejudices" (HE iv 395), and this may suggest that historiography is not as effective as all that. However, consider a side effect of exposition that is both emotionally engaging and as repetitive as a methodology built around the amassing of evidence re-quires. Hume was a British Empiricist, and endorsed a psychology on which repeated assessments of a given kind make the mind more likely to move in the same paths on subsequent occasions. So those assessments will operate as *moral drill*: in reading the *History*, one is practicing for the ethical assessments one will subsequently make in one's day-to-day life.[24] History told with moderation will be drill in moderation, and Hume hopes that "the greater moderation we ... employ in representing past events; the nearer shall we be to produce a full coalition of parties" (EMPL 500). That is, a sufficiently lengthy and sufficiently moderate history is a means of habituation to judiciousness, and thereby an antidote to the extremism of party politics.[25]

History provides a domain in which one can exercise one's evaluative skills, without having them swamped by political or self-interested pas-sions, and there may be a lesson for today's philosophical pedagogy here. It has become routine for teachers of philosophy to attempt to engage their students by asking them to debate current hot-button issues, and introductory ethics classes nowadays use any number of these as their hooks. The teachers share the motivations which Hume attributed to the poets: the drive to boost course enrollments and student evaluations (their version of the author's need to acquire and entertain readers) is an overwhelming incentive to attract and excite students. If Hume is right about the poets, these classes train students in blind and misdirected passion, rather than judicious and intelligent moral deliberation. The dialectical skills students bring to such courses are (anyway in American colleges) normally quite weak, and easily swamped by emotion and political loyalties. Better to follow Hume, and find a safer ground on which to exercise the skill set; only when the students have become stronger reasoners will they be able to return to the hot-button topics, and actually reason about them.

6

Hume, then, took himself to have solutions to the problems he found pressing: to the theoretical need to account for the look and feel of political and moral argumentation, given his nihilism about practical reasoning, and the political need to conduct such argument in a way that could arrive at a shared and calmly held resolution. Contemporary noncognitivists would do well to follow his lead, that is, to treat the challenge of reconstructing moral and ethical argument as best responded to, not with handwaving, but with an extended demonstration of how it is done. Still, in the background to those solutions we find views about practical reasoning and moral psychology that are not widely held today. So to what extent can Hume's ideas be adapted to the problem of Political Noncognitivism?

First of all, for a number of reasons, Hume's expectations of historical writing may seem to us unrealistically high. I mentioned earlier that Hume was proposing his own *History of England* as a nonpartisan treatment, one which he hoped would create common ground between the parties of his own day; it is an indicator of how deep the problem he was struggling with goes that he was immediately accused of – and is still presented as – taking sides.[26] Hume may have been underestimating how much training good history takes. Hume's observation that historians come down on the side of virtue seems, in our day and age, to be controverted by the history of historiography.[27] The idea that amassing historical evidence allows one to trump or sidestep controversy over particular events is likely to seem naive: there is not just revisionist history, but revisionist history of everything. (Why should we think that historians cannot disagree with each other up and down the line?) Last in the present list, faculties of the human mind can be turned upon themselves, and when they are, sometimes they prove to be self-reinforcing (as, Hume thought, our moral sense is: we approve of our dispositions to approve of some things and not others); sometimes they discredit themselves (as did, Hume thought, the faculty of theoretical rationality, by providing arguments for skepticism).[28] What happens when we turn (what we could think of as) the historical faculty on itself? It is a slightly more recent commonplace that historical narrative, when carefully reexamined, tends to dissolve into a welter of detail, detail which dislodges the initial narrative. Altogether, twenty-first century readers are likely to be more skeptical about the prospects of historical argument than was Hume.

But there is a further and strategic obstacle to appropriating Hume's ideas. As a nihilist about practical reasoning, Hume had no alternative to understanding the problems he identified as having to do with the manipulation, modulation, and control of the passions. It was not an option for him to worry that something in political contexts derails genuine inference, and forestalls argument properly so called. If we are not nihilists ourselves, however, we cannot avoid framing the problem of Political Noncognitivism in these terms.

There is an obvious enough explanation for Political Noncognitivism, one having to do with the function of public political argument. Successful politics is in large part a matter of building winning coalitions of supporters. Such coalitions need to be robust and stable. If supporters could be talked out of a position by exposing them to the problems with the arguments for it, political coalitions would be tenuous at best, for, as practicing philosophers further know, arguments usually have problems. Being sensitive to the indefinitely many objections to one's position means that one's support for the position is not robust, and so that sort of sensitivity will be, over the medium to long term, weeded out of political practice. Political effectiveness precisely requires *in*sensitivity to the problems with your reasons for your policies; it's not a coincidence that politicians are regularly accused of, rather than praised for, flip-flopping on the issues.[29] So public political argument will not be about arriving at conclusions supported by the available evidence. Normally its real function is to display unswerving support for the political position: to show that it has dedicated and vocal advocates who will not be moved by opposition (or opposing advocacy). If this is correct, however, a position very much like emotivism seems to be, not just true, but *required* of most political argument; it is politically necessary that it serve to *express commitment* to a policy or party, and that it not be held to the standards appropriate to reasoning about belief.

The explanation can be adapted to accommodate the way that Political Noncognitivism seems to hold of moral (as opposed to specifically political) argumentation. Morals are, after all, about mores; customs and practices require a type of stability analogous to that required for political coalition building. For instance, you need to know that your interlocutor's unwillingness to deceive you is not overly sensitive to the many objections one could find or invent to any argument he could give for honesty. And you need to be assured that his honesty does not depend on his being a moral philosopher, someone capable of following the arguments; professional training of this kind is just too rare. This is perhaps why moral and political philosophy are so much less intellectually adventuresome than debates about other philosophical topics.

There is a second and supplementary explanation. Political coalitions will be successful only if their members grasp the ideas they are supporting. (If they do not, they will fail to be motivated by them, and will fail to implement them effectively.) Most educations do not provide much in the way of training in argumentation; the percentage of the population with a competence in rigorous reasoning is vanishingly small. Moreover, argument quickly complicates hypotheses and proposals, and complicated ideas are harder to grasp. So argument-based political coalitions will also be small, and since, in politics, size and numbers matter, argument-based coalitions will tend to be displaced by coalitions in which argument properly so called does not play much of a role.

To complain that arguments – real arguments – do not play a real role in politics, when real arguments are not suitable for political use, is to ask political players to sacrifice their political effectiveness and standing to an unrealistic standard of intellectual purity; that is, it is to engage in ineffectual and unproductive kvetching. The point, please note, is not that commitment in politics is a bad thing. (It is certainly not a bad thing in many other domains; you had better not be asking yourself, every morning, whether the family you're in is the right one for you.) The question is whether there is a way to make argumentation the source of political commitment, rather than its epiphenomenon.

While there has been some recent discussion, under the slogan "deliberative democracy," of how to make the political process more reason- and argument-driven, if we see where in the territory that discussion has been located, we will see that the underlying problem has not been addressed. There are diagnoses and proposals already in circulation which focus on the conditions surrounding political debate, rather than the forms such argument takes. For instance, James Fishkin takes the problem to be a relative of the Voter's Paradox: in a large body politic, the chances of your opinions making a difference are so low that there's no good reason to spend time and other resources developing them. And so his solution is to create circumstances in which a representative sample of citizens will think, in a focused and informed manner, about political issues. But spending more time, in better surroundings, thinking harder about the arguments that ought to decide some policy question is not a way of resolving your policy questions if, the more you think, the more problems you find with the arguments.[30] Or again, Gutmann and Thompson try to specify the sorts of considerations that ought to play a role in political argument (roughly, the sorts of considerations that your opponent can respect, even if not agree with), and how they ought to be deployed (roughly, respectfully and with open ears).[31] But if the objections to the arguments which deploy such considerations do not run out, it does not matter how respectfully you listen, and how respectfully you choose your premises.

Call an argument *politically valid* if its form is robust: if the movement to its conclusions is not going to be interrupted by the sorts of objections that will come up in the regions of political debate where it is likely to be used. And call an argument *politically sound* if its premises are (or can be made) shared ground in those regions of political debate. The theoreticians of deliberative democracy have been spending their time worrying about political soundness, and about the circumstances in which the arguments are conducted.[32] Equal attention has not been devoted to the *forms* such arguments can take. But if arguments cannot be made politically valid, then it is irrelevant how sound they are, or how ideal are the circumstances in which the debate is conducted.

If we are trying to satisfy the requirement that usable political argument be robust, in virtue of its form, in a way that philosophical argument normally is not, historical argumentation, as Hume understands and conducts it, takes on the appearance of a model proposal – the *kind* of proposal we are looking for (even if in the end we reject it). Humean argument in history works very differently from argument in philosophy, just because the *weight* of evidence matters to the former in a way it does not to the latter. You do not decide which philosophical position is correct by counting up the arguments for and against; and, as we have already remarked, any individual argument for a philosophical conclusion will be very sensitive to the indefinitely many objections to it which one can find or invent. But while a rendering or interpretation of any particular historical event may be controversial, a preponderance of evidence, collected from a thousand years of history, and resulting from the treatment of one historical incident after another after another, can settle certain sorts of historical question – or so Hume thinks. The right conclusion is determined by the cumulative force of the considerations, and objections to this or that retelling of some occurrence are filtered out as so much noise.[33]

Political debates will not turn on real arguments until there are modes of real argument that are not too delicate to cement stable coalitions. That does seem to entail that political argument had better turn out to be a very different sort of beast than philosophical argument. When I teach, I routinely ask my students to tell me what's wrong with the argument we are examining, and they rise to the occasion – even though the philosophical arguments that get taken up in a schoolroom are normally classics of their kind. Nevertheless, even if the arguments we are looking for prove different from the ones philosophers deploy, a substantive account of political validity may, in the academic division of labor, be a suitable task for the philosophers.

We do need to be aware that we are not anywhere close to the finish line. Why think that types of arguments and their components *can* be divided up into the politically valid and invalid, sound and unsound? Even if they can, will they be usable in political debate? (Hume's *History* was a bestseller, but how many voters today are going to take the time to read six volumes of *anything*?) Providing such modes of argument is not the same thing as getting them used. (But if they are not available, they certainly will not be used.) Possibly, relying on one class of arguments and excluding others will introduce an unwanted bias into political debate (if some forms of argument tend to support certain kinds of conclusions rather than others). And of course it would be utopian to expect political debate to be entirely argument-driven, even if there are usable modes of argumentation on hand. Still, we cannot usefully take up these further issues until we have live candidates with which to think them through.

Whether or not historical narrative is a form of argument that is suitably robust, thinking about it under this heading shows us what we are looking for. Real political argument can only be effective (and so will only play a significant role in politics) if it can be constructed so that controversial details don't matter. Perhaps identifying forms of argument with this feature ought to be one of the short- to medium-term goals of political philosophy.

Notes

I'm grateful to Chrisoula Andreou, Sarah Buss, Don Garrett, Gabi Juvan, and Hillel Millgram for comments on an earlier draft, and to Alyssa Bernstein, Jon Bendor, Pepe Chang, David Friedheim, Jenann Ismael, Amy Johnson, Nadeem

Hussain, Brenda Lyshaug, Clif MacIntosh, Sherri Roush, Yonatan Shemmer, and Steve Stich for helpful conversation.

1. Hume, 1985, p. 486; further citations by EMPL and page. Hume, 1778/1983, will be cited as HE, by volume and page; see note 3 to Chapter 6 for the conventions to be used in referring to Hume's *Treatise* and *Enquiries*. The interpretation of Hume as a nihilist is defended in Chapters 6 and 7 of this volume.

2. Perhaps even if the premise sets do not overlap, the doctrines belong together because they *cohere* with one another.

   But notice first that without a clear specification of what is meant by "coherence," compelling arguments cannot be constructed to support this objection (Millgram, 2000): any tight argument would have to help itself to a crisp description of coherence. With one-and-a-half exceptions (Thagard, 1989; Thagard and Verbeurgt, 1998), which I expect are unsuitable for these purposes, there aren't any clear specifications available. In plain English: philosophers (other than Thagard) who use the word "coherence" haven't decided what they mean by it.

   Moreover, notice that the objection does not fit the practice of political discourse it is meant to save. The objection supposes that partisan packages of political positions will all be largely coherent (even if one of them is slightly more coherent than another). But this is not how participants in political argument regard matters. They all see their *own* package of positions as coherent, and other packages as extremely incoherent. (Think of how American Democrats and Republicans delight in pointing out the inconsistencies in the others' views – and of how rare the acknowledgment of inconsistency is.) So my working hypothesis is that conviction as to the coherence of one's own political views should be regarded as *part* of the phenomenon I am calling Political Noncognitivism, and should not be taken at face value.

3. For emotivism, see Ayer, 1951, ch. 6, Stevenson, 1963, ch. 2; the "merely" is an important component of the characterization, registering as it does a thin and dismissive conception of the emotions. The logical positivists thought of the emotions as something like itches or twinges (in one terminology of the time, as *qualia*). Adding richer conceptions of the emotions to the identification of evaluative assertion with expression of emotion will give you positions that could not by any means be characterized as noncognitivist. For an example of such a position, attributed to the ancient Stoics, see Nussbaum, 1987.

   For prescriptivism, see Hare, 1961.

   For projectivism, see Mackie, 1977, ch. 1. Unlike emotivism and prescriptivism, projectivism allows that moral judgments are full-fledged (albeit invariably false) assertions; so calling Political Noncognitivism – a position on which political claims may yet be true or false – a form of noncognitivism has precedent.

4. For a short recapitulation of the early and still standard objections to emotivism, see MacIntyre, 1981, pp. 12–13. For the so-called Frege-Geach argument, which seems to have been accepted as decisive as regards both emotivism and prescriptivism, see Geach, 1972; I'll give a condensed version

in note 10. For a very interesting variation on the Frege-Geach argument, see Williams, 1973b, pp. 209–12.

I'm confining myself to early twentieth-century noncognitivism just now because later noncognitivist theories were constructed specifically to sidestep these objections. For an example, see Gibbard, 1990.

5. Pocock, 1999–, vol. ii, p. 176. Hume took the test of time very seriously himself; see EMPL 233, and compare HE vi 151–4, on Milton, Hobbes, and Harvey. (For remarks with an opposite tendency, see HE i 336–7.)

6. For an eye-opening contrast with present practice, see HE i 167–8.

7. HE iii 76, iv 384; for other arguments, see "Of Refinement in the Arts," at EMPL 268–80; or HE i 103; or HE v 132, where Hume argues that opulence reduces stiffness and formality.

8. Gibbon, 1906; I have been much helped by the discussion of the aims of the *Decline and Fall,* and of Hume's *History* as its background and context, in Pocock, 1999–.

9. Interestingly, one can find in Hume anticipations of some of the elements of Gibbon's argument. However, Hume takes the problem to lie in the distance of military encampments from the capital and court, and so to affect the nobility of "enormous monarchies," from which category he seems to be excluding Britain (EMPL 341).

Gibbon has a second agenda that is worth remark, that of constructing an Enlightenment argument against a body of Christian theology, one which works by exhibiting the historical contingency of its elements. For instance, learning that Catholicism came to include the Nicene Creed, rather than the monophysite doctrine, because Cyril of Alexandria brought a squad of thugs along to the second Council of Ephesus, has the intended effect of undercutting one's belief in that component of the theology (Gibbon, 1906, ch. 47).

10. For instance, the Frege-Geach argument departed from the premise that simple inferences with moral terms are obviously valid. (E.g.: if it's wrong to torment the cat, then it's wrong to get your little brother to torment the cat; it's wrong to torment the cat; ergo, it's wrong to get your little brother to torment the cat.) The objection was that an emotivist, for instance, could not accommodate their validity.

Very quickly, the argument ran as follows. Emotivism is the claim that moral statements are actually expressions of emotion rather than genuine propositions. So every moral statement must express emotion. In order for the inference about tormenting the cat to be valid, "wrong" has to mean the same thing all the way through; otherwise the inference would turn on an equivocation. In the moral statements embedded in the conditional ("if it's wrong to torment the cat, then it's wrong to get your little brother to torment the cat"), no emotion is being expressed; the conditional "brackets" the force of its antecedent and consequent clauses. Therefore the meaning of the free-standing occurences of "wrong" can't be a matter of expressing emotion, either. Consequently, emotivism is false.

11. This is not a new observation; see, e.g., Tomorrow, 1996, p. 87. But for empirical work that helps delineate the extent of the phenomenon, see

Zaller, 1992, p. 241. Zaller's work also preempts the objection that perhaps the direction of explanation is the other way around: that people belong to their party because they have independently arrived at their party's beliefs.

If one thought that inference properly performed was coherentist, that coherentist inference could rationally underwrite accepting the premises of an argument because one already accepted its conclusions, and that political positions were in the relevant sense coherent, then one could allow the phenomenon, while not taking it to demonstrate Political Noncognitivism. But see note 2 for the obstacles to maintaining this objection.

12. There is a very interesting exception that proves the rule (in the current, rather than the original and more Popperian sense of that phrase), a book called *Cities and the Wealth of Nations* (Jacobs, 1984). An essay in what used to be called political economy, and written in a popular style, its author argues that every urban area ought to have its own currency – certainly a startling and unfamiliar conclusion. While I don't want to take a stand on whether the argument works, the style of argument is likely to elicit a philosopher's recognition: *this* is what political argument would look like, if its premises were adopted independently of the familiar range of conclusions, and if the inferences followed the trail of reasons wherever it led ... that is, it is what political argument would look like if it were performed in the style of the more agile subdisciplines of philosophy. But (and this is why the exception really does prove the rule) its conclusion is politically irrelevant. We do not have to take the trouble to assess how good the argument is, because, whether it is good or not, the conclusion is not already on anyone's political agenda, and advocating it would, in the world of politics, consequently be merely cranky.

13. Cavell, 1999, part III.

14. Depending on what the explanation is when it does not, softening the claim may reinforce rather than undercut Political Noncognitivism. For example, Zaller, 1992, claims that when the opinions in a package are not found together, often the reason is that politically uninformed respondents have not been "cued." (In the 1980s, Republican respondents who scored low on "political awareness" measures failed to endorse funding the Contras, because they didn't know who the Contras were. When the question was changed to "cue" the respondents, by tagging the Contras as an anticommunist insurgency, they corrected their response to match the party position.) The earlier work of Converse, 1964, argued that when beliefs are unconstrained by ideology, that is normally because the persons in question scarcely engage in political debate at all. That is, independently reasoned argument is not necessarily what accounts for failure to toe the party line.

Zaller is also a very useful reminder that Political Noncognitivism need not mean, as in the early metaethical noncognitivists, the substitution of emotions expressed for beliefs. In his rather discouraging model, most voters do not have political opinions at all; that is, they have not integrated the various political "messages" they have assimilated on a topic into a single belief that they endorse. Rather, when asked for an opinion, they search for relevant "considerations" (the products of assimilated "messages"), and reply on the basis of the first (few) they remember. Consequently, polls, elections, and so on are highly sensitive to salience effects. Salience (for these purposes, what happens to come to mind first) may be emotion-driven in some cases, but need not be so generally.

Zaller seems to think that while the masses do not engage in political reasoning, the elites who produce the political positions and "messages" (academics in particular) *do.* That strikes me as a locus of naiveté in an otherwise hard-bitten treatment, but one that is importantly typical: it is in general much easier to be noncognitivist about other people than about oneself, and noncognitivist positions tend to have their greatest difficulties making sense of the first-person deliberative perspective.

15. To return to the case of note 12, there is a certain amount of discussion within economics of optimal currency areas (see Kawai, 1998, for a quick overview), which has played a role in the recent dramatic modifications to the European currency system. Because politicians (sometimes) respect economic expertise, sophisticated economic arguments can be brought to bear on policy decisions even when they are not a part of the public political debate.

16. The dismissiveness makes this an emotionally and politically charged claim, which is likely to prompt uptake of the claim as political argument – in the very sense I have been discussing. I would like to preempt this response; after all, one of the burdens of the discussion so far has been that engaging in this sort of political argument is not an intellectually productive use of one's time. So here is a request to the reader.

In calling my reasons for Political Noncognitivism "reminders," I am marking the fact that I haven't assembled a thorough, lengthy, and airtight argument, one that would force a believer in the surfaces of public political argumentation over to my view of it. I'm taking the diagnosis to be obvious enough for present purposes, and I'm inviting you to see it that way as well, but a natural response is to argue back. That's fine, but only helpful if you conduct your argument in a way that is not properly described by the list of reminders. So please (and here is the request) don't let the commitment to cognitivism about political debate explain your acceptance of the premises which get you that conclusion; don't let the rejection of Political Noncognitivism become part of a package of logically unrelated views that nevertheless have coalesced into a partisan position; and so on.

17. EMPL 465. Hume also made a number of attempts to explain religious fanaticism, and since he regarded it as continuous with political fanaticism, we can treat them as evidence of his persistent concern with the topic: for instance, "enthusiasm" is the effect of manipulation by self-interested clergy (EMPL 60–3), or of heightened metabolism inducing "raptures" and "transports" (EMPL 74), or of a natural tendency for members of a group to imitate one another (EMPL 523; compare the analogous explanation of national character at 202–3).

See Livingston, 1984, pp. 312–23, for a discussion of Hume on "metaphysical" political parties.

18. HE vi 438. But it is not just the worst that are corrupted by political ideology: "During the violence ... of such popular currents ... all private

considerations are commonly lost in the general passion; and the more
principle any person possesses, the more apt is he, on such occasions, to
neglect and abandon his domestic duties" (HE vi 513; compare HE v 527:
"the more sincere and more disinterested they are, they only become the
more ridiculous and more odious").

19. HE ii 518–19; compare HE ii 525: "An acquaintance with the distant periods
of their government is chiefly *useful* by instructing [a civilized nation] to
cherish their present constitution, from a comparison or contrast with the
condition of those distant times." Hume wrote the volumes of the *History* in
pairs, and backwards; the end of the second volume is the chronologically
last writing of the work (HE i xii). So these remarks, written at the completion
of the work, give us Hume's most mature look backwards, and the lessons he
himself is still willing to endorse at the endpoint of his project.

20. While this essay was withdrawn from later editions of the *Essays*, the likeliest
reason is the way it addressed itself to Hume's "female readers," and bumbled
"into a kind of raillery against the ladies" (EMPL 563, 565). Hume seems to
have had second thoughts about the essays to which he had given this form,
and we need not infer, from his having decided not to reprint them, that he
had changed his mind about their contents. He also excised short passages
with this tone from the essays he retained (EMPL 603, 628ff; EMPL 134 is
an exception).

21. EPM 274; 229:18–19; 228:18–22. Here again moral resembles aesthetic judgment; compare Hume's essay, "Of the Standard of Taste," EMPL 226–49.

22. EMPL 567–8. History may also do better at enlivening the sentiments than
fiction, because history is believed to be true; belief, on Hume's psychology,
is a matter of the vivacity of the idea; that greater vivacity is then available
to be communicated to the passions. As early as the *Treatise*, Hume had
claimed:

> If one person sits down to read a book as a romance, and another as a true history,
> they plainly receive the same ideas, and in the same order; nor does the incredulity of
> the one, and the belief of the other hinder them from putting the same sense upon
> their author.... The latter [however] has a more lively conception of all the incidents.
> He enters deeper into the concerns of the persons: represents to himself their actions,
> and characters, and friendships, and enmities ... While the former, who gives no credit
> to the testimony of the author, has a more faint and languid conception of all these
> particulars ... (T 97:21–98:12)

This view may seem unrealistic and quaint to modern readers, for whom it
is fiction that excites, and documentaries that are dull. In Hume's day, the
novel was a novel genre, and much more slow moving, while Hume's own
historical prose was a model of lively writing.

Over and above the contrast between fiction and nonfiction, history exploits our tendency to be impressed by great antiquity. (Livingston, 1984,
pp. 122–5, reconstructs Hume's explanation of the phenomenon.) If (older)
history makes more of an impression (of reflection) on us, moral argument
that invokes it will have greater effectiveness.

23. EMPL xxxiv (emphasis removed), xxxviii. Hume points out on another occasion that "though argument and reasoning could not give conviction, an

historical fact, well supported, was able to make impression on [men's] understandings" (HE iii 141).

24. But if you are resisting a moral that Hume wants you to draw from history, won't repeated efforts on the part of the historian merely strengthen your resistance? Perhaps Hume would want to say that in the vast expanses of the past there must be very many events about which you have no entrenched views; you cannot have encountered them all. Where you have no entrenched views, you will exhibit no resistance.

Because, while reading such a history, one is to a great extent sympathetically occupying the shared point of view of a past society, these historical assessments can diverge from those we would make of a similar character today. Hume on occasion corrects a likely assessment by a naive reader, for example of Queen Elizabeth: even by the lights of Hume's day (and much more so by those of our own), Elizabeth was an autocratic and intolerant ruler, but Hume reminds his readers of the standards of the time – and of her popularity, a defeasible indication that she was taken to live up to them (HE iv 354ff, 351). He also reminds his readers not to invoke gender-based codes in the course of evaluating the character of someone who is being considered as a monarch, rather than, say, as a potential spouse (HE iv 352–3).

25. It is not, of course, the sole such technique; more important is the "police": "general virtue and good morals in a state, which are so requisite to happiness, can never arise from the most refined precepts of philosophy, or even the severest injunctions of religion; but must proceed entirely from the virtuous education of youth, the effect of wise laws and institutions" (EMPL 55). The consumption of history books may make up part of a virtuous education, but surely by no means the most important part.

It is perhaps ironic that "Moderate" became, in Hume's own time, a label for a political camp (Mossner, 1980, ch. 25).

26. Mossner, 1980, p. 403. For antecedents and reception, see Forbes, 1975, pp. 233–63, 290–2, 296 n. 1.

27. There is nonetheless a Humean argument we can now offer for Hume's view. If historians become so by reading history, if extant history mostly comes down on the side of virtue, and if reading history drills you in its ethical attitudes, then we can expect later historians to inherit the virtuous outlook of their predecessors.

28. Korsgaard, 1997, pp. 51–63.

29. Philosophers may also fail, often enough, to have their minds changed by the arguments. (And sometimes the explanation is institutional; philosophers reap professional rewards when they become the flagbearer for a position.) But that it is a philosophical *failing* is exhibited by this contrast: philosophers do not get accused of flip-flopping.

30. Fishkin's proposal (1997) is structurally similar to "informed desire" conceptions of deliberation and of welfare, still popular in mainstream ethics: what you really want, and what is really good for you, is what you *would* want if you were to reconsider at length, with more information than you now have, etc. That is, the idea is that if you take care (perhaps counterfactually) of the

surrounding circumstances (the time and care devoted to deliberation, the respectful attitudes of the participants, and so on), the rationality will take care of itself. Our worry, however, is that the rationality will *not* take care of itself.

Unless you know what substantive features of argument or reasoning you are trying to foster, you cannot show that any particular set of (actual or counterfactual) circumstances promotes them; even if Fishkin's subjects were to converge on some policy proposal, we would not know, without checking their deliberations against prior norms of argumentation, whether that was merely an effect of exhaustion, or the desire to look good on national television, or whether it was because they had found the right answer. However, if you do know, you might as well cut to the chase, and make those prior norms your criteria of success.

31. Gutmann and Thompson, 1996; see p. 348 for a representative remark to the effect that "the content of deliberation often matters as much as the conditions." And see Gutmann and Thompson, 2000, for a shorter restatement of the view.

32. My own preference would be to see more empirical work on what counts as politically sound, before endorsing one or another view of political soundness. For instance, in his investigation of numerically driven inference (Munnich, Ranney, and Appel, 2004), Michael Ranney found that subjects were willing to accept as factual National Institutes of Health figures for the annual number of legal abortions in the US, but unwilling to accept estimates of illegal immigration. (Personal communication.) It would be very helpful to have a much fuller map of such dispositions.

33. Are there candidates other than this one? Perhaps the once well-known argument of Meadows et al., 1972, is suggestive: that exponential growth swamps closed systems, that the global economy is growing exponentially in the closed system that is the planet, and that therefore we need to rein in economic growth. An argument like this one, which turns on the behavior of functions of a certain form, is relatively insensitive to values of controversial parameters. (It does not really matter for the argument if reserves of tin are four, or even forty, times the current best estimates.)

9

Incommensurability and Practical Reasoning

Worries about the incommensurability of ends or of values arise when practical reasoning – that is, reasoning directed toward decision or action, contrasted with reasoning that aims only at arriving at belief – seems to run out: the thought that ends or values are incommensurable is prompted by facing a decision in which they must be jointly brought to bear and it is not clear how this is to be done. If the difficulty persists, frustration may give rise to the thought that there *is* no way to do this, that one *cannot*, here, reason one's way to a practical conclusion; and that this is because the relevant considerations cannot be measured or weighed against each other. So far, so familiar.

I myself do not know what "values" are; like William Bennett, when I hear the word "values," I reach for my Sears catalog. So I am going to consider only the incommensurability of ends (or equivalently, as I will claim, the incommensurability of desires), on the supposition that the incommensurability of values is a closely related phenomenon, and that a treatment of the former could, if necessary, be adapted to the latter. "Incommensurability" is a word applied to a number of distinct, though related, phenomena. I will use it, provisionally, to say of pairs (or sets) of ends or desires that one is not more important than another (or the others), and that they are not equally important. And I will restrict myself to the case in which all ends or desires in question are those of a single human being.

I will first show how the worry that ends are incommensurable is framed by a widely shared model of practical reasoning. I will then suggest that the standard way of introducing incommensurability as a philosophical problem has things backwards: commensurability is the result, rather than the precondition, of practical deliberation. I will give two examples of ways in which desires or ends are commensurated, and show how they indicate imprecise, but rather near, boundaries to the effectiveness of practical reasoning. Then I will consider how, despite the nearness of these boundaries, it can be brought about that practical deliberation provides an agent resources sufficient to negotiate the decisions he faces. Along the way, I will try to indicate the role that the achievement of commensurability plays in the constitution of the practically unified agent; if I am right in thinking that commensurability is a product of practical deliberation, practical deliberation is important not only for successful action, but for the construction of an acting self.

1

Failure of deliberation is one thing, and incommensurability (on the etymology, inability to measure) is another. We need an explanation for their being so often connected, evidently one identifying practical deliberation, or some central part of it, with measurement. I take the explanation to lie in the widespread, if often only implicit, acceptance of an instrumentalist model of practical reasoning, by which I mean the following.

In the formal mode, instrumentalism is the view that to justify an action or a plan or a goal, one must adduce a further goal, such that attaining the former goal (or performing the action, or executing the plan) would be a means (or a satisfactory means, or the best means) of attaining the latter. (I will from here on out mention only ends or goals, and will omit such qualifications as "satisfactory," "the best," and so on.) In the psychological mode, it is the view that all practical reasoning consists in, or can be without loss reconstructed as, deriving a desire (or intention, or action; again, I will not continue to repeat this) from another desire via a bridging belief to the effect that attaining the object of the former desire would be a way of attaining the object of the latter desire. I desire to lower my cholesterol levels and I believe that the best way of doing this is to cut back on eggs and butter and cheese. So I come to desire to cut back on eggs and butter and cheese. In the formal mode: the goal of lowering my cholesterol levels, together with the fact that cutting back on the butter and so on will lower them, justifies my goal of cutting back. On the instrumentalist model, all practical reasoning, and all practical justification, while perhaps more elaborate, comes to something very much like this; practical deliberation consists *only* in means-end reasoning. The point of practical reasoning, on this model, can only be to satisfy some already existing desire or attain some already adopted goal, and practical justification can do no more than exhibit the fact that some action or desire serves the satisfaction of some further desire.

That instrumentalism is more or less the received view, and that it is mistaken, are claims which I will not argue for now.[1] Rather, I want to consider problems that arise within the instrumentalist model, and how addressing these problems leads to the idea that ends may be incommensurable.

We live in a world in which ends or goals or desires can conflict, that is, in which desires that one has cannot be jointly satisfied. Such conflicts are pervasive: it is *normally* true that, for any desire one has, one has a conflicting desire. A purchase requires money with which I could buy something else I want; activities compete for time with other activities. So a sane instrumentalism must supplement the raw claim that practical reasoning consists in finding ways to satisfy one's desires with an explanation of how conflicts between desires can be resolved.

Now instrumentalism is an exclusionist doctrine: it counts *only* deliberation directed toward the satisfaction of desires as practical reasoning. Since only desires give rise to practical reasons, conflicts between desires must be adjudicated by appeal to features of those desires whose satisfaction deliberation can address. At this point, the notion of the strength or weight of a desire enters the picture, as an intrinsic feature of the desire that can be used to resolve conflicts between desires. Some desires are intrinsically more demanding than others; conflict between desires is resolved by satisfying the stronger of the conflicting desires, or, in more complicated conflicts, by satisfying the desires that have the greatest summed strength or weight.

This version of instrumentalism requires that we be able to determine the weights or strengths of desires or goals in a way that allows them to be compared, one to another and in larger groups: deliberation proceeds by measuring and comparing the respective weights or strengths of one's ends. It is in this context that failure of deliberation is construed – is bound to be construed – as failure of commensuration. If one is clear about what is a means to what – and attaining this kind of clarity is not, it has been pointed out, properly speaking practical deliberation at all[2] – then the remaining locus of difficulty is the task of comparing weights or strengths of ends or desires.

Naive instrumentalists – early utilitarians, perhaps – might have thought that desires resembled sensations and came with their strengths somehow inscribed on them; and if desires *did* come this way (and if the view of sensations that tends to be relied on in this context were satisfactory), then incommensurability would be quite unusual. But the sophisticated instrumentalist realizes that "desire," in his use of it, must be a term of art, the correlate in his moral psychology of a goal or end, and that there is no particular phenomenological aspect it must wear. A desire need not *feel* like anything at all, and so its strength need not feel like anything at all either. The strength of a desire, considered logically rather than phenomenologically, is simply a way of expressing or summarizing the relations of comparative importance in which the object of desire stands to other objects of (actual or possible) desire.

Expressions like "strength" or "weight" normally indicate a quantitative conception of the comparison-enabling intrinsic feature of desires. I will return to the link between the comparison of ends or desires and the measurement of quantities associated with them. For now, note that a quantitative conception of the relations of importance among an agent's desires requires only that those relations satisfy a few familiar formal conditions.[3] But because the instrumentalist wishes to *explain* those relations in terms of features internal to the desire, when he believes those formal conditions are satisfied, he will be pressured to construe the comparison-enabling features as measurable quantities of something within the desires (their strengths or weights), and ascertaining the presence of the feature as measuring.

There is no reason to expect that when agents conceive an interest in some object, they at the same time consider and settle the relations of comparative importance in which it stands to all other possible objects of desire. (When you decide you want a piece of apple pie, do you ask yourself whether you would prefer it to an order of vegetable samosas? If samosas are not on the menu, probably not; and even if for some reason you do consider the samosas, there are indefinitely many items that you do not consider, at least if you are ever to get around to ordering.) A desire is formed in a particular practical context, and we should not expect its content to address demands not made by that context. Of course desires will quite often come with contents supplemented by habit, or by references to judgments of relative importance invoking previously formed desires, as when finishing the pie is unproblematically overridden by a babysitter emergency. But a newly formed desire will generally not contain within itself the resources needed to adjudicate conflicts between it and many other actual and possible desires. Desires have only the contents that are put into them, and since human beings are finite

creatures, those contents will be quite limited.[4] So, because it is characteristic of human beings to find themselves in circumstances in which
desires conflict in novel ways, we should expect desires to be frequently
incommensurable.

This is not to say that one *could* not form only desires that contained
the resources needed to adjudicate arbitrary conflicts – for example, by
making a real number intended to be used for all such comparisons part
of the content of each desire. But our desires are normally not like that,
and there is a reason they are not. If you *did* form desires equipped
with these resources – whether in the crude way just mentioned or in
some more sophisticated fashion – you would be foolishly committing
yourself to a position whose practical upshots you could not have seriously
considered. Forming desires in this way would be imprudent, thoughtless,
and rash.

The instrumentalist take on practical reasoning is an essential ingredient of the problem. If I have already formed a desire that allows me
to choose between *A*, *B*, and *C*, and another desire that allows me to
choose between *D*, *E*, and *F*, why can I not repeat the procedure when
a situation arises that requires me to face the hitherto uncontemplated
choice between *A*, *D*, and *G*? The difficulty is that instrumentalism insists
that if the way in which the choice between *A*, *D*, and *G* is made is to
count as practical *reasoning*, it must be justifiable entirely by reference to
the already available desires; simply *coming to have* a further desire is not
reasoning. If we accept the instrumentalist model of practical reasoning,
the pervasiveness of conflicting desires and the inevitability of novel conflicts, the severe limitations on the deliberative resources we can suppose
are located within reasonably adopted desires, and the consequent pervasiveness of incommensurable desires, we must conclude that practical
reasoning should almost *never* work. If the optional member of this package is instrumentalism, then the price of instrumentalism is quite high.

That one can't successfully navigate one's life by rational deliberation
alone is a conclusion that might be accepted with composure. Faced
with decisions between incommensurable options, it will be suggested,
we have resources other than deliberation. For example, one can decide
on impulse; and there are presumably more sophisticated methods of
adjudication. If the considerations supporting the competing options
are genuinely incommensurable, then one's choice will at any rate not
have been *wrong*.

Against this counsel of complacency, let me briefly indicate the
kind of trouble into which choice on the basis of incommensurable

considerations is likely to get one. Selection techniques whose results are not entirely explicable in terms of their sensitivity to what is important in the choice situation will to that extent produce results that are arbitrary with respect to what is important in that choice situation; they will rehearse, piecemeal, the foolhardiness of forming desires whose demands significantly outrun the thought that one has put into them. And experiment with such techniques shows that there are further problems. Choice that does not reflect a resolution of the competing considerations should not be expected to be consistent across choice situations; for example, an agent acting on a systematic policy of impulsive choice – the most naive member of this family of techniques – would be almost bound to end up at cross-purposes with himself.[5] Because the competing considerations are not decisively resolved, is it easy to find oneself reconsidering one's choice and discovering that the overridden consideration now seems more salient, more central, and simply more important. Such reconsideration is likely to give rise to a family of related and not always distinguishable forms of impaired agency: vacillation, akrasia,[6] an inability to free oneself of second thoughts and to commit oneself to a single course of action, and, last but not least, regret avoidable only by a cultivated blindness to the persisting merits of the discarded choice.[7] That is, choice on the basis of incommensurable desires undermines unified agency in one of several ways: either by successively propelling the agent in different directions, or by encouraging indecisiveness, both of which prevent the adoption of coherent and effective approaches to practical problems; or, where agents are able to avoid indecisiveness and waffling by dint of the sheer determination not to change their minds once they are made up, by committing them to dogged and unintelligent responses to as yet unanticipated circumstances; or, where agents prop up the arbitrary choice by adopting equally arbitrary ways of viewing the choice situation, by trading in akrasia for self-deception.[8]

Faced with this catalog of the risks taken in using alternatives to rational deliberation to bridge the gap between competing desires and choice, the instrumentalist might reply that not all candidate techniques have been considered. (These techniques might add new desires to one's stock, or modify those already in it; or they might select an action while leaving one's desires and evaluative judgments unchanged – if one cannot settle which option is better, one can always flip a coin, or ask one's mother.) Perhaps a technique will be found that does not involve these risks – a method sufficiently intelligent, even when systematically applied, to support rather than weaken agency; sensitive enough to its surroundings to deflect charges that its use is ill-considered, and so on. But when a technique that deserves these encomiums is found, the time will have come to ask whether the instrumentalist is not being dogmatic in refusing to call it a form of practical reasoning.

2

Within the instrumentalist model of practical reasoning, the bases for comparison of desires are their intrinsic features; and so one can determine whether given desires are commensurable simply by examining them. Ends or desires considered generally are either always (or almost always) commensurable – so that instrumental practical reasoning is in principle equipped to solve the problems it is given – or they are often incommensurable, so that practical reasoning must be frequently unsuccessful. Instrumentalists who have not realized how quickly the resources available in desires run out are bound to ask which option we are stuck with.

On the one hand, they may observe that many ends do not, when carefully and sensitively considered, seem to be commensurable. Should I become a lawyer or a clarinetist? Exactly how much money should Judy take her friendship with John to be worth, anyway?[9] If a prospective graduate student attends institution *A*, she will live in Los Angeles, with its automobile-oriented lifestyle, study with the teachers at institution *A*, and become much closer with her LA-dwelling friends and acquaintances. But if she goes to institution *B*, she will live in the Bay Area, with its more bohemian lifestyle, receive a very differently flavored education, live in proximity to a number of relatives, and so on. Would it be better to study with the Wittgensteinian at *A*, or the philosopher of physics at *B*? How much better? If one teacher is preferred to the other, how is the difference between them to be weighed against the availability of used books and an endless supply of perfectly prepared cappucinos? The ends being compared seem resistant to measurement and even to ranking, both within and across categories of goods. From the observation that many ends are plausibly incommensurable, an instrumentalist is likely to draw the conclusion that there are many questions that practical reasoning cannot answer. Choices have to be made, and they will be made without sufficient reason.

On the other hand, instrumentalists might observe that even in circumstances of this kind deliberation quite often terminates in reasoned choice. The considerations presented at the outset may seem incommensurable, but we deliberate and decide anyway. The prospective graduate student visits the respective institutions, talks to friends, advisors, and other students, searches her soul, decides – and is subsequently able to justify her decision. Since, on the instrumentalist view, getting the answer right through rational deliberation requires commensurability, the apparently incommensurable considerations must have been commensurable after all. The problem is then to explain why the considerations had been mistakenly thought to be incommensurable and to reconstruct the underlying metric.[10]

On the one hand, we have convincing examples of agents faced with considerations that do not contain within them the means of commensuration; on the other, we have agents successfully completing deliberations in equally difficult circumstances, and who are subsequently prepared to pronounce on the relative importance of the considerations that entered into their decision. The competing arguments that proceed from these observations are mirror images of each other; each argument requires dismissing the opposing and recalcitrant observation. We should accommodate both observations if we can; they can be reconciled if we suppose that the considerations to which deliberation appeals *are* incommensurable at the outset of the deliberation, but that the process of deliberation *renders* them commensurable. The prospective graduate student begins deliberating unable to commensurate her desires to study under the guidance of the teachers at institution *A* with her desires to study under those at *B*, and these desires with other goals having to do with the way she wants the texture of her day-to-day life to feel. Eventually, she decides to attend one of the two, having on the way seen how to commensurate the conflicting and initially incommensurable ends. Commensurability is not the precondition but the *product* of successful deliberation. At any rate, I propose to proceed on this hypothesis.

Some philosophers have come this far only to conclude that deliberation must be self-deceiving. In an influential but under-discussed paper, Aurel Kolnai writes that

> However enlightened by reason and based on or rather supported by reasons, choice is shot through with arbitrariness . . .

> Placed before significant choices, man cannot but deliberate, weighing ends as if they were means, comparing them as if they were fixed data accessive to theoretical measurement, whereas their weight depends on the seesaw of his own tentative willing and on his emergent *parti-pris* as well as the other way around.

In some sense, it is an inherently deceptive, not to say deceitful operation, with loaded dice as it were; the agent cannot help weighting what he is weighing, though neither can he do the weighting without a vague but imperative reliance on the results of his weighing, some would say the illusion of his manipulating fixed weights.[11]

If competing ends do not have content sufficient to resolve conflict between them into a choice, choice proceeding from resolution rather than impulse, or something on a par with impulse, will involve *augmenting* the content of those ends; for example, by arriving at fixed weights for them. That is to say, choice in the face of incommensurability involves deliberation of ends. Kolnai's difficulty is that deliberation is, as he affirms, of ends, but he takes rationality to be of means: deliberation's "primary habitat and starting-point is indeed, so Aristotle's dictum remains valid, the consideration of means in view of ends."[12] Deliberation of ends was required because instrumental rationality did not have enough to go on; but deliberation of ends, on Kolnai's view, amounts to a form of instrumental rationality. So he concludes that obtaining results in the face of incommensurable considerations must involve some sleight of hand.

We saw earlier that within the instrumentalist model successful practical reasoning presupposes commensurability. So it is not surprising that accepting the suggestion that commensurability is the product of practical reasoning will force an instrumentalist to construe the practical reasoning that produces commensuration as dishonest. If we want to continue to explore the suggestion, we will have to leave instrumentalism behind.

Abandoning instrumentalism means revising our provisional notion of incommensurability. Instrumentalism entails that whenever we are able to render a judgment as to the relative importance of the objects of our desires, we can do so on the basis of the desires themselves; consequently, when we cannot render such a judgment, we can determine that we cannot simply by examining the competing desires. So an instrumentalist can use the notion of commensurability without distinguishing between ends or desires standing in relations of relative importance in whatever way, and their standing in relations of relative importance specified by the desires' contents. When we reject instrumentalism, we need to make the distinction, and to decide what the term "incommensurable" is going to label. Continuity suggests adhering to the following revised usage: Desires or ends are incommensurable when they do not contain within themselves the resources to resolve conflict between them into a judgment of relative importance or into choice.

3

The next item on the agenda is to lay out reasonably representative examples of practical deliberation that manages to commensurate initially incommensurable ends. Consider a standard case of conflicting desires. My roommate has announced that we are welcome to the raspberry chocolate cake in the fridge; it is from Rosie's, and is bound to be delicious. However, I am on a diet, and the cake is fattening. It may help to think of the two considerations as the major premises of competing practical syllogisms ("Eat delicious things," and "Do not eat fattening things"). A practical syllogism proceeding from one major premise might well be defeasible by the major premise of the other: if something is delicious *enough*, and the occasion special enough, making an exception to the diet is probably the right thing to do; conversely, if something is fattening enough, I should make an exception to my policy of eating delicious items. I know that both of these considerations are important to me, but the cake is both delicious and fattening, and, faced with it, I realize that I do not know *how* important the two considerations are with respect to one another in this particular case. I want this, I want that, and I cannot tell which one I want more. How do I resolve this very practical problem?

There are many ways one might address a question like this; let me run through one. Desires, as Anscombe pointed out, come with desirability characterizations; or, equivalently, major premises of practical syllogisms have *points*. What are the points of my competing major premises? The point of eating delicious things will be the sensual pleasure involved; that seems clear enough.[13] And while there are of course many kinds of diets, mine is a response to my body image. I am fat, and ashamed of how I seem to others, especially when I dwell on my thighs, of which I am particularly conscious. Because I do not believe that anyone could find me attractive, I don't date. I feel guilt for my body and contempt and hatred for myself. A successful diet would change my body (and, I perhaps naively think, my body image) for the better.

How can I bring these two desirability characterizations to bear on each other? One thought that might occur to me is that my body makes me so unhappy that I should not deny myself this bit of pleasure. But this thought is self-pitying, and realizing this may lead me to examine more closely the pleasure that I will experience when eating the cake. It might occur to me that there are, after all, different kinds of pleasure: on the one hand, the expansive, joyous pleasure that I might have sharing dessert with old friends, and, on the other, the pleasure of escape: alone in my kitchen at night, the only light that from the open door of the refrigerator, hunched over and completely absorbed in the cake I am greedily devouring, I can forget, for as long as I am eating, that I am ashamed of my body and unhappy with myself. Now I realize that as long as I see myself the way I do, it is the latter pleasure, rather than the former, that I would experience on eating the cake. And once I realize this, my mind is made up. The pleasure of escaping from my body into food is a pleasure I do not want; it is part of the life of self-hatred I am striving to be rid of. It is not that this pleasure has undesirable side effects (though I imagine it does); not all pleasures are intrinsically good, and this, I firmly believe, is one that is not. I will forgo the cake.[14]

In this example, deliberation has rendered initially incommensurable ends commensurable, and done so by enriching their contents. I can now say that my diet has turned out to matter more than the pleasure of eating the cake, and I can say this because I have developed a more articulated picture of the objects of my desires. My indiscriminate desire for sensual pleasure has become a more nuanced family of attitudes toward different varieties of sensual pleasure.[15]

Here is a second example. I am trying to choose between two potential roommates. One of them, I can see, will be clean to a fault, but her conversation loud and uninteresting. The other is quite personable, well read, and clearly will be fun to talk to, but admits to leaving half-full cups of coffee on the floor, dishes in the sink, and laundry on the furniture, often for weeks on end. I know that I care about both aspects of a roommate's behavior, but find myself unable to say which is more important. The competing considerations are incommensurable.

When the summer is over, I *know* which is more important. I shudder when I think about the kitchen sink. My roommate and I have settled into a kind of trench warfare over taking out the garbage. And I find myself saying things like, "I had no idea that cleanliness mattered so much." It is clear to me that a dull conversationalist who has learned to pick up after herself is much to be preferred to a witty slob.

Here it looks like I have *discovered* how much cleanliness matters. I could not have simply made up my mind, enriching my desire by conceiving a further interest, as it were, in one quality or the other. And the problem is not, or not obviously, something I could, at the outset, have reasoned or imagined my way through. (The story could just as easily have been told the other way; I might have found slovenliness tolerable, but dull and whiny conversation obnoxious and infuriating. Ahead of time, there is no way to tell which of these imaginable outcomes I will be brought up against by events.) Rather, I learn what is important (and *how* it is important) in the way I learn many other things: from experience.[16]

If so, then one form that practical deliberation can take is something analogous to inductive or experimental reasoning. In cases like these, we are unable rationally to decide – and the competing considerations are incommensurable – because we simply do not yet know enough about how they matter. Experience and inductive deliberation may supply the information that content-poor desires could not.

Aristotle holds that *phronesis*, or practical intelligence, comes only with experience. We can now give reasons for thinking him correct on this point. Practical intelligence is in large part a matter of being able to choose correctly in the face of competing considerations; on Aristotle's view, intelligent choice appeals to a conception of what matters (which he calls *eudaemonia*).[17] By determining how the different ways in which our ends are important fit together, this conception commensurates the major premises of one's practical syllogisms. But the agent's conception of *eudaemonia* is an achievement. It is acquired piecemeal, beginning with parental instruction, and supplemented by experience when disappointment and pleasant surprises supply one with new premises for one's practical syllogisms, or correct and augment premises already accepted. When circumstances press one to resolve conflicts between one's ends into a locally coherent understanding of what, in the case at hand, matters more, one articulates, bit by bit, the gradually more global, coherent and systematic conception of what matters that serves as a guide to subsequent choice. That is, the process of rendering ends commensurable is the process of acquiring one's conception of what matters.

4

I have suggested that incommensurability works to undermine agency. I now wish to claim that rendering competing considerations commensurable is a central part of the process through which unified agency, or the practical unity of the self, is achieved.

Consider the would-be agent whose would-be practical syllogisms are not at all defeasible by competing considerations – that is, a creature equipped with reflexes rather than the logical apparatus of the practical syllogism. In such a creature, the joint acknowledgment of the major and minor premises of a practical syllogism suffices for forming the intention or executing the action that is its conclusion. The major premise functions as an exceptionless rule, and where rules conflict, conflicts must be resolved in an arbitrary manner – perhaps simply on the basis of which rule happens to be triggered first. Decision making of this kind is familiar enough: Skinner's pigeons, unwieldy bureaucracies, and rule-based expert systems are examples. We think of the behaviorist's conditioned pigeons and rule-bound bureaucracies as mindless; and it is instructive that expert systems, although now a commercial technology, are considered one of the dead ends of Artificial Intelligence, precisely because intelligence was what they could not be made to exhibit.

Now a rough and ready rule of thumb for use in discussions of unity of the self at a time (or synchronic as opposed to diachronic personal identity) might be this: if two thoughts belong to the same mind, then there are trains of thought they could both figure in. And since unity of the self is a matter of degree, we can add that the mind's unity is in part a matter of how *likely* it is that, when thinking that deploys one thought makes it appropriate to invoke the other, the other will in fact be invoked. If this is right, then unity of agency – the practical dimension of personal identity at a time – will be exhibited in the agent's ability to bring to bear in a train of thought leading to a practical conclusion various desires, concerns, and so on, as they become relevant. But this ability is just what makes the difference between reflex and that essentially defeasible inference pattern, the practical syllogism: so achieving unity of agency is a matter of transmuting one's reflexes into practical syllogisms. However, bringing competing considerations to bear in the course of deploying a practical syllogism – contrasted now with the mere juxtaposition of impulses – requires commensurating its major premise with the various considerations that are its potential defeaters. Consequently, a central part of the enterprise of attaining unified agency is commensurating one's ends or desires.

Like our conception of *eudaemonia*, unified agency is an achievement – in fact, the same achievement, seen from a different point of view. The process resembles the day-to-day activities of a sculptor I know. He begins work with a pile of found metal objects – rebar, cotter pins, washers, steel plate, and so on – which he pieces together to form larger units: the head of a hoe is joined to a length of bent reinforcement rod, and is now a hand. Similarly, we start our practical lives with haphazard collections of desires so content-poor as to amount to no more than reflexes – some innate, some conditioned, and some supplied by adults around us. Pressured by experience to resolve practical conflicts, we weld disparate desires into larger and more structured practical judgments. When we do, they are transformed in two not entirely distinguishable ways. First, the desires may be reshaped, just as the sculptor might cut or bend the hoe to make it fit its role as a hand. Second, the desire acquires a role or location in a larger whole, in roughly the way the hoe has; this location is displayed in the defeasibility of the practical syllogisms in which the desire figures.

We are now in a position to reconnect measurement and commensurability. My deliberations regarding the relative merits of diets and cakes, or different kinds of roommates, allowed me to say, retroactively, that my diet and a roommate's cleanliness mattered more than their competitors. But these conclusions did not involve a judgment, or at any rate a very precise judgment, as to *how much* more they mattered. A quantitative conception of the competing merits does not seem to have figured large in my deliberations.

That is in part because of the locality and small number of comparisons. As more of the judgments of relative importance that make up one's picture of what matters are put in place, it will often happen that more patterns of comparability will seem to be expressible using notions of measurement.[18] Recall the sculptor: as parts of the sculpture are assembled, a scale is gradually brought into play with respect to which parts of the sculpture can be too big, or too small, or against which one can be bigger than another, and bigger by such and such an amount. (The respective *physical* sizes of the pieces do not themselves determine their respective sculptural sizes. Painting two physically identical pieces of metal red and blue, respectively, will typically have the effect of making one larger with respect to the other. For comparison, think of the way adding painted items to an initially blank canvas creates the perspectival space in which the items have their relative pictorial sizes.) Similarly, the development of an overall and coherent conception of what matters gradually puts in place a background against which one can judge not only that one consideration is more important than another, but *how much* more important.

Now if, as the instrumentalist has it, the direction of explanation proceeds from what is already there (that is, from the contents of one's desires) to comparisons, then the ability to perform the full range of comparisons presupposes that this background is fully in place; and a background with enough structure to guarantee the feasibility of the full range of possible comparisons is normally one that supports measurability. This is why the strengths or weights of desires are thought of as *quantities*; and it explains why commensurability has so often been thought of as a question of what quantities are measurable against what other quantities. But if the instrumentalist has the direction of explanation back to front, and the contents of one's desires are constructed, piece by piece, through the deliberation of ends, then quantitative measurability will be a cumulative by-product of successive commensurations. Over the course of one's deliberations, one constructs a conception of what matters, and in doing so, one may come to an understanding of some things mattering measurably more or less than others.

Measurability of this kind will appear only when the successive commensurations produce results that satisfy the formal conditions required for a quantitative construal. We should not expect that this will always occur – just as we should not expect every sculpture or painting to put in place enough perspective and scale to fully determine the absolute and relative pictorial and sculptural sizes of all their elements.[19] A satisfactory conception of *eudaemonia* is more likely to look like Matisse's *Red Room* than Raphael's *School of Athens*.

5

We began with the worry that incommensurability threatens the effectiveness of practical reasoning. Now we can see that we have better things to worry about: that the ineffectiveness of practical deliberation might threaten the commensurability of ends and thus the practical unity of the self. And, it seems, there is reason to worry. I am not going to claim that all commensurating practical deliberation looks like one or the other of the two examples of Section 3. After all, we do not have the theory of practical reasoning it would take to underwrite such a claim. But I do think that instances of deliberation that resemble them are not unusual; and if they are not, then practical reasoning is likely to run out precisely when we need it most.

First, experience has a way of coming along too late to be of use. I discover that cleanliness in a roommate is more important than wit only after I have made my choice of whom to live with. To be sure, the lesson I have learned here may stand me in good stead in similar future choices, and if so the experience will not have been wasted. But if it is the case that the larger the decision to be made, the less likely it is to be repeated, then the larger the decision to be made, the less likely one is to come to it prepared by experience. And of course the larger the decision, the more important the ability of practical reasoning to resolve it will be.

Second, recall the way in which the competing considerations relevant to eating the chocolate cake were brought to bear on each other. The approach to the problem was opportunistic and ad hoc. It seems to follow that my arriving at a solution was a matter of pure luck. It was fortuitous that I noticed that there were relevantly different kinds of pleasures at stake in the problem, fortuitous that one of these was disqualified as an end, and fortuitous that this disqualification solved the practical problem. While it is possible that surveying more examples and developing a theory to account for them would bring to light a general technique guaranteeing solution, I see no reason to expect such a guarantee, and I am going to push forward on the assumption that there is not going to be one. Although we may on occasion be lucky enough to find a way to square one end with another, it looks like we should count on being left high and dry most of the time.

Third, notice that in this example the number of relevant considerations was quite small. To arrive at a practical conclusion I had only to make clear the relation between my interest in my diet and the kind of pleasure that wolfing down the cake would entrain. The more complex the situation, the harder it will be successfully to bring the respective considerations to bear on each other in this kind of way – and not only because we can only keep seven or so items in mind at once.[20] It will simply be less likely that there *is* a story that does the job of showing how, here, this decision would be the right one. If this is right, then in order to be successful practical deliberators, the number of considerations facing us in each of our choices must usually be few. But the situations in which we need practical guidance most are bound to be the ones in which the considerations are multifarious.

It appears that we are back very near where we started. Incommensurability looks to be the rule rather than the exception, and successful practical deliberation the odd lucky hit. All we have succeeded in doing, it might be thought, is reversing the direction of explanation: instead of explaining the failures of practical reasoning by appealing to the prevalence of incommensurability, we are now explaining the prevalence of incommensurability by adducing the failures of practical reasoning. And if this is the position we are in, then there is something we are not seeing. The reason is that if we are to take it for granted that we *are* more or less unified agents, our successes in commensurating competing considerations must be much more frequent than the argument so far has led us to suppose.

Our stake in our own agency should lead us to treat this as a *practical* problem: how can sufficient commensurability be brought about to make integrated persons the rule and fragmented would-be agents the exception? If the problem is that arbitrary desires and goals will be too infrequently amenable to deliberative commensuration, then evidently the solution is to ensure that the competing considerations that we face are not simply drawn at random from the space of possible desires and goals. If the machinery of practical reasoning is effective only for a relatively narrow range of inputs, we can safeguard the unity of agency that depends on successful practical reasoning by making it likely that practical reasoning by and large receives inputs on which it is likely to be effective.

While there are steps the individual can take toward this end, I want now to consider social dimensions of the solution to this problem. Christine Korsgaard has pointed out that one of the more important functions of social organization is to remove occasions for means-end reasoning: when I want to fly to Prague, instead of spending time and effort considering how this is to be done, I call my travel agent.[21] There is a parallel point to be made about the role of social organization in making possible deliberation of ends: we ought to judge social arrangements in part by the degree to which they provide the missing guarantee that the premises of competing practical syllogisms can be (often enough) commensurated.

Many of the major premises of our practical syllogisms are *bequeathed* to us by our social surroundings. (Parents and friends play a particularly important role in this regard.) By contriving to equip our children with aims, maxims, and evaluative judgments that we know to be amenable to joint commensuration, we will have stacked the deck in favor of successful practical deliberation. Now we know that ends, evaluative judgments, and so on are amenable to joint commensuration if we have derived them from a unified and systematic conception of what matters that captures a way in which they can be commensurated. This suggests telling our children to do and value those things that belong to our own picture of the well-lived life – remembering, of course, that we should not expect them to simply reconstruct, in the course of growing up and deliberating, precisely the conception of *eudaemonia* from which these dicta were derived.

If we need experience in order to discover what matters and why, then proper upbringing will involve not just the right parental injunctions, but arrangements that ensure the range of experience that an agent needs to develop his practical intelligence. Saying what the appropriate range of experience would be is not a task I want to take up now; in any case, it will vary with the deliberative demands the agent is likely to face later on in life. But there may well be an argument in the vicinity of this point against our current practices of committing childhood and youth almost entirely to formal schooling.

Lastly for now, a social organization must arrange matters for those who live in it so that they are presented with manageable choices, both with regard to the number of considerations involved in any particular choice, and the ability of the agent to square considerations of particular kinds with one another. Policies to the end of presenting agents with manageable choices do not need to be carried to extremes: our choices need not be quite as predigested as those we are given on commerical airlines. ("Sir? Would you like the chicken or the beef?") Choices can be prestructured and remain genuine choices. Such policies may smack of paternalism, but there is a Kantian argument for paternalism of this kind. If autonomy consists in resolving or, at any rate, in a willingness to attempt to resolve, practical problems by bringing to bear the resources of practical rationality, respect for autonomy demands doing what one can to make sure the resources of practical deliberation are not too often swamped. For when they are, failure to deliberate successfully will normally result in heteronomous choice, and consistent failure will lead the agent to abandon deliberation as quixotic and simply surrender himself to heteronomy.

If we are adequately unified agents, we may conclude that we have been given starting points that are good enough, and choices that are manageable enough. That is no surety for the future. Unified agency is fragile: technological and social change may force us into choices that we are unequipped to make; a personality that counts as a unified and practically intelligent deliberator when faced with one menu of options may be irrational, habit-bound, and impulse-driven when faced with a different menu. It is up to us to do our best to make sure that the menus we face are the right ones, and that we come equipped to meet them as rational deliberators.

6

Experience shows that the account I have been sketching is likely to prompt a number of related objections; I will conclude by briefly addressing these. Taken jointly, they amount to a dilemma.

On the one hand, I have claimed that incommensurability can often be resolved by appealing to experience. This suggests that what I have been describing as a problem arising from incommensurable desires is actually a problem of incomplete information about something like values, where these are thought of as mind-independent objects of perception and theorizing. But if this is the right way to think about the problem, experience will only be able to help square incommensurable desires if the values they reflect or express are themselves commensurable; and if so, the commensurability of values will be the prior, and deeper, philosophical problem. Moreover, if this *is* the right picture of the problem, my suggestion that we can adequately respond to the threat posed by incommensurability to unified agency by supplying agents with ends made to be commensurated should seem beside the point. If what matters is the responsiveness of our practical judgments to an already existing Good, it is not merely unhelpful but positively pernicious to supply agents with motivational materials that they will fit into patterns which do not correspond to that Good. (The point of moral education, on such a view, must be the transmission of a discovered truth.) Finally, if one can simply *observe* what matters more than what, one would expect a good deal of agreement about what matters. But different people can have different – even conflicting – yet nonetheless adequate understandings of what matters, and these differences are often to be accounted for in terms of the agents' differing deliberative histories.

On the other hand, I have been suggesting that deliberation that commensurates ends is something like the construction by the agent of a conception of what matters – and, implicitly, a scale against which relative importance can be, sometimes, measured – out of raw materials such as desires, ends, preferences, and reflexes. But if *this* is the right picture of the problem, why isn't the process of commensurating competing desires or ends after all only a sophisticated member of that camp of strategies, represented by choice on impulse, to which it was supposed to be an alternative? How can it differ from the self-deceiving deliberation of ends characterized by Kolnai? And, lastly, if an agent's conception of what matters is his own construction, how can it be experience- and observation-driven as well?

As I remarked at the outset of the paper, I do not understand what "values" are. But I suspect that if there *are* items to which the much-abused term can be applied, they arise out of and in the course of the kind of experience-driven deliberation at which I have been gesturing. So the question is whether there are processes of noninstrumental deliberation that sidestep the dilemma; since an answer will have to wait on a far more definite characterization of the usable deliberative techniques than I can give here, I will just say what I think. It is a mistake to imagine that experience can play a role in the construction of a picture of what matters only if that picture is taken to be a *copy* of something else. (Think of the role of experience in painting, when painting is not merely a mimetic exercise.) It is also a mistake – the same mistake – to suppose that if something is not meant as a copy of something else, then there is no possible source of correction to and constraint on it. (Think again of painting, or for that matter of mathematics.) Whether the impression of constraint is genuine rather than self-deceiving, and what forms the evaluative by-products of choice that commensurates incommensurables are likely to take, depend on whether there are in fact patterns of noninstrumental practical reasoning, and what they look like. If this is right, the next step in understanding the achievement of commensurability, of conceptions of *eudaemonia*, and of unity of agency is to advance an account of the forms that noninstrumental practical reason can take.

Notes

I'm grateful to Alyssa Bernstein, Hilary Bok, Sarah Buss, Ruth Chang, Alice Crary, Wilfried Hinsch, Geoff Sayre-McCord, Adria Quiñones, Bill Talbott, and Kayley Vernallis for commenting on earlier drafts, and to Rebecca Entwisle, Christoph Fehige, David Friedheim, Amy Gutmann, and audiences at Williams College, the Hebrew University, and the conference on Incommensurability and Value for discussion.

1. There is a terminological point to be cleared up here, however. A number of philosophers have identified forms of reasoning that are directed toward the satisfaction of desires but which are not simply finding ways of *causing* the desire to be satisfied; see, for example, the much-discussed list at Williams, 2001, p. 80, which adduces, among others, "thinking how the satisfaction [of one's desires] can be combined, e.g., by time-ordering," or "finding constitutive solutions, such as deciding what would make for an entertaining evening, granted that one wants entertainment." Such philosophers may be instrumentalists on my use of the term but not necessarily on their own. For some reason to think that instrumentalism, in my sense, *is* the received view, see Millgram, 1996b; for an argument against instrumentalism, see Millgram, 1997, ch. 2.

2. Cf. Kolnai, 2001, pp. 260, 262–3; Williams, 2001, p. 80.

3. See Griffin, 1986, ch. 6, Broome, 1991, ch. 4.

4. The claim needs to be qualified by the now familiar point, due to Hilary Putnam, that meanings aren't only in the head. I won't pursue the qualification because it doesn't seem to me to change the course of the current argument.

5. Seuss, 1982.

6. Akrasia is by a philosophers' convention characterized as acting against one's all things considered best judgment. If I am right, akratic action is often to be

explained by the background awareness that one's all things considered best judgment does not have that much to be said for it. For a discussion of the related question of whether incommensurability is *required* in order to make sense of akrasia, see Stocker, 1990.

7. Regret will be most likely in those cases where the satisfactoriness of the chosen option is assessed on the basis of its relative standing vis-à-vis other live options. (If I have not bought the winning lottery ticket, I do not regret it; things are fine as they are now. But if I had *almost* bought the winning lottery ticket, I will probably regret not having done so, and things as they are now may no longer seem fine to me.) Incommensurability, by tempting agents into retrospective reversal of their comparative assessments, will tend to bring agents – for part of the time, at any rate – to regard their choices as having been regrettable.

8. Barring self-deception, vacillation will rearise when there are alternative ways of viewing the situation corresponding to and perhaps expressive of the competing considerations; here it will take the form of oscillation between the different ways of viewing the choice.

9. The examples are from Raz, 1986, ch. 13.

10. An interesting variation on this theme concedes that deliberation presupposes commensurability, and that ends are incommensurable; commensurability is then advanced as a reform that would make successful deliberation possible across the board. See Nussbaum, 2001.

11. Kolnai, 2001, pp. 268, 272.

12. Ibid., p. 273; he has in mind Aristotle's controversial pronouncement at NE 1112b.

13. These points don't have to be further *ends*, though they might be: sensual pleasure is not a *further* end, above and beyond eating delicious things.

14. Cf. Jaglom, 1990.

15. We may stipulate that I am not simply rendering explicit already present but tacit attitudes; the revulsion I feel at the image of myself guiltily reaching into the refrigerator, the focus of my awareness narrowing down to the creamy chocolate icing melting on my palate, allowing me to forget my body . . . all this is a new realization, an attitude I have arrived at in the course of this train of practical reasoning. One way to give force to such a stipulation is to point out that the practical judgments in question depend on conceptual apparatus arrived at in the course of the reasoning: if you do not have the concept F, there are attitudes you cannot have towards Fs. I will not here pursue questions about the normative constraints on the introduction of concepts, and of attitudes involving them, into one's cognitive economy.

We also need to stipulate that the way in which I now see my desire for the cake is not the upshot of arbitrary choice between two competing ways of seeing the choice situation that are tied to the respective desires. (Cf. note 8.) If I were also to have the realistic option of seeing my desire for a better body as the expression of a degrading and destructive standard of beauty (which would prompt me to celebrate my liberation from the standard by wolfing down the cake), and have no nonarbitrary way of determining which of the two ways of seeing to adopt, my actual choice would be a matter of impulse, self-deception, or something similar to these. I mean to be considering a choice situation in which alternatives of this kind do not pose a problem.

16. There are a number of problems we can bracket here. First, my discovery may be no such thing if, had I chosen the other roommate, I would have ended up thinking the grass greener on *this* side of the fence. But such situations can arise in theoretical reasoning as well, and we do not think they show that one cannot learn from experience; we need merely stipulate that this example is not a case of this kind. Second, one might demand an account of how my experience has supported my conclusion. But there are principled reasons to resist this demand. For one, it is important that one can learn from experience without being able to give an account of how one has done so: often, one *just sees* that *p*, without being able to explain further why one is now justified in asserting *p*.

   Third, philosophers may be inclined to resist my interpretation of the second example. I could not have been learning, from experience, what *matters*; only facts, and not values, can be discovered by observation and experimental reasoning; and so – the objection would run – what we have had described must actually have been either the simple acquisition of a new desire, or the discovery that such and such circumstances would have the effect of satisfying desires or preferences I already had. I consider these responses elsewhere (Millgram, 1996b, Millgram, 1997, ch. 6).

17. Though *eudaemonia*, or the well-lived life, is a narrower notion than that of what matters: one might have the view that what matters does not add up, or even contribute, to a well-lived life.

18. The point here is *not* that piling up ordinal comparisons is somehow going to produce cardinality. (Though there are special cases – the well-known von Neumann-Morgenstern construction of utility functions from preferences is one – which could be described in that way.)

19. See Raz, 1986, pp. 345–57, for reasons to think that in satisfactory human lives the perspective grid will remain incomplete.

20. Cf. Miller, 1956.

21. Korsgaard, 1990, ch. 3.

10

Commensurability in Perspective

Complete commensurability of ends is a good deal like single-point perspective. When a picture is rendered in perspective, there is a definite answer to the question: of two objects in the picture, which is larger? The answer, in fact, can be made numerically precise; with the perspective grid in place, it is possible to say not only which of the two is larger, but how many times larger it is. Likewise, in a rendering of our practical world that insists on complete commensurability (such as that of Benthamite utilitarians), there is always a fact of the matter as to which of two states of affairs is more important, and that fact allows of numerical precision. There is an answer to the question, "*How much* more important is this than that?"[1]

"Incommensurability" is a word with different meanings in different areas of philosophy; here, to say that two ends are incommensurable is to say that it is not true that one is more important than the other, and also that it is not true that they are as important (or even roughly as important) as one another. To say that ends are commensurable is usually to say somewhat more than that gloss on "incommensurable" would indicate; it is to imply that they can be, not just compared, but compared using a single measure, and that the comparisons are (something like) quantitative. The analogy between perspective in painting, and the kind of full-fledged agent-wide commensurability of ends that allows the agent's preferences to be represented by a vNM utility function, can, I hope, help us see our way past a handful of ideas that for the most part get taken for granted in the debate over the (in)commensurability of ends.[2] The first of these ideas is that the debate should be about whether ends are *already* commensurable or not – metaphysically, as it were, and merely in virtue of their being ends. Paralleling the thought that there has to be some metaphysical fact of the matter as to whether all ends are necessarily commensurable would be the notion that it is worth arguing over the metaphysical question of whether all paintings are necessarily in single-point perspective. That of course would be just silly; some are, and some are not: compare, for example, Crivelli's elaborate and fastidious *Annunciation with Saint Emidius* with a piece like Picasso's rather less fastidious *Les Desmoiselles d'Avignon*.[3] Whether a painting is in perspective is up to the painter, and depends on how he has painted it, and so our comparison suggests a more interesting question than whether ends *are* (necessarily) commensurable: *when* ends are commensurable, how did they get that way?

1

First of all, a painting will not be in perspective until there is *enough* of it on the canvas. If there are, so far, only a couple of items painted onto the blank space, we will not yet have enough in place to induce a perspective grid. Now human beings start out their own pictures of what matters very early on, by placing on or in them collections of found objects: things their mothers told them about crossing the street, not very articulately formulated urges for sweets or parental attention, lessons learned from unexpected delights and disappointments, role models taken from television and children's books, and so on. For the most part, there just will not be enough in place to amount to a system of commensurable ends, and so, normally, a small child's ends will often not allow answers to the kinds of questions about their relative importance that we have on the table. (Of course, such answers may nonetheless be demanded and produced, as when a child is asked which of its divorced parents it likes most.[4]) As one's life proceeds, the canvas naturally fills up, but it is worth emphasizing that, except in unfortunate cases of arrested emotional development, one's picture of what matters is, unlike the painting ready for purchase on the gallery wall, never actually finished. Only persons whose lives have gone distressingly awry have arrived at a "reflective equilibrium" about what matters.

Second, a painting will not be in perspective unless it is planned that way from the beginning. Grids must be laid out in advance, and the carefully measured contents of one's image placed in preallocated positions on it, if the pictorial space created by painting objects onto a canvas is to have the structural properties that will generally allow definite answers to questions regarding the relative pictorial sizes of the items represented in the picture. Other methods of composition, for instance, painting items onto the canvas in the order in which they occur in a narrative, will produce a pictorial space in which many questions of the form "Which is bigger, and by how much?" simply fail to have answers. This suggests that, even once we have gotten past childhood, we will continue to find our ends often to be incommensurable. For at the outset of our lives, when we begin composing our picture of what matters, we are in no position to design the analog of a perspectival space in which to insert the various goods we will later encounter; infants and small children possess neither the intellectual sophistication nor the motivation to pursue such a project. (Just for instance, one must already be fairly sophisticated to understand, say, the Sure-Thing Principle, and one must be sophisticated indeed to have made conformity to it a priority.[5]) What is more, the haphazard character of the materials out of which the picture is to be assembled means that it is likely to resist the imposition of this kind of design in any case; perspective is much easier to achieve in a painting than in a collage.[6]

Whether or not ends are always commensurable, they are certainly sometimes commensurable. So, if the placement of one and another demand, attraction, and so on, on a child's initially blank mattering map cannot itself explain the subsequent adult's commensurable ends, we need to ask what is done to the canvas after that initial placement (and after later accretions of the same kind) that could impose something like a perspectival grid on it.[7] Now, faced with a half-finished painting in which the perspectival space was out of kilter, we might, if perspective mattered enough to us, simply paint parts of it over in order to achieve the desired effect. And in fact contemporary decision theory presses us to do something very much like this. When one's preferences satisfy a small number of what are traditionally called "consistency conditions," then those preferences can be represented by a utility function; we are told to adjust our preferences so that we have well-defined utility functions.[8]

This is not, however, normally a satisfactory way of achieving commensurability in one's ends, because the process of constructing a picture of what matters is, differently described, the process of constructing a self. While some ends, and the preferences that express them, are not central to who one is – think of a car salesman's thoroughly worked out view of just what the vehicles on his lot are worth, and then imagine that this is, for him, just a job – other ends cannot be given up or greatly modified without giving up on one's person or character.[9] When it is those more central ends that are in question (and we can expect that they normally will be in question, when one is after full-fledged, across the board commensurability in one's ends), the price of the suggested revisions can be quite high, since making the recommended revisions would amount to deleting core components of one's personality. Unless one is so thoroughly unhappy that anything that would be one's *own* life has simply become unliveable, it is hard to believe that the benefits of complete commensurability so achieved are worth it.[10]

2

If commensurability in one's picture of what matters were a product of this kind of wholesale painting over of one's personality, it would not, except in desperate cases, be reasonably arrived at. So what commensurability there rationally is in one's system of ends must emerge not simply by fiat, but from operations appropriately performed on the raw materials that are available to (and that for practical purposes constitute) us at one time and another in our lives. The changes in one's priorities brought about by practical reasoning seem to me to be the best place to look, because suitable deliberative connections between past and future priorities can form a bridge over even fairly radical motivational change that allows one to see oneself both as the same agent, and as having a stake in one's (possibly very different) future self.

What model of practical reasoning should we use to explore this option? The default is still instrumentalism, the widely held view that figuring out what to do consists exclusively in finding ways to satisfy the desires one has, and so entirely in means-end reasoning.[11] And this take on practical reasoning is especially salient here, since worries about the incommensurability of ends have been framed by instrumentalism, and in particular, by two further and ensuing ideas: that if there are ends that are not already of themselves commensurable, then there will be no rational basis for choices involving them, and that having ends that are commensurable is consequently a precondition for practical rationality.[12]

Nonetheless, I think we would do best to put instrumentalism to one side. First, it looks particularly unpromising when viewed through the analogy we have been developing. Instrumentalism has it that one's reasons for action must be found *inside* one's desires, and so, in particular, must the reasons for making tradeoffs between ends that compete. The internal feature that must be already present is thought of as the desire's strength or weight; in the pictorial metaphor, it is as though the item to be placed on one's picture of what matters must *already* have a pictorial size, internal to its being what it is, and prior to its placement on the canvas. But of course elements of a picture are not like this: a cut-out picture of a giraffe may have a physical size, but that does not itself settle the pictorial size the giraffe will have when it is placed on my painting. That will depend, for instance, on whether the giraffe is put down in the foreground, or in the background.

Second, because instrumental deliberation is tethered to ends or desires that one already has, it seems unlikely to solve the problem on our plate, that of showing how changes in motivation and evaluation that are sufficient to resolve incommensurability can be something other than merely overwriting sizable sectors of one's personality.[13] And third, for the reasons we have just highlighted, means-end reasoning will not, by itself, resolve incommensurabilities in one's system of ends. If there are not, already, relative strengths to one's desires, there is no rational way (or so the instrumentalist presumes) of proceeding when they conflict. That means that if we are going to pursue the idea that practical reasoning is a way to account for rational commensurability of ends, we will want to consider other forms of practical inference.

I don't have an exhaustive list of the forms that practical reasoning can take, and so I can't be sure what the results of doing practical reasoning over the course of a life ought to look like. But I'm willing to hazard a guess on the basis of methods of practical reasoning that have already been described, and that guess is that, done right, practical reasoning will not, except rarely and by coincidence, produce the analog of full (rather than partial or gappy) perspective in one's picture of what matters and what is important. I will consider two forms of practical inference, beginning in the next section with the specification of ends, and taking up empirical practical reasoning in the section following.

3

The specificationist view has it that at least some practical reasoning consists in filling in overly abstract ends to arrive at richer and more concretely specified versions of those ends. This seems necessary if one is to get on to taking steps in many cases, because many of the ends we have are not the kind of thing to which it yet makes sense to look for means. If what I want is to write a very good paper, I am not yet in a position to do anything about it; I must first settle on a much more definite conception of what sort of paper it is I wish to write.[14]

Now, what happens when I engage in practical deliberation of this kind? Sometimes further specifying my ends introduces commensurability where there had been none before, and this is how Aurel Kolnai, who kicked off the current discussion of the subject, seems to have thought of it as working. Ends are further specified in respect of (*inter alia*) their *weights*, and this additional content puts one in a position to make trade-offs between them. (Kolnai argued that the process is inevitably irrational and self-deceiving, a conclusion he labelled "the fundamental paradoxy of Practice.") The specification of the weight of an end is typically in-direct: having already decided to go for a walk, I do not now simply choose a strength for my desire to walk; rather, I choose a direction, thus further specifying what that walk will be – and thereby determine, by settling whether it will be merely a stroll through the streets, or an occasion to commune with nature, its relative importance vis-à-vis dinner and a movie. Here, practical deliberation, by producing priorities where there had been none, makes some ends commensurable with respect to one another, and introduces elements of a perspectival organization into one's picture of what matters. Notice the role played by the actually available options (here, what kinds of walks are to be had by going in different directions). The successful specification of one's ends does not normally proceed in a vacuum, but is given traction by a terrain of live possibilities.

But that is by no means the only upshot that specificationist delibera-tion can have for the commensurability of one's ends. Henry Richardson has suggested that cospecifying apparently conflicting ends jointly can remove the need to trade them off against each other. If I want to go for a walk, and I want to get exercise, and these ends conflict (how will I find time for both?), I could further specify the walk as the uphill, brisk kind, and the exercise as low-key, outdoor, not necessarily aerobic activity. In cases like these, the need for commensuration is sidestepped: because my more fully specified ends no longer conflict, I do not have to arrive at a view as to how they trade off against one another. Sometimes, then, spec-ificationist deliberation preempts the need for (and so the achievement of) commensurability.[15]

Sometimes it also creates fresh loci of incommensurability. In my own view, the design of technologically innovative systems and products pro-vides a better testbed for specificationism than the ethics-centered cases to which its advocates have generally confined themselves; so let's take for our example Bruno Latour's full-dress reconstruction of the attempt to settle on a specification for Aramis, a futuristic guided transportation system into which various French government bodies and Matra Transport, over the course of the seventies and eighties, sunk around half a billion francs. At the early stages, the priorities of the relevant competing ends had seemed fairly clear (in the view of the project team, if not of the Budget Office): for instance, the added convenience and comfort of point-to-point transportation was more than worth the financial costs of developing and constructing the system. However, at one phase of the design process, at which passengers were to be seated in ten-person vehicles (as opposed to the smaller four-seaters of earlier designs), a study of the potential clientele was commissioned, and it was discovered that such a "small-group situation confers an exaggerated importance on interpersonal relations," and that potential clients were concerned about losing "the benefits of anonymity." This was an end that the engineers simply had never thought of, and so they were brought up short. They had not given any consideration to how anonymity should be prioritized with respect to other ends in play, and it was, quite rightly, not (yet) commensurable with those other ends. Specifying the indefinite end, Aramis, had put a *new* concern into the picture, one whose priority relations to other concerns were not yet defined.[16]

Moreover, even if one's thinly specified ends are already ranked (and even quantitatively comparable), more concretely and more richly specifying an end may render it incommensurable with one's other ends. The Mayor of Paris regarded the thinly specified end (Aramis: a high-tech, futuristic showpiece) as worth the costs and trouble, but not a further specified Aramis. (Is something that's futuristic and high-tech in *this* way worth *this* kind of trouble?) Or again, pretty much everyone involved agreed that the thinly specified goal ("nominal Aramis") was worth pursuing, but as more and more of the design fell into place, and more and more of the necessary compromises were made, it became, for all the actors, progressively more difficult to see whether Aramis *was* worth doing. Eventually, as it became harder to give clear and unequivocal answers as to whether the system was worth the costs, support for it eroded and in 1987 the project was discontinued.[17]

My sense of the territory is that the specificationist variety of practical reasoning is as likely to introduce incommensurability into one's system of ends as it is to remove it. If that is right, then we should not expect that the result of a lifetime of practical deliberation that includes the specification of ends on a regular basis will produce the fully commensurated system of ends or preferences that we were taking to be the analog of single-point perspective.

   In fact, if such specification is a regular demand of practical rationality, finding an agent with fully commensurable ends is prima facie but rather strong evidence of *irrationality*. I will return to this point after we have taken a look at a further form of practical reasoning. In the meantime, our very partial picture of how deliberation proceeds suggests that too much coherence of preferences *at* a time is usually paid for by incoherence *over* time. The common view that preferences can be tested for rationality by testing them for decision-theoretic consistency is a little like the idea that you can test a set of beliefs for rationality by checking it for consistency. But this way of thinking about the matter is a mistake. First, consistency is *not enough*: you can no more tell whether a conclusion is rational just by looking at *it* than you can tell whether it is a *conclusion* just by looking at it; you need to look to how it was arrived at, as well. Second, consistency is also *too much*: if eliminating previous inconsistency in a system of ends (or beliefs, for that matter) must have involved illegitimate inferential transitions, then consistency turns out to be a mark, not of rationality, but of irrationality.

4

An advocate of global commensurability, perhaps one with moral realist leanings, might, at several points in the argument we have been traversing, have wanted to invoke *values*. Pictures are in perspective, an analogous type of realist might insist, when they are properly rendered from life (or from still life); objects in the painting have pictorial sizes because the real objects in the scene have spatial sizes. Our ends are (or ought to be) commensurable because they are rendered from the values, and the values are already commensurable. Let me register being more than a little uncomfortable with talk of values; it comes with metaphysical baggage I dislike, and values are usually thought of in a way that begs the questions about commensurability that we are now considering. I am happy, however, to countenance practical reasoning that deploys something very much like perception to determine what things matter, and how they are important. You can learn that one thing is more important than another from experience; you can move, inductively, from such observations to generalizations about what matters; and you can manage, in both ways, conclusions about *how much* things matter.[18] ("I used to think that taste mattered more than presentation, but now that I've been exposed to

Japanese cuisine, I realize that presentation matters as much as, maybe more than, taste.") And since I do want to give the objection a run for its money, as far as possible on its own terms, I will go along with talk of values for the duration.

What guarantee have we got that practical observations will deliver priorities that are coordinate with one another, in a way that makes them add up to a unified perspectival structure? Perhaps such coordination will be rare, and the likeliest outcome of such exercises a take on what matters that resembles, in its structural features (though not, one hopes, in its thematic or tonal qualities), Piranesi's Carceri etchings. The problem here is that moral realists cannot have commensurability in the values for free, and the explanation they owe us must satisfy two constraints that seem offhand to conflict. On the one hand, values must be shaped by and for human life. Even the abstractly characterized objects of import that preoccupy philosophers (such as happiness or autonomy or virtue), and more obviously the down-to-earth goods prized by nonphilosophers (such as intimacy or thrills or a cold beer), can only be valuable for creatures with the idiosyncratic mode of life our species has cobbled together. (Autonomy is not a good for ants; intimacy doesn't benefit mountain lions; and starfish aren't in it for the thrills.) If, for instance, the values were objects that froze out of the plasma during the Big Bang, their relevance to human life would be a mind-boggling coincidence.

On the other hand, commensurability in values cannot now be merely the projection of an agent's psychological states. Such a projection would require commensurability already internally achieved (marked by a pattern of preferences, or of evaluations, that could be captured in a cardinal utility function). But we were in the course of trying to account for such commensuration as was psychologically present by looking to values outside the agent's psychology that were already themselves commensurable.

Giving moral realism the courtesy of a realistic treatment evidently means asking how human *activity* (rather than passive human psychology) makes values commensurable. And this means identifying activities in which comparative evaluative observations figure, and ways in which those comparisons are systematized so as to be capturable by a meaningfully cardinal (that is, quantitative) index. Exchanges are one of the obvious and very important types of such relations, and I will begin with them. (But there are others, one of which I will discuss later.)

In a primitive barter economy, patterns of exchange may fail to be capturable by a cardinal (or quantitative) representation. But in developed economies, market pressures, assisted by the availability of money – that is, a unit of account that is also a medium of exchange – systematize and regiment those transactions in a way that makes the objects exchanged (largely) commensurable: they now have market values, denominated in the relevant currency.[19] (Markets with these effects are complicated and hands-on social institutions. For instance, financial market prices are insured by the presence of "market makers," players who have assumed a commitment to serving as the transaction partner of last recourse.) Marx, it will be recalled, discusses this process early on in *Capital*, but where he regards the market values that stand over and against the economic agents as a kind of projection (that is, in roughly the way that Mackie regards *all* values), I am happy to take them on board as genuine values that have been made to be commensurable by human activity. That is, the values are in fact produced by the market (this is especially vivid when, as Marx again noticed, the commodities themselves come to be manufactured so as to be more easily commensurated), and it's not at all "commodity fetishism" to treat them as real.[20]

When the price of a commodity is both public and relatively stable, consumers often develop a sense of "what it is worth." (They are chagrined to learn that they have paid more than the going rate; they will not spend the money when the prices are out of line with their sensibilites; they are not so quietly proud to have gotten a really good deal.) Rendering a system of ends from a set of prices of this kind will (in favorable circumstances, but to be sure, not always) produce ends that are commensurable with one another. The extreme case – say, of the Wall Street analysts for whom, at least while they are on the job, nothing matters but the relative rates of return – is unusual, but less extreme versions of the effect are frequent enough.

Markets, then, are one way to generate the commensurable values appealed to by the moral realist – which, in conjunction with empirical practical reasoning, could account for a system of ends, or concerns more generally, that is perspectivally structured. When the human activity that gives content to the commensuration of value is trade, the commensurating value turns out to be the means of exchange: money. But it is not the only way to come by external commensurable values. Human beings themselves are still to some extent outside the money economy, the outright purchase and sale of persons being prohibited nowadays; the evaluation of human beings is exhibited in respect for them, in an interest in their company, in admiration and attention, and so on. I am told that, in American middle and high schools, peer pressure produces a regimentation of these attitudes, and along with it, an ordinally rigid, and roughly cardinal evaluative hierarchy of persons: a football player and a cheerleader, who are worth most, occupy the top slots, and there is a pretty definite matter of fact as to who is worth how much (less) all the rest of the way down the pecking order.[21] American adolescents rapidly learn the nuances of these evaluative hierarchies, and when they internalize these rankings, we may find that they end up with commensurable systems of ends: they know not only that having Jane as a friend is worth more than a friendship with Joan, but just how *much* more.

Ends are commensurable, we allowed, when they are rendered, through some form of empirical practical reasoning, from values that are commensurable. But values are commensurable when they have been made so by human activity, and we have just gotten a glimpse at the kinds of human activity that produce commensurable values, and at the kinds of values that such activities produce. The upshot for the *overall* commensurability of ends is not promising. First, complete commensurability of ends would require complete commensurability of value – for example, a world in which every object of human interest was a commodity, or a world that was an American high school writ very large – and we are just not there (yet).[22]

And second, commensuration of this kind fails to solve the problem for which we turned to practical deliberation in the first place. Deliberation, recall, promised to account for sizable change in the structure of one's concerns that was not tantamount to having one's personality erased. Learning from experience that something matters to you, or matters more or less than you had imagined, does seem to face up to this problem: you can understand yourself to have a stake in what practical reasoning of this kind will one day show to be important to you. But, even if it does involve empirical practical reasoning, copying all of one's evaluations and preferences from the commodity pages of the *Wall Street Journal,* or from the social rankings of one's high school peers, looks nonetheless like a way of not having a personality of one's own. (This is why we normally regard disengagement from such systems of evaluation as a part of *growing up.*) The moral realist route to a perspectively structured system of ends is not actually that at all.

5

The argument we now have on the table is not by any means airtight. Perhaps there are alternative methods of revising one's system of ends that we have not considered: methods of revision that are not practical reasoning, but which do not amount to self-deletion, or perhaps forms of practical reasoning that do after all produce commensuration in one's ends. And of course there is the possibility of an agent growing up, by chance or by contrivance, with a system of ends that does not need revision because the ends are commensurable in the first place. But I think the conclusion I am about to endorse is by now quite plausible.

Perspective was once regarded as mandatory, and is now understood to be optional; if, however, the argument to this point has been on track, the globally commensurating mattering map is not normally even optional. That might seem surprising, for a reason that the analogy between perspective and commensurability makes vivid. A perspectivally structured rendering would be a good navigational guide to the scene it depicts; it will allow you to figure out how to move around in it, in a way that many nonperspectival renderings will not.[23] Likewise, a globally commensurable system of ends is an unconfusing guide to action, and since the point of having ends is to guide action, shouldn't they be commensurable?

But the presumption that ends serve *simply* as guides to action is at least an oversimplification. If ends and other ingredients of practical deliberation can be thought of as constituting the agent, then we may have other demands to make on them. An image that is in perspective presents just that visual information that can be taken in from a single and constant vantage point, and cubists sometimes said that their paintings displayed objects from many points of view simultaneously.[24] They were not deterred by their paintings being less than useful as navigational guides, and likewise, while a practical rendering of the world that saw things from more than one vantage point at a time might complicate and even impede one's decision making, it could nevertheless allow a kind of personal advantage that one would not want to sacrifice.

We care about being able to see (as we say) more than one side of a question; even more importantly, we care about the deliberative rationality exhibited in arriving at our concerns; I have been suggesting that it is this rationality that allows us to see many of those concerns as our own. Now, it is widely believed that to be a practically rational agent is to have preferences that can be represented by a utility function. If I am right, however, and practical reasoning correctly performed does not produce preferences (or systems of ends) that satisfy the conditions for an agent's possessing a well-defined utility function, then the utility-maximizing agent is a model, not of practical rationality, but of practical *irrationality*. And if that is so, attempts to justify claims in moral and political philosophy, or, for that matter, public policy decisions, by appealing to this model are perverse.

Notes

An earlier draft of this paper benefited from comments from Lori Alward, Carla Bagnoli, Alice Clapman, Alice Crary, Bob Ehman, Gregg Horowitz, Henry Richardson, Amy Schmitter, and Valerie Tiberius, and was presented at an APA session in memory of Gregory Kavka. I'm grateful to the supporters of the Gregory Kavka Memorial Prize, to panelists Bill Talbott and Candace Vogler for their responses, and to members of the audience. The paper was read at a conference on Justification and Meaning, hosted by the University of Siena. I was also helped by conversation with Irene Appelbaum, Dedre Gentner, and John McDowell. For comments on a distant predecessor, I'm grateful to Sarah Buss, Tamar Gendler, Kathy Gaca, Tim Leonard, and Susan Sauve Meyer. Work on this paper was supported by fellowships from the National Endowment for the Humanities and the Center for Advanced Study in the Behavioral Sciences; I am grateful for the financial support provided through the Center by the Andrew W. Mellon Foundation.

1. Both claims need qualification and elaboration. First, the pictorial grid is in fact not always enough; for instance, a bird painted against a background of sky might be a small bird relatively close by, or a larger bird farther away. For perspective to give you information about the relative sizes of pictorial objects, the objects must be anchored to the perspective grid – as the bird would be were it to alight on a branch. Anchoring is a complicated and artificial matter, and best addressed by devices such as tiled floors; it never has a fully principled solution, since in general there are indefinitely many arrangements of objects in three dimensions that can project a given two-dimensional image; it may have quite unprincipled solutions, as when familiarity with the sizes of objects represented is used to make up for the sparseness of an image.

    Second, in the Expected Utility model (which is today the most influential model for the commensurability of ends), there are no answers to how much, absolutely, this or that matters to the agent; utility functions are unique only up to linear transformation (which means that both the units and the zero point are arbitrary; think of Fahrenheit-Celsius temperature conversions). In this respect they further resemble paintings in perspective. Given only the perspective structure of the painting, there's no fact of the matter as to how large, absolutely, the objects in the paintings are; all one can say is how large they are with respect to one another. (Alberti's own recommendation for fixing the absolute size of the objects in the picture was to provide a man for purposes of comparison, on the charmingly innocent grounds that "man is the thing best known to man" [1956, p. 55].)

2. For current overviews of the commensurability debate, see Richardson, 2001, and Chang, 1997. (The definition of "incommensurable" is taken from

Chang's Introduction.) For expositions of vNM utility theory, see Mandler, 2001, Luce and Raiffa, 1957.

3. Perhaps I am dismissing the question too hastily: after all, in the Transcendental Aesthetic, Kant thought it reasonable to insist that the spatial map we construct of our surroundings necessarily conforms to the perspectival conventions. But then again, this has been a constraint that philosophers appropriating Kant, from Strawson to Heidegger, have hastened to relax.

4. The example is due to Carla Bagnoli.

5. And of course even the sophisticates can balk; see, e.g., Ellsberg, 1961.

6. There is a view, due to Donald Davidson and Susan Hurley, to the effect that we do not need a substantive explanation of the evaluative analog of perspective, that is, of preferences that induce utility functions. More carefully, the view is that we do not need an explanation that adduces features of the *process* of preference formation. (Hurley, 1989; Davidson, 1984.) I will borrow a tag from Gopal Sreenivasan (2001), and call this the Hurley-Davidson view. On the Hurley-Davidson view, it is a constraint on the interpretation of agents that the preferences ascribed to them satisfy, at any rate for the most part, the classical utility-inducing constraints.

Davidson's metaphysics has a massiveness that makes it hard to nudge out of the way both quickly and fairly, but for now the following will do. The comparison with perspective puts us in a position to see how very implausible the Hurley-Davidson view really is. The analogous suggestion would be that perspective is a constraint on visual interpretation, and so that paintings *must* be in perspective. Now, it may well be true that we (nowadays) generally try to parse pictorial representations perspectivally. But it is *not* true that we either succeed in seeing them as conforming to the laws of perspective, or fail to see them at all – as a stroll through either the ancient Egyptian or the contemporary wing of your local museum will in short order persuade you. (Compare Gombrich, 1984, p. 2.) And even if that *were* true, it wouldn't follow that we don't need substantive explanations of how paintings that are in perspective got that way: all those manuals on perspective weren't written for no reason at all.

7. The phrase "mattering map" is lifted from Rebecca Goldstein's *roman a clef* of hanky-panky at Princeton (1983).

8. There are various reasons given for so doing, such as the risk of being made into a "money pump" (Davidson, McKinsey, and Suppes, 1955). For a discussion of ways to resist such arguments, see Mandler, 2001.

9. The distinction between personal identity and character is taken from Bernard Williams, who uses it to allow for a future personality being literally one's own, on one's preferred metaphysical theory of personal identity, even when the stake one has in that future personality and its concerns has been undercut. See, e.g., Williams, 1981.

10. The point is related to one famously made by Aristotle (NE 1159a5–15). I'm leaving to one side for now the question of whether this kind of revision is generally feasible, but for reason to think it's not, see Millgram, 1997, ch. 2.

11. Many authors restrict the terms "instrumental reasoning" and "means-end reasoning" to finding a cause of the end that is physically distinct from it,

presumably because they take it that a "means" must be a cause, and a cause must be physically distinct from its effects. This does not seem to me to be a useful distinction to introduce into discussions of practical deliberation, and I will describe as "means-end" or "instrumental" practical reasoning aimed solely toward the satisfaction of given desires, even when the ways one finds of satisfying those desires are "constitutive" (as when, looking for a laptop with such and such technical specifications, I select a particular brand). However, we will shortly discuss a contrasting form of constitutive deliberation that cannot be so understood.

12. Although that is the way the threat of incommensurability is generally perceived, the move is just a little too fast. Simon, for instance, has suggested that a satisficer can decide in the face of incommensurability by setting satisficing thresholds for each of the incommensurable dimensions of value that figure in his decision, and taking the first option to come in above all those thresholds (1957, pp. 250–2).

13. Bernard Williams, in a paper that deserves more uptake that it has gotten (1973a), suggests that we face a dilemma: maintaining a fixed character, and eventually, one's life span permitting, being too bored with oneself for life to be worth living; or radically altering one's character, and so facing the prospect of becoming someone in whose concerns one does not now have a stake. If I am right, there is a route between the horns of the dilemma. Understanding one's very different future concerns as having been arrived at via one's own deliberations allows one correctly to see oneself as having a stake in the future self that has those concerns. This possibility, however, depends on the legitimacy of alternatives to means-end reasoning, since reasons that are anchored to the satisfaction of one's current desires cannot be made to reach concerns that are very distant. I take it that Williams's commitment to internalism (to practical reasons bottoming out in one's desires, that is, to instrumentalism as I am using the term) is what prevents him from seeing this route through the problem. For his internalism, see Williams, 2001.

14. The example is due to Allen Coates. Advocates of specificationism include Kolnai, 2001, Wiggins, 2001, and Richardson, 1994. For some discussion of the position, see Millgram, 1996a, Millgram, 1997, sec. 6.7.

15. Ends are not always, however, properly specified in a way that removes conflict. Consider an example from Williams (2001): if what I want is (so far, *just*) to be entertained this evening, I am not yet in a position to do anything about it: I must first settle on what I want by way of entertainment. Now if one of my other ends for the evening is to keep a depressed (and so unentertaining) friend company, I could specify my end of being entertained as being entertained passively, and that keeping company will take the form of sitting side by side in silence in a dark movie theater. But the solution I have just given may eliminate the conflict, while raising, in some circumstances anyway, the question of just what kind of a friend I am. Sometimes the right thing to do is to *acknowledge* a conflict, rather than to specify one's way around it.

16. Latour, 1996, pp. 185–8. Here's another example with a similar structure. Early on in the design process, the engineers realized that in order to

accommodate high traffic volumes the cars would have to form trains, but that, because the cars would be joining and leaving the moving trains, they could not be mechanically coupled. The solution, virtual or "nonmechanical" coupling (that is, having the cars compute and maintain their own positions in the train, without physical contact), was an entirely novel idea, and at the outset it was not settled just how important it was. Surprisingly, nonmechanical coupling ended up being more important, in the design team's eyes, than almost any other element of Aramis: it became the one feature on which no compromise was possible (p. 112).

17. I should acknowledge that the example is in some ways a tricky one, and that there are two contrasting objections that need to be fielded. The first begins with the fact that Aramis, taken as a whole, is a *failed* case of practical reasoning: no specification was ever settled on, and the system was never built. My own reading of it is that Latour is recounting precisely that: a case of failed practical reasoning. But one might take the view that the failure was so bad that we should not really regard it as an instance of practical reasoning at all (in roughly the way we would not regard certain kinds of monkeying around in the kitchen as cooking at all). For this reason I have been (with the exception of this last example) focusing on shorter deliberative episodes in the history of Aramis. (I'm grateful to Candace Vogler for pressing me on this point.)

     The contrasting objection (due to Henry Richardson) is that, one's initial reactions notwithstanding, the Aramis episode is a *successful* instance of practical reasoning; after all, they ended up deciding to cancel it, which meant that they must have come to see the competing considerations as, anyway, commensurable *enough*. Here I think we need to distinguish between the decision to sit tight that results from commensuration, and the kind of throwing up one's hands in confusion that results in sitting tight. Latour describes an autobiographical character engaged to do the post-mortem because, after all that argument (and all that money), no one knew *what* to think.

     Latour's protagonist was asked to determine whether Aramis had been technically feasible and economically viable, but these are questions he adroitly ducks. It's easy to mistake this for a bad case of French antirealism, but in fact Latour's resistance here is well motivated, and has to do with specificationist deliberation in particular. Surely whether Aramis is technically feasible depends on how it is specified, and (especially since fully specified versions may well not actually satisfy the thin, "nominal" description) *some* of the Aramises that might have been specified would have been feasible. Before the specification is fairly far along, there is no straight answer to the question.

18. I develop a view of this kind in Millgram, 1997.

19. Money is indispensible, and various reasons have been given for its ubiquity: it is a store of value; it is a way of facilitating economic interaction between spatially separated agents; currency can be understood as a communication device or as carrying information about previous interactions with the state (Townsend, 1990). An earlier tradition emphasized the role of legal tender in resolving disputes: like it or not, you *have* to take payment in money, and then

the debt is settled (Commons, 1924/1957, pp. 240ff; for related discussion, see Nussbaum, 1950, ch. 1). Money (but not credit cards) depersonalizes and anonymizes transactions; you don't need to know anything more about the other parties than that they have the cash in hand (Hart, 1986). If I am right, we should be highlighting a different effect: the increased tractability of decisions in which the various considerations have been commensurated. A medium of exchange is a device for simplifying deliberation; that is, its explanation and justification is to be found in its cognitive benefits. Partly this is a matter of simplifying calculation on the basis of the preferences one already has; but partly it is a matter of altering those preferences to make the calculations easier.

20. Marx, 1967, vol. 1, ch. 1; see also ch. 3, sec. 1. Marx does not give a particularly high-resolution explanation of the regimentation of exchanges that permits exchange-value to be represented quantitatively, probably because he understands "congealed labor" to be itself already homogenous. From our perspective, of course, the commensurability of labor cannot be an explanatory stopping-point.

21. The story is just slightly more complicated than I have made it out to be. See Stone and Brown, 1998, and esp. p. 164, for their reconstruction of the adolescents' "symbolic social space"; for a description of American high schools as a battlefield between two warring evaluative systems, see Eckert, 1989.

22. There are familiar complaints about processes that push the world in this direction. See, e.g., Schwartz, 1986, pp. 171–81, 231–325, Anderson, 1996, chs. 7–9. Nussbaum, 2001, considers and objects to another version of this kind of radical restructuring of human concern.

23. Of course, maps are not usually in perspective, and they do not have to indicate relative sizes. There are many ways of encoding navigationally useful information: think of subway maps that are topologically, but not geometrically, accurate.

24. We are not quite on the road to a theory that could be happily described as "cubist ethics." A cubist painting shows the same thing from different perspectives (that is, the perspectives speak consistently about the thing they depict from different points of view). But just as "what's important for *me*" is not captured by a perspective rendering – the view from here of the values as they are really sized – so seeing the different sides of a question is not seeing, simultaneously, different sides of the *same* thing. (I'm grateful to David Gauthier for pressing me on this point.)

Varieties of Practical Reasoning and Varieties of Moral Theory

Practical reasoning is reasoning directed toward decision or action, as contrasted with theoretical reasoning, which is directed toward belief. Deciding to pass your dinner companions the salt instead of the sugar, because you've always meant to find out if they would notice the difference, and now, you realize, is your chance, would be an example of practical reasoning, though not, perhaps, of the best table manners. Since everyone is an agent, everyone has a fairly direct interest in understanding the forms that practical reasoning takes: just as understanding the logic of theoretical reasoning can lead to better arguments and better beliefs, a like grasp of the logic of practical reasoning might improve one's decisions. Moral philosophers, however, have, in addition, a more focused and professional interest in the workings of practical rationality, in virtue of its consequences for systematic ethics.

1

It should not be surprising that a theory of practical reasoning can have consequences for moral philosophy. Moral reasoning is reasoning about what to do in which specifically moral issues are at stake. Because moral reasoning is practical reasoning, practical reasoning stands (or *should* stand) to moral theory as process to product. So a moral philosopher's view of practical reasoning is likely to account for many of the deeper structural features of his or her moral theory.

By way of an example, consider instrumentalism, which is still, despite a certain amount of recent dissent, the default view of the subject. The instrumentalist holds that practical reasoning is simply means-end reasoning: that what practical reasoning is *for* is to figure out how to get whatever it is you happen to want. If instrumentalism is right, then, because only thinking about how to get what you want counts as practical reasoning, there is no such thing as thinking about what to want in the first place.

When instrumentalists follow a chain of means-end links back to its origin, they find desires that cannot, on the instrumentalist view, be the products of reasoning. In the beginning, there are things you *just want*; we can label these desires *arbitrary*. So instrumentalist moral philosophers are likely to run up against the following problem: morality ought to be rationally motivating, but all rational motivation is derived from arbitrary desires, and these desires might be entirely selfish, or directed toward unusual objects, or actually cruel. If what, as it so happens, I most want is to witness the abject misery of innocents, how likely is it – Nietzschean considerations to one side – that the most effective means of satisfying my desire will turn out to be laid down by the prescriptions of a more or less conventional moral theory?

An instrumentalist moral theorist might try to show that it is rational to be moral by arguing that, despite appearances, rationality can lead you from your not necessarily moral desires to doing the right thing: arguments that morality is in one's interest are supposed to ground moral action in desires that it is (perhaps naively) supposed one is bound to have. Another strategy would be to try to find some way to exclude the inconvenient desires or preferences from the moral accounting: for instance, by filtering out desires that are, in one way or another, antisocial. Or, finally for now, one could simply adopt the expedient of addressing one's moral theory only to those who have a prior desire to be moral. There are different ways of tackling the problem, but, however one goes about it, to the extent that one's moral theory is a response to the problem of arbitrary desires, its architecture will be induced by that problem. Now the problem of arbitrary desires is generated by instrumentalism. If instrumentalism is not in fact the correct theory of practical reasoning, then the architectural alterations in one's moral theory induced by the problem of arbitrary desires are at best unnecessary, and probably pernicious.

2

Theories of practical reasoning are important for moral theory not just as a source of lurking errors and pitfalls: work on practical reasoning can be expected to drive progress in systematic ethics. It is probably still not unfair to describe the state of systematic moral theory as a three-way showdown between utilitarianism and its descendants, deontological moral theory taking after Kant, and, more recently, virtue theory with an Aristotelian bent. And it is probably also not unfair to say that the showdown has become a decades-old stalemate: systematic ethics is stuck in a rut – a rut from which arguments that proceed by appealing to moral intuitions have been unable to extricate it.

Now each of these moral theories (or rather, families of theories) is associated with a conception of the workings of practical reasoning. John Stuart Mill argued for utilitarianism by appealing to his instrumentalist account of deliberation; and I think it is accurate to describe utilitarianism's contemporary consequentialist offspring as sharing that account. (Consequentialist theories justify actions, rules, dispositions, or whatever, by showing that they are the *means* to the best available consequences.) Kant explicitly anchored his moral theory to an account of practical reasoning, one according to which universalizability is central to something's being a satisfactory reason at all; and, again, this feature of his view has been inherited by its prominent descendants. The connection between Aristotle's theory of practical reasoning and virtue ethics is slightly more indirect, but no less real. Aristotle's practical syllogism is *defeasible*: that delicious things ought to be eaten, and that the cake is delicious may, ordinarily, jointly amount to a perfectly good reason to eat it; but if I discover that the cake has been baked with rat poison, the otherwise warranted conclusion is defeated, and I ought not to draw it. Because a practical syllogism has indefinitely and unsystematizably many defeating conditions, the theory of practical inference to which the practical syllogism is central ends up focusing its attention on the sensibilities of the practically intelligent agent that are indispensible in deploying the inference pattern. What turns out to make the difference, practical and moral, between getting it right and getting it wrong, is whether the agent is intelligent enough, steadfast enough, and sufficiently aware of the proper priorities to draw the conclusions of practical syllogisms only when they are not defeated. And as the list of character traits just given suggests, attention to these deliberative sensibilities is continuous with the attention to the ethical dispositions of agents that is the core of virtue theory.[1]

This overview of the connections between theories of practical reasoning and moral theories suggests two ways in which settling questions about how practical reasoning works can address questions in moral theory. First, if each of the major contenders in the field of systematic moral theory is underwritten by a different theory of practical reasoning, then we should be able to figure out which of them, if any, is the correct moral theory by figuring out which theory of practical reasoning is the right one. This is a promising approach because we ought to be able to decide what the correct theory of practical reasoning is without knowing what the correct moral theory is: because most practical reasoning is not moral reasoning, we can test our theories of practical reasoning on well-understood problems that are uncontaminated by our moral intuitions. An account of practical reasoning thus provides an Archimedean point from which we can get the leverage we need to move debate in ethics from its current impasse.[2]

Second, if systematic ethics is deadlocked, perhaps it is because none of the competing styles of moral theory has what it takes to win. After all, one might think that if one of utilitarianism, deontological moral theory, or virtue theory *were* a satisfactory rendition of our moral world, there would by now be no remaining dissenters. If none of these theories have gained anything close to consensus, their very able advocates and the amount of time they have had to exhibit their merits notwithstanding, a likely explanation of the persistent dissatisfaction is that there is something seriously and fairly obviously wrong with each. If that is right, then to make progress in systematic ethics we need to expand the menu by developing new and different moral theories. But where might these theories come from?

If the hypothesis that patterns of practical reasoning tend to generate characteristic styles of moral theory has anything to it, then one way of introducing novelty into the apparently fixed terrain of systematic ethics would be to look for hitherto unnoticed or unexploited patterns of practical reasoning. We have no good reason to think that the patterns of practical reasoning that have so far held center stage are all there are. Over two millennia after Aristotle, Kant thought logic complete, and John Stuart Mill believed the theory of the syllogism to be the last word on the subject;[3] so one thing that Frege-Russell logic shows is that even extremely basic patterns of inference can go unnoticed for a very long time. Perhaps there are also hitherto unnoticed forms of practical inference; and if there are, perhaps examining them will suggest new, different, and more convincing moral theories.

3

An expedition into largely unmapped territory requires navigational aids. I will adopt the heuristic of looking for analogs of the forms taken by theoretical reasoning (that is, reasoning aimed at belief rather than action), in the hope that a domain we understand better can help us in making sense of one we don't yet know our way around. If the heuristic is effective, that will raise further questions about the underlying relations between the two domains; but I do not propose to address those questions now. Note that I have no reason to think that the list of forms of practical reasoning that I'm about to produce is exhaustive – even if considered as a supplement to the short catalog we've already been through. When the list runs out, I'll finish up with some speculation as to what kind of ethical theorizing attention to the items on it is likely to generate.

Induction is one of the more obviously important forms of theoretical reasoning: to get by in the world, we need to learn from experience what the world is like, and for our conclusions to be useful, we have to generalize from the past we have seen to the future we have not. Our heuristic suggests a parallel form of practical reasoning, which we can label *practical induction*. Like theoretical induction, practical induction proceeds from instances to generalizations that cover them, and, again like theoretical induction, practical induction bottoms out in experience. Practical induction is the medium through which experience teaches us what matters.

Here is a very simple example of practical induction at work. Some time back, Harriet went out with Joe, which turned out to be a painful mistake. Subsequently, she went out with Jim, which was even worse, and with Jack, which she regrets most of all. She eventually performs the practical induction, and concludes: "*Men. Why bother?*"

This isn't the place to argue that practical induction is a legitimate form of inference.[4] (By way of anecdotal support, recall Eva Heller's very funny novel, *Beim nächsten Mann wird alles anders*.[5] The title achieves its intended rhetorical effect because it is clear that its speaker is allowing wishful thinking to prevent her from executing the practical induction that she obviously ought to have performed.) Here I only want to remark on a few of the more interesting features of the inference pattern. First of all, Harriet's desires have been corrected by experience. We may imagine that her initial motivating desires were simply copied – as so many of our desires are – from those of acquaintances and role models. Having performed the induction, she no longer has those desires (or at any rate she believes that taking them to be a reason to act would be an error). And this need not be because she has found that satisfying them conflicts with other desires she had, or that the desires are unsatisfiable. (Whatever conflicting desires she ends up having we can suppose to have been acquired inductively; and, these things being what they are, the worst part of her experiences might well have been satisfying her desires.) Notice also that Harriet's conclusion need not have been mediated by any purely theoretical (as opposed to practical) induction. It is not that there is some nonevaluative *fact* about men that Harriet has noticed; rather, from "I shouldn't have gone out with Joe," "I shouldn't have gone out with Jim," and so on, she infers, directly, that she shouldn't go out with any of them.

Second, like traditional theoretical inductions, Harriet's inference is defeasible. If Harriet learns that Joe, Jim, and Jack were hired by her so-called friends as an overly elaborate practical joke, she will, let's suppose correctly, retract her inference; as with other defeasible inference patterns, sensitivity to the defeating conditions of the inference is a condition of mastery of the inference pattern. The adequacy of the inference depends not just on its instantiating some formally specifiable pattern, but on a body of domain-specific background knowledge. (Here, that you are likely to do better, or at least differently, with people who are not tormenting you for pay.)

Third, again like theoretical induction, inference from particular judgments to general ones raises the further question of the provenance of the premises. In the theoretical case, if we leave to one side inductive premises that are supplied by further inductions, the most important sources seem to be observation and testimony: to obtain information about particulars, you can go and look, or you can ask. This suggests that we should consider whether the practical domain contains analogs of observation and of testimony; and I think our example suggests that it does. That dating Jim was a terrible mistake was a practical observation: face to face with Jim, Harriet realized that this was a man who ought to be declared a National Disaster Area. And while I did not originally tell the story this way, we can supplement it by having Harriet take into account not only her own experiences, but the dismal reports of her friends.

A second form of theoretical reasoning for which we can seek a practical analog is the resolution of contradictions in one's system of beliefs. Like induction, this type of reasoning is not very well understood: logic books ignore it, telling you, unrealistically, to infer anything from a contradiction, or to reject an unhelpfully unspecified premise. But it is a kind of reasoning that, because we all have inconsistent beliefs, we cannot do without.

To explain what its practical analog is, I need to distinguish two ways in which desires can be at odds. Sometimes desires *conflict*, in that the world does not allow us to satisfy them jointly. If I want the house in

Mendocino and the apartment in Oakland, and I cannot afford them both, then while I need to choose which desire to pursue, I am not under pressure to cease desiring either option. Sometimes, however, desires are *directly incompatible.* Recall Saul Kripke's "puzzle about belief": in his example, Pierre believes that Londres is pretty, and that London is not, and does not realize that London *is* Londres. (Kripke poses the third-person question: what does Pierre believe about London?[6]) What is important for us is that when Pierre learns that London is Londres, he will, if he is rational, lose one or both of his beliefs: perhaps he will simply decide that London is hideous, or perhaps, more interestingly, that like most very large cities, it has many sides, some very pretty, and some decidedly not.[7] Now suppose that Pierre also had desires to spend time in Londres, but to avoid London at all costs.[8] Leaving to one side the question of what Pierre can be said to have wanted, let us imagine that one day he learns that London and Londres are identical. He has discovered that his desires are directly incompatible: he wants, and does not want, the very same thing. In such circumstances we do not expect him to treat the problem by asking himself, say, which desire he finds stronger, in order to satisfy the stronger desire at the expense of the weaker. Rather, we should expect his motivational system to readjust so as to remove the incompatibility. He will perhaps end up wanting to stay as far away from London as possible, or, maybe, develop a more nuanced attitude toward the city, involving enthusiasm for its high culture and aversion to its seamy underside (or the other way around). It is characteristic of the resolution of such direct incompatibilities, though, that his subsequent choice will not require him to leave a residual desire unsatisfied. If he ends up wanting to spend time in London, he will not also have the mirroring desire not to.

Directly incompatible desires require revision in one's system of motivations that is very similar to the revision of inconsistent systems of belief. (Saying when desires merely conflict, and when they are directly incompatible, is a hard problem: I won't try to solve it here.[9]) Notice that admitting the need to revise directly incompatible desires is a sharp departure from instrumentalism: on the instrumentalist view, while one can have reason to abandon desires for the means to one's ultimate desires, one's ultimate desires are immune to such threats; direct incompatibility, however, can force one to leave even one's ultimate desires behind.

When direct incompatibility between desires forces revision in one's motivational system, how does that revision take place? Examining cases in which inconsistent systems of belief are revised suggests that coherence considerations play a large role: of the various possible adjustments that would remove the inconsistency, one ought to choose the revision that results in the most coherent system of belief. When I turn up at Fatapples, and find my belief that Robin would be there confronted by my observation that she is not, I settle on the explanation that best hangs together with my other beliefs: we had forgotten that there are now two Fatapples, and she has gone to the other one. Or again, Pierre settles on a view about London that not only hangs together with other things he thinks, but which makes other things he thinks hang together: that French tourists see some parts of London, and that poor residents see other parts.

Once again, our guiding heuristic directs our attention to a parallel phenomenon in the practical domain: incompatibility-driven readjustment of our motivational systems presses in the direction of greater motivational coherence. Forced to choose between desires, I am likely to – and, other things being equal, I *ought* to – go with the one that, together with my other desires, intentions, and so on, best fits into the most coherent available motivational pattern. (We can call this "inference to the best plan."[10])

Why is coherence so important to motivation? This is not the place to attempt a full-fledged answer, so a couple of remarks will have to stand in for one. The point of practical reasoning is successful action. Goals that cohere with one another so as to form coherent plans, and plans that cohere with one another rather than proceeding at cross-purposes, are more likely to eventuate in successful action than goals and plans that do not. Again, human beings engage in practical reasoning because they are trying to live their lives, and for something to amount to a life, it must be sufficiently coherent.[11] Because the demand for coherence in the results of practical reasoning should be reflected in the methods used to obtain them, coherence-driven adjustment of our motivational systems makes sense.[12]

Perhaps one contributor to the coherence of one's plans with one another and one's overall scheme of action with itself is the like treatment of like cases. Kant is known for the most extreme possible version of this demand; he insisted that it be possible to reformulate reasons for action as universal laws. Now Kant's model of practical reasoning has a number of shortcomings. First, it takes defeasibility, which Aristotle noticed was so important a feature of practical inference, insufficiently seriously. (For instance, Kant notoriously concluded that if the fact that a proposed action is a lie is a sufficient reason not to do it, it is *always* a sufficient reason not to do it – even if the occasion for lying involves a murderer in hot pursuit of your nearest and dearest friend.[13]) Second, Kant requires of agents a degree of clarity about their motives that it is normally unrealistic to expect; we are often able to think our way through practical problems without being able to extract the features of a situation that would lend themselves to formulating general principles in their terms.

Analogical reasoning does not have these disadvantages. Analogical reasoning allows one the benefits of using a solved problem to solve another that is relevantly similar; importantly, it does not require that one be able to reformulate the similarity and shared solution into a universally applicable and exceptionless rule. Philosophers have often been inclined to treat analogical reasoning as a derivative pattern of inference; it has been supposed that whatever there is to analogical reasoning must be the application of some general principle, and that the analogy could be, and would be better off, dispensed with in favor of applying the principle. But it is likely that this gets things backwards. Crisply articulated general principles are available only when a category of problems is so well understood that its treatment can be completely routinized. But how is that understanding arrived at in the first place? Evidently, it is the end product of processes of deliberation that do not use the not yet available principles. And I think that examining those processes will show that, typically, analogy figures large in them. Rather than analogical reasoning being reducible to rule-based reasoning, it seems that rule-based reasoning presupposes the independent viability of analogical reasoning.[14]

As before, what we find in the theoretical domain is a very helpful guide to the practical domain. Analogical reasoning is widely used to solve new practical problems on the basis of previously solved practical problems. Analogical reasoning not only identifies strategies that are likely to work; it is a guide to what *counts* as working. Faced with a novel and disorienting set of circumstances, analogy helps us see what is important in those circumstances, and what are goals that we can intelligently adopt.[15]

Finally for now, consider the recently popular doctrine of specificationism: the claim that one form taken by practical inference is the specification of vague or overly general goals or rules. For example, perhaps we wish to be entertained this evening. Entertainment is too vaguely specified a goal to serve as a starting point for successful means-end reasoning. Before we have decided, say, to see a movie, or a particular movie, instrumental deliberation is premature; first, we need to find a more concrete and focused rendering of our goal.[16]

I do not know that specificationists arrived at their view by using the heuristic I have been following, but perhaps it is worth pointing out that the method has a parallel in theoretical reasoning. Nancy Cartwright has pointed out that the laws of physics are very often too general to be applied to the situations of interest to physicists: working scientists proceed by first developing more specific characterizations of the circumstances they are trying to understand.[17] The process of arriving at these more specific characterizations of situations is poorly understood, but resembles in many ways the pattern of reasoning highlighted by specificationism.

4

I believe that all the forms of practical reasoning I have just mentioned deserve further investigation; once again, I don't have any reason to think that these are all there are. Now recall that I proposed turning to new forms of practical reasoning as a way of breaking the deadlock in systematic ethics. If I am right in thinking that *all* of these (and perhaps others) are ways we reason about what to do, and if I am right in believing that traditional moral theories have been generated and underwritten by far more restrictive conceptions of practical deliberation, then there are grounds for suspicion that none of the three competing families of moral theory can be on target: whether or not they are right as far as they go, it's hard to believe that any one of them is, or all of them together are, the whole picture. And if that's right, then we need to ask what styles of moral theory we can expect to be generated by these further inference patterns.

One common thread running through several of the patterns of practical inference we have surveyed is the scope allowed for empirical investigation of what is ultimately important, and the degree to which what does matter is, in one way or another, contingent. This is in striking contrast to traditional moral theory, which is both avowedly and in practice apriorist. What desires and preferences people may actually have, utilitarians admit they may not yet know; but that what *matters* is the satisfaction of people's desires and preferences, utilitarians believe not to require empirical investigation. Kantians may not have detailed recommendations already on hand as to what courses of action one should take – although then again they might: recall Kant's discussion of lying – but they take themselves to have settled, in advance of empirical investigation of any kind, the overriding importance of even-handedness and impartiality. And while Aristotle took *endoxa*, things people think, as his starting point, he does not seem to have considered seriously the idea that he and his fellows had not had enough experience to say what living well is.

But if practical induction is how we learn what matters, then whether, and how, the satisfaction of desires and preferences is important is an open question, not to be settled by thumping the upholstery of one's philosophical armchair. Sane parents, for example, quickly learn that many, perhaps most, of a small child's desires are frivolous, and should be corrected or ignored rather than satisfied. (Certainly the mere *strength* of the child's desires does not, and should not, count for much: it may want to throw its food so badly that it will cry if it is not allowed to, but even though its desires are stronger than those of the surrounding, less tear-prone adults, it should not be allowed to throw its food.) Similarly, the importance of treating people impartially is open to *empirical* investigation. Recall the Marxist appraisal of economic equality and basic economic needs as more important than the easy availability of consumer luxuries and the advantages of distributing goods through the market. This perhaps initially very plausible assessment has been challenged – *empirically* challenged – by the recent history of Israel, a formerly socialist state whose electorate, in the mid-seventies, gave the then opposition a mandate to dismantle a working socialist economy: having gotten equality and basic economic needs (in a form unadulterated by gulags, a controlled press, mock-parliaments, and so on – Israel actually managed "socialism with a human face"), Israelis decided they didn't want it, after all. Likewise, we can imagine a Kantian world turning out to produce in its inhabitants the same disillusionment and cynicism about treating others as ends in themselves that talk of socialist ideals provokes in some formerly socialist countries. If it did, that would be a large part of an empirical argument against the importance of treating others as ends in themselves, and for the claim that universalizability is not as important as all that.

Practical reasoning driven by the need to revise a motivational system containing directly incompatible desires is another locus of epistemic contingency, and speaks for empirical investigation and against armchair philosophizing. The Evening Star and the Morning Star (or London and Londres) may be, if identical, then necessarily identical; but there is no nonempirical way to find out that they are. One may come to a situation prepared with a priori, overriding injunctions against lying and against murder: but one can find out that, in this situation, not lying just *is* murder; and then one will have to revise one's apriorist injunctions. No armchair-manufactured moral theory can be secure against this kind of discovery: not consequentialist theories, where a higher-ranked outcome may be surprisingly identified with a lower-ranked outcome; not virtue ethics, where a virtue may prove to be a vice; not Kantian theories, where one's clear-headed intentions may suddenly turn out to be strikingly incoherent. (Wilfred Owen's depiction of what the military virtues of World

War I soldiery actually came to would, if correct, provide examples of all of these.[18])

Coherentist revision of motivational systems introduces still further contingency into our conception of what matters. I have not here tried to spell out what deliberative coherence amounts to, but let us adopt the plausible working assumption that when attaining one goal facilitates attaining another, both goals cohere with each other, that when attaining two goals jointly facilitates attaining a further goal, they all cohere, and that when two goals are difficult to accomplish jointly, this detracts from their mutual coherence.[19] I suggested that it makes sense to adopt goals that hang together with one's other aims and purposes: for example, one might adopt an overarching goal because it unifies and organizes many disparate pursuits to which one is already committed into a way of life. But if what hangs together with what is partly a matter of what facilitates what, and of what impedes what, then what it makes sense for one to care about is a deeply contingent matter: after all, what facilitates what is an entirely contingent matter.

And, to wrap up the list, specificationism introduces an empirical element into practical reasoning as well. Consider the problem, mentioned earlier, of arriving at a more definite version of the aim of having an entertaining evening. Solving this problem requires knowing, of at least some of the options on the table, whether they *are* entertaining; and the knowledge that something is entertaining is both a practical matter, and to be empirically discovered. Often enough, all the flatly factual description one can come by will not settle whether the show is entertaining or not, and the only way to find out is to go and see it.

5

If moral theory, when reconceived in the light of a broadened view of practical reasoning, proves to be empirical through and through, it may, like Hegel's owl of Minerva, arrive on the scene too late to be of use. Even apriorist theory provides no guarantee that results will appear in a timely manner; theorems and concepts and even whole branches of mathematics may be still unproved or uninvented when they are needed. But the tardiness of moral theory may be inevitable in a way which that of mathematics is not.

Other domains of empirical investigation also seem to do better in this regard than moral theory. The world investigated by the hard sciences is one of fixed laws, discoverable once and for all, or very slowly changing biological species, or long-lasting geological facts; however long it takes to find out how things work, eventually, one can hope, one will be done and that will be that. The moral sciences differ in that the human world is constantly reinventing itself, and always contains a population of novel meanings, artifacts, social structures and much more. If only experiment will tell us how these things matter and why they are important, then our ready-made moral theories will constantly prove themselves stodgy and out of date, their scripts only sometimes useful in what turns out to be improvisational theater.

The intersubjectivity of the hard sciences means that the results of one's predecessors can be appropriated in the most straightforward manner possible: one sees far because one stands on the shoulders of giants, and one can stand on the shoulders of giants because what they saw from their vantage point is what one would see oneself. But human lives and their meanings differ from one another. What your mother discovered was important for her may not turn out to be important for you. Practical reasoning does not start from scratch – advice is essential – but one cannot always make another's empirically acquired wisdom one's own. If empirical practical reasoning is less intersubjective than our paradigms of empirical theoretical reasoning are, we may find confirmed Iris Murdoch's insistence that moral theory, when it does not succumb to moral laziness, will be private and idiosyncratic.[20]

The upshot is that one may find that one could not but have learned the moral facts of life too late. Perhaps one's ideals could only have been unmasked by pursuing them for the better part of one's life; the realization that one has wasted one's best years comes too late to be of practical value. One faces the situation with integrity, and it is only because of the terrible way it goes wrong that one comes to see that integrity should not always override human concern.

If this is right, perhaps the closure for which systematic ethics strives is overly ambitious. And if this is right in turn, then perhaps the largest difference a more comprehensive account of practical reasoning could make for systematic ethics would be to impress upon us this lesson.

Notes

I'm grateful to Christoph Fehige, Konstanze Feigel, Gopal Sreenivasan, Rachel Shuh, and Yael Tamir for comments on an earlier draft of this paper, and to Jenann Ismael for helpful discussion.

1. My Chapters 2, 3, and 4 lay out these connections in greater detail.

2. There are ways in which the dependencies are more complicated than this quick sketch suggests. In particular, one frequently executed manuever is to attempt to make an ethical theory of one pattern assume the form of another, or, equivalently, to attempt to make a foundation of one kind justify the superstructure of another. Examples include rule-utilitarianism (for critical discussion, see Lyons, 1965), Hare's attempt to move from a universalization-based account of moral reasoning to utilitarian results (1982), the consequentialist justification of virtue ethics advanced by Driver (2001), and the recent attempt by a host of Kantian ethicists to pull off a hostile takeover, of the kind popular on Wall Street in the eighties, of the Aristotelian competition, with the aim of making it a kind of corporate subsidiary. (I'm grateful to John Rawls for, long ago, having pressed me on this point.)

It's hard to give a straightforward and uniformly applicable treatment of these quite varied and often ingenious constructions. I think, however, that if one proceeds case by case, one will start to see a pattern emerging: mix-and-match theories get themselves in trouble, and the trouble has to do with the seam where the substantive ethical theory is grafted onto the account of practical reasoning. By way of example, consider rule-utilitarianism, which has been taken to task for its inability to command on-the-spot practical allegiance: if you know that the point of the rule is to maximize utility, and you also know that in this instance, following the rule will fail to maximize utility, then you will end up not following the rule. What is happening here is that the instrumental mode of reasoning prescribed by the foundational theory is conflicting with the mode of reasoning prescribed by the theory that has been grafted onto it. My sense of the territory is that mix-and-match theories make such conflicts hard to avoid, and that, consequently, they will lose out to the "pure" theories – to which we can accordingly restrict our attention.

3. Kant, 1781/1787/1998, B viii; Mill, 1872/1973, pp. 164ff.

4. I do that in Millgram, 1997.

5. Heller, 1987. An English rendering of the title might be: "With the next man, everything will be different."

6. Kripke, 1979. I'm riding roughshod over the many niceties in Kripke's treatment of the puzzle; I don't think they make a difference here.

7. Again, this is begging the question of what it was Pierre believed before his discovery; for now, that question isn't important.

8. Let's further suppose that these desires are associated with his beliefs as to the city's prettiness, but not instrumentally derived from them: it is not that he desires to visit pretty cities, and thinks of a trip to Londres as a means of satisfying that desire.

9. The idea that incompatibility of desires of this kind might rationally require their revision is due to Candace Vogler.

10. Thagard and Millgram, 1995. The item at the head of the coherentist agenda must be the task of saying just what is meant by coherence, and to specify when one system of beliefs, or of motivations, is more coherent than another; see Millgram, 2000.

It is perhaps worth emphasizing that coherence is probably not the sole proper determinant of a person's system of motivations. Recall the importance of diversity in one's commitments: one does not want one's motivations to collapse into a single, Parmenidean end.

11. To say this is to defer the explanation of the need for coherence, but not to discharge it: we have not yet said why lives must be coherent.

12. Let me connect issues regarding the justification of coherentist (and other) forms of inference with a point we will arrive at shortly. In this century, the kind of argument that has carried most justificatory weight has been the reconstruction of a large and very prestigious body of already accepted inference, together with its conclusions, using the proposed inference patterns. (Whitehead and Russell, 1929/1963; I take it that Thagard, 1992, is meant as an argument of this kind also, in which science plays the role of the body of already accepted inference.) Now there is a difficulty in reproducing this form of argument in the practical domain: there does not seem to be a body of practical doctrine with anything like the prestige of mathematics or the hard empirical sciences, and it's going to be difficult to show a pattern of inference to be legitimate by using it to reconstruct a prestigious body of inference if the latter is not to be had. We will soon have a possible explanation for its absence.

13. Kant, 1902–, vol. 8, pp. 423–30.

14. For recent discussions of analogy, see Holyoak and Thagard, 1995, Gentner, Holyoak, and Kokinov, 2001, Hofstadter and the Fluid Analogies Research Group, 1995, Holyoak and Thagard, 1989.

15. Robert Nozick has proposed that "symbolic utility" – treating something as valuable because it symbolizes something else that is valuable – serves the cognitive function of helping us stick to our guns in the face of temptation (1993). If I am right, it has a deeper cognitive role: symbolic utility is a necessary part of the process of mapping one practical problem onto another. It allows us to use an already solved practical problem to show us what is important in a new practical problem by making the analogs of what is important in the old problem symbolically important in the new one.

16. The example is due to Bernard Williams (2001). Specificationists include Kolnai (2001), Wiggins (2001), and Richardson (1990). See Broadie, 1987, for an objection to the view.

17. Cartwright, 1983.

18. Owen, 1963. I'm grateful to Cora Diamond for bringing Owen's poems to my attention as an instance of this point.

19. This of course is not meant to be anything like a complete specification of a notion of coherence. Recall, for example, my earlier suggestion that uniform treatment of relevantly similar cases also increases coherence.

20. See Chapter 5.

References

Albee, E., 1957. *A History of English Utilitarianism*. Macmillan, New York.

Alberti, L. B., 1956. *On Painting*. Translated by John R. Spencer, Routledge and Kegan Paul, London.

Allen, W., 1983. *Zelig*. Produced by Jack Rollins, Charles Joffe, and Robert Greenhut, Metro-Goldwyn-Mayer, Santa Monica. Film.

Anderson, E., 1991. "John Stuart Mill and Experiments in Living." *Ethics*, 102: 4–26.

———, 1996. *Value in Ethics and Economics*. Harvard University Press, Cambridge.

Anderson, R. L., 2001. "Synthesis, Cognitive Normativity, and the Meaning of Kant's Question, 'How Are Synthetic Cognitions A Priori Possible?'" *European Journal of Philosophy*, 9 (3): 275–305.

Anscombe, G. E. M., 1985. *Intention*, second edition. Cornell University Press, Ithaca.

———, 1997. "Modern Moral Philosophy." In Crisp, R., and Slote, M., editors, *Virtue Ethics*, 26–44, Oxford University Press, Oxford.

Asimov, I., 1991. *Foundation*. Bantam Books, New York.

Atkinson, R. F., 1968. "Hume on 'Is' and 'Ought': A Reply to Mr. MacIntyre." In Chappell, V. C., editor, *Hume: A Collection of Critical Essays*, 265–77, University of Notre Dame Press, Notre Dame.

Ayer, A. J., 1951. *Language, Truth and Logic*. Victor Gollancz, London.

Baier, A., 1991. *A Progress of Sentiments*. Harvard University Press, Cambridge.

Bakhurst, D., 2000. "Ethical Particularism in Context." In Hooker, B., and Little, M., editors, *Moral Particularism*, 157–77, Clarendon Press, Oxford.

Bendor, J., 2003. "Herbert A. Simon: Political Scientist." *Annual Review of Political Science*, 6: 433–71.

Bentham, J., 1789/1970. *An Introduction to the Principles of Morals and Legislation*. Edited by J. H. Burns and H. L. A. Hart, Clarendon Press, Oxford.

Bok, H., 1998. *Freedom and Responsibility*. Princeton University Press, Princeton.

Borges, J. L., 1998. "Pierre Menand, Author of the *Quixote*." In *Collected Fictions*, translated by Andrew Hurley, 88–95, Penguin, New York.

Brandom, R., 2001. "Action, Norms, and Practical Reasoning." In Millgram, E., editor, *Varieties of Practical Reasoning*, MIT Press, Cambridge.

Brandt, R., 1979. *A Theory of the Good and the Right.* Clarendon Press, Oxford.

Brännmark, J., 1999. "Rules and Exceptions." *Theoria*, 65 (2–3): 127–43.

Bratman, M., 1987. *Intention, Plans and Practical Reason.* Harvard University Press, Cambridge.

———, 1999. *Faces of Intention.* Cambridge University Press, Cambridge.

———, 2001. "Taking Plans Seriously." In Millgram, E., editor, *Varieties of Practical Reasoning*, MIT Press, Cambridge.

———, 2004. "Shared Valuing and Frameworks for Practical Reasoning." In Wallace, R. J., Pettit, P., Scheffler, S., and Smith, M., editors, *Reason and Value: Themes from the Moral Philosophy of Joseph Raz*, 1–27, Oxford University Press, Oxford.

Brickman, P., Coates, D., and Janoff-Bulman, R., 1978. "Lottery Winners and Accident Victims: Is Happiness Relative?" *Journal of Personality and Social Psychology*, 36: 917–27.

Broad, C. D., 1930/1951. *Five Types of Ethical Theory.* Humanities Press, New York.

Broadie, S. W., 1987. "The Problem of Practical Intellect in Aristotle's Ethics." In Cleary, J., editor, *Proceedings of the Boston Area Colloquium in Ancient Philosophy*, Vol. III, 229–52, University Press of America, Lanham.

Broome, J., 1991. *Weighing Goods: Equality, Uncertainty and Time.* Blackwell, Oxford.

Carnap, R., 1937. *The Logical Syntax of Language.* Kegan Paul, Trench, Trubner and Co., London.

Cartwright, N., 1983. *How the Laws of Physics Lie.* Clarendon Press, Oxford.

Cavell, S., 1999. *The Claim of Reason.* Oxford University Press, New York.

Chang, R., 1997. *Incommensurability, Incomparability, and Practical Reason.* Harvard University Press, Cambridge.

Chi, M., Feltovich, P., and Glaser, R., 1981. "Categorization and Representation of Physics Problems by Experts and Novices." *Cognitive Science*, 5: 121–52.

Churchland, P., and Hooker, C., 1985. *Images of Science: Essays on Realism and Empiricism.* University of Chicago Press, Chicago.

Cohon, R., 1994. "On an Unorthodox Account of Hume's Moral Psychology." *Hume Studies*, 20 (2): 179–94.

Commons, J., 1924/1957. *Legal Foundations of Capitalism.* University of Wisconsin Press, Madison.

Converse, P., 1964. "The Nature of Belief Systems in Mass Publics." In Apter, D., editor, *Ideology and Discontent*, 206–61, Free Press of Glencoe, New York.

Cooper, J., 1986. *Reason and Human Good in Aristotle.* Hackett, Indianapolis.

Cooter, R., and Rappoport, P., 1984. "Were the Ordinalists Wrong about Welfare Economics?" *Journal of Economic Literature*, 22: 507–30.

Copp, D., and Sobel, D., 2004. "Morality and Virtue: An Assessment of Some Recent Work in Virtue Ethics." *Ethics*, 114 (3): 514–54.

Coupland, D., 1991. *Generation X.* St. Martin's Press, New York.

Csikszentmihalyi, M., 1990. *Flow: The Psychology of Optimal Experience.* Harper-Collins, New York.

Cummins, R., Poirier, P., and Roth, M., 2004. "Epistemological Strata and the Rules of Right Reason." *Synthese*, 141 (3): 287–331.

Dancy, J., 1985. "The Role of Imaginary Cases in Ethics." *Pacific Philosophical Quarterly*, 66: 141–53.

———, 1993. *Moral Reasons*. Blackwell, Oxford.

———, 1999. "On the Logical and Moral Adequacy of Particularism." *Theoria*, 65 (2–3): 144–55.

———, 2000. "The Particularist's Progress." In Hooker, B., and Little, M., editors, *Moral Particularism*, 130–56, Clarendon Press, Oxford.

Daniels, N., 1979. "Wide Reflective Equilibrium and Theory Acceptance in Ethics." *Journal of Philosophy*, 76 (5): 256–82.

———, 1980. "On Some Methods of Ethics and Linguistics." *Philosophical Studies*, 37 (1): 21–36.

Davidson, D., 1980. "Mental Events." In *Essays on Actions and Events*, 207–27, Clarendon Press, Oxford.

———, 1984. *Expressing Evaluations*. University of Kansas, Lawrence. Lindley Lecture.

Davidson, D., McKinsey, J. C. C., and Suppes, P., 1955. "Outlines of a Formal Theory of Value, I." *Philosophy of Science*, 22 (2): 140–60.

Dawes, R., 1994. *House of Cards*. Free Press, Englewood Cliffs.

de Groot, A. D., 1965. *Thought and Choice in Chess*. Mouton and Co., The Hague.

Deacon, T., 1997. *The Symbolic Species*. W. W. Norton, New York.

Diamond, C., 1996. "'We Are Perpetually Moralists': Iris Murdoch, Fact, and Value." In Antonaccio, M., and Schweiker, W., editors, *Iris Murdoch and the Search for Human Goodness*, 79–109, University of Chicago Press, Chicago.

Dick, P. K., 1992. "Faith of our Fathers." In *The Collected Stories of Philip K. Dick*, vol. 5, 197–222, Carol Publishing, New York.

Doris, J., 2002. *Lack of Character*. Cambridge University Press, Cambridge.

Driver, J., 2001. *Uneasy Virtue*. Cambridge University Press, Cambridge.

Duncker, K., 1945. *On Problem-Solving*. Translated by Lynne S. Lees. *Psychological Monographs* 58 (Whole No. 270). American Psychological Association, Washington, DC.

Eckert, P., 1989. *Jocks and Burnouts*. Teachers College Press, New York.

Ellsberg, D., 1961. "Risk, Ambiguity, and the Savage Axioms." *Quarterly Journal of Economics*, 75: 643–69.

Elster, J., 1983. *Sour Grapes: Studies in the Subversion of Rationality*. Cambridge University Press, Cambridge.

Engstrom, S., 1986. "The Principle of Sufficient Reason in Kant's Practical and Theoretical Philosophy." Ph.D thesis, University of Chicago.

Fehige, C., 1994. "The Limit Assumption in Deontic (and Prohairetic) Logic." In Meggle, G., and Wessels, U., editors, *Analyomen 1*, de Gruyter, Berlin.

Fishkin, J., 1997. *The Voice of the People*. Yale University Press, New Haven.

Fodor, J., 1994. *The Elm and the Expert*. MIT Press, Cambridge.

Fogelin, R. J., 1985. *Hume's Skepticism in the* Treatise of Human Nature. Routledge and Kegan Paul, Boston.

Foot, P., 2001. *Natural Goodness*. Clarendon Press, Oxford.

Forbes, D., 1975. *Hume's Philosophical Politics*. Cambridge University Press, Cambridge.

Ford, R., 1995. *Independence Day*. Vintage/Random House, New York.

Garrett, D., 1981. "Hume's Self-doubts about Personal Identity." *Philosophical Review*, 90 (3): 337–58.

Gass, W., 1957. "The Case of the Obliging Stranger." *Philosophical Review*, 66 (2): 193–204.

Geach, P., 1956. "Good and Evil." *Analysis*, 17: 33–42.

———, 1972. "Assertion." In *Logic Matters*, 251–69, University of California Press, Berkeley.

Geertz, C., 1973. *The Interpretation of Cultures*. Basic Books, New York.

Gentner, D., Holyoak, K., and Kokinov, B., editors, 2001. *The Analogical Mind: Perspectives from Cognitive Science*. MIT Press, Cambridge.

Gerard, S., 1997. "Desire and Desirability: Bradley, Russell and Moore versus Mill." In Tait, W. W., editor, *Early Analytic Philosophy: Frege, Russell, Wittgenstein*, 37–74, Open Court Press, Chicago.

Gerstenblith, P., 1995. "Associational Structures of Religious Organizations." *Brigham Young University Law Review*, (2): 439–80.

Gibbard, A., 1990. *Wise Choices, Apt Feelings: A Theory of Normative Judgment*. Harvard University Press, Cambridge.

Gibbon, E., 1906/1776–88. *The Decline and Fall of the Roman Empire*. Edited by J. B. Bury. Fred de Fau and Company, New York.

Gigerenzer, G., Todd, P., and the ABC Research Group, 1999. *Simple Heuristics That Make Us Smart*. Oxford University Press, Oxford.

Gilbert, D. and Wilson, T., 2000. "Miswanting: Some Problems in the Forecasting of Future Affective States." In Forgas, J., editor, *Feeling and Thinking: The Role of Affect in Social Cognition*, 178–97, Cambridge University Press/Editions de la Maison des Sciences de l'Homme, Cambridge/Paris.

Gilbert, D., Pinel, E., Wilson, T., Blumberg, S., and Wheatley, T., 1998. "Immune Neglect: A Source of Durability Bias in Affective Forecasting." *Journal of Personality and Social Psychology*, 75 (3): 617–38.

Goldberg, R., 2000. *Inventions*. Edited by Maynard Frank Wolfe. Simon and Schuster, New York.

Goldstein, R., 1983. *The Mind-Body Problem*. Laurel/Dell, London.

Gombrich, E. H., 1984. *Art and Illusion*. Princeton University Press, Princeton.

Goodman, N., 1983. *Fact, Fiction, and Forecast*, fourth edition. Foreword by Hilary Putnam. Harvard University Press, Cambridge.

Griffin, J., 1986. *Well-Being*. Clarendon, Oxford.

Gunn, J., 1961. *The Joy Makers*. Bantam, New York.

Gutmann, A., and Thompson, D., 1996. *Democracy and Disagreement*. Harvard University Press, Cambridge.

———, 2000. "Why Deliberative Democracy is Different." *Social Philosophy and Policy*, 17 (1): 161–80.

Hall, P., and Soskice, D., editors, 2001. *Varieties of Capitalism*. Oxford University Press, New York.

Hampshire, S., 1954. "Logic and Appreciation." In Elton, W., editor, *Aesthetics and Language*, 161–9, Basil Blackwell, Oxford.

Hare, R. M., 1961. *The Language of Morals*. Clarendon Press, Oxford.

———, 1963. *Freedom and Reason*. Oxford University Press, Oxford.

———, 1982. "Ethical Theory and Utilitarianism." In Sen, A., and Williams, B., editors, *Utilitarianism and Beyond*, 23–38, Cambridge University Press, Cambridge.

Harman, G., 1976. "Practical Reasoning." *Review of Metaphysics*, 29 (3): 431–63.

———, 1982. "Critical Review: Richard B. Brandt, *A Theory of the Good and the Right*." *Philosophical Studies*, 42: 119–39.

Harrison, J., 1976. *Hume's Moral Epistemology*. Clarendon Press, Oxford.

Hart, K., 1986. "Heads or Tails? Two Sides of the Coin." *Man, N. S.* 21 (4): 637–56.

Hawks, H. 1940. *His Girl Friday*. Script by Ben Hecht, Charles MacArthur, and Charles Lederer. Columbia Picture Corporation. Film.

Hayek, F. A., 1948. *Individualism and Economic Order*. University of Chicago Press, Chicago.

———, 1989. *Order – With or Without Design?* Edited by Naomi Moldofsky. Centre for Research into Communist Economies, London.

Hearne, V., 1987. *Adam's Task: Calling Animals by Name*. Vintage/Random House, New York.

Heller, E., 1987. *Beim nächsten Mann wird alles anders*. Fischer, Frankfurt a. M.

Henrich, D., 1975. "Die Deduktion des Sittengesetzes: Über die Gründe der Dunkelheit des letzten Abschnittes von Kants 'Grundlegung zur Metaphysik der Sitten'." In *Denken im Schatten des Nihilismus*, 55–112, Wissenschaftliche Buchgesellschaft, Darmstadt.

Herman, B., 1990. *Morality as Rationality: A Study in Kant's Ethics*. Reprint of 1976 doctoral dissertation. Garland, New York.

———, 1993. *The Practice of Moral Judgment*. Harvard University Press, Cambridge.

Hill, T., 1992. "Making Exceptions without Abandoning the Principle: Or How a Kantian Might Think about Terrorism." In *Dignity and Practical Reason in Kant's Moral Theory*, 196–225, Cornell University Press, Ithaca.

Himmelfarb, G., 1990. *On Liberty and Liberalism: The Case of John Stuart Mill*. Institute for Contemporary Studies Press, San Francisco.

Hofstadter, D., and the Fluid Analogies Research Group, 1995. *Fluid Concepts and Creative Analogies*. Basic Books, New York.

Holyoak, K., and Thagard, P., 1989. "Analogical Mapping by Constraint Satisfaction." *Cognitive Science*, 13: 295–355.

———, 1995. *Mental Leaps: Analogy in Creative Thought*. MIT Press, Cambridge.

Hooker, B., 2000. "Moral Particularism: Wrong and Bad." In Hooker, B., and Little, M., editors, *Moral Particularism*, 1–22, Clarendon Press, Oxford.

Hooker, B., and Little, M., editors, 2000. *Moral Particularism*. Clarendon Press, Oxford.

Hrdy, S. B., 1981. *The Woman That Never Evolved*. Harvard University Press, Cambridge.

Hsee, C., and Abelson, R., 1991. "Velocity Relation: Satisfaction as a Function of the First Derivative of Outcome Over Time." *Journal of Personality and Social Psychology*, 60 (3): 341–7.

Hsee, C., Abelson, R., and Salovey, P., 1991. "The Relative Weighting of Position and Velocity in Satisfaction." *Psychological Science*, 2 (4): 263–6.

Hudson, W. D., 1968. "Hume on *Is* and *Ought*." In Chappell, V. C., editor, *Hume: A Collection of Critical Essays*, 295–307, University of Notre Dame Press, Notre Dame.

————, 1983. *Modern Moral Theory,* second edition. St. Martin's Press, New York.

Hume, D., 1777/1978. *Enquiries Concerning Human Understanding and Concerning the Principles of Morals,* third edition. Edited by L. A. Selby-Bigge and P. H. Nidditch. Clarendon Press, Oxford.

————, 1778/1983. *The History of England from the Invasion of Julius Caesar to the Revolution in 1688.* Introduction by William Todd. Liberty Fund, Indianapolis.

————, 1888/1978. *A Treatise of Human Nature,* second edition. Edited by L. A. Selby-Bigge and P. H. Nidditch. Clarendon Press, Oxford.

————, 1985. *Essays: Moral, Political, and Literary,* revised edition. Edited by Eugene Miller. Liberty Fund, Indianapolis.

Hurley, S., 1989. *Natural Reasons: Personality and Polity.* Oxford University Press, Oxford.

Hursthouse, R., 1999. *On Virtue Ethics.* Oxford University Press, Oxford.

Hutchinson, D. S., 1995. "Ethics." In Barnes, J., editor, *The Cambridge Companion to Aristotle,* 195–232, Cambridge University Press, Cambridge.

Huxley, A., 1998. *Brave New World.* HarperPerennial, New York.

Jackson, F., Pettit, P., and Smith, M., 2000. "Ethical Particularism and Patterns." In Hooker, B., and Little, M., editors, *Moral Particularism,* 79–99, Clarendon Press, Oxford.

Jacobs, J., 1984. *Cities and the Wealth of Nations.* Random House, New York.

Jacobson, D., 2003. "J. S. Mill and the Diversity of Utilitarianism." *Philosophers' Imprint,* 3 (2). Online Journal.

Jaglom, H., 1990. *Eating.* Produced by Judith Wolinsky. International Rainbow, Los Angeles. Film.

Jarry, A., 1996. *Exploits and Opinions of Dr. Faustroll, Pataphysician.* Translated by Simon Watson Taylor. Exact Change, Boston.

Jaworska, A., 1999. "Respecting the Margins of Agency: Alzheimer's Patients and the Capacity to Value." *Philosophy and Public Affairs,* 28 (2): 105–38.

Kahneman, D., Diener, E., and Schwarz, N., 1999. *Well-Being: The Foundations of Hedonic Psychology.* Russell Sage Foundation, New York.

Kahneman, D., Fredrickson, B., Schreiber, C. M., and Redelmeir, D., 1993. "When More Pain is Preferred to Less: Adding a Better End." *Psychological Science,* 4: 401–5.

Kant, I., 1755/1992. "A New Elucidation of the First Principles of Metaphysical Cognition." In *Theoretical Philosophy, 1755–1770,* translated and edited by David Walford and Ralf Meerbote, 1–45, Cambridge University Press, Cambridge.

————, 1781/1787/1998. *Critique of Pure Reason.* Translated by Paul Guyer and Allen Wood. Cambridge University Press, Cambridge.

————, 1785/1981. *Grounding for the Metaphysics of Morals.* Translated by James Ellington. Hackett, Indianapolis.

————, 1788/1997. *Critique of Practical Reason.* Translated by Mary Gregor. Cambridge University Press, Cambridge.

————, 1793/1998. *Religion within the Boundaries of Mere Reason and other Writings.* Translated by Allen Wood and George di Giovanni. Cambridge University Press, Cambridge.

————, 1797/1994. "Metaphysical Principles of Virtue." In *Ethical Philosophy,* Translated by James Ellington. 31–161, Hackett, Indianapolis.

———, 1902–. *Kants gesammelte Schriften.* 29 vols., edited by the German Academy of Sciences (formerly the Royal Prussian Academy of Sciences). de Gruyter, Berlin.

———, 1992. *Lectures on Logic.* Translated by Michael Young. Cambridge University Press, Cambridge.

Kantorowicz, E., 1957. *The King's Two Bodies: A Study in Mediaeval Political Theology.* Princeton University Press, Princeton.

Katz, L., 1986. "Hedonism as Metaphysics of Mind and Value." Ph.D thesis, Princeton University.

Kawai, M., 1998. "Optimum Currency Areas." In Eatwell, J., Milgate, M., and Newman, P., editors, *The New Palgrave*, Palgrave Publishers, New York.

Kenny, A., 1992. *What Is Faith?* Oxford University Press, Oxford.

Kolnai, A., 1970. "A Defense of Intrinsicalism Against 'Situation Ethics'." In *Situationism and the New Morality*, 232–71, Appleton-Century-Crofts, New York.

———, 2001. "Deliberation Is of Ends." In Millgram, E., editor, *Varieties of Practical Reasoning*, MIT Press, Cambridge.

Komar, V., and Melamid, A., 1999. *Painting by Numbers: Komar and Melamid's Scientific Guide to Art.* University of California Press, Berkeley.

Korsgaard, C., 1990. *The Standpoint of Practical Reason.* Reprint of 1981 doctoral dissertation. Garland Press, New York.

———, 1996a. *Creating the Kingdom of Ends.* Cambridge University Press, Cambridge.

———, 1996b. *The Sources of Normativity.* Cambridge University Press, Cambridge.

———, 1997. "The Normativity of Instrumental Reason." In Cullity, G., and Gaut B., editors, *Ethics and Practical Reason*, 215–54, Clarendon Press, Oxford.

———, 1999. "Self-constitution in the Ethics of Plato and Kant." *Journal of Ethics*, 3: 1–29.

Kretzmann, N., 1971. "Desire as Proof of Desirability." In Gorowitz, S., editor, *Utilitarianism with Critical Essays*, 231–41, Bobbs-Merrill, Indianapolis.

Kripke, S., 1979. "A Puzzle about Belief." In Margalit, A., editor, *Meaning and Use*, 239–83, D. Reidel, Dordrecht.

Kubrick, S. 1971. *A Clockwork Orange.* Adapted from the novel by Anthony Burgess. Warner Studios. Film.

Landesman, C., 1995. "When to Terminate a Charitable Trust?" *Analysis*, 55 (1): 12–13.

Latour, B., 1996. *Aramis, or the Love of Technology.* Translated by Catherine Porter. Harvard University Press, Cambridge.

Lear, J., 1998a. *Love and Its Place in Nature.* Yale University Press, New Haven.

———, 1998b. *Open Minded: Working Out the Logic of the Soul.* Harvard University Press, Cambridge.

Lewis, D., 1988. "Desire as Belief." *Mind*, 97: 323–32.

Lippert-Rasmussen, K., 1999. "On Denying a Significant Version of the Constancy Assumption." *Theoria*, 65 (2–3): 90–113.

Little, M., 2000. "Moral Generalities Revisited." In Hooker, B., and Little, M., editors, *Moral Particularism*, 276–304, Clarendon Press, Oxford.

———, 2001a. "On Knowing the 'Why': Particularism and Moral Theory." *Hastings Center Report*, 31 (4): 32–40.

————, 2001b. "Wittgensteinian Lessons on Moral Particularism." In Elliott, C., editor, *Slow Cures and Bad Philosophers: Essays on Wittgenstein, Medicine, and Bioethics,* Duke University Press, Durham.

Livingston, D., 1984. *Hume's Philosophy of Common Life.* University of Chicago Press, Chicago.

Lowenstein, G., and Schkade, D., 1999. "Wouldn't It Be Nice? Predicting Future Feelings." In Kahneman, D., Diener, E., and Schwarz, N., editors, *Well-Being: The Foundations of Hedonic Psychology,* 85–105, Russell Sage Foundation, New York.

Luce, R. D., and Raiffa, H., 1957. *Games and Decisions.* John Wiley and Sons, New York.

Lukes, S., 1995. *The Curious Enlightenment of Professor Caritat.* Verso, New York.

Lyons, D., 1965. *The Forms and Limits of Utilitarianism.* Clarendon Press, Oxford.

McDowell, J., 1998. *Mind, Value, and Reality.* Harvard University Press, Cambridge.

MacIntyre, A., 1981. *After Virtue.* University of Notre Dame Press, Notre Dame.

————, 1999. *Dependent Rational Animals.* Open Court, Chicago.

Mackie, J. L., 1977. *Ethics: Inventing Right and Wrong.* Penguin, New York.

————, 1980. *Hume's Moral Theory.* Routledge and Kegan Paul, Boston.

Macmillan, M., 1890. *The Promotion of Happiness.* Swan Sonnenschein, London.

McNaughton, D., 1989. *Moral Vision: An Introduction to Ethics.* Blackwell, Oxford.

McNaughton, D., and Rawling, P., 2000. "Unprincipled Ethics." In Hooker, B., and Little, M., editors, *Moral Particularism,* 256–75, Clarendon Press, Oxford.

Maier, N. R. F., 1931. "Reasoning in Humans: II. The Solution of a Problem and its Appearance in Consciousness." *Journal of Comparative Psychology,* 12: 181–94.

Mandler, M., 2001. "A Difficult Choice in Preference Theory." In Millgram, E., editor, *Varieties of Practical Reasoning,* MIT Press, Cambridge.

Marx, K., 1967. *Capital.* Edited by Frederick Engels; translated by Samuel Moore and Edward Aveling. International Publishers, New York.

Meadows, D., Meadows, D., Randers, J., and Behrens, W., 1972. *The Limits to Growth.* Universe Books, New York.

Merritt, M., 2000. "Virtue Ethics and Situationist Personality Psychology." *Ethical Theory and Moral Practice,* 3: 365–83.

Mill, J., 1878. *Analysis of the Phenomena of the Human Mind,* second edition. With Notes Illustrative and Critical by Alexander Bain, Andrew Findlater, and George Grote, Edited with Additional Notes by John Stuart Mill. Longmans, London.

Mill, J. S., 1872/1973. *A System of Logic: Ratiocinative and Inductive.* University of Toronto Press, Toronto.

————, 1967–1989. *Collected Works of John Stuart Mill.* University of Toronto Press/Routledge and Kegan Paul, Toronto/London.

Miller, G., 1956. "The Magical Number Seven, Plus or Minus Two: Some Limits on Our Capacity for Processing Information." *Psychological Review,* 63: 81–97.

Millgram, E., 1987. "Aristotle on Making Other Selves." *Canadian Journal of Philosophy,* 17 (2): 361–76.

————, 1993. "Pleasure in Practical Reasoning." *The Monist,* 76 (3): 394–415.

———, 1995. "Inhaltsreiche ethische Begriffe und die Unterscheidung zwischen Tatsachen und Werten." In Fehige, C., and Meggle, G., editors, *Zum moralischen Denken*, 354–88, Suhrkamp, Frankfurt a.M.

———, 1996a. "Review of Henry Richardson, *Practical Reasoning about Final Ends.*" *Mind*, 105 (419): 504–6.

———, 1996b. "Williams' Argument Against External Reasons." *Nous*, 30 (2): 197–220.

———, 1997. *Practical Induction.* Harvard University Press, Cambridge.

———, 1998. "Review of Iris Murdoch, *Existentialists and Mystics.*" *Boston Review*, 23 (1): 45–6.

———, 1999. "Moral Values and Secondary Qualities." *American Philosophical Quarterly*, 36 (3): 253–5.

———, 2000. "Coherence: The Price of the Ticket." *Journal of Philosophy*, 97 (2): 82–93.

———, 2002. "How to Make Something of Yourself." In Schmidtz, D., editor, *Robert Nozick*, 175–98, Cambridge University Press, Cambridge.

———, 2004. "On Being Bored Out of Your Mind." *Proceedings of the Aristotelian Society*, 104 (2): 163–84.

———, editor, 2001. *Varieties of Practical Reasoning.* MIT Press, Cambridge.

Mossner, E. C., 1980. *The Life of David Hume*, second edition. Clarendon Press, Oxford.

Munnich, E., Ranney, M., and Appel, D., 2004. "Numerically-driven Inferencing in Instruction." In Forgus, K., Gentner, D., and Regier, T., editors, *Proceedings of the Twenty-Sixth Annual Conference of the Cognitive Science Society*, Erlbaum, Mahwah, NJ.

Murdoch, I., 1967. *The Italian Girl.* Penguin, New York.

———, 1970. *The Sovereignty of Good.* Routledge and Kegan Paul, London.

———, 1989. *Sartre: Romantic Rationalist.* Penguin, New York.

———, 1992. *Metaphysics as a Guide to Morals.* Allen Lane/Penguin, New York.

———, 1998. *Existentialists and Mystics.* Edited by Peter Conradi. Allen Lane/Penguin, London.

Nehamas, A., 1985. *Nietzsche: Life as Literature.* Harvard University Press, Cambridge.

Nell, O., 1975. *Acting on Principle: An Essay on Kantian Ethics.* Columbia University Press, New York.

Nietzsche, F., 1886/1966. *Beyond Good and Evil.* Translated by Walter Kaufmann. Vintage Books/Random House, New York.

———, 1887/1974. *The Gay Science.* Translated by Walter Kaufmann. Random House, New York.

Norman, R., 1997. "Making Sense of Moral Realism." *Philosophical Investigations*, 20 (2): 117–35.

Nozick, R., 1993. *The Nature of Rationality.* Princeton University Press, Princeton.

Nussbaum, A., 1950. *Money in the Law.* Foundation Press, Brooklyn.

Nussbaum, M., 1987. "The Stoics on the Extirpation of the Passions." *Apeiron*, 20: 129–77.

———, 2001. "The *Protagoras*: A Science of Practical Reasoning." In Millgram, E., editor, *Varieties of Practical Reasoning*, MIT Press, Cambridge.

O'Neill, O., 1989. *Constructions of Reason.* Cambridge University Press, Cambridge.

Owen, W., 1963. *The Collected Poems.* New Directions Publishing, New York.

Pocock, J. G. A., 1999–. *Barbarism and Civilization.* Currently three vols. Cambridge University Press, Cambridge.

Putnam, H., 1979. "The Logic of Quantum Mechanics." In *Mathematics, Matters and Method,* 174–97, Cambridge University Press, Cambridge.

——, 1981. *Reason, Truth and History.* Cambridge University Press, Cambridge.

Quinn, W., 1993a. "Putting Rationality in its Place." In Foot, P., editor, *Morality and Action,* 228–55, Cambridge University Press, Cambridge.

——, 1993b. "Rationality and the Human Good." In Foot, P., editor, *Morality and Action,* 210–27, Cambridge University Press, Cambridge.

Raphael, D. D., 1947. *The Moral Sense.* Oxford University Press, London.

Rawls, J., 1971. *A Theory of Justice.* Harvard University Press, Cambridge.

——, 1989. "Themes in Kant's Moral Philosophy." In Förster, E., editor, *Kant's Transcendental Deductions,* 81–113, Stanford University Press, Stanford.

——, 1999. "The Independence of Moral Theory." In Freeman, S., editor, *Collected Papers,* 286–302, Harvard University Press, Cambridge.

——, 2000. *Lectures on the History of Moral Philosophy.* Edited by Barbara Herman. Harvard University Press, Cambridge.

Raz, J., 1986. *The Morality of Freedom.* Clarendon Press, Oxford.

——, 2000. "The Truth in Particularism." In Hooker, B., and Little, M., editors, *Moral Particularism,* 48–78, Clarendon Press, Oxford.

Richardson, H. S., 1990. "Specifying Norms as a Way to Resolve Concrete Ethical Problems." *Philosophy and Public Affairs,* 19 (4): 279–310.

——, 1994. *Practical Reasoning about Final Ends.* Cambridge University Press, Cambridge.

——, 2001. "Commensurability." In Becker, L. C. and Becker, C. B., editors, *The Encyclopedia of Ethics,* second edition, 258–62, Routledge, New York.

Sayre-McCord, G., 1996. "Hume and the Bauhaus Theory of Ethics." *Midwest Studies in Philosophy,* 20: 280–98.

——, G., 2001. "Mill's 'Proof' of the Principle of Utility: A More than Half-hearted Defense." *Social Philosophy and Policy,* 18 (2): 330–60.

Schapiro, T., 2001. "Three Conceptions of Action in Moral Theory." *Nous,* 35 (1): 93–117.

Scheffler, S., 1994. *The Rejection of Consequentialism.* Oxford University Press, Oxford.

Schwartz, B., 1986. *The Battle for Human Nature: Science, Morality and Modern Life.* Norton, New York.

Seuss, D., 1982. *Hunches in Bunches.* Random House, New York.

Shope, R., 1978. "The Conditional Fallacy in Contemporary Philosophy." *The Journal of Philosophy,* 75 (8): 124–35.

Sidgwick, H., 1907/1981. *The Methods of Ethics.* Hackett, Indianapolis.

Simon, H., 1957. *Models of Man.* John Wiley and Sons, New York.

Skorupski, J., 1989. *John Stuart Mill.* Routledge, New York.

Smith, M., 1987. "The Humean Theory of Motivation." *Mind,* 96 (381): 36–61.

Sreenivasan, G., 2001. "Understanding Alien Morals." *Philosophy and Phenomenological Research,* 62 (1): 1–32.

Starbuck, W., 1963. "Level of Aspiration." *Psychological Review*, 70 (1): 51–60.

Stevenson, C. L., 1963. *Facts and Values*. Yale University Press, New Haven.

Stocker, M., 1990. *Plural and Conflicting Values*. Clarendon Press, Oxford.

Stone, M., and Brown, B. B., 1998. "In the Eye of the Beholder: Adolescents' Perceptions of Peer Crowd Stereotypes." In Muuss, R., and Porton, H., editors, *Adolescent Behavior and Society*, fifth edition, 158–69, McGraw-Hill, Boston.

Stroud, B., 1977. *Hume*. Routledge and Kegan Paul, Boston.

Thagard, P., 1989. "Explanatory Coherence." *Behavioral and Brain Sciences*, 12: 435–67.

———, 1992. *Conceptual Revolutions*. Princeton University Press, Princeton.

Thagard, P., and Millgram, E., 1995. "Inference to the Best Plan: A Coherence Theory of Decision." In Leake, D., and Ram, A., editors, *Goal-Driven Learning*, 439–54, MIT Press, Cambridge.

Thagard, P., and Verbeurgt, K., 1998. "Coherence as Constraint Satisfaction." *Cognitive Science*, 22 (1): 1–24.

Thesiger, W., 1959. *Arabian Sands*. Longmans, London.

Thompson, M., 1995. "The Representation of Life." In Hursthouse, R., Lawrence, G., and Quinn, W., editors, *Virtues and Reasons: Philippa Foot and Moral Theory*, 247–96, Clarendon Press, Oxford.

———, 2003. Tre gradi di bontà naturale. Translated by Lorenzo Greco. *Iride*, 16 (38): 191–7. (English title: Three Degrees of Natural Goodness.)

———, 2004. "Apprehending human form." In O'Hear, A., editor, *Modern Moral Philosophy*, 47–74, Cambridge University Press, Cambridge.

Tomorrow, T., 1996. *The Wrath of Sparky*. St. Martin's Press, New York.

Townsend, R., 1990. *Financial Structure and Economic Organization*. Basil Blackwell, Cambridge.

Trudeau, G. B., 1996. *Virtual Doonesbury*. Andrews and McMeel, Kansas City.

Turing, A. M., 1950. "Computing Machinery and Intelligence." *Mind*, 59 (236): 433–60.

van Fraassen, B., 1980. *The Scientific Image*. Clarendon Press, Oxford.

Vogler, C., 1995. "Philosophical Feminism, Feminist Philosophy." *Philosophical Topics*, 23 (2): 295–319.

———, 2000. "Review of Elijah Millgram, *Practical Induction*." *Mind*, 109 (435): 630–4.

———, 2001a. "Anscombe on Practical Inference." In Millgram, E., editor, *Varieties of Practical Reasoning*, 437–64, MIT Press, Cambridge.

———, 2001b. *John Stuart Mill's Deliberative Landscape*. Garland Publishing, New York.

———, 2002. *Reasonably Vicious*. Harvard University Press, Cambridge.

Watson, G., 1990. "On the Primacy of Character." In Flanagan, O., and Rorty, A. O., editors, *Identity, Character, and Morality*, MIT Press, Cambridge.

Watterson, B., 1996. *It's a Magical World*. Andrews and McMeel, Kansas City.

Weir, P. 1981. *Gallipoli*. Produced by Patricia Lovell and Robert Stigwood. Paramount/Associated R and R Films, Hollywood. Film.

Whitehead, A. N. and Russell, B., 1929/1963. *Principia Mathematica*, second edition. Cambridge University Press, Cambridge.

Wiggins, D., 2001. "Deliberation and Practical Reason." In Millgram, E., editor, *Varieties of Practical Reasoning*, MIT Press, Cambridge.

Williams, B., 1973a. "The Makropulos Case: Reflections on the Tedium of Immortality." In *Problems of the Self*, 82–100, Cambridge University Press, Cambridge.

———, 1973b. "Morality and the Emotions." In *Problems of the Self*, 207–29, Cambridge University Press, Cambridge.

———, 1981. "Persons, Character and Morality." In *Moral Luck*, 1–19, Cambridge University Press, Cambridge.

———, 1985. *Ethics and the Limits of Philosophy*. Harvard University Press, Cambridge.

———, 1995. "Replies." In Altham, J. E. J., and Harrison, R., editors, *World, Mind and Ethics: Essays on the Ethical Philosophy of Bernard Williams*, Cambridge University Press, Cambridge.

———, 2001. "Internal and External Reasons (with postscript)." In Millgram, E., editor, *Varieties of Practical Reasoning*, MIT Press, Cambridge.

Williamson, O., 1985. *The Economic Institutions of Capitalism*. Free Press, New York.

Winston, P. H., 1977. *Artificial Intelligence*. Addison-Wesley, Menlo Park.

Zaller, J., 1992. *The Nature and Origins of Mass Opinion*. Cambridge University Press, Cambridge.

Index

accident victims, 35, 36
affective forecasting, 52
agency, 97, 99, 188
   end-setting, 93, 99, 105
   human, 94, 97, 98, 100
   unified, 21, 22, 274, 278, 284–90
Alberti, L., 307
Allen, W., 152
analogy, reasoning by, 320
Anderson, E., 87
Anscombe, G. E. M., 128, 191, 196,
   282
Aquinas, T., 196
Aramis, 5, 301
Aristotle, 17, 18, 20, 133–8, 142, 145–6,
   152, 162, 163, 166, 172, 284, 314, 315,
   319, 321
   on becoming a god, 308
   conception of the person, 188
   as instrumentalist, 79, 198, 281
autonomy, 49, 90, 112, 117, 130, 161, 290,
   303

Baier, A., 215
Bakhurst, D., 191
belief-desire psychology, 47, 55, 208,
   274
Bennett, W., 273
Bentham, J., 15, 42, 49, 68, 275,
   295
Borges, J. L., 177
Brandt, R., 51, 54, 69
Bratman, M., 140–1, 151, 197
Bridging Problem, 13–15, 31

Broad, C. D., 243
Broadie, S. W., 166

capitalism, varieties of, 154
Cartwright, N., 320
Categorical Imperative, 16, 18, 89–132,
   161, 196
   See also CI-procedure
causal chain, 205, 219–20, 222–3
causal resemblance theory, 205, 208, 219,
   232, 236, 237
causation, 116–18, 213, 223, 230, 231, 244
   intelligible, 117
Cavell, S., 253
ceteris paribus clause, *see* defeasibility
chess, 106, 144
Chomsky, N., 107, 164
CI-procedure, 17, 89–132, 141–5
   See also Categorical Imperative
Coffeeshop Responses, 9
coherence, 7, 9, 26, 61, 91, 114, 266, 268,
   302, 318–19, 323
commensurability, 25, 273–94, 295–311
   definition of, 273, 281, 295
complexity, 126, 263, 288
   computational, 127
   of perturbed social worlds, 106–7,
      144
   of syntax, 107
Comte, A., 72
conditional fallacy, 193
consequentialism, 12, 26, 71, 91, 157, 158,
   314, 322
   virtue-, 325